More praise for The Reading Teacher's Book of Lists, *Fifth Edition*

"Ed Fry and Jackie Kress's book of lists have served me well as a researcher and served my teacher-students in the preparation of lessons. In short, these lists are very valuable resources."
—Isabel Beck, professor of education,
University of Pittsburgh

"Drs. Fry and Kress hit another homerun. *The Reading Teacher's Book of Lists* will be every bit as valuable to classroom teachers as all of their previous books of lists. This one is a ready-made friend to all teachers because it helps them with their most important reading, vocabulary, phonics, and spelling tasks—choosing the most important words to teach their children."
—Dr. James Flood and Dr. Diane Lapp,
distinguished professors, San Diego State University

"*The Reading Teacher's Book of Lists* is one of the most useful and handy teaching resources a teacher can own. Fry and Kress have done it again."
—Dr. Robert B. Ruddell, professor emeritus,
University of California, Berkeley

Jossey-Bass Teacher

Jossey-Bass Teacher provides K–12 teachers with essential knowledge and tools to create a positive and lifelong impact on student learning. Trusted and experienced educational mentors offer practical classroom-tested and theory-based teaching resources for improving teaching practice in a broad range of grade levels and subject areas. From one educator to another, we want to be your first source to make every day your best day in teaching. *Jossey-Bass Teacher* resources serve two types of informational needs—essential knowledge and essential tools.

Essential knowledge resources provide the foundation, strategies, and methods from which teachers may design curriculum and instruction to challenge and excite their students. Connecting theory to practice, essential knowledge books rely on a solid research base and time-tested methods, offering the best ideas and guidance from many of the most experienced and well-respected experts in the field.

Essential tools save teachers time and effort by offering proven, ready-to-use materials for in-class use. Our publications include activities, assessments, exercises, instruments, games, ready reference, and more. They enhance an entire course of study, a weekly lesson, or a daily plan. These essential tools provide insightful, practical, and comprehensive materials on topics that matter most to K–12 teachers.

The
Reading
Teacher's
BOOK OF LISTS
Fifth Edition

Edward B. Fry, Ph.D.
Jacqueline E. Kress, Ed.D.

 JOSSEY-BASS
A Wiley Imprint
www.josseybass.com

Published by Jossey-Bass
A Wiley Imprint
989 Market Street, San Francisco, CA 94103-1741   www.josseybass.com

Library of Congress Cataloging-in-Publication Data
Fry, Edward Bernard, 1925-
   The reading teacher's book of lists / Edward B. Fry, Jacqueline E. Kress.-- 5th ed.
     p. cm.
   ISBN-13: 978-0-7879-8257-7
   ISBN-10: 0-7879-8257-1
   1. Reading--Miscellanea. 2. Curriculum planning--Miscellanea. 3. Tutors and tutoring--Miscellanea. 4. Handbooks, vade-mecums, etc. I. Kress, Jacqueline E. II. Title.
   LB1050.2.F79 2005
   428.4--dc22
                          2006002641

Printed in the United States of America
FIRST EDITION
PB Printing 10 9 8 7 6 5 4 3 2 1

About the Authors

Edward B. Fry, Ph.D., Professor Emeritus of Education at Rutgers University (New Brunswick, NJ) where, for 24 years, he was director of the Reading Center. At Rutgers, Dr. Fry taught graduate and undergraduate courses in reading, curriculum, and other educational subjects, and served as chairman and dissertation committee member for doctoral candidates in reading and educational psychology. As the Reading Center director, he provided instruction for children with reading problems, trained teacher candidates, and conducted statewide reading conferences. Dr. Fry is known internationally for his Readability Graph which is used by teachers, publishers, and others to judge the reading difficulty of books and other materials. He is also well known for his Instant Words, high-frequency word list, and for reading, spelling, and secondary curriculum materials. He works as a curriculum author and skis and swims whenever possible.

Jacqueline E. Kress, Ed.D., is Dean and Professor of Education at New York Institute of Technology (Old Westbury, NY) where she teaches reading methods courses and works with college and school faculty in the preparation and development of teachers, educational technology specialists, and other educators. She is an experienced reading teacher and teacher educator, having taught developmental and remedial reading in urban elementary schools, and reading skills and methods courses at the undergraduate and graduate levels. Dr. Kress has designed numerous educational programs, including programs to increase P-12 students' literacy and school achievement. She is the author of *The ESL Teacher's Book of Lists* and coauthor of *The Readability Machine* (both published by Jossey-Bass).

This book is dedicated to the many teachers,
professors, volunteers, homeschoolers, and editors who are
actively engaged in opening the world of knowledge and thought to children and
adults through literacy instruction
in their schools, community centers, homes,
and publishing houses.

Contents

SECTION 6: Writing   227

SECTION 7: Teaching Ideas   257

SECTION 12: **Spelling**   **369**

SECTION 13: **The Internet**   **393**

SECTION 14: **English Language Learners (ESL or ELL)**   **419**

SECTION 15: **Language**   **437**

SECTION 16: **Alphabets and Symbols**   **451**

SECTION 17: **Word Play**   471

SECTION 18: **Reference**   505

Preface to the Fifth Edition

It is surprising to us, and also a great pleasure, that hundreds of thousands of teachers, publishers, tutors, homeschoolers, and other individuals have used previous editions of this book. Part of its popularity is due to word of mouth where one teacher tells another, or one editor tells an author, that there is a wealth of creative ideas and helpful information in *The Reading Teacher's Book of Lists.* We are sure that you, too, will find many useful lists in this new edition.

We thought a good deal about the extraordinary changes in reading and literacy education that have occurred since the first edition was published in 1984 while developing the lists for this fifth edition. The long-running argument about the best way to teach beginning reading seems to have been fairly settled. Most now agree that a balanced approach is best, employing a broad range of phonics and word recognition skills, comprehension strategies, and using a wide variety of reading materials to further teach and reinforce these skills.

In even less time, the Internet (World Wide Web), and other technologies have entered our business and daily life, and are now in many classrooms across the nation. In addition, as we reviewed each list, we marveled at the rapidity of change in the English language itself.

The Reading Teacher's Book of Lists, Fifth Edition reflects these changes and more, while preserving a great deal of the material that has made the earlier editions so recognized and well-used. It contains substantially updated versions of most of the lists found in the fourth edition, plus many new ones. For example, our Phonics section includes new research-based lists that will help you balance your reading and literacy programs. In this section, you'll also find updated lists that are the cornerstone of our earlier editions, like Phonograms and Phonics Example Words.

This new edition has a whole new section on Fluency (Section 9) as it has become more important due to recommendations of the National Reading Panel. We also have major updates on all our Content Words (Section 4) for Mathematics and Social Studies Vocabulary lists based on the newest school textbooks. The ever-changing field of the Internet has also influenced a thorough revision of our Internet section (Section 13). Web addresses have been added to our updated List of Publishers in the Reference section (Section 18).

You will find a new section devoted to Alphabets and Symbols (Section 16), not just handwriting charts for traditional penmanship, but something for the curious like the Ancient Egyptian Alphabet for hieroglyphs. And our useful Word Wall Lists are totally new.

Research is a more pressing demand for curriculum materials so we have included specific researched lists for Prefixes, Suffixes, and Phoneme-Grapheme correspondences (phonics). But we would like to remind readers that our older lists of Instant Words and Phonics Example Words are research-based also. We have included some new Spanish Word and Phrase lists for teachers struggling with our largest immigrant populations.

Some lists demand updating, like recent Award-Winning Books for Caldecott and Newbery Medals. But there are literally hundreds of minor additions and updates to the basic lists found in the earlier editions and a number of reproducible worksheets (see list on page xviii).

We suggest that you take a little time and just turn each page. By skimming through the book you will get a better idea of its contents and where you might be able to use some of these lists. We all but guarantee that you will learn something or at least pick up a few new words for your vocabulary. But the real purpose of this book is to help you to help a non-reader, or poor reader, to read better. And that is one of the most important things you can do with your life or your student's life.

Edward Fry
Jacqueline Kress

A User's Guide

This is a big and complex book. If you take a little time to get to know it, it will be much more useful for you. Try turning every page, not reading, just skimming. You will be amazed at what you will find. For a quicker, broader overview, glance at the section headings in the Table of Contents.

The wide diversity of lists in this book makes it possible for teachers to pick and choose those that meet specific classroom and teaching needs. Some lists may be appropriate for different types of teaching or for various grade levels. The following list suggestions are designed to help you and to make this book of lists even more useful.

1
PHONICS

LIST 1. CONSONANT SOUNDS

The following are all the beginning consonant sounds for either words or syllables (except for final consonant blends). They constitute what some linguists call the "onset" for the syllable. The rest of the syllables must have a vowel or a vowel plus consonant (a vowel plus a consonant is called a phonogram or rime).

The Reading Teacher's Book of Lists, Fifth Edition, © 2006 by John Wiley & Sons, Inc.

Single Consonants

b	h	n	v
c	j	p	w
d	k	r	y
f	l	s	z
g	m	t	

Important Exceptions

qu = /kw/ as in "quick"
  (the letter "q" is never used without "u")
ph = /f/ as in "phone"
c = /s/ before e, i, or y as in "cent," "city,"
  or "cycle"
c = /k/ before a, o, or u as in "can," "cot," or "cub"
g = /j/ before e, i, or y as in "gem," "giraffe,"
  or "gym"
x = /ks/ blend as in "fox"
s = /z/ sound at the end of some words as in "is"
ng = /ng/ phoneme as in "sing"
ck = /k/ often at the end of a word as in "luck"

Consonant Digraphs

ch as in "chin"   **ph** as in "phone"
sh as in "shut"   **gh** as in "rough"
th (voiced) as in "thin"
th (voiceless) as in "this"
wh (hw blend) as in "which"

Rare Exceptions

ch = /k/ as in "character"
ch = /sh/ as in "chef"
ti = /sh/ as in "attention"
s = /sh/ as in "sure"
x = /gz/ as in "exact"
x = /z/ as in "xylophone"
s = /zh/ as in "measure"
si = /zh/ as in "vision"

Silent Consonants

gn = /n/ as in "gnat"
kn = /n/ as in "knife"
wr = /r/ as in "write"
gh = /silent/ as in "high"
mb = /m/ as in "lamb"
lf = /f/ as in "calf"
lk = /k/ as in "walk"
tle = /l/ as in "castle"

INITIAL CONSONANT BLENDS

r family	l family	s family	3-letter s family	no family
br as in "bride"	**bl** as in "blend"	**sc** as in "scare"	**sch** as in "school"	**dw** as in "dwell"
cr as in "crop"	**cl** as in "clay"	**sk** as in "skunk"	**scr** as in "scrub"	**tw** as in "twin"
dr as in "drive"	**fl** as in "fly"	**sm** as in "smile"	**squ** as in "squall"	**thr** as in "threw"
fr as in "free"	**gl** as in "glass"	**sn** as in "snack"	**str** as in "strong"	
gr as in "grand"	**pl** as in "plug"	**sp** as in "spell"	**spr** as in "sprout"	
pr as in "prize"	**sl** as in "slow"	**st** as in "sting"	**spl** as in "splash"	
tr as in "trust"		**sw** as in "swipe"	**shr** as in "shrank"	
wr as in "write"				

FINAL CONSONANT BLENDS

(Note: These are usually learned best with rhymes.)

ct as in "act"	**lt** as in "salt"	**nk** as in "think"	**sk** as in "tusk"
ft as in "lift"	**mp** as in "jump"	**nt** as in "hunt"	**sp** as in "lisp"
ld as in "old"	**nc**(e) as in "since"	**pt** as in "kept"	**st** as in "lost"
lm as in "calm"	**nch** as in "lunch"	**rd** as in "word"	
lp as in "pulp"	**nd** as in "band"	**rt** as in "art"	

See also List 7, Suggested Phonics Teaching Order; List 9, Phonics Example Words; List 111, Games and Methods for Teaching.

LIST 2. VOWEL SOUNDS

There are about 21 vowel sounds in English (the actual number is dialect dependent), including vowel sounds affected by the consonant "r." For words that use these vowel sounds, refer to List 9—Phonics Example Words.

Short Vowels
a = /ă/ as in "cat"
e = /ĕ/ as in "end"
i = /ĭ/ as in "sip"
o = /ŏ/ as in "hot"
u = /ŭ/ as in "cup"

Vowel Y
y = /ī/ as in "try," "cycle"
y = /ē/ as in "funny"

Schwa
a = /ə/ as in "ago"
e = /ə/ as in "happen"
o = /ə/ as in "other"

Diphthongs
oi = /oi/ as in "oil"
oy = /oi/ as in "boy"
ou = /ou/ as in "out"
ow = /ou/ as in "how"

Vowel Exceptions
ea = /ĕ/ as in "bread" or /ē/ as in "seat"
e = /silent/ as in "come" and "make"

y = /y/ as in "yes"

le = /əl/ as in "candle"
al = /əl/ as in "pedal"
ul = /əl/ as in "awful"

Long Vowels—Final E Rule
a = /ā/ as in "make"
e = /ē/ as in "these"
i = /ī/ as in "five"
o = /ō/ as in "hope"
u = /ū/ as in "cube"

Long Vowels— Open Syllable Rule
a = /ā/ as in "baby"
e = /ē/ as in "we"
i = /ī/ as in "tiger"
o = /ō/ as in "open"

Double O
oo = /o͞o/ as in "soon"
oo = /o͝o/ as in "good"
u = /o͞o/ as in "truth"
u = /o͝o/ as in "put"

Long Vowel Digraphs
ai = /ā/ as in "aid"
ay = /ā/ as in "say"
ea = /ē/ as in "eat"
ee = /ē/ as in "see"
oa = /ō/ as in "oat"
ow = /ō/ as in "own"
ew = /ū/ as in "new"

Vowel Plus R
ar = /är/ as in "far"
er = /ər/ as in "her"
ir = /ər/ as in "sir"
or = /ôr/ as in "for"
ur = /ər/ as in "fur"

Broad O
o = /ô/ as in "long"
a(l) = /ô/ as in "also"
a(w) = /ô/ as in "saw"
a(u) = /ô/ as in "auto"

"ea" makes both a long and short E sound.

E at the end of a word is usually silent, and often makes the preceding vowel long.

Y is a consonant at the beginning of a word (yes), but is a vowel in the middle or end of other words. See Vowel Y shown above.

Final "le" makes a schwa plus l sound.
Final "al" makes a schwa plus l sound.
Final "ul" makes a schwa plus l sound.

See also List 3, The Final "E" Rule; List 4, Double Vowels; List 7, Suggested Phonics Teaching Order; List 9, Phonics Example Words.

The Reading Teacher's Book of Lists, Fifth Edition, © 2006 by John Wiley & Sons, Inc.

LIST 3. THE FINAL "E" RULE

Often, an "e" at the end of a word makes the preceding vowel long. Here are some short vowel words contrasted with long vowel words that illustrate this rule. These words make interesting and instructive word walls, flash cards, or spelling lessons.

A Words

fad—fade	rag—rage	wag—wage
stag—stage	cam—came	dam—dame
tam—tame	sham—shame	ban—bane
can—cane	pan—pane	Sam—same
cap—cape	gap—gape	fat—fate
tap—tape	scrap—scrape	rat—rate
hat—hate	mat—mate	

I Words

hid—hide	rid—ride	slid—slide
dim—dime	rim—rime	Tim—time
grim—grime	prim—prime	slim—slime
din—dine	fin—fine	pin—pine
shin—shine	spin—spine	tin—tine
twin—twine	win—wine	rip—ripe
grip—gripe	snip—snipe	strip—stripe
bit—bite	kit—kite	lit—lite
quit—quite	spit—spite	sit—site

O Words

lob—lobe	rob—robe	glob—globe
cod—code	nod—node	rod—rode
cop—cope	hop—hope	mop—mope
pop—pope	slop—slope	tot—tote

U Words

cub—cube	tub—tube	cut—cute

Exceptions to the final e rule.   The letter "e" is nearly always silent at the end of a word. Here are some words that have a silent final "e," but *do not* follow the final e rule.

- most words ending in -le*:   circle, cattle, middle, apple, single, trouble
- most words ending in -ce: since, notice, voice, force, dance, office, practice
- most words ending in -se: house, else, horse, course, praise, sense, else, whose, please
- most words ending in -re: before, sure, figure, are, measure, square, store
- most words ending in -ve: give, love, believe, have, serve
- others: come, some, one, there, large, eye, edge, gone, done

*The final -le is sometimes called a syllabic l when the letter l acts like a vowel.

See also List 7, Suggested Phonics Teaching Order; List 9, Phonics Example Words.

LIST 4. DOUBLE VOWELS

The following are long vowel digraphs contrasted with short vowels in closed syllables. The old double vowel rule has too many exceptions like "oo" or "ou" to be generalized.

Short a /ă/	Long a /ā/	Short e /ĕ/	Long e /ē/	Short i /ĭ/	Short o /ŏ/
lad	laid	red	reed	did	crock
mad	maid	bed	bead	lid	clock
pad	paid	fed	feed		rod
clam	claim	led	lead	**Long i**	sop
man	main	Ned	need	/ī/	cot
pan	pain	wed	weed	died	got
ran	rain	bled	bleed	lied	
van	vain	bred	breed		**Long o**
bran	brain	Fred	freed		/ō/
plan	plain	sped	speed		croak
span	Spain	stem	steam		cloak
pant	paint	Ben	bean		road
bat	bait	Ken	keen		soap
		men	mean		coat
		ten	teen		goat
		fend	fiend		
		pep	peep		
		rep	reap		
		step	steep		
		bet	beet		
		bet	beat		
		met	meet		
		met	meat		
		net	neat		
		pet	peat		
		set	seat		
		den	dean		
		best	beast		

The Reading Teacher's Book of Lists, Fifth Edition, © 2006 by John Wiley & Sons, Inc.

LIST 5. SOUND DETERMINED BY LETTER POSITION

Another way of teaching phonics is to show how the sound of the letter or grapheme is determined by its position or environment within a word. For example, 1 shows that many consonants make the same sound no matter where they are, but 2 shows that the position in a syllable or other factors change the sound.

1. Position-independent letter correspondences (doesn't matter where the letter is)

Single Consonants

t	/t/	top	f	/f/	fish
n	/n/	nut	v	/v/	valentine
r	/r/	ring	h	/h/	hand
m	/m/	man	k	/k/	kite
d	/d/	dog	w	/w/	window
l	/l/	letter	j	/j/	jar
p	/p/	pen	z	/z/	zebra
b	/b/	book			

2. Position-dependent letter correspondences (position changes sound)
Closed Syllable Rule (If syllable ends in a consonant, the vowel is short.)

a	/a/	at
e	/e/	end
i	/i/	is
o	/o/	hot
u	/u/	pup

Second Sounds

s	/s/	saw	(at the beginning)
s	/z/	his	(frequently at the end)
y	/y/	yes	(at the beginning)
y	/ē/	funny	(at the end)
y	/ī/	my	(middle or end)
e	/silent/	come	(at the end)

Open Syllable Rule (If syllable ends in a vowel, the vowel is long.)

a	/ā/	table	o	/ō/	donut
e	/ē/	before	u	/ū/	music
i	/ī/	tiny			

Schwa (always in an unaccented syllable when word has two or more syllables)

a	/ə/	principal	o	/ə/	canyon
e	/ə/	happen	u	/ə/	radium
i	/ə/	pencil			

Letter X (always at end)

x	/ks/	box

3. Marker-dependent letter correspondences (marker is another letter in the word that changes sound)

Final E Rule (always "VCe")

a	/ā/	cake	o	/ō/	home
e	/ē/	these	u	/ū/	use
i	/ī/	ice			

When a single vowel is followed by a single consonant and a silent final e, the vowel is long.

Consonant Second Sounds

c	/k/	cake	(followed by a, o, u)
c	/s/	city	(followed by i, e, y)
g	/g/	gate	(followed by a, o, u)
g	/j/	gem	(followed by i, e, y)

R Modified Vowels (always where "r" follows)

a	/är/	far	o	/or/	for
e	/ûr/	her	u	/ûr/	fur
i	/ûr/	fir			

4. Digraph correspondences (two letters positioned together)

Consonant Digraphs

sh	/sh/	shoe
ch	/ch/	church
th	/th/	this
th	/th/	thing
wh	/hw/	white
mb	/m/	bomb

Long Vowel Digraphs

ea	/ē/	eat
ee	/ē/	see
ai	/ā/	aid
ay	/ā/	say
oa	/ō/	oat
ow	/ō/	know

Broad O Digraphs

au	/o/	auto
aw	/o/	saw

Double O

oo	/o͞o/	moon
oo	/o͝o/	look

Exceptions

qu	/kw/	quick
ea	/e/	bread
ph	/f/	phone
ng	/ng/	sing

Silent Consonants

gn	/n/	gnat
kn	/n/	knife
wr	/r/	write
gh	/silent/	right
ck	/k/	back

Diphthongs

ou	/ou/	out
ow	/ou/	now
oy	/oi/	boy
oi	/oi/	boil
ew	/ew/	few

See also List 156, Double-Letter Spelling Patterns.

LIST 6. PHONICS AWARENESS

The English language uses 26 alphabetic letters in more than 100 combinations to represent between 44 and 45 speech sounds. Phonics helps new as well as experienced readers make connections between letter patterns and the speech sounds for which they stand. It begins with an awareness and recognition of letters and sounds, then builds connections between them, starting with the most frequent and distinct correspondences.

Letter Knowledge	Recognize, name, and distinguish upper- and lower-case letters.
Word Segmentation	Recognize individual words within a sentence. Example: "I went to the store." (5 words)
Syllable Segmentation	Recognize and separate syllables within words. Examples: Bill-y, Ton-ya, a-bout, talk-ing
Syllable Blending	Can listen to simple polysyllabic words spoken in separate syllables and can say the complete blended word. Example: let-ter → letter
Phonemic Awareness—Consonants	Upon hearing two similar words with different initial consonants, tell whether the initial sounds are the same or different. Examples: mat—sat; big—beg
	Upon hearing two similar words with different final consonants, tell whether the final sounds are the same or different. Examples: sat—sad; met—mat
	Do the same with consonant endings.
Phonemic Awareness—Vowels	Upon hearing two similar words with different vowel sounds, tell whether the vowel (medial) is the same or different. Examples: mane—cane; pin—pen
Phonemic Blending	Upon hearing separate phonemes, blend them and say the complete word. Example: /t/ /o/ /m/ → Tom
Phonemic Segmentation	Upon hearing a complete word, separate and pronounce the individual sounds. Example: cat → /c/ /a/ /t/
Rhyming	Recognize and produce rhyming pairs. Examples: tan/pan; big/pig; get/set; sap/tap
	Upon hearing a series of onset consonants and a phonogram, blend them to produce rhyming words. Examples: /k/ /ab/ → cab; /d/ /ab/ → dab; /g/ /ab/ → gab; /j/ /ab/ → jab
	Upon hearing a series of rhymes, break the rhyme into onset and rime. Examples: set → / s / / et / ; bet → /b/ /et/; let → /l/ /et/

The Reading Teacher's Book of Lists, Fifth Edition, © 2006 by John Wiley & Sons, Inc.

See also List 186, Handwriting Charts.

LIST 7. SUGGESTED PHONICS TEACHING ORDER

This suggested teaching order is based on research (see List 8). It is simplified and combines consonants and vowels so it will be more useful for the classroom teacher.

	Letter(s)	Sound	Example	Letter(s)	Sound	Example
Easy Consonants (high frequency/ high contrast)	t	/t/	tap	l	/l/	lap
	n	/n/	nap	c	/k/	cat
	r	/r/	rat	p	/p/	pat
	m	/m/	mat	b	/b/	bat
	d	/d/	dog	f	/f/	fat
	s	/s/	sat	v	/v/	vet
Short Vowels	a	/ă/	cat	o	/ŏ/	hot
	e	/ĕ/	let	u	/ŭ/	cut
	i	/ĭ/	hit			
Long Vowels (final e rule)	a_e	/ā/	make	o_e	/ō/	bone
	e_e	/ē/	these	u_e	/ū/	use
	i_e	/ī/	nine			
Long Vowels (open syllable rule-end of word)	e	/ē/	me	o	/ō/	go
Other Single Consonants	g	/g/	get	x	/ks/	box
	h	/h/	hot	qu	/kw/	quit
	k	/k/	kit	z	/z/	zip
	w	/w/	wet	y	/y/	yes
	j	/j/	jet			
Initial Consonant Digraphs	th	/t̶h̶/	thin	sh	/sh/	ship
	th	/th/	these	wh	/hw/	when
	ch	/ch/	chin			
Y Vowels	-y	/ī/	my	y	/ē/	funny
Consonant Second Sounds	c	/s/	city	g	/j/	gym
	s	/z/	his	x	/gs/	exam
Consonants Q and X	qu	/kw/	queen			
	x	/ks/	box			
Long Vowel Digraphs	ea	/ē/	meat	ay	/ā/	day
	ee	/ē/	feet	oa	/ō/	boat
	ai	/ā/	pain	ow	/ō/	tow
Initial Consonant Blends	pr	/pr/	prize	fr	/fr/	free
	tr	/tr/	trip	st	/st/	step
	gr	/gr/	greet	sp	/sp/	spin
	br	/br/	Brad	sk	/sk/	skip
	cr	/cr/	crib	sc	/sc/	scan
	dr	/dr/	drive	sw	/sw/	swim

SUGGESTED PHONICS TEACHING ORDER CONTINUED

	Letter(s)	Sound	Example	Letter(s)	Sound	Example
Initial Consonant Blends (cont.)	sm	/sm/	smell	fl	/fl/	flip
	sn	/sn/	snap	sl	/sl/	slap
	pl	/pl/	play	gl	/gl/	glow
	cl	/cl/	clip	tw	/tw/	twin
	bl	/bl/	blip	str	/str/	street
Final Consonant Blends	ld	/ld/	cold	nt	/nt/	ant
	lf	/lf/	elf	mb	/mb/	lamb
	sk	/sk/	ask	mp	/mp/	camp
	st	/st/	pest	ng	/ng/	sing
	nk	/nk/	ink			
R-Vowels	ar	/är/	far	air	/âr/	fair
	er	/ûr/	her	are	/âr/	bare
	ir	/ûr/	fir	ear	/ēr/	tear
	or	/ôr/	for	eer	/ēr/	beer
	ur	/ûr/	fur			
Broad O Vowels	aw	/aw/	awful	al	/aw/	also
	au	/aw/	auto	o	/aw/	off
Other Vowels— Diphthongs	ow	/ou/	owl	oi	/oi/	boil
	ou	/ou/	out	oy	/oi/	boy
Double O Vowels	oo	/o͞o/	pool	u	/o͞o/	truth
	oo	/o͝o/	foot	u	/o͝o/	push
Schwa in Unaccented Syllable	a	/ə/	about	o	/ə/	onion
	e	/ə/	letter	u	/ə/	circus
	i	/ə/	holiday			
Other Spellings/ Silent Letters	gn	/n/	gnu	kn	/n/	knew
	ph	/f/	phone	wr	/r/	write
Other Vowel Spellings	ough	/aw/	ought	igh	/ī/	sight
	ea	/ea/	head			

The Reading Teacher's Book of Lists, Fifth Edition, © 2006 by John Wiley & Sons, Inc.

See also List 8, Phonics Research Basis; List 9, Phonics Example Words.

LIST 8. PHONICS RESEARCH BASIS

These tables give the research basis for including all the common phoneme-grapheme (phonics) correspondences. The numbers tell how many times each correspondence occurs in a 17,310-word vocabulary study done at Stanford University and funded by the U.S. Department of Education (Hanna).

The grouping gives a research-based teaching order; List 7 gives a teaching order using a vowel–consonant mix based on this data.

Vowel Graphemes Arranged by Rule and/or Sound Grouping and Phoneme-Grapheme Frequency in a 17,310-Word Vocabulary Study

Long and Short Vowels

Short Vowels 16,135
Closed Syllable Rule

I	5,346	is
A	4,192	at
E	3,316	end
U	1,723	up
O	1,558	hot

Long Vowels 6,105
Open Syllable Rule

O	1,876	go
E	1,765	me
A	1,007	baby
U/o͞o/	907	music
I	555	idea

Long Vowels 1,789
Final E Rule

A	790	ate
O	370	home
I	339	ice
U	290	use

Long Vowels 1,083
Vowel Digraphs
Long E

EE	249	see
EA	245	eat

Long A

AI	208	aid
AY	131	say

Long O

OA	126	oat
OW	124	own

Vowel Y 2,012

Y = /ē/	1,801	very
Y = /ī/	211	my

Other Vowel Sounds

Vowel Dipthongs 438

OU/ou/	227	out
OW/ou/	119	owl
OI/oi/	92	oil
OY/oi/	45	toy

R Modified Vowels 3,271

ER/er/ or /ər/	1,979	her
AR/är/	474	arm
OR/ar/ or er/	312	labor
UR/ər/ or/er	234	turn
AR/âr/	168	vary
IR/er/ or/ər/	104	sir

Schwa 1,252

E/ə/	763	item
O/ə/	321	atom
A/ə/	114	ago

Broad O/ô/Vowel 509

AL/ôl/	165	all
AU/ô/	146	auto
O/ô/	123	off
AW/ô/	75	saw

Long & Short OO 487

U/o͝o/ or/u̇/	200	pull
OO/o͞o/	173	moon
OO/o͝o/	114	look

PHONICS RESEARCH BASIS CONTINUED

Consonant Graphemes Ranked by Frequency of Regular Phoneme-Grapheme Correspondence in a 17,310-Word Vocabulary

Consonant Sounds

Very Common	**R**	9,134	Rare	**Z**	299
	T	7,528		**X**/ks/	245[5]
	N	7,452		**Qu**/kw/	191[3]
	L	4,894		**Y**	53[6]
	S/s/	4,599[4]			
Common	**D**	3,611	Consonant	**TH** /th/	411
	C/k/	3,452[1]	Digraphs	**SH**	398
	M	3,302		**CH**	311
	P	3,296		**TH**/TH/	149
	B	2,342		**WH**	89
Less Common	**F**	1,580			
	V	1,485			
	G/g/	1,178[2]			
	H	762			
	J	218			
	K	601			
	W	578			

Notes:

[1]The letter C is ranked by its regular sound of /k/ as in "cat" (3,452); however; the letter C frequently makes the /s/ sound as in "city" (1,067).

[2]The regular sound of G is /g/ as in "good (1,178); however, G makes the /j/ sound as in "general" (647) more often than letter J does (218).

[3]The letter Q has no sound of its own and always appears with a U, so this ranking is when QU makes the /kw/ sound as in "queen" (191).

[4]The regular sound of S is /s/ as in "so" (4,599); however, S makes the /z/ sound as in "is" (640) more often than letter Z does (299).

[5]The letter X has no sound of its own, so this ranking is for when it makes the /ks/ sound as in "box" (245).

[6]The letter Y is usually a vowel; however, this ranking is when it makes its consonant sound /y/ as in "yes" (53).

Reference:

Fry, E. B. (2004). Phonics: A large phoneme-grapheme frequency chart revised. *Journal of Literacy Research, 36-1.*

LIST 9. PHONICS EXAMPLE WORDS

This is an important list at the heart of phonics instruction. It alphabetically lists 99 single phonemes (speech sounds) and consonant blends (usually two phonemes), and it gives example words for each of these; often for their use in the beginning, middle, and end of words. These example words are also common English words, many taken from the list of Instant Words. This list solves the problem of coming up with a good common word to illustrate a phonics principle for lessons and worksheets.

/a/ SHORT A, CLOSED SYLLABLE RULE

Initial			Medial		
and	add	am	that	has	began
at	act	animal	can	than	stand
as	adjective	ant	had	man	black
after	answer	ax	back	hand	happen
an	ask	Africa	last	plant	fast

apple

/ā/ LONG A, OPEN SYLLABLE RULE

Initial	Medial			
able	paper	lazy	label	vibration
acre	lady	flavor	equator	basis
agent	baby	tomato	relation	hazy
apron	radio	navy	vapor	potato
Asia	crazy	station	enable	ladle
apex	labor	basic	volcano	vacation
April				tablecloth

table

/ā/ LONG A, FINAL E RULE

Initial		Medial			
ate	ape	make	late	gave	baseball
age	ace	made	tale	base	spaceship
ache		face	place	plane	racetrack
ale		same	name	game	shapeless
		came	wave	shape	
		state	space		

cake

/ā/ LONG A, AI DIGRAPH

Initial	Medial				
aim	rain	mail	claim	obtain	faint
aid	train	pain	detail	paid	grain
ailment	wait	sail	explain	remain	rail
ail	tail	strait	fail	wait	
	chain	afraid	gain	plain	
	jail	brain	main	laid	

nail

See also List 7, Suggested Phonics Teaching Order; List 8, Phonics Research Basis.

PHONICS EXAMPLE WORDS CONTINUED

/ā/ LONG A, AY DIGRAPH

Medial			Final		
always	gayly	jaywalk	day	pay	repay
mayor	haystack	player	say	gray	anyway
layer	wayside	daylight	away	bay	way
maybe	payment		play	stay	pray
	rayon		may	birthday	lay
			today	highway	gay
					hay

crayon

/ə/ SCHWA, A SPELLING

Initial		Medial		Final	
about	appear	several	canvass	antenna	china
above	away	national	familiar	algebra	comma
ago	again	senator	career	alfalfa	idea
alone	ahead	thousand	purchase	banana	
America	another	magazine	compass		
alike	agree	breakfast	diagram		

announce

/ô/ AL DIGRAPH SPELLING

Initial		Medial		Final	
all	altogether	talk	scald	call	baseball
always	alternate	walk	walnut	tall	wall
also	altar	chalk	fallen	fall	stall
already	albeit	salt		overall	recall
almost	almanac	false		hall	
although	almighty	falter		small	

ball

/ô/ AU DIGRAPH SPELLING

Initial		Medial			
August	Australia	audible	because	cause	sausage
author	autoharp	authentic	caught	dinosaur	overhaul
autumn	auction	auditor	laundry	sauce	launch
auditorium	auburn		haul	caution	faucet
autograph	auxiliary		daughter	exhaust	
audience	automatic		fault	fraud	

auto

/ô/ AW DIGRAPH SPELLING

Initial	Medial			Final	
awful	lawn	yawn	crawl	law	paw
awkward	drawn	tawny	squawk	jaw	claw
awning	lawyer	drawer	scrawl	draw	flaw
awe	hawk	shawl		straw	gnaw
awl	lawful	bawl		thaw	caw
awfully				taw	

saw

The Reading Teacher's Book of Lists, Fifth Edition, © 2006 by John Wiley & Sons, Inc.

/air/ AIR VOWEL, AR AND ARE SPELLINGS

Initial	Medial			Final	
area	January	February	declare	care	fare
	dictionary	tiara	beware	rare	stare
	vary	parent	flare	aware	glare
	primary	wary		share	welfare
	secretary	careful		spare	hare
	canary	scare		bare	square
	daring	scarcely		dare	

library

/ar/ AR VOWEL, AR SPELLING

Initial	Medial			Final	
are	argument	card	garden	car	mar
arm	article	March	start	far	par
army	arch	farm	dark	bar	scar
art	armor	hard	yard	jar	
artist	ark	part	party	tar	
arctic	arbor	large			

star

/b/ REGULAR B CONSONANT SOUND

Initial	Medial			Final	
be	back	number	subject	tub	job
by	but	problem	baby	cab	club
boy	because	remember		rob	rub
been	below	object		cub	grab
box	before	probably		rib	adverb
big	better			verb	bulb

book

/bl/ CONSONANT BLEND

Initial				Medial	
black	blame	blank	blink	oblige	obliterate
blue	bloom	blast	blur	emblem	grumbling
bleed	blossom	blend	blow	tumbler	oblivious
blood	blond	blue	blanket	nosebleed	gambler
blind	blade	blot	bleach	ablaze	rambling
				nimbly	

block

/br/ CONSONANT BLEND

Initial			Medial		
bread	bring	brush	library	daybreak	algebra
break	breath	breeze	umbrella	cobra	embrace
brick	branch	bridge	celebrate	membrane	lubricate
broad	bright	brain	vibrate	outbreak	
brother	broken	brass	abroad	zebra	
brown	brave	breakfast			

broom

PHONICS EXAMPLE WORDS CONTINUED

/k/ HARD C, REGULAR CONSONANT K SOUND

Initial		Medial		Final		
can	call	because	across	back	check	
come	country	picture	become	rock	stick	
came	cut	American	quickly	sick	black	
camp	car	second		lock	pick	
color	cold			kick	thick	
could	carry			music	electric	

cat

/s/ SOFT C, REGULAR CONSONANT S SOUND

Initial			Medial		Final	
cent	certain	cigar	pencil	decide	face	
circle	civil	cyclone	fancy	Pacific	since	
cycle	ceiling	cellar	concert	percent	ice	
circus	celebrate	cease	acid	precise		
center	cereal		dancing	process		
cell	cinder		peaceful	sincere		

city

/ch/ CH CONSONANT DIGRAPH SOUND

Initial		Medial		Final		
children	chief	pitcher	searching	which	catch	
church	chart	attached	stretched	each	branch	
change	chin	purchase	exchange	much	touch	
chance	chest	merchant		such	inch	
cheer	chain			teach	reach	
check	chase			rich	watch	

chair

/cl/ CONSONANT BLEND

clock

Initial				Medial		
clean	clear	clever	climb	enclose	eclipse	
cloth	class	cliff	click	include	acclaim	disclose
clay	clap	close		cyclone	conclude	decline
claim	claws	cloud		exclaim	reclaim	proclaim
club	clerk	clues		exclude	declare	incline

/cr/ CONSONANT BLEND

Initial				Medial		
cry	crew	cried	cruel	across	aircraft	recruit
crack	crazy	crops	credit	secret	sacred	scarecrow
crowd	cross	crayon		increase	concrete	screen
crash	crow	creek		microscope	disease	
cream	create	crown		democrat	decree	

crab

/d/ REGULAR D CONSONANT SOUND

Initial		Medial		Final	
do	does	study	order	and	find
day	door	under	Indians	good	need
did	done	idea	didn't	had	did
dear	different	body		said	old
down	during			red	around
deep	don't			would	end

dog

/dr/ CONSONANT BLEND

Initial			Medial		
dry	dream	drift	address	undress	hydrogen
draw	dragon	drama	hundred	withdraw	laundress
drug	drill	drain	children	daydream	redress
drove	drink	drip	dandruff	eardrum	dewdrop
drop	drive	drench	cathedral	laundry	
dress	drew	droop			

drum

/e/ SHORT E, CLOSED SYLLABLE RULE

Initial			Medial			
end	empty	ever	when	let	set	men
egg	energy	edge	then	them	went	spell
every	explain	enter	get	very	help	next
extra	enjoy	elf	left	tell	well	red
enemy	engine	else				

elephant

/ē/ LONG E, OPEN SYLLABLE RULE

Initial	Medial			Final	
even	cedar	meter	being	me	we
equal	demon	prefix	recent	he	be
ether	secret	react	legal	she	maybe
evil	zebra	area	really		
ecology		female	depot		

Egypt

/ē/ LONG E, EE DIGRAPH

Initial	Medial		Final		
eel	sleep	seem	see	bee	fee
eerie	green	teeth	three	degree	spree
	keep	sweet	tree	flee	referee
	street	week	free	knee	
	feet	screen	agree	glee	
	wheel	fifteen			
	feel				

deer

PHONICS EXAMPLE WORDS CONTINUED

/ē/ LONG E, EA DIGRAPH

Initial			Medial		Final
eat	eager	ease	neat	leaf	sea
each	easel	eaves	read	feast	tea
east	Easter	easily	least	peach	flea
easy	eaten		beat	meat	plea
eagle	eastern		clean	weak	pea
			deal	peanut	

peach

/e/ SHORT E, EA SPELLING

Medial

head	breath	feather	meadow	threaten	heaven
heavy	dear	death	pleasant	treasure	dread
ready	ahead	measure	spread	weapon	pleasure
thread	breakfast	instead	heading	weather	widespread
steady	already	leather	sweat	overhead	gingerbread
dead					

bread

/ə/ SCHWA, E SPELLING

Initial		Medial			
efface	effective	happen	scientist	fuel	label
effect	efficient	problem	item	given	absent
efficiency		hundred	united	level	agent
erratic		arithmetic	quiet	heaven	hundred
essential		children	diet	even	often
erroneous		calendar	different	happen	

eleven

/er/ ER VOWEL, ER SPELLING

Medial		Final			
camera	afternoon	her	better	another	river
allergy	liberty	mother	sister	baker	winter
bakery	operate	over	under	wonder	liver
wonderful	federal	other	after	ever	shower
dangerous	battery	were	water	offer	lower

letter

/f/ REGULAR F CONSONANT SOUND

Initial		Medial		Final	
for	father	after	different	if	chief
first	face	before	Africa	half	stuff
find	family	often	beautiful	myself	brief
four	follow	careful		off	cliff
funny	far			leaf	itself
food	few			himself	wolf

fish

The Reading Teacher's Book of Lists, Fifth Edition, © 2006 by John Wiley & Sons, Inc.

/fl/ CONSONANT BLEND

Initial

flower	floor	fleet	flea
flat	flavor	flow	fluffy
flight	flood	flap	
flew	flute	flock	
fly	flame	fling	
float	flash	flip	

Medial

afflict	inflame
inflict	afloat
conflict	reflect
influence	inflate
aflame	inflexible
snowflake	

flag

/fr/ CONSONANT BLEND

Initial

free	frost	fruit	frisky
from	frank	freedom	freighter
front	freshman	frozen	fragile
friend	frame	France	
Friday	fresh		
fry	fraction		

Medial

afraid	defraud
affront	infringe
befriend	leapfrog
bullfrog	refrain
carefree	refresh
confront	infrequent

frog

/g/ REGULAR G CONSONANT SOUND

Initial | | **Medial** | | **Final** |

Initial		Medial		Final	
go	gun	again	segment	dog	frog
good	game	ago	regular	big	pig
got	gas	began	figure	egg	log
gave	gift	sugar		leg	bag
girl	gone	wagon		fig	
get	garden	signal		flag	

gate

/j/ SOFT G, REGULAR CONSONANT J SOUND

Initial		Medial		Final	
gem	gym	gesture	danger	change	page
gentlemen	gypsy	genius	energy	large	village
geography	ginger	genuine	region	bridge	huge
generous	gelatin	generate	engine	age	strange
gently	germ	giant	original		
	general		vegetable		
			oxygen		

giraffe

/gl/ CONSONANT BLEND

Initial

glad	glisten	glare	glider
glass	gloom	glade	glimpse
glow	glue	gleam	glitter
glory	glum	glee	glance
glove	glamour		glaze

Medial

eyeglass	hourglass
jingling	bugler
spyglass	angler
smuggling	mangling
wiggling	singly

globe

PHONICS EXAMPLE WORDS CONTINUED

/gr/ CONSONANT BLEND

Initial			Medial		
grade	grand	grant	hungry	program	disgrace
great	green	grin	angry	regret	fragrant
grow	ground	gradual	congress	degrade	outgrow
grew	group	grandfather	agree	engrave	engross
grass	grab	gravity	degree		
gray	grain				

grapes

/h/ REGULAR H CONSONANT SOUND

Initial				Medial	
he	help	half	high	behind	rehearse
had	here	his	hit	ahead	behold
have	happy	hen	house	unhappy	unhook
her	home	hero		behave	ahoy
him	hard	hide		overheard	
how	has	hill		autoharp	

hand

/ĭ/ SHORT I, CLOSED SYLLABLE RULE

Initial			Medial		
in	it	ill	with	will	different
is	invent	include	did	big	until
if	important	isn't	this	still	miss
into	insect	inside	little	give	begin
inch	instead		which	his	city
				him	

India

/ī/ LONG I, OPEN SYLLABLE RULE

Initial		Medial			
I	icy	bicycle	pilot	variety	title
idea	Irish	tiny	quiet	dinosaur	spider
I'll	iodine	silent	triangle	giant	diagram
iris	Iowa	rifle	climate	lion	China
I'm	ivory				
item					

iron

/ī/ LONG I, FINAL E RULE

Initial	Medial				
idle	five	fire	nine	mile	drive
ire	white	write	bite	size	wire
isle	ride	life	like	wide	mine
I've	time	side	line	describe	wife

ice

The Reading Teacher's Book of Lists, Fifth Edition, © 2006 by John Wiley & Sons, Inc.

/er/ ER VOWEL, IR SPELLING

Medial   **Final**

girl	skirt	thirteen	shirk	circuit	fir
first	birthday	girth	mirth	girdle	sir
third	thirsty	birth	confirm	stirrup	stir
shirt	affirm	circus	Virginia	dirty	tapir
dirt	circle	thirty	firm		whir
					astir

girl

/j/ REGULAR J CONSONANT SOUND

Initial   **Medial**

just	jet	June	object	project	unjust
jump	job	jungle	enjoy	adjust	majesty
January	joke	junior	subject	dejected	majority
jaw	joy	jacket	major	overjoyed	rejoice
July	juice	join	banjo	adjoin	
			adjective	reject	

jar

/k/ REGULAR K CONSONANT SOUND

Initial   **Medial**   **Final**

kind	kiss	monkey	market	like	work
key	kitten	broken	packing	make	mark
kill	kid	turkey	stroking	book	speak
king	kettle	worker		look	milk
keep	kick			cake	bank
kin	keen			cook	break

kite

/n/ SOUND, KN SPELLING

Initial   **Medial**

knee	knelt	knack	knockout	knell	unknown
knew	knit	kneel	knickers	kneecap	doorknob
know	knock	knapsack	knothole	knotty	penknife
knowledge	knight	knob	knoll	known	acknowledge
knife	knuckle	knead	knave		knickknack
					knock-kneed

knot

/l/ REGULAR L CONSONANT SOUND

Initial   **Medial**   **Final**

little	large	only	really	will	oil
like	last	below	follow	all	tell
long	line	along	family	girl	until
look	learn	children		school	spell
live	left			shall	well
land	light			small	vowel

letter

The Reading Teacher's Book of Lists, Fifth Edition, © 2006 by John Wiley & Sons, Inc.

PHONICS EXAMPLE WORDS CONTINUED

/m/ REGULAR M CONSONANT SOUND

Initial		Medial		Final	
me	more	number	important	from	farm
my	mother	American	example	them	room
make	move	something	family	am	arm
much	must	complete		seem	team
many	made			warm	form
may	men			him	bottom

man

/n/ REGULAR N CONSONANT SOUND

Initial		Medial		Final	
not	name	many	until	in	man
no	number	under	any	on	even
new	need	answer	animal	can	own
night	never	country		when	open
next	near			an	been
now	next			then	than

nut

/ng/ CONSONANT DIGRAPH SOUND

Medial		Final			
slingshot	gangster	sing	long	bang	spring
lengthen	singer	bring	song	lung	strong
longing	hanger	thing	gang	wing	fang
kingdom	gangplank	going	hang	ring	hung
youngster	gangway	swing	young	fling	string
					wrong

king

/o/ SHORT O, CLOSED SYLLABLE RULE

Initial		Medial			
odd	opera	not	fox	follow	rock
olive	oxygen	hot	drop	got	bottom
oxen	operate	body	pop	problem	copy
October	occupy		clock	product	cannot
opportunity					

box

/ō/ LONG O, OPEN SYLLABLE RULE

Initial		Medial	Final		
open	odor	October	go	zero	echo
over	omit	program	no	cargo	volcano
obey	oboe	Roman	so	piano	
ocean	okra	moment	hello	potato	
Ohio		poem	ago	hero	
		total	also		
		broken	auto		

radio

The Reading Teacher's Book of Lists, Fifth Edition, © 2006 by John Wiley & Sons, Inc.

/ō/ LONG O, FINAL E RULE

Initial	Medial				
owe	home	rode	whole	rose	stove
	those	nose	slope	spoke	awoke
	hope	stone	bone	smoke	phone
	note	joke	tone	drove	
	along	globe	pole	vote	

rope

/ō/ LONG O, OA DIGRAPH

Initial	Medial				
oak	coat	toast	approach	croak	coal
oat	soap	goat	loaf	soak	toad
oath	road	goal	groan	cloak	moan
oatmeal	coast	loan	foam	roach	throat
oaf	load	float	roast	boast	coach

boat

/ō/ LONG O, OW DIGRAPH

Initial	Medial		Final		
own	bowl	crowbar	show	follow	mow
owe	stowaway	bowling	low	tomorrow	glow
owing	snowball	mower	slow	throw	know
owner	towboat		snow	blow	crow
			row	grow	arrow
			yellow	flow	borrow

window

/ou/ OU DIPHTHONG, OW SPELLING

Medial			Final		
down	crown	towel	how	somehow	endow
town	cowboy	powder	now	eyebrow	vow
brown	power	tower	cow	bow	prow
flower	vowel	chowder	plow	scow	avow
crowd	downward	shower	allow	sow	snowplow

owl

/oi/ OI DIPHTHONG, OY SPELLING

Initial	Medial		Final		
oyster	royal	joyous	toy	decoy	convoy
	voyage	disloyal	joy	newsboy	envoy
	loyal	loyalty	enjoy	annoy	corduroy
	boycott	enjoyment	employ	soy	
	annoying	joyful	destroy	viceroy	
	employer	boyish	coy	Troy	
	boyhood		cowboy	alloy	

boy

PHONICS EXAMPLE WORDS CONTINUED

/ə/ SCHWA, O SPELLING

Initial		Medial		Final
other	oblige	mother	action	kimono
original	obstruct	money	canyon	
official	oppose	atom	weapon	
observe	occasion	second	period	
opinion	oppress	nation	mission	
objection	opossum	method	riot	

violin

/oi/ OI DIPHTHONG, OI SPELLING

Initial	Medial				
oilcloth	join	broil	coil	sirloin	joint
oilwell	point	spoil	moisture	disappoint	embroider
oily	voice	avoid	exploit	toil	typhoid
ointment	coin	poison	doily	void	
	choice	boil	soil	broiler	
	noise	turmoil	rejoice		

oil

/ou/ OU DIPHTHONG, OU SPELLING

Initial		Medial			Final
out	outer	hour	aloud	doubt	thou
our	outline	sound	found	count	
ounce	outside	about	council	boundary	
oust	outlook	around	ground		
ourselves	outcry	round	loud		
outdoors	outfield	scout	cloud		
ouch		amount	mountain		

house

/ô/ O SPELLING

Initial			Medial		
off	onto	offhand	soft	wrong	moth
office	offset	offshore	long	cloth	frost
officer	offspring	ostrich	along	toss	cross
often	onward		cost	coffee	belong
on	onset		across	strong	
offer	oncoming			song	

dog

/or/ OR VOWEL, OR SPELLING

Initial		Medial			Final
or	Oregon	short	score	corner	for
order	organ	horn	form	store	more
ore	ordinary	forget	before	north	nor
orbit	oral	born	horse	force	
orchestra	orchard	cord	story		
	orchid		important		

fork

The Reading Teacher's Book of Lists, Fifth Edition, © 2006 by John Wiley & Sons, Inc.

/oo/ SHORT DOUBLE O, OO SPELLING

Medial

look	took	foot	shook	brook	cook
good	wood	stood	goodbye	wool	dogwood
book	rook	soot	lookout	notebook	rookie
afoot	hoof	cookie	football	understood	handbook
hood	crook	nook	wooden	neighborhood	overlook
motherhood					

hook

/o͞o/ LONG DOUBLE O, OO SPELLING

Initial	**Medial**			**Final**	
ooze	soon	tooth	mood	too	bamboo
	school	cool	roof	zoo	cuckoo
	room	goose	loose	shampoo	boo
	food	troop	balloon	woo	igloo
	shoot	fool	noon	coo	
	smooth	boot		tattoo	
	pool	took		kangaroo	

moon

/p/ REGULAR P CONSONANT SOUND

Initial		**Medial**		**Final**	
put	point	open	perhaps	up	ship
people	piece	example	happy	sleep	top
page	pass	paper		jump	step
pair	person	important		help	map
part	paper	upon		stop	deep
picture	pull			group	drop

pencil

/f/ SOUND, PH SPELLING

Initial		**Medial**		**Final**	
photo	phase	alphabet	cellophane	photograph	telegraph
phonics	phantom	orphan	emphasis	phonograph	graph
phrase	phonetic	nephew	gopher	autograph	triumph
physical	pharmacy	sulphur	graphic	paragraph	
physician	phoenix	geography	trophy		
pheasant	phenomenon	sophomore			

telephone

/pl/ CONSONANT BLEND

Initial			**Medial**		
play	place	player	supply	display	applaud
plant	plan	pleasant	multiply	explain	apply
plain	plane	plot	employ	supplying	complain
please	planets	plank	reply	surplus	
plow	plastic	plug	perplex		
plus	platform	plate	imply		

airplane

PHONICS EXAMPLE WORDS CONTINUED

/pr/ CONSONANT BLEND

Initial

pretty	president	present	probably
price	prince	problem	prove
press	program	produce	pray
print	practice	property	products
	prepare	provide	propeller

Medial

surprise	approach
April	approximate
improve	appropriate
apron	impression
express	

prize

/kw/ QU CONSONANT BLEND SOUND

Initial

quart	quiet	quote	
quite	quack	quill	
question	quail	quality	
quick	quake		
quit	quilt		
queer	quiz		

Medial

square	liquid	squirm
equal	equipment	sequence
squirrel	equator	squeak
frequent	equivalent	inquire
require	squash	
equation	earthquake	

queen

/r/ REGULAR R CONSONANT SOUND

Initial

run	rest
red	ride
right	road
ran	rock
read	room
rat	rod

Medial

very	large
part	story
word	form
around	

Final

our	other
their	over
for	water
year	her
dear	after
your	near

ring

/s/ REGULAR S CONSONANT SOUND

Initial

some	sound
so	say
see	sentence
said	side
soon	same
set	sea

Medial

also	question
person	inside
answer	system
himself	

Final

this	less
us	across
likes	its
makes	gas
yes	bus
miss	perhaps

saw

/z/ Z CONSONANT SOUND, S SPELLING

Medial

music	observe	please
easy	museum	cheese
busy	present	wise
those	result	these
because	season	
desert	poison	

Final

is	odds	news
as	says	hers
was	suds	does
his	yours	
has	tongs	
ours	days	

eyes

The Reading Teacher's Book of Lists, Fifth Edition, © 2006 by John Wiley & Sons, Inc.

/sc/ CONSONANT BLEND

Initial

score	scatter	scream	scoop
school	scholar	scallop	scrub
screen	scout	screw	
scratch	scare	scared	
scarf	scramble	scab	
scar	scrape		

Medial

describe	inscribe
telescope	unscramble
description	microscopic
microscope	unscrupulous
nondescript	telescoping
unscrew	descriptive

scale

/sh/ CONSONANT BLEND

Initial

she	shot
shall	shirt
show	shell
ship	sheet
short	shop
shape	shut

Medial

dashed	ashes
splashing	friendship
sunshine	
worship	
fisherman	

Final

wish	rush
wash	dish
fish	crash
push	bush
finish	flash
fresh	establish

shoe

/sk/ CONSONANT BLEND

Initial

sky	skeleton	skillet
skin	skull	skirmish
skill	skid	skinny
skunk	sketch	skylark
skirt	ski	skeptic
skip	skim	skate

Medial

outskirts
askew
muskrat
rollerskate
muskmelon
masked

Final

desk	mask
task	husk
ask	dusk
brisk	

desk

/sl/ CONSONANT BLEND

Initial

slow	sled	slope	sly
sleep	slave	slam	slash
slept	sleeve	slate	slab
slip	slant	slipper	sleek
slid	slice	sleet	slimy
slap	slight	slim	

Medial

asleep	oversleep
landslide	snowslide
onslaught	grandslam
enslave	nonslip
bobsled	
manslaughter	

slide

/sm/ CONSONANT BLEND

Initial

smile	smash	smock	smote	smuggler
smooth	smear	smoky	smokestack	smelt
smell	smith	smudge	smattering	smite
small	smolder	smuggle	smorgasbord	
smart	smack	smug	smithy	
smother	smog	smitten	smoker	

Medial

blacksmith
gunsmith
silversmith
locksmith

smoke

PHONICS EXAMPLE WORDS CONTINUED

/sn/ CONSONANT BLEND

Initial

snow	snuggle	snapshot	sniff	snooze	snuff
snowball	snip	sneak	sniffle	snorkel	snowman
snare	snarl	snatch	snipe	snort	sniper
sneeze	snap	sneakers	snob	snout	snowy
snore	snack	sneer	snoop	snub	
snug	snail				

snake

/sp/ CONSONANT BLEND

Initial			**Medial**		**Final**
sports	speed	spider	inspect	despair	clasp
space	spell	spend	respect	inspire	crisp
speak	spot	spark	respond	despite	gasp
spring	spin		despise		grasp
spread	spoke		unspeakable		wasp
special	spare		respectful		lisp
					wisp

spoon

/st/ CONSONANT BLEND

Initial			**Medial**		**Final**
stop	story	stick	instead	restless	best
step	street	stone	destroy	poster	cast
stay	stand	stood	restore	tasty	dust
state	star		westward		fast
still	study		haystack		least
store	strong		destruction		past
					west

stamp

/sw/ CONSONANT BLEND

Initial

swim	switch	sweet	swollen	swampy	swarthy
swell	swallow	swift	sway	swirl	swat
swept	swung	swan	swine	swarm	swerve
sweat	swam	swagger	swoop	swear	sworn
swing	swamp	swap	swindle	swelter	swish
sweep					

sweater

/t/ REGULAR T CONSONANT SOUND

Initial		**Medial**		**Final**	
to	took	city	later	not	what
two	top	into	sentence	at	set
take	ten	water	until	it	part
tell	talk	after		out	got
too	today			get	put
time	told			but	want

table

The Reading Teacher's Book of Lists, Fifth Edition, © 2006 by John Wiley & Sons, Inc.

The Reading Teacher's Book of Lists, Fifth Edition, © 2006 by John Wiley & Sons, Inc.

/t̶h̶/ VOICELESS TH CONSONANT DIGRAPH SOUND

Initial		Medial		Final	
thank	thought	something	toothbrush	with	truth
think	thread	author	python	both	death
thing	threw	nothing		ninth	south
third	thumb	athlete		worth	fifth
thirty	thunder	faithful		cloth	bath
thick	threat	bathtub		teeth	

three

/th/ VOICED TH CONSONANT DIGRAPH SOUND

Initial		Medial		Final
the	though	mother	weather	smooth
that	thus	other	gather	
them	thy	brother	breathing	
they	thence	father	rhythm	
this	their	although	farther	
there	then	bother	leather	
than	thou	clothing	northern	
these		either		

feather

/tr/ CONSONANT BLEND

Initial			Medial		
track	trick	trouble	extra	control	country
tractor	travel	trap	electric	sentry	patrol
train	tree	trail	central	waitress	
trade	trim	triangle	attract	contract	
truly	trip	traffic	entry	patron	
try	true		subtract	contrast	

truck

/tw/ CONSONANT BLEND

Initial					Medial
twelve	twirl	twinkle	twinge	twelfth	between
twenty	twine	twist	twang	twill	entwine
twice	tweed	twitter	twentieth	twiddle	untwist
twig	twilight	twitch	tweet		intertwine

twins

/u/ SHORT U, CLOSED SYLLABLE RULE

Initial			Medial		
up	unhappy	unless	but	number	such
us	upon	umpire	run	must	hunt
under	usher		much	study	summer
until	unusual		just	hundred	jump
ugly	uproar		cut	sudden	gun
uncle	upset		funny	sun	

umbrella

PHONICS EXAMPLE WORDS CONTINUED

/ū/ LONG U, OPEN SYLLABLE RULE

Initial		Medial			Final
unit	unify	future	humid	fugitive	menu
united	unique	human	museum	funeral	
Utah	utilize	valuable	continuous	beautiful	
uniform		humor	fuel	unusual	
universe		January	bugle	musician	
usual		pupil	cubic	puny	
university		community	communicate		

music

/o͝o/ SHORT DOUBLE O, U SPELLING

Medial					
bullet	bush	cushion	bull's-eye	pulpit	bulldog
full	bushel	ambush	bushy	fully	armful
pull	sugar	bulletin	pullet	bullfrog	bully
push	pudding	handful	pushcart	fulfill	bullfight
put	butcher	pulley	bulldozer	bulwark	output

bull

/o͞o/ LONG DOUBLE O, U, AND U_E SPELLINGS

Medial					
June	flute	tune	punctuation	revolution	tuna
July	prune	conclusion	constitution	ruby	influence
truth	cruel	tube	duty	prudent	solution
junior	numeral	February	nutrition	situation	rhubarb
rule	parachute	aluminum	reduce	ruin	truly
crude					

ruler

/er/ ER VOWEL, UR SPELLING

Initial	Medial			Final	
urn	turn	purple	further	fur	spur
urban	burn	hurt	purpose	sulfur	cur
urchin	hurry	turkey	burst	murmur	bur
urge	curl	curb	surf	concur	
urgent	Thursday	nurse	church	occur	
	purse	surface		slur	

turtle

/v/ REGULAR V CONSONANT SOUND

Initial		Medial		Final	
very	vowel	over	however	give	live
visit	van	even	cover	five	move
voice	verb	never	several	love	above
vote	vase	river		gave	leave
view	violin			twelve	wave
vest	valley			have	believe

Valentine

The Reading Teacher's Book of Lists, Fifth Edition, © 2006 by John Wiley & Sons, Inc.

/w/ REGULAR W CONSONANT SOUND

Initial   **Medial**

we	way	wave	away	awake	halfway
with	were	win	reward	aware	sidewalk
will	word	woman	forward	unwind	upward
was	week	wait	sandwich	highway	midway
work	would	want		backward	tapeworm
water					

window

/wh/ WH CONSONANT BLEND SOUND

Initial   **Medial**

when	white	whip	whiskey	awhile	buckwheat
what	while	whisper	whack	bobwhite	cartwheel
which	why	whistle	whiff	overwhelm	somewhere
whether	wheat	wheeze	whimper	somewhat	anywhere
where	whale	wharf	whiz	everywhere	nowhere
					meanwhile

wheel

/r/ SOUND, WR SPELLING

Initial   **Medial**

write	wrestle	wretch	wrung	awry	typewriter
writing	wrist	wrinkle	wry	rewrite	typewritten
written	wreath	wrapper	wrangle	handwriting	
wrote	wring	wrathful		unwrap	
wrong	wreck	wreckage		playwright	
wrap	wren	wriggle		shipwreck	

wrench

/ks/ REGULAR X CONSONANT SOUND

Medial   **Final**

Mexico	explain	fox	fix	complex	vex
Texas	axis	ax	relax	index	wax
mixture	oxen	six	mix	lax	sex
extremely	extra	tax	prefix	hex	perplex
sixty	excuse	ox		lox	
expert	exclaim				

box

/y/ REGULAR Y CONSONANT SOUND

Initial   **Medial**

you	youth	yam	yew	lawyer	vineyard
year	yawn	yank	yeast	canyon	papaya
yellow	yard	yak	yen	beyond	dooryard
yes	yet	yodel	yolk	courtyard	stockyard
yell	your	yacht	yonder	barnyard	backyard
young					

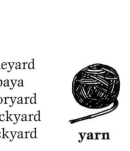

yarn

PHONICS EXAMPLE WORDS CONTINUED

/ē/ LONG E, Y SPELLING

Medial	Final			
anything	very	happy	country	early
babysit	any	lady	city	money
everyone	many	story	really	quickly
ladybug	pretty	family	body	heavy
bodyguard	only	study	usually	ready
copying	funny	every	easy	energy
everything				

baby

/ī/ LONG I, Y SPELLING

Medial		Final			
myself	type	my	sky	shy	reply
nylon	lying	by	July	defy	sly
cycle	rhyme	why	fry	dry	deny
dying	python	buy	apply	ally	
style	hyena	cry	pry	spy	

fly

/z/ REGULAR Z CONSONANT SOUND

Initial		Medial		Final	
zero	zipper	lazy	citizen	size	quiz
zoo	zoom	crazy	frozen	freeze	whiz
zone		puzzle	grazing	prize	buzz
zest		dozen		realize	fizz
zenith		magazine		breeze	fuzz
zigzag				organize	jazz
zinc				seize	adz

zebra

See also List 1, Consonant Sounds; List 7, Suggested Phonics Teaching Order; List 11, Phonograms; List 13, Phonically Irregular Words.

The Reading Teacher's Book of Lists, Fifth Edition, © 2006 by John Wiley & Sons, Inc.

LIST 10. PHONICS WORKSHEET

Name _____   **Date** _____

Here is the grapheme we are studying today:

_____

Here is a word that uses this grapheme:

_____

Here are five words I have found using this grapheme to make this sound:

    1. _____

    2. _____

    3. _____

    4. _____

    5. _____

(As a word source for these five words, you can use the Instant Words (List 16) or a book you are reading.)

Here are two words using this grapheme and sound in words I thought up all by myself without using any list or book:

    1. _____

    2. _____

See also List 7, Suggested Phonics Teaching Order.

LIST 11. PHONOGRAMS

A phonogram is a vowel plus a final consonant sound; for example, the "ab", in "cab." As teachers, we found it difficult to find a complete list of phonograms, so we developed our own using many available lists and a rhyming dictionary. We think this is the most complete one in existence. These are useful for all kinds of games and practice in reading and spelling. Phonograms, or rimes, have been used in the teaching of reading since Colonial times and are currently used in regular classrooms, remedial/corrective reading instruction, English as a Second Language classes, and in adult literacy instruction. Because syllable rimes also include just vowel endings like -ay in "say" or -ea in "tea," we have included some of them in this list. These phonograms are all one-syllable words; however, the same phonograms appear in many polysyllabic words.

-ab	hack	gad	**-aft**	gage	**-ain**	pair
/a/	Jack	had	/a/	page	/ā/	chair
cab	lack	lad	daft	rage	lain	flair
dab	Mack	mad	raft	sage	main	stair
gab	pack	pad	waft	wage	pain	
jab	quack	sad	craft	stage	rain	**-aise**
lab	rack	tad	draft		vain	/ā/
nab	sack	Brad	graft	**-aid**	wain	raise
tab	tack	Chad	shaft	/ā/	brain	braise
blab	black	clad		laid	chain	chaise
crab	clack	glad	**-ag**	maid	drain	praise
drab	crack	shad	/a/	paid	grain	
flab	knack		bag	raid	plain	**-ait**
grab	shack		gag	braid	slain	/ā/
scab	slack	**-ade**	hag	staid	Spain	bait
slab	smack	/ā/	jag		sprain	gait
stab	snack	bade	lag	**-ail**	stain	wait
	stack	fade	nag	/ā/	strain	strait
	track	jade	rag	bail	train	trait
-ace	whack	made	sag	fail		
/ā/		wade	tag	Gail		**-ake**
face		blade	wag	hail	**-aint**	/ā/
lace	**-act**	glade	brag	jail	/ā/	bake
mace	/a/	grade	crag	mail	faint	cake
pace	fact	shade	drag	nail	paint	fake
race	pact	spade	flag	pail	saint	Jake
brace	tact	trade	shag	quail	taint	lake
grace	tract		slag	rail	quaint	make
place			snag	sail		quake
space	**-ad**	**-aff**	stag	tail	**-air**	rake
trace	/a/	/a/	swag	wail	/er/ or /ar/	take
	bad	gaff		flail	fair	wake
-ack	cad	chaff	**-age**	snail	hair	brake
/a/	dad	quaff	/ā/	trail	lair	drake
back	fad	staff	cage			

See also List 1, Consonant Sounds; List 2, Vowel Sounds; List 12, The Most Common Phonograms.

The Reading Teacher's Book of Lists, Fifth Edition, © 2006 by John Wiley & Sons, Inc.

The Reading Teacher's Book of Lists, Fifth Edition, © 2006 by John Wiley & Sons, Inc.

flake
shake
snake
stake

-ale
/ā/
bale
dale
gale
hale
male
pale
sale
tale
scale
shale
stale
whale

-alk
/aw/
balk
calk
talk
walk
chalk
stalk

-all
/ô/
ball
call
fall
gall
hall
mall
pall
tall
wall
small
squall
stall

-alt
/aw/
halt

malt
salt

-am
/a/
cam
dam
ham
jam
Pam
ram
Sam
tam
yam
clam
cram
dram
gram
scam
scram
sham
slam
swam
tram

-ame
/ā/
came
dame
fame
game
lame
name
same
tame
blame
flame
frame
shame

-amp
/a/
camp
damp
lamp
ramp
tamp
vamp

champ
clamp
cramp
scamp
stamp
tramp

-an
/a/
ban
can
Dan
fan
man
pan
ran
tan
van
bran
clan
flan
plan
scan
span
than

-ance
/a/
dance
lance
chance
France
glance
prance
stance
trance

-anch
/a/
ranch
blanch
branch
stanch

-and
/a/
band

hand
land
sand
bland
brand
gland
stand
strand

-ane
/ā/
bane
cane
Jane
lane
mane
pane
sane
vane
wane
crane
plane

-ang
/ā/
bang
fang
gang
hang
pang
rang
sang
tang
clang
slang
sprang
twang

-ank
/ā/
bank
dank
hank
lank
rank
sank
tank
yank

blank
clank
crank
drank
flank
Frank
plank
prank
shank
stank
thank

-ant
/a/
can't
pant
rant
chant
grant
plant
scant
slant

-ap
/a/
cap
gap
lap
map
nap
pap
rap
sap
tap
yap
chap
clap
flap
scrap
slap
snap
strap
trap
wrap

-ape
/ā/
cape

gape
nape
rape
tape
drape
grape
scrape
shape

-ar
/ar/
bar
car
far
jar
mar
par
tar
char
scar
spar
star

-ard
/ar/
bard
card
guard
hard
lard
yard
shard

-are
/air/
bare
care
dare
fare
hare
mare
pare
rare
ware
blare
flare
glare
scare

share
snare
spare
square
stare

-arge
/ar/
barge
large
charge

-ark
/ar/
bark
dark
hark
lark
mark
park
Clark
shark
spark
stark

-arm
/ar/
farm
harm
charm

-arn
/ar/
barn
darn
yarn

-arp
/ar/
carp
harp
tarp
sharp

-art
/ar/
cart

PHONOGRAMS CONTINUED

dart
mart
part
tart
chart
smart
start

-ase
/ā/
base
case
vase
chase

-ash
/a/
bash
cash
dash
gash
hash
lash
mash
rash
sash
brash
clash
flash
slash
smash
stash
thrash
trash

-ask
/a/
ask
cask
mask
task
flask

-asm
/a/
chasm
plasm
spasm

-asp
/a/
gasp
hasp
rasp
clasp
grasp

-ast
/a/
cast
fast
last
mast
past
vast
blast

-aste
/ā/
baste
haste
paste
taste
waste
chaste

-ass
/a/
bass
lass
mass
pass
brass
class
glass
grass

-at
/a/
bat
cat
fat
gnat
hat
mat
pat
rat

sat
tat
vat
brat
chat
drat
flat
scat
slat
spat
that

-atch
/a/
batch
catch
hatch
latch
match
patch
scratch
thatch

-ate
/ā/
date
fate
gate
hate
Kate
late
mate
rate
crate
grate
plate
skate
state

-ath
/ă/
bath
lath
math
path
wrath

-aught
/aw/
caught

naught
taught
fraught

-aunch
/aw/
haunch
launch
paunch

-aunt
/aw/
daunt
gaunt
haunt
jaunt
taunt
flaunt

-ave
/ā/
cave
Dave
gave
pave
rave
save
wave
brave
crave
grave
shave
slave
stave

-aw
/aw/
caw
gnaw
jaw
law
paw
raw
saw
claw
draw
flaw
slaw
squaw
straw

-awl
/aw/
bawl
brawl
crawl
drawl
shawl
scrawl
trawl

-awn
/aw/
dawn
fawn
lawn
pawn
yawn
brawn
drawn
prawn
spawn

-ax
/a/
lax
Max
tax
wax
flax

-ay
/ā/
bay
day
gay
hay
jay
lay
may
nay
pay
quay
ray
say
way
bray
clay
cray
fray

gray
play
pray
slay
spray
stay
stray
sway
tray

-aze
/ā/
daze
faze
gaze
haze
maze
raze
blaze
craze
glaze
graze

-ea
/ē/
pea
sea
tea
flea
plea

-each
/ē/
beach
leach
peach
reach
teach
bleach
breach
preach
screech

-ead
/e/
dead
head
lead
read

bread
dread
spread
thread
tread

-ead
/ē/
bead
lead
read
knead
plead

-eak
/ē/
beak
leak
peak
teak
weak
bleak
creak
freak
sneak
speak
squeak
streak
tweak

-eal
/ē/
deal
heal
meal
peal
real
seal
teal
veal
zeal
squeal
steal

-ealth
/e/
health
wealth
stealth

The Reading Teacher's Book of Lists, Fifth Edition, © 2006 by John Wiley & Sons, Inc.

The Reading Teacher's Book of Lists, Fifth Edition, © 2006 by John Wiley & Sons, Inc.

-eam /ē/	**-ear** /e/	**-ed** /e/	**-eed** /ē/	**-een** /ē/	sheet	dell
beam	bear	bed	deed	keen	skeet	fell
ream	pear	fed	feed	queen	sleet	hell
seam	wear	led	heed	seen	street	jell
cream	swear	Ned	kneed	teen	sweet	knell
dream		red	need	green	tweet	Nell
gleam	**-east**	Ted	reed	preen		sell
scream	/ē/	wed	seed	screen	**-eeze**	tell
steam	beast	led	weed	sheen	/ē/	well
stream	feast	bred	bleed		breeze	yell
team	least	fled	breed		freeze	dwell
	yeast	Fred	creed	**-eep**	sneeze	quell
-ean		shed	freed	/ē/	squeeze	shell
/ē/	**-eat**	shred	greed	beep	tweeze	smell
bean	/ē/	sled	speed	deep	wheeze	spell
dean	beat	sped	steed	Jeep		swell
Jean	feat		treed	keep	**-eft**	
lean	heat		tweed	peep	/e/	
mean	meat	**-edge**		seep	deft	**-elp**
wean	neat	/e/		weep	heft	/e/
clean	peat	hedge	**-eek**	cheep	left	help
glean	seat	ledge	/ē/	creep	cleft	kelp
	bleat	wedge	leek	sheep	theft	yelp
	cheat	dredge	meek	sleep		
-eap	cleat	pledge	peek	steep		
/ē/	pleat	sledge	reek	sweep	**-eg**	**-elt**
heap	treat		seek		/e/	/e/
leap	wheat		week		beg	belt
reap		**-ee**	cheek		keg	felt
cheap		/ē/	creek	**-eer**	leg	knelt
	-eave	bee	Greek	/ē/	meg	melt
	/ē/	fee	sleek	beer	peg	pelt
-ear	heave	knee		deer		welt
/ē/	leave	lee		jeer		dwelt
dear	weave	see	**-eel**	leer	**-eigh**	smelt
fear	cleave	tee	/ē/	peer	/ā/	
gear	sheave	wee	feel	queer	neigh	
hear		flee	heel	seer	weigh	
near		free	keel	sneer	sleigh	**-em**
rear	**-eck**	glee	peel	steer		/e/
sear	/e/	tree	reel			gem
tear	deck		creel		**-eld**	hem
year	heck		steel		/e/	stem
clear	neck	**-eech**	wheel		held	them
shear	peck	/ē/		**-eet**	meld	
smear	check	beech		/ē/	weld	
spear	fleck	leech	**-eem**	beet		**-en**
	speck	breech	/ē/	feet	**-ell**	/e/
	wreck	screech	deem	meet	/e/	Ben
		speech	seem	fleet	bell	den
			teem	greet	cell	hen

PHONOGRAMS CONTINUED

	-ent /e/	-ern /er/	-et /e/	they	flick	dried
Ken	bent	fern	bet	whey	slick	fried
men	cent	tern	get		stick	tried
pen	dent	stern	jet	-ib	thick	
ten	gent		let	/i/	trick	-ief
yen	Kent	-erve	met	bib		/ē/
glen	lent	/er/	net	fib	-id	brief
then	rent	nerve	pet	jib	/i/	chief
when	sent	serve	set	rib	bid	grief
wren	tent	verve	wet	crib	did	thief
	vent	swerve	yet	glib	hid	
-ence	went		Chet		kid	-ield
/e/	scent	-esh	fret	-ibe	lid	/ē/
fence	spent	/e/	whet	/ī/	mid	field
hence		mesh		jibe	quid	yield
whence	-ep	flesh	-etch	bribe	rid	shield
	/e/	fresh	/e/	scribe	grid	
-ench	pep		fetch	tribe	skid	-ier
/e/	rep	-ess	retch		slid	/ī/
bench	prep	/e/	sketch	-ice		brier
wench	step	Bess	wretch	/ī/	-ide	crier
clench		guess		dice	/ī/	drier
drench	-ept	less	-ew	lice	bide	flier
French	/e/	mess	/ōō/	mice	hide	
quench	kept	bless	dew	nice	ride	-ies
stench	wept	chess	few	rice	side	/ī/
trench	crept	dress	hew	vice	tide	dies
wrench	slept	press	Jew	price	wide	lies
	swept	stress	knew	slice	bride	pies
-end		tress	new	splice	chide	ties
/e/	-erge		pew	thrice	glide	cries
bend	/er/	-est	blew	twice	pride	dries
end	merge	/e/	brew		slide	flies
fend	serge	best	chew	-ick	snide	fries
lend	verge	guest		/i/	stride	skies
mend		jest	-ex	Dick		tries
rend	-erk	lest	/e/	hick	-ie	
send	/er/	nest	hex	kick	/ī/	-ife
tend	jerk	pest	sex	lick	die	/ī/
vend	clerk	rest	vex	Nick	fie	fife
wend		test	flex	pick	lie	knife
blend	-erm	vest		quick	pie	life
spend	/er/	west	-ey	Rick	tie	rife
trend	berm	zest	/ā/	sick	vie	wife
	germ	blest	hey	tick		strife
-ense	term	chest	gray	wick	-ied	
/e/	sperm	crest	prey	brick	/ī/	-iff
dense		quest		chick	died	/i/
sense		wrest		click	lied	miff
tense						

The Reading Teacher's Book of Lists, Fifth Edition, © 2006 by John Wiley & Sons, Inc.

tiff
cliff
skiff
sniff
whiff

-ift
/i/
gift
lift
rift
sift
drift
shift
swift
thrift

-ig
/i/
big
dig
fig
gig
jig
pig
rig
wig
brig
sprig
swig
twig

-igh
/ī/
high
nigh
sigh
thigh

-ight
/ī/
knight
light
might
night
right
sight

tight
blight
bright
flight
fright
plight
slight

-ike
/ī/
bike
dike
hike
like
Mike
pike
spike
strike

-ild
/ī/
mild
wild
child

-ile
/ī/
bile
file
mile
Nile
pile
tile
vile
smile
stile
while

-ilk
/i/
bilk
milk
silk

-ill
/i/
bill

dill
fill
gill
hill
ill
Jill
kill
mill
pill
quill
rill
sill
till
will
chill
drill
frill
grill
skill
spill
still
swill
thrill
trill
twill

-ilt
/i/
gilt
jilt
hilt
kilt
tilt
wilt
quilt
stilt

-im
/i/
dim
him
Jim
Kim
rim
Tim
vim
brim

grim
prim
slim
swim
trim
whim

-ime
/ī/
dime
lime
mime
time
chime
clime
crime
grime
prime
slime

-imp
/i/
limp
chimp
crimp
primp
skimp
blimp

-in
/i/
bin
din
fin
gin
kin
pin
sin
tin
win
chin
grin
shin
skin
spin
thin
twin

-ince
/i/
mince
since
wince
prince

-inch
/i/
cinch
finch
pinch
winch
clinch
flinch

-ind
/ī/
bind
find
hind
kind
mind
rind
wind
blind
grind

-ine
/ī/
dine
fine
line
mine
nine
pine
tine
vine
wine
brine
shine
shrine
spine
swine
whine

-ing
/i/
bing

ding
king
ping
ring
sing
wing
zing
bring
cling
fling
sling
spring
sting
string
swing
thing
wring

-inge
/i/
binge
hinge
singe
tinge
cringe
fringe
twinge

-ink
/i/
kink
link
mink
pink
rink
sink
wink
blink
brink
chink
clink
drink
shrink
slink
stink
think

-int
/i/
hint
lint
mint
tint
glint
print
splint
sprint
squint
stint

-ip
/i/
dip
hip
lip
nip
quip
rip
sip
tip
zip
blip
chip
clip
drip
flip
grip
ship
skip
slip
snip
strip
trip
whip

-ipe
/ī/
pipe
ripe
wipe
gripe
snipe
stripe
swipe
tripe

PHONOGRAMS CONTINUED

-ir
/er/
fir
sir
stir
whir

-ird
/er/
bird
gird
third

-ire
/ī/
fire
hire
tire
wire
spire

-irk
/er/
quirk
shirk
smirk

-irt
/er/
dirt
flirt
shirt
skirt
squirt

-irth
/er/
birth
firth
girth
mirth

-ise
/ī/
guise
rise
wise

-ish
/i/
dish

fish
wish
swish

-isk
/i/
disk
risk
brisk
frisk
whisk

-isp
/i/
lisp
wisp
crisp

-iss
/i/
hiss
kiss
miss
bliss
Swiss

-ist
/i/
fist
list
mist
wrist
grist
twist

-it
/i/
bit
fit
hit
kit
knit
lit
pit
quit
sit
wit
flit
grit

skit
slit
spit
split
twit

-itch
/i/
ditch
hitch
pitch
witch
switch

-ite
/ī/
bite
kite
mite
quite
rite
site
white
write
sprite

-ive
/ī/
dive
five
hive
jive
live
chive
drive
strive
thrive

-ix
/i/
fix
mix
six

-o
/oo/
do
to
who

-o
/ō/
go
no
so
pro

-oach
/ō/
coach
poach
roach
broach

-oad
/ō/
goad
load
road
toad

-oak
/ō/
soak
cloak
croak

-oal
/ō/
coal
foal
goal
shoal

-oam
/ō/
foam
loam
roam

-oan
/ō/
Joan
loan
moan
groan

-oar
/or/
boar

roar
soar

-oast
/ō/
boast
coast
roast
toast

-oat
/ō/
boat
coat
goat
moat
gloat
float
throat

-ob
/o/
Bob
cob
fob
gob
job
knob
lob
mob
rob
sob
blob
glob
slob
snob

-obe
/ō/
lobe
robe
globe
probe

-ock
/o/
dock
hock
knock

lock
mock
rock
sock
tock
block
clock
crock
flock
frock
shock
smock
stock

-od
/o/
cod
God
mod
nod
pod
rod
sod
Tod
clod
plod
prod
shod
trod

-ode
/ō/
code
lode
mode
node
rode
strode

-oe
/ō/
doe
foe
hoe
Joe
toe
woe

-og
/o/
bog

cog
dog
fog
hog
jog
log
tog
clog
flog
frog
grog
slog
smog

-ogue
/ō/
brogue
rogue
vogue

-oil
/oi/
boil
coil
foil
soil
toil
spoil
broil

-oin
/oi/
coin
join
loin
groin

-oist
/oi/
foist
hoist
joist
moist

-oke
/ō/
coke
joke
poke
woke

The Reading Teacher's Book of Lists, Fifth Edition, © 2006 by John Wiley & Sons, Inc.

yoke	**-olt**	**-one**	**-ood**	**-oon**	**-op**	**-ore**
broke	/ō/	/ō/	/o͞o/	/o͞o/	/o/	/or/
choke	bolt	bone	food	coon	bop	bore
smoke	colt	cone	mood	loon	cop	core
spoke	jolt	hone	brood	moon	hop	fore
stoke	molt	lone		noon	mop	gore
stroke	volt	tone		soon	pop	more
		zone	**-oof**	croon	sop	pore
		clone	/o͞o/	spoon	top	sore
-old	**-om**	crone	goof	swoon	chop	tore
/ō/	/o/	drone	roof		crop	wore
bold	Mom	phone	proof		drop	chore
cold	Tom	prone	spoof	**-oop**	flop	score
fold	prom	shone		/o͞o/	plop	shore
gold		stone		coop	prop	snore
hold			**-ook**	hoop	shop	spore
mold	**-ome**		/o͝o/	loop	slop	store
old	/ō/	**-ong**	book	droop	stop	swore
sold	dome	/aw/	cook	scoop		
told	home	bong	hook	sloop		
scold	Nome	dong	look	snoop		
	Rome	gong	nook	stoop	**-ope**	**-ork**
	tome	long	took	swoop	/ō/	/or/
-ole	gnome	song	brook	troop	cope	cork
/ō/	chrome	tong	crook		dope	fork
dole		prong	shook		hope	pork
hole		strong		**-oor**	lope	York
mole	**-ome**	thong		/oo/	mope	stork
pole	/u/	wrong	**-ool**	poor	nope	
role	come		/o͞o/	boor	pope	
stole	some		cool	moor	rope	**-orm**
whole			fool	spoor	grope	/or/
	-omp	**-oo**	pool		scope	dorm
	/o/	/o͞o/	tool		slope	form
	pomp	boo	drool	**-oose**		norm
-oll	romp	coo	school	/o͞o/		storm
/ō/	chomp	goo	spool	goose	**-orch**	
poll	stomp	moo	stool	loose	/or/	
roll		poo		moose	porch	**-orn**
toll		too		noose	torch	/or/
droll	**-on**	woo	**-oom**		scorch	born
knoll	/u/	zoo	/o͞o/			corn
scroll	son	shoo	boom	**-oot**		horn
stroll	ton		doom	/o͞o/		morn
troll	won		loom	boot	**-ord**	torn
			room	hoot	/or/	worn
	-ond	**-ood**	zoom	loot	cord	scorn
-oll	/o/	/o͝o/	bloom	moot	ford	shorn
/o/	bond	good	broom	root	lord	sworn
doll	fond	hood	gloom	toot	chord	thorn
loll	pond	wood	groom	scoot	sword	
moll	blond	stood		shoot		
	frond					

PHONOGRAMS CONTINUED

-ort	hot	**-oud**	croup	wove	**-owl**	coy
/or/	jot	/ow/	group	clove	/ow/	joy
fort	knot	loud	stoup	drove	fowl	Roy
Mort	lot	cloud		grove	howl	soy
port	not	proud	**-our**	stove	jowl	toy
sort	pot		/ow/	trove	growl	ploy
short	rot	**-ough**	hour		prowl	
snort	tot	/u/	sour	**-ove**	scowl	**-ub**
sport	blot	rough	flour	/u/		/u/
	clot	tough	scour	dove	**-own**	cub
-ose	plot	slough		love	/ow/	dub
/ō/	shot		**-ouse**	glove	down	hub
hose	slot	**-ought**	/ow/	shove	gown	nub
nose	spot	/aw/	douse		town	pub
pose	trot	bought	house	**-ow**	brown	rub
rose		fought	louse	/ō/	clown	sub
chose	**-otch**	ought	mouse	bow	crown	tub
close	/o/	sought	rouse	know	drown	club
prose	botch	brought	souse	low	frown	drub
those	notch	thought	blouse	mow		flub
	blotch		grouse	row	**-own**	grub
-oss	crotch	**-ould**	spouse	sow	/ō/	scrub
/aw/	Scotch	/oo/		tow	known	shrub
boss		could	**-out**		mown	snub
loss	**-ote**	would	/ow/	**-ow**	sown	stub
moss	/ō/	should	bout	/ow/	blown	
toss	note		gout	blow	flown	**-ube**
cross	quote	**-ounce**	lout	crow	grown	/o͞o/
floss	rote	/ow/	pout	flow	shown	cube
gloss	vote	bounce	rout	glow	thrown	rube
	wrote	pounce	tout	grow		tube
-ost		flounce	clout	show	**-owse**	
/ô/	**-oth**	trounce	flout	slow	/ow/	**-uck**
cost	/aw/		grout	snow	dowse	/u/
lost	moth	**-ound**	scout	stow	browse	buck
frost	broth	/ow/	shout		drowse	duck
	cloth	bound	snout	**-ow**		luck
-ost	froth	found	spout	/ow/	**-ox**	muck
/ō/	sloth	hound	sprout	bow	/o/	puck
host		mound	stout	cow	box	suck
most	**-ouch**	pound	trout	how	fox	tuck
post	/ow/	round		now	lox	Chuck
ghost	couch	sound	**-outh**	row	pox	cluck
	pouch	wound	/ow/	sow		pluck
-ot	vouch	ground	mouth	vow	**-oy**	shuck
/o/	crouch		south	brow	/oi/	stuck
cot	grouch	**-oup**		chow	boy	struck
dot	slouch	/o͞o/	**-ove**	plow		truck
got		soup	/ō/	prow		
			cove	scow		

The Reading Teacher's Book of Lists, Fifth Edition, © 2006 by John Wiley & Sons, Inc.

The Reading Teacher's Book of Lists, Fifth Edition, © 2006 by John Wiley & Sons, Inc.

-ud /u/	muff puff ruff bluff fluff gruff scuff sluff snuff stuff	hulk sulk	flume plume spume	tune prune	**-up** /u/ cup pup sup	**-us** /u/ bus pus plus thus
bud cud dud mud spud stud thud		**-ull** /u/ cull dull gull hull lull mull skull	**-ump** /u/ bump dump hump jump lump pump rump chump clump frump grump plump slump stump thump trump	**-ung** /u/ dung hung lung rung sung clung flung sprung stung strung swung wrung	**-ur** /er/ cur fur blur slur spur	**-use** /ū/ fuse muse ruse
-ude /ōō/ dude nude rude crude prude	**-ug** /u/ bug dug hug jug lug mug pug rug tug chug drug plug shrug slug smug snug thug	**-ull** /ŏŏ/ bull full pull			**-ure** /ū/ cure lure pure sure	**-ush** /u/ gush hush lush mush rush blush brush crush flush plush slush thrush
-udge /u/ budge fudge judge nudge drudge grudge sludge smudge trudge		**-um** /u/ bum gum hum mum rum sum chum drum glum plum scum slum strum swum	**-un** /u/ bun fun gun nun pun run sun shun spun stun	**-unk** /u/ bunk dunk funk hunk junk punk sunk chunk drunk flunk plunk shrunk skunk slunk spunk stunk trunk	**-url** /er/ burl curl furl hurl purl churl knurl	**-uss** /u/ buss cuss fuss muss truss
-ue /ōō/ cue due hue Sue blue clue flue glue true	**-uke** /ōō/ duke nuke puke fluke	**-umb** /u/ dumb numb crumb plumb thumb	**-unch** /u/ bunch hunch lunch munch punch brunch crunch		**-urn** /er/ burn turn churn spurn	
	-ule /ū/ mule pule rule yule			**-unt** /u/ bunt hunt punt runt blunt grunt shunt stunt	**-urse** /er/ curse nurse purse	**-ust** /u/ bust dust gust just lust must rust crust thrust trust
-uff /u/ buff cuff huff	**-ulk** /u/ bulk	**-ume** /ōō/ fume	**-une** /ū/ June		**-urt** /er/ curt hurt blurt spurt	

PHONOGRAMS CONTINUED

-ut	Tut	hutch	mute	putt	fry	why
/u/	glut	clutch	brute		ply	
but	shut	crutch	chute	-y	pry	-ye
cut	smut		flute	/ī/	shy	/ī/
gut	strut	-ute		by	sky	aye
hut		/ū/	-utt	my	sly	dye
jut	-utch	cute	/u/	cry	spy	eye
nut	/u/	jute	butt	dry	spry	lye
rut	Dutch	lute	mutt	fly	try	rye

See also List 1, Consonant Sounds; List 2, Vowel Sounds.

The Reading Teacher's Book of Lists, Fifth Edition, © 2006 by John Wiley & Sons, Inc.

LIST 12. THE MOST COMMON PHONOGRAMS

A phonogram, or rime, is usually a vowel sound plus a consonant sound, but it is often less than a syllable and therefore less than a word. When a consonant sound is added at the beginning, or at the onset, the two form many recognizable words. Adding single consonants or consonant blends to common phonograms is an excellent way to quickly build reading and spelling vocabulary. This list includes the most common phonograms ranked in the order of the number of words they can form.

Rime	Example Words				Rime	Example Words			
-ay	jay	say	pay	day	play	**-ug**	rug	bug	hug	dug	tug
-ill	hill	Bill	will	fill	spill	**-op**	mop	cop	pop	top	hop
-ip	dip	ship	tip	skip	trip	**-in**	pin	tin	win	chin	thin
-at	cat	fat	bat	rat	sat	**-an**	pan	man	ran	tan	Dan
-am	ham	jam	dam	ram	Sam	**-est**	best	nest	pest	rest	test
-ag	bag	rag	tag	wag	sag	**-ink**	pink	sink	rink	link	drink
-ack	back	sack	Jack	black	track	**-ow**	low	slow	grow	show	snow
-ank	bank	sank	tank	blank	drank	**-ew**	new	few	chew	grew	stew
-ick	sick	Dick	pick	quick	chick	**-ore**	more	sore	tore	store	score
-ell	bell	sell	fell	tell	yell	**-ed**	bed	red	fed	led	Ted
-ot	pot	not	hot	dot	got	**-ab**	cab	dab	jab	lab	crab
-ing	ring	sing	king	wing	thing	**-ob**	cob	job	rob	Bob	knob
-ap	cap	map	tap	clap	trap	**-ock**	sock	rock	lock	dock	block
-unk	bunk	sunk	junk	skunk	trunk	**-ake**	cake	lake	make	take	brake
-ail	pail	jail	nail	sail	tail	**-ine**	line	nine	pine	fine	shine
-ain	rain	pain	main	chain	plain	**-ight**	light	night	right	fight	sight
-eed	feed	seed	weed	need	freed	**-im**	him	Kim	rim	grim	brim
-y	my	by	dry	try	fly	**-uck**	duck	luck	buck	truck	stuck
-out	pout	trout	scout	shout	spout	**-um**	gum	bum	hum	drum	plum

See also List 11, Phonograms.

The Reading Teacher's Book of Lists, Fifth Edition, © 2006 by John Wiley & Sons, Inc.

LIST 13. PHONICALLY IRREGULAR WORDS

As every reading teacher knows, there are many words that do not follow regular phonics or spelling rules. This list contains common words that are not pronounceable using regular phonics rules. Students need to learn to recognize them on sight and to memorize their spellings. See also words with silent letters in Consonant Sounds, List 1.

a	does	listen	said	usually
adjective	door	live	science	want
again	earth	many	should	was
although	enough	measure	sign	watch
answer	example	most	some	water
any	eyes	mother	something	where
are	father	mountain	stretch	were
become	feather	move	subtle	what
been	find	of	sure	who
both	four	off	the	woman
bread	friends	often	their	women
brought	from	old	there	words
climbed	give	on	they	work
cold	great	once	though	world
color	group	one	thought	would
come	have	only	through	you
could	heard	other	to	young
country	island	people	today	your
design	kind	picture	two	youth
do	learn	piece		

LIST 14. STANDALONES

Words in the English language often follow patterns—similar sounds and/or spellings. Just take a look at the number of phonograms in List 11. Or think about how easy it is to rhyme most longer words. The list below contains words that have no "close cousins" or rhymes. Can you think of any other words for which there is no true rhyme?

bulb	hundred	nothing	tablet
dreamt	hungry	orange	wasp
druggist	infant	purple	Wednesday
exit	month	silver	zebra
film	noisy	sixth	

The Reading Teacher's Book of Lists, Fifth Edition, © 2006 by John Wiley & Sons, Inc.

LIST 15. SYLLABICATION RULES*

The teaching of syllabication rules is somewhat controversial. Some say you should, and some say it is not worth the effort. Syllables sometimes are part of phonics lessons because syllabication affects vowel sounds (for example, an open vowel rule), and sometimes they are part of spelling or English lessons. There is no close agreement on various lists of syllabication rules, and some of the rules have plenty of exceptions. We are not urging you to teach them, but neither are we urging you to refrain from doing so.

Rule 1. VCV†   A consonant between two vowels tends to go with the second vowel unless the first vowel is accented and short.
Examples: *bro'-ken, wag'-on, e-vent'*

Rule 2. VCCV   Divide two consonants between vowels unless they are a blend or digraph. (See List 1.)
Examples: *pic-ture, ush-er*

Rule 3. VCCCV   When there are three consonants between two vowels, divide between the blend or the digraph and the other consonant.
Example: *an-gler*

Rule 4. Affixes
a. Prefixes always form separate syllables (*un-hap-py, re-act*).
b. Suffixes form separate syllables if they contain a vowel sound.
c. The suffix *-y* tends to pick up the preceding consonant to form a separate syllable.
Example: *fligh-ty*
d. The suffix *-ed* tends to form a separate syllable only when it follows a root that ends in *d* or *t*.
Example: *plant-ed* (not in stopped)
e. The suffix *-s* never forms a syllable except sometimes when it follows an *e*.
Examples: *at-oms, cours-es*

Rule 5. Compounds   Always divide compound words.
Example: *black-bird*

Source: Costigan, P. (1977) *A Validation of the Fry Syllabification Generalization.* Unpublished master's thesis, Rutgers University, New Brunswick, NJ. Available from ERIC.

†V = vowel: C = consonant.

NOTE: These rules tend to give phonetic (sound) division of syllables that is in harmony with phonics instruction. Dictionaries tend to favor morphemic (meaning) division for main entries. Often, this does not conflict with the phonetic (pronunciation) division but sometimes it does; for example, "skat-er" morphemic versus "ska-ter" phonetic. The "er" is a morphemic (meaning) unit meaning "one who."

SYLLABICATION RULES CONTINUED

Rule 6. Final *le*   Final *le* picks up the preceding consonant to form a syllable. Example: *ta-ble*

Rule 7. Vowel Clusters   Do not split common vowel clusters, such as:

    a. *R*-controlled vowels (*ar, er, ir, or,* and *ur*). Example: *ar-ti-cle*

    b. Long vowel digraphs (*ea, ee, ai, oa,* and *ow*). Example: *fea-ture*

    c. Broad *o* clusters (*au, aw,* and *al*). Example: *au-di-ence*

    d. Diphthongs (*oi, oy, ou,* and *ow*). Example: *thou-sand*

    e. Double *o* like *oo*. Examples: *moon, look*

Rule 8. Vowel Problems   Every syllable must have one and only one vowel sound.

    a. The letter *e* at the end of a word is usually silent. Example: *come*

    b. The letter *y* at the end or in the middle of a word operates as a vowel. At the beginning of a word it is a consonant. Examples: *ver-y, cy-cle, yes*

    c. Two vowels together with separate sounds form separate syllables. Example: *po-li-o*

See also List 29, More Prefixes, List 31, More Suffixes.

2

USEFUL WORDS

LIST 16. INSTANT WORDS

These are the most common words in English, ranked in frequency order. The first 25 make up about a third of all printed material. The first 100 make up about half of all written material, and the first 300 make up about 65 percent of all written material. Is it any wonder that all students must learn to recognize these words instantly and to spell them correctly also?

FIRST HUNDRED

WORDS 1–25	WORDS 26–50	WORDS 51–75	WORDS 76–100
the	or	will	number
of	one	up	no
and	had	other	way
a	by	about	could
to	word	out	people
in	but	many	my
is	not	then	than
you	what	them	first
that	all	these	water
it	were	so	been
he	we	some	call
was	when	her	who
for	your	would	am
on	can	make	its
are	said	like	now
as	there	him	find
with	use	into	long
his	an	time	down
they	each	has	day
I	which	look	did
at	she	two	get
be	do	more	come
this	how	write	made
have	their	go	may
from	if	see	part

Common suffixes: *-s, -ing, -ed, -er, -ly, -est*

INSTANT WORDS CONTINUED

SECOND HUNDRED

WORDS 101–125	WORDS 126–150	WORDS 151–175	WORDS 176–200
over	say	set	try
new	great	put	kind
sound	where	end	hand
take	help	does	picture
only	through	another	again
little	much	well	change
work	before	large	off
know	line	must	play
place	right	big	spell
year	too	even	air
live	mean	such	away
me	old	because	animal
back	any	turn	house
give	same	here	point
most	tell	why	page
very	boy	ask	letter
after	follow	went	mother
thing	came	men	answer
our	want	read	found
just	show	need	study
name	also	land	still
good	around	different	learn
sentence	farm	home	should
man	three	us	America
think	small	move	world

Common suffixes: -s, -ing, -ed, -er, -ly, -est

The Reading Teacher's Book of Lists, Fifth Edition, © 2006 by John Wiley & Sons, Inc.

THIRD HUNDRED

The Reading Teacher's Book of Lists, Fifth Edition, © 2006 by John Wiley & Sons, Inc.

WORDS 201–225	WORDS 226–250	WORDS 251–275	WORDS 276–300
high	saw	important	miss
every	left	until	idea
near	don't	children	enough
add	few	side	eat
food	while	feet	facet
between	along	car	watch
own	might	mile	far
below	close	night	Indian
country	something	walk	really
plant	seem	white	almost
last	next	sea	let
school	hard	began	above
father	open	grow	girl
keep	example	took	sometimes
tree	begin	river	mountain
never	life	four	cut
start	always	carry	young
city	those	state	talk
earth	both	once	soon
eye	paper	book	list
light	together	hear	song
thought	got	stop	being
head	group	without	leave
under	often	second	family
story	run	later	it's

Common suffixes: *-s, -ing, -ed, -er, -ly, -est*

INSTANT WORDS CONTINUED

FOURTH HUNDRED

WORDS 301–325	WORDS 326–350	WORDS 351–375	WORDS 376–400
body	order	listen	busy
music	red	wind	pulled
color	door	rock	draw
stand	sure	space	voice
sun	become	covered	seen
question	top	fast	cold
fish	ship	several	cried
area	across	hold	plan
mark	today	himself	notice
dog	during	toward	south
horse	short	five	sing
birds	better	step	war
problem	best	morning	ground
complete	however	passed	fall
room	low	vowel	king
knew	hours	true	town
since	black	hundred	I'll
ever	products	against	unit
piece	happened	pattern	figure
told	whole	numeral	certain
usually	measure	table	field
didn't	remember	north	travel
friends	early	slowly	wood
easy	waves	money	fire
heard	reached	map	upon

FIFTH HUNDRED

WORDS 401–425	WORDS 426–450	WORDS 451–475	WORDS 476–500
done	decided	plane	filled
English	contain	system	heat
road	course	behind	full
halt	surface	ran	hot
ten	produce	round	check
fly	building	boat	object
gave	ocean	game	bread
box	class	force	rule
finally	note	brought	among
wait	nothing	understand	noun
correct	rest	warm	power
oh	carefully	common	cannot
quickly	scientists	bring	able
person	inside	explain	six
became	wheels	dry	size
shown	stay	though	dark
minutes	green	language	ball
strong	known	shape	material
verb	island	deep	special
stars	week	thousands	heavy
front	less	yes	fine
feel	machine	clear	pair
fact	base	equation	circle
inches	ago	yet	include
street	stood	government	built

The Reading Teacher's Book of Lists, Fifth Edition, © 2006 by John Wiley & Sons, Inc.

SIXTH HUNDRED

WORDS 501–525	WORDS 526–550	WORDS 551–575	WORDS 576–600
can't	picked	legs	beside
matter	simple	sat	gone
square	cells	main	sky
syllables	paint	winter	glass
perhaps	mind	wide	million
bill	love	written	west
felt	cause	length	lay
suddenly	rain	reason	weather
test	exercise	kept	root
direction	eggs	interest	instruments
center	train	arms	meet
farmers	blue	brother	third
ready	wish	race	months
anything	drop	present	paragraph
divided	developed	beautiful	raised
general	window	store	represent
energy	difference	job	soft
subject	distance	edge	whether
Europe	heart	past	clothes
moon	sit	sign	flowers
region	sum	record	shall
return	summer	finished	teacher
believe	wall	discovered	held
dance	forest	wild	describe
members	probably	happy	drive

SEVENTH HUNDRED

WORDS 601–625	WORDS 626–650	WORDS 651–675	WORDS 676–700
cross	already	hair	rolled
speak	instead	age	bear
solve	phrase	amount	wonder
appear	soil	scale	smiled
metal	bed	pounds	angle
son	copy	although	fraction
either	free	per	Africa
ice	hope	broken	killed
sleep	spring	moment	melody
village	case	tiny	bottom
factors	laughed	possible	trip
result	nation	gold	hole
jumped	quite	milk	poor
snow	type	quiet	let's
ride	themselves	natural	fight
care	temperature	lot	surprise
floor	bright	stone	French
hill	lead	act	died
pushed	everyone	build	beat
baby	method	middle	exactly
buy	section	speed	remain
century	lake	count	dress
outside	consonant	cat	iron
everything	within	someone	couldn't
tall	dictionary	sail	fingers

INSTANT WORDS CONTINUED

EIGHTH HUNDRED

WORDS 701–725	WORDS 726–750	WORDS 751–775	WORDS 776–800
row	president	yourself	caught
least	brown	control	fell
catch	trouble	practice	team
climbed	cool	report	God
wrote	cloud	straight	captain
shouted	lost	rise	direct
continued	sent	statement	ring
itself	symbols	stick	serve
else	wear	party	child
plains	bad	seeds	desert
gas	save	suppose	increase
England	experiment	woman	history
burning	engine	coast	cost
design	alone	bank	maybe
joined	drawing	period	business
foot	east	wire	separate
law	pay	choose	break
ears	single	clean	uncle
grass	touch	visit	hunting
you're	information	bit	flow
grew	express	whose	lady
skin	mouth	received	students
valley	yard	garden	human
cents	equal	please	art
key	decimal	strange	feeling

NINTH HUNDRED

WORDS 801–825	WORDS 826–850	WORDS 851–875	WORDS 876–900
supply	guess	thick	major
corner	silent	blood	observe
electric	trade	lie	tube
insects	rather	spot	necessary
crops	compare	bell	weight
tone	crowd	fun	meat
hit	poem	loud	lifted
sand	enjoy	consider	process
doctor	elements	suggested	army
provide	indicate	thin	hat
thus	except	position	property
won't	expect	entered	particular
cook	flat	fruit	swim
bones	seven	tied	terms
tail	interesting	rich	current
board	sense	dollars	park
modern	string	send	sell
compound	blow	sight	shoulder
mine	famous	chief	industry
wasn't	value	Japanese	wash
fit	wings	stream	block
addition	movement	planets	spread
belong	pole	rhythm	cattle
safe	exciting	eight	wife
soldiers	branches	science	sharp

TENTH HUNDRED

The Reading Teacher's Book of Lists, Fifth Edition, © 2006 by John Wiley & Sons, Inc.

WORDS 901–925	WORDS 926–950	WORDS 951–975	WORDS 976–1000
company	sister	gun	total
radio	oxygen	similar	deal
we'll	plural	death	determine
action	various	score	evening
capital	agreed	forward	nor
factories	opposite	stretched	rope
settled	wrong	experience	cotton
yellow	chart	rose	apple
isn't	prepared	allow	details
southern	pretty	fear	entire
truck	solution	workers	corn
fair	fresh	Washington	substances
printed	shop	Greek	smell
wouldn't	suffix	women	tools
ahead	especially	bought	conditions
chance	shoes	led	cows
born	actually	march	track
level	nose	northern	arrived
triangle	afraid	create	located
molecules	dead	British	sir
France	sugar	difficult	seat
repeated	adjective	match	division
column	fig	win	effect
western	office	doesn't	underline
church	huge	steel	view

See also List 17, Primary Students' Most Used Words (in Writing); List 18, Picture Nouns; List 111, Games and Methods for Teaching; List 155, Spelling—Traditional Teaching Methods.

LIST 17. PRIMARY STUDENTS' MOST USED WORDS (IN WRITING)

In case you wondered whether primary students (K–2) used words different from the Instant Words, here is a list based on 176 samples of primary students' writing. You'll see that they are not much different from the Instant Words.

Frequently Used Words by Primary Students

I	like	have
the	was	see
to	run	am
my	can	snow
and	play	because
a	that	dad
is	eat	get
it	mom	going
we	for	tree
turkey	go	favorite
in	on	story
you	when	are
me	with	buy
then	he	family
of	at	out

See also List 16, Instant Words; List 18, Picture Nouns.

The Reading Teacher's Book of Lists, Fifth Edition, © 2006 by John Wiley & Sons, Inc.

LIST 18. PICTURE NOUNS

Combined with the first hundred Instant Words, these picture words make a powerful beginning reading and writing vocabulary.

1. People	2. Toys	3. Numbers	4. Clothing
boy	ball	one	shirt
girl	doll	two	pants
man	train	three	dress
woman	game	four	shoes
baby	skateboard	five	hat

5. Pets	6. Furniture	7. Eating Objects	8. Transportation
cat	table	cup	bicycle
dog	chair	plate	truck
rabbit	sofa	bowl	bus
bird	chest	fork	plane
fish	desk	spoon	boat

9. Food	10. Drinks	11. Zoo Animals	12. Fruit
bread	water	elephant	fruit
meat	milk	giraffe	orange
soup	juice	bear	grape
fruit	soda	lion	pear
cereal	malt	monkey	banana

13. Plants	14. Sky Things	15. Earth Things	16. Farm Animals
bush	sun	water	horse
flower	moon	rock	cow
grass	star	dirt	pig
tomatoes	cloud	field	chicken
tree	rain	hill	duck

17. Workers	18. Entertainment	19. Writing Tools	20. Reading Things
farmer	television	pen	book
police officer	radio	pencil	newspaper
cook	movie	crayon	magazine
doctor	ball game	typewriter	sign
nurse	band	computer	letter

See also List 16, Instant Words; List 111, Games and Methods for Teaching.

LIST 19. HOMOPHONES

Homophones are words that sound the same but have different meanings and usually different spellings. Recognizing homophones is particularly important because computer "spell check" programs do not recognize them as spelling errors. There are many ways to teach homophones, including reading and spelling games, jokes and riddles, and workbook exercises. See List 111, Games and Methods for Teaching, for suggestions.

This list contains only homophones that have different spellings. If a pair has the same spelling (for example, *bat* meaning a flying animal and *bat* meaning a club), they are included in the homograph list. The term *homonym* can include both homophones (same sound) and homographs (same spelling).

Easy Homophones

add	creek	I	oh	road
ad	creak	eye	owe	rode
		aye		rowed
air	dear	in	one	
heir	deer	inn	won	sale
				sail
already	die	its	or	
all ready	dye	it's	oar	see
			ore	sea
ant	fair	led		
aunt	fare	lead	our	seem
			hour	seam
ate	feet	loan		
eight	feat	lone	pair	sell
			pare	cell
ball	find	made	pear	
bawl	fined	maid		sent
			peace	cent
bare	flower	meet	piece	scent
bear	flour	meat		
			plane	shoe
be	for	might	plain	shoo
bee	four	mite		
	fore		principal	side
beat		missed	principle	sighed
beet	great	mist		
	grate		rain	so
been		morn	reign	sew
bin	heard	mourn	rein	sow
	herd			
blue		need	read	some
blew	here	knead	reed	sum
	hear			
brake		new	real	son
break	hi	knew	reel	sun
	high	gnu		
by			red	steal
bye	hole	night	read	steel
buy	whole	knight		
			right	tail
close	horse	no	write	tale
clothes	hoarse	know		
cloze				

The Reading Teacher's Book of Lists, Fifth Edition, © 2006 by John Wiley & Sons, Inc.

their   toe   way   week   wood
there   tow   weigh   weak   would
they're

through   told   we   where   you
threw   tolled   wee   wear   you're
                      weather   ware
to   whether

two

too

Homophone Master List

acts (deeds)
ax (tool)

ad (advertisement)
add (addition)

ads (advertisements)
adz (axlike tool)

aid (assistance)
aide (a helper)

ail (be sick)
ale (beverage)

air (oxygen)
heir (successor)

aisle (path)
I'll (I will)
isle (island)

all (everything)
awl (tool)

all together (in a group)
altogether (completely)

already (previous)
all ready (all are ready)

allowed (permitted)
aloud (audible)

altar (in a church)
alter (change)

ant (insect)
aunt (relative)

ante (before)
anti (against)

arc (part of a circle)
ark (boat)

ascent (climb)
assent (agree)

assistance (help)
assistants (those who help)

ate (did eat)
eight (number)

attendance (presence)
attendants (escorts)

aural (by ear)
oral (by mouth)

away (gone)
aweigh (clear anchor)

awful (terrible)
offal (entrails)

aye (yes)
eye (organ of sight)
I (pronoun)

bail (throw water out)
bale (bundle)

bait (lure)
bate (to decrease)

ball (round object)
bawl (cry)

band (plays music)
banned (forbidden)

bard (poet)
barred (having bars)

bare (nude)
bear (animal)

bark (dog's sound)
barque (ship)

baron (nobleman)
barren (no fruit)

base (lower part)
bass (deep tone)

based (at a base)
baste (cover with liquid)

bases (plural of base)
basis (foundation)

bask (warm feeling)
Basque (country)

bazaar (market)
bizarre (old)

be (exist)
bee (insect)

beach (shore)
beech (tree)

bearing (manner, machine)
baring (uncovering)

beat (whip)
beet (vegetable)

beau (boyfriend)
bow (decorative knot)

been (past participle of be)
bin (box)

beer (drink)
bier (coffin)

bell (something you ring)
belle (pretty woman)

berry (fruit)
bury (put in ground)

berth (bunk)
birth (born)

better (more good)
bettor (one who bets)

bight (slack part of rope)
bite (chew)
byte (computer unit)

HOMOPHONES CONTINUED

billed (did bill)
build (construct)

blew (did blow)
blue (color)

block (cube)
bloc (group)

boar (hog)
bore (drill; be tiresome)

boarder (one who boards)
border (boundary)

boll (cotton pod)
bowl (dish; game)

bolder (more bold)
boulder (big stone)

born (delivered at birth)
borne (carried)

borough (town)
burro (donkey)
burrow (dig)

bough (of a tree)
bow (of a ship)

bouillon (clear broth)
bullion (uncoined gold or silver)

boy (male child)
bouy (floating object)

brake (stop)
break (smash)

bread (food)
bred (cultivated)

brewed (steeped)
brood (flock)

brews (steeps)
bruise (bump)

bridal (relating to bride)
bridle (headgear for horse)

Britain (country)
Briton (Englishman)

broach (bring up)
brooch (pin)

but (except)
butt (end)

buy (purchase)
by (near)
bye (farewell)

cache (hiding place)
cash (money)

callous (unfeeling)
callus (hard tissue)

cannon (big gun)
canon (law)

canvas (cloth)
canvass (survey)

capital (money; city)
Capitol (building of U.S. Congress)

carat (weight of precious stones)
caret (proofreader's mark)
carrot (vegetable)

carol (song)
carrel (study space in library)

cast (throw; actors in a play)
caste (social class)

cause (origin)
caws (crow calls)

cede (grant)
seed (part of a plant)

ceiling (top of room)
sealing (closing)

cell (prison room)
sell (exchange for money)

cellar (basement)
seller (one who sells)

censor (ban)
sensor (detection device)

cent (penny)
scent (odor)
sent (did send)

cereal (relating to grain)
serial (of a series)

cession (yielding)
session (meeting)

chance (luck)
chants (songs)

chased (did chase)
chaste (modest)

cheap (inexpensive)
cheep (bird call)

chews (bites)
choose (select)

chic (style)
sheik (Arab chief)

chilly (cold)
chili (hot pepper)

choir (singers)
quire (amount of paper)

choral (music)
coral (reef)

chorale (chorus)
corral (pen for livestock)

chord (musical notes)
cord (string)

chute (slide)
shoot (discharge gun)

cite (summon to court)
sight (see)
site (location)

claws (nails on animal's feet)
clause (part of a sentence)

click (small sound)
clique (small exclusive subgroup)

climb (ascend)
clime (climate)

close (shut)
clothes (clothing)
cloze (test)

The Reading Teacher's Book of Lists, Fifth Edition, © 2006 by John Wiley & Sons, Inc.

coal (fuel)
cole (cabbage)

coarse (rough)
course (path; school subject)

colonel (military rank)
kernel (grain of corn)

complement (complete set)
compliment (praise)

coop (chicken pen)
coupe (car)

core (center)
corps (army group)

correspondence (letters)
correspondents (writers)

council (legislative body)
counsel (advise)

cousin (relative)
cozen (deceive)

creak (grating noise)
creek (stream)

crews (groups of workers)
cruise (sail)
cruse (small pot)

cruel (hurting)
crewel (stitching)

cue (prompt)
queue (line up)

currant (small raisin)
current (recent, fast part of a stream)

curser (one who curses)
cursor (moving pointer)

cymbal (percussion instrument)
symbol (sign)

deer (animal)
dear (greeting; loved one)

desert (abandon)
dessert (follows main course of meal)

die (expire)
dye (color)

dine (eat)
dyne (unit of force)

disburse (pay out)
disperse (scatter)

discreet (unobtrusive)
discrete (noncontinuous)

doe (female deer)
dough (bread mixture)
do (musical note)

do (shall)
dew (moisture)
due (owed)

done (finished)
dun (demand for payment; dull color)

dual (two)
duel (formal combat)

duct (tube)
ducked (did duck)

earn (work for)
urn (container)

ewe (female sheep)
yew (shrub)
you (personal pronoun)

eyelet (small hole)
islet (small island)

fain (gladly)
feign (pretend)

faint (weak)
feint (pretend attack)

fair (honest; bazaar)
fare (cost of transportation)

fawn (baby deer)
faun (mythical creature)

faze (upset)
phase (stage)

feat (accomplishment)
feet (plural of *foot*)

find (discover)
fined (penalty of money)

fir (tree)
fur (animal covering)

flair (talent)
flare (flaming signal)

flea (insect)
flee (run away)

flew (did fly)
flu (influenza)
flue (shaft)

flour (milled grain)
flower (bloom)

for (in favor of)
fore (front part)
four (number 4)

foreword (preface)
forward (front part)

forth (forward)
fourth (after third)

foul (bad)
fowl (bird)

franc (French money)
frank (honest)

freeze (cold)
frees (to free)
frieze (sculptured border)

friar (brother in religious order)
fryer (frying chicken)

gate (fence opening)
gait (foot movement)

gilt (golden)
guilt (opposite of innocence)

gnu (antelope)
knew (did know)
new (opposite of *old*)

gorilla (animal)
guerrilla (irregular soldier)

grate (grind)
great (large)

HOMOPHONES CONTINUED

groan (moan)
grown (cultivated)

guessed (surmised)
guest (company)

hail (ice; salute)
hale (healthy)

hair (on head)
hare (rabbit)

hall (passage)
haul (carry)

handsome (attractive)
hansom (carriage)

hangar (storage building)
hanger (to hang things on)

halve (cut in half)
have (possess)

hart (deer)
heart (body organ)

hay (dried grass)
hey (expression to get attention)

heal (make well)
heel (bottom of foot)
he'll (he will)

hear (listen)
here (this place)

heard (listened)
herd (group of animals)

heed (pay attention)
he'd (he would)

hertz (unit of wave frequency)
hurts (pain)

hew (carve)
hue (color)

hi (hello)
hie (hasten)
high (opposite of *low*)

higher (above)
hire (employ)

him (pronoun)
hymn (religious song)

hoarse (husky voice)
horse (animal)

hole (opening)
whole (complete)

holey (full of holes)
holy (sacred)
wholly (all)

horde (crowd)
hoard (hidden supply)

hostel (lodging for youth)
hostile (unfriendly)

hour (sixty minutes)
our (possessive pronoun)

hurdle (jump over)
hurtle (throw)

idle (lazy)
idol (god)
idyll (charming scene)

in (opposite of *out*)
inn (hotel)

insight (self knowledge)
incite (cause)

instance (example)
instants (short periods of time)

insure (protect against loss)
ensure (make sure)

intense (extreme)
intents (aims)

its (possessive pronoun)
it's (it is)

jam (fruit jelly)
jamb (window part)

knit (weave with yarn)
nit (louse egg)

lam (escape)
lamb (baby sheep)

lain (past participle of *lie*)
lane (narrow way)

lay (recline)
lei (necklace of flowers)

lead (metal)
led (guided)

leak (crack)
leek (vegetable)

lean (slender; incline)
lien (claim)

leased (rented)
least (smallest)

lessen (make less)
lesson (instruction)

levee (embankment)
levy (impose by legal authority)

liar (untruthful)
lyre (musical instrument)

lichen (fungus)
liken (compare)

lie (falsehood)
lye (alkaline solution)

lieu (instead of)
Lou (name)

lightening (become light)
lightning (occurs with thunder)

load (burden)
lode (vein or ore)

loan (something borrowed)
lone (single)

locks (plural of lock)
lox (smoked salmon)

loot (steal)
lute (musical instrument)

low (not high; cattle sound)
lo (interjection)

The Reading Teacher's Book of Lists, Fifth Edition, © 2006 by John Wiley & Sons, Inc.

made (manufactured)
maid (servant)

mail (send by post)
male (masculine)

main (most important)
Maine (state)
mane (hair)

maize (Indian corn)
maze (confusing network of passages)

mall (courtyard)
maul (attack)

manner (style)
manor (estate)

mantel (over fireplace)
mantle (cloak)

marry (join together)
merry (gay)
Mary (name)

marshal (escort)
martial (militant)

massed (grouped)
mast (support)

maybe (perhaps, adj.)
may be (is possible, v.)

meat (beef)
meet (greet)
mete (measure)

medal (award)
meddle (interfere)

might (may; strength)
mite (small insect)

miner (coal digger)
minor (juvenile)

missed (failed to attain)
mist (fog)

moan (groan)
mown (cut down)

mode (fashion)
mowed (cut down)

morn (early day)
mourn (grieve)

muscle (flesh)
mussel (shellfish)

naval (nautical)
navel (depression on abdomen)

nay (no)
neigh (whinny)

need (require)
knead (mix with hands)

new (not old)
knew (remembered)
gnu (animal)

night (evening)
knight (feudal warrior)

no (negative)
know (familiar with)

none (not any)
nun (religious sister)

not (in no manner)
knot (tangle)

oar (of a boat)
or (conjunction)
ore (mineral deposit)

ode (poem)
owed (did owe)

oh (exclamation)
owe (be indebted)

one (number)
won (triumphed)

overdo (go to extremes)
overdue (past due)

overseas (abroad)
oversees (supervises)

pail (bucket)
pale (white)

pain (discomfort)
pane (window glass)

pair (two of a kind)
pare (peel)
pear (fruit)

palate (roof of mouth)
palette (board for paint)
pallet (tool)

passed (went by)
past (former)

patience (composure)
patients (sick persons)

pause (brief stop)
paws (feet of animals)

peace (tranquility)
piece (part)

peak (mountaintop)
peek (look)
pique (offense)

peal (ring)
peel (pare)

pearl (jewel)
purl (knitting stitch)

pedal (ride a bike)
peddle (sell)

peer (equal)
pier (dock)

per (for each)
purr (cat sound)

pi (Greek letter)
pie (kind of pastry)

plain (simple)
plane (flat surface)

plait (braid)
plate (dish)

pleas (plural of *plea*)
please (to be agreeable)

plum (fruit)
plumb (lead weight)

pole (stick)
poll (vote)

pore (ponder; skin gland)
pour (flow freely)

pray (worship)
prey (victim)

presents (gifts)
presence (appearance)

principal (chief)
principle (rule)

profit (benefit)
prophet (seer)

HOMOPHONES CONTINUED

rack (framework; torture)
wrack (ruin)

rain (precipitation)
reign (royal authority)
rein (harness)

raise (put up)
raze (tear down)
rays (of sun)

rap (hit; talk)
wrap (cover)

read (peruse)
reed (plant)

read (perused)
red (color)

real (genuine)
reel (spool)

reek (give off strong odor)
wreak (inflict)

rest (relax)
wrest (force)

review (look back)
revue (musical)

right (correct)
rite (ceremony)
write (inscribe)

rime (ice, or rhyme)
rhyme (same end sound)

ring (circular band)
wring (squeeze)

road (street)
rode (transported)
rowed (used oars)

roe (fish eggs)
row (line; use oars)

role (character)
roll (turn over; bread)

root (part of a plant)
route (highway)

rose (flower)
rows (lines)

rote (by memory)
wrote (did write)

rude (impolite)
rued (was sorry)

rumor (gossip)
roomer (renter)

rung (step on a ladder; past tense of *ring*)
wrung (squeezed)

rye (grain)
wry (twisted)

sail (travel by boat)
sale (bargain)

scene (setting)
seen (viewed)

scull (boat; row)
skull (head)

sea (ocean)
see (visualize)

seam (joining mark)
seem (appear to be)

sear (singe)
seer (prophet)

serf (feudal servant)
surf (waves)

sew (mend)
so (in order that)
sow (plant)

shear (cut)
sheer (transparent)

shoe (foot covering)
shoo (drive away)

shoot (use gun)
chute (trough)

shone (beamed)
shown (exhibited)

side (flank)
sighed (audible breath)

sign (signal)
sine (trigonometric function)

slay (kill)
sleigh (sled)

sleight (dexterity)
slight (slender)

slew (killed)
slue (swamp)

soar (fly)
sore (painful)

sole (only)
soul (spirit)

some (portion)
sum (total)

son (male offspring)
sun (star)

staid (proper)
stayed (remained)

stair (step)
stare (look intently)

stake (post)
steak (meat)

stationary (fixed)
stationery (paper)

steal (rob)
steel (metal)

step (walk)
steppe (prairie of Europe or Asia)

stile (gate)
style (fashion)

straight (not crooked)
strait (channel of water)

suite (connected rooms)
sweet (sugary)

surge (sudden increase)
serge (fabric)

tacks (plural of *tack*)
tax (assess; burden)

tail (animal's appendage)
tale (story)

The Reading Teacher's Book of Lists, Fifth Edition, © 2006 by John Wiley & Sons, Inc.

The Reading Teacher's Book of Lists, Fifth Edition, © 2006 by John Wiley & Sons, Inc.

taught (did teach)
taut (tight)

tea (drink)
tee (holder for golf ball)

teas (plural of *tea*)
tease (mock)

team (crew)
teem (be full)

tear (cry)
tier (level)

tear (rip apart)
tare (weight deduction)

tern (sea bird)
turn (rotate)

their (possessive pronoun)
there (at that place)
they're (they are)

theirs (possessive pronoun)
there's (there is)

threw (tossed)
through (finished)

throne (king's seat)
thrown (tossed)

thyme (herb)
time (duration)

tic (twitch)
tick (insect; sound of clock)

tide (ebb and flow)
tied (bound)

to (toward)
too (also)
two (number)

toad (frog)
towed (pulled)

toe (digit on foot)
tow (pull)

told (informed)
tolled (rang)

trussed (tied)
trust (confidence)

vain (conceited)
vane (wind indicator)
vein (blood vessel)

vale (valley)
veil (face cover)

vary (change)
very (absolutely)

vice (bad habit)
vise (clamp)

vile (disgusting)
vial (small bottle)

wade (walk in water)
weighed (measured heaviness)

wail (cry)
whale (sea mammal)

waist (middle)
waste (trash)

wait (linger)
weight (heaviness)

waive (forgive)
wave (swell)

want (desire)
wont (custom)

ware (pottery)
wear (have on)
where (what place)

way (road)
weigh (measure heaviness)
whey (watery part of milk)

ways (plural of *way*; shipyard)
weighs (heaviness)

we (pronoun)
wee (small)

weak (not strong)
week (seven days)

weal (prosperity)
we'll (we will)
wheel (circular frame)

weather (state of atmosphere)
whether (if)

weave (interlace)
we've (we have)

we'd (we would)
weed (plant)

weir (dam)
we're (we are)

wet (moist)
whet (sharpen)

which (what one)
witch (sorceress)

while (during)
wile (trick)

whine (complaining sound)
wine (drink)

who's (who is)
whose (possessive of *who*)

wood (of a tree)
would (is willing to)

worst (most bad)
wurst (sausage)

yoke (harness)
yolk (egg center)

you (pronoun)
ewe (female sheep)
yew (evergreen tree)

you'll (you will)
yule (Christmas)

your (possessive pronoun)
you're (you are)

Note. For a more complete list of homophones, see *The Vocabulary Teacher's Book of Lists* (Fry, 2004)

See also List 20, Homophone Teaching Suggestions; List 22, Homographs and Heteronyms; List 23, Easily Confused Words.

LIST 20. HOMOPHONE TEACHING SUGGESTIONS

Have some fun. Both you and the students can develop jokes and riddles.
What is a large animal without its fur? (**a bare bear**)
What is an insect's relative? (**an aunt ant**)

Proofread and correct sentences.
Please drink sum milk.
Turn write at the end of the street.

Make flash cards. Write one of a homophone pair on each side. Student sees one side, and tries to spell the other. Then discuss the meanings or use the words in a sentence.

Make playing cards for a "Go Fish" or "Rummy" game.
Use the same cards for a "Concentration" game.

Make some worksheets.
Write the homophone pair: "sell— ___ ___ ___ ___"
Select the correct word: "Dogs have (for—four) legs."

Make a game in which half of a pair of homophones is provided.
Bingo cards
Crossword puzzles

Make teaching devices.
Spinner games
Board games (example: racetrack and shake dice)

Have an old-fashioned bee.

Find homophones in other materials: social studies, math, art.
Have classroom teams compete for three days.

Have a word wall or corner of a chalkboard with a pair of homophones.
Discuss the words for two minutes and change them periodically.

Use a Worksheet like the one in List 21 or make one of your own.

Spelling Test. Use homophone pairs. You say word and definition.

See also List 19, Homophones; List 111, Games and Methods for Teaching.

The Reading Teacher's Book of Lists, Fifth Edition, © 2006 by John Wiley & Sons, Inc.

LIST 21. HOMOPHONE WORKSHEET

Name _____   **Date** _____

Fill in a Homophone A and B pair.

1.   Homophone **A**: _____   **A** in syllables: _____

      Write **A** without vowels: _____

      Meaning of **A**: _____

      Use **A** in a phrase: _____

      Homophone **B**: _____   **B** in syllables: _____

      Write **B** without vowels: _____

      Meaning of **B**: _____

      Use **B** in a phrase: _____

Fill in a Homophone C and D pair.

2.   Homophone **C**: _____   **C** in syllables: _____

      Write **C** without vowels: _____

      Meaning of **C**: _____

      Use **C** in a phrase: _____

      Homophone **D**: _____   **D** in syllables: _____

      Write **D** without vowels: _____

      Meaning of **D**: _____

      Use **D** in a phrase: _____

See also List 19, Homophones; List 20, Homophone Teaching Suggestions.

LIST 22. HOMOGRAPHS AND HETERONYMS

Homographs are words that are spelled the same but have different meanings and different origins. Many other words have multiple meanings, but according to dictionary authorities, what makes these words homographs is that they have different origins as well. Some homographs are also heteronyms, which means that they have a different pronunciation often caused by changing syllable stress (con′·sole vs. con·sole′) or vowel shift. These can also be called homonyms. These are marked with an asterisk (*).

*affect (influence)
affect (pretend)

alight (get down from)
alight (on fire)

angle (shape formed by two connected lines)
angle (to fish with hook and line)

arch (curved structure)
arch (chief)

arms (body parts)
arms (weapons)

*august (majestic)
August (eighth month of the year)

*axes (plural of *ax*)
axes (plural of *axis*)

bail (money for release)
bail (handle of a pail)
bail (throw water out)

ball (round object)
ball (formal dance)

band (group of musicians)
band (thin strip for binding)

bank (mound)
bank (place of financial business)
bank (row of things)
bank (land along a river)

bark (tree covering)
bark (sound a dog makes)
bark (sailboard)

base (bottom)
base (morally low)

*bass (low male voice)
bass (kind of fish)

baste (pour liquid on while roasting)
baste (sew with long stitches)

bat (club)
bat (flying animal)
bat (wink)

batter (hit repeatedly)
batter (liquid mixture used for cakes)
batter (baseball player)

bay (part of a sea)
bay (aromatic leaf used in cooking)
bay (reddish brown)
bay (alcove between columns)
bay (howl)

bear (large animal)
bear (support; carry)

bill (statement of money owed)
bill (beak)

bit (small piece)
bit (tool for drilling)
bit (did bite)

blaze (fire)
blaze (mark a trail or a tree)
blaze (make known)

blow (hard hit)
blow (send forth a stream of air)

bluff (steep bank or cliff)
bluff (fool or mislead)

bob (weight at the end of a line)
bob (move up and down)
Bob (nickname for Robert)

boil (bubbling of hot liquid)
boil (red swelling on the skin)

boom (deep sound)
boom (long beam)
boom (sudden increase in size)

boon (benefit)
boon (merry)

The Reading Teacher's Book of Lists, Fifth Edition, © 2006 by John Wiley & Sons, Inc.

bore (make a hole)
bore (make weary)
bore (did bear)

bound (limit)
bound (obliged)
bound (spring back)
bound (on the way)

*****bow** (weapon for shooting arrows)
bow (forward part of a ship)
bow (bend in greeting or respect)

bowl (rounded dish)
bowl (play the game of bowling)

box (four-sided container)
box (kind of evergreen shrub)
box (strike with the hand)

bridge (way over an obstacle)
bridge (card game)

brush (tool for sweeping)
brush (bushes)

buck (male deer)
buck (slang for *dollar*)

buffer (something that softens)
buffer (pad for polishing)

*****buffet** (cabinet for dishes and linens)
buffet (self-serve meal)
buffet (strike)

butt (thicker end of a tool)
butt (object of ridicule)

can (able to)
can (metal container)

capital (money)
capital (punishable by death)

carp (complain)
carp (kind of fish)

case (condition)
case (box or container)

chap (crack or become rough)
chap (boy or man)

chop (cut with something sharp)
chop (jaw)

chop (irregular motion)
chop (cut of meat)

chord (two or more musical notes)
chord (together)
chord (an emotional response)

Chow (breed of dog)
chow (slang for *food*)

chuck (throw or toss)
chuck (cut of beef)

cleave (cut)
cleave (hold on to)

clip (cut)
clip (fasten)

*****close** (shut)
close (near)

clove (fragrant spice)
clove (section of a bulb)

cobbler (one who mends shoes)
cobbler (fruit pie with one crust)

cock (rooster)
cock (tilt upward)

colon (mark of punctuation)
colon (lower part of the large intestine)

*****commune** (talk intimately)
commune (group of people living together)

*****compact** (firmly packed together)
compact (agreement)

con (swindle)
con (against)

*****console** (cabinet)
console (ease grief)

*****contract** (written agreement)
contract (withdraw)

*****content** (all things inside)
content (satisfied)

*****converse** (talk)
converse (opposite)

corporal (of the body)
corporal (low-ranking officer)

count (name numbers in order)
count (nobleman)

counter (long table in a store or restaurant)
counter (one who counts)
counter (opposite)

HOMOGRAPHS AND HETERONYMS CONTINUED

crow (loud cry of a rooster)
crow (large black bird)
Crow (tribe of Native American Indians)

cue (signal)
cue (long stick used in a game of pool)

curry (rub and clean a horse)
curry (spicy seasoning)

date (day, month, and year)
date (sweet dark fruit)

defer (put off)
defer (yield to another)

demean (lower in dignity)
demean (humble oneself)

*__desert__ (dry barren region)
desert (go away from)

die (stop living)
die (tool)

*__do__ (act; perform)
do (first tone on the musical scale)

dock (wharf)
dock (cut some off)

*__does__ (plural of *doe*)
does (present tense of *to do*)

*__dove__ (pigeon)
dove (did dive)

down (from a higher to a lower place)
down (soft feathers)
down (grassy land)

dredge (dig up)
dredge (sprinkle with flour or sugar)

dresser (one who dresses)
dresser (bureau)

drove (did drive)
drove (flock; herd; crowd)

dub (give a title)
dub (add voice or music to a film)

duck (large wild bird)
duck (lower suddenly)
duck (type of cotton cloth)

ear (organ of hearing)
ear (part of certain plants)

egg (oval or round body laid by a bird)
egg (encourage)

elder (older)
elder (small tree)

*__entrance__ (going in)
entrance (delight; charm)

*__excise__ (tax)
excise (remove)

fair (beautiful; lovely)
fair (just; honest)
fair (showing of farm goods)
fair (bazaar)

fan (devise to stir up the air)
fan (admirer)

fast (speedy)
fast (go without food)

fawn (young deer)
fawn (try to get favor by slavish acts)

fell (did fall)
fell (cut down a tree)
fell (deadly)

felt (did feel)
felt (type of cloth)

file (drawer; folder)
file (steel tool to smooth material)
file (material)

fine (high quality)
fine (money paid as punishment)

firm (solid; hard)
firm (business; company)

fit (suitable)
fit (sudden attack)

flag (banner)
flag (get tired)

flat (smooth)
flat (apartment)

The Reading Teacher's Book of Lists, Fifth Edition, © 2006 by John Wiley & Sons, Inc.

fleet (group of ships)
fleet (rapid)

flight (act of flying)
flight (act of fleeing)

flounder (struggle)
flounder (kind of fish)

fluke (lucky stroke in games)
fluke (kind of fish)

fly (insect)
fly (move through the air with wings)

foil (prevent carrying out plans)
foil (metal sheet)
foil (long narrow sword)

fold (bend over on itself)
fold (pen for sheep)

forearm (part of the body)
forearm (prepare for trouble ahead)

forge (blacksmith shop)
forge (move ahead)

****forte** (strong point)
forte (loud)

found (did find)
found (set up; establish)

founder (sink)
founder (one who establishes)

frank (hot dog)
frank (bold talk)
Frank (man's name)

fray (become ragged)
fray (fight)

fresh (newly made, not stale)
fresh (impudent, bold)

fret (worry)
fret (ridges on a guitar)

fry (cook in shallow pan)
fry (young fish)

fuse (slow-burning wick)
fuse (melt together)

gall (bile)
gall (annoy)

game (pastime)
game (lame)

gauntlet (challenge)
gauntlet (protective glove)

gin (alcoholic beverage)
gin (apparatus for separating seeds from cotton)
gin (card came)

gore (blood)
gore (wound from a horn)
gore (three-sided insert of cloth)

grate (framework for burning fuel in a fireplace)
grate (have an annoying effect)

grave (place of burial)
grave (important, serious)
grave (carve)

graze (feed on grass)
graze (touch lightly in passing)

ground (soil)
ground (did grind)

grouse (game bird)
grouse (grumble; complain)

gull (water bird)
gull (cheat; deceive)

gum (sticky substance from certain trees)
gum (tissue around teeth)

guy (rope; chain)
guy (fellow)

hack (cut roughly)
hack (carrier or car for hire)

hail (pieces of ice that fall like rain)
hail (shouts of welcome)

hamper (hold back)
hamper (large container or bucket)

hatch (bring forth young from an egg)
hatch (opening in a ship's deck)

hawk (bird of prey)
hawk (peddle goods)

haze (mist; smoke)
haze (bully)

heel (back of the foot)
heel (tip over to one side)

Homographs and Heteronyms Continued

hide (conceal; keep out of sight)
hide (animal skin)

hinder (stop)
hinder (rear)

hold (grasp and keep)
hold (part of ship or place for cargo)

husky (big and strong)
husky (sled dog)

impress (have a strong effect on)
impress (take by force)

*__incense__ (substance with a sweet smell when burned)
incense (make very angry)

*__intern__ (force to stay)
intern (doctor in training at a hospital)

*__intimate__ (very familiar)
intimate (suggest)

*__invalid__ (disabled person)
invalid (not valid)

jam (fruit preserve)
jam (press or squeeze)

jerky (with sudden starts and stops)
jerky (strips of dried meat)

jet (stream of water, steam, or air)
jet (hard black soil)
jet (type of airplane)

jig (dance)
jig (fishing lure)

*__job__ (work)
Job (Biblical man of patience)

jumper (person or thing that jumps)
jumper (type of dress)

junk (trash)
junk (Chinese sailing ship)

key (instrument for locking and unlocking)
key (low island)

kind (friendly; helpful)
kind (same class)

lap (body part formed when sitting)
lap (drink)
lap (one course traveled)

lark (small songbird)
lark (good fun)

lash (cord part of a whip)
lash (tie or fasten)

last (at the end)
last (continue; endure)

launch (start out)
launch (type of boat)

*__lead__ (show the way)
lead (metallic element)

league (measure of distance)
league (group of persons or nations)

lean (stand slanting)
lean (not fat)

leave (go away)
leave (permission)

left (direction)
left (did leave)

lie (falsehood)
lie (place oneself in a flat position; rest)

light (not heavy)
light (not dark)
light (land on)

like (similar to)
like (be pleased with)

lime (citrus fruit)
lime (chemical substance)

limp (lame walk)
limp (not stiff)

line (piece of cord)
line (place paper or fabric inside)

list (series of words)
list (tilt to one side)

*__live__ (exist)
live (having life)

loaf (be idle)
loaf (shaped as bread)

The Reading Teacher's Book of Lists, Fifth Edition, © 2006 by John Wiley & Sons, Inc.

lock (fasten door)
lock (curl of hair)

long (great measure)
long (wish for)

loom (frame for weaving)
loom (threaten)

low (not high)
low (cattle sound)

lumber (timber)
lumber (move along heavily)

mace (club; weapon)
mace (spice)

mail (letters)
mail (flexible metal armor)

maroon (brownish red color)
maroon (leave helpless)

mat (woven floor covering)
mat (border for picture)

match (stick used to light fires)
match (equal)

meal (food served at a certain time)
meal (ground grain)

mean (signify; intend)
mean (unkind)
mean (average)

meter (unit of length)
meter (poetic rhythm)
meter (device that measures flow)

might (past tense of *may*)
might (power)

mine (belonging to me)
mine (hole in the earth to get ores)

*__minute__ (sixty seconds)
minute (very small)

miss (fail to hit)
miss (unmarried woman or girl)

mold (form; shape)
mold (fungus)

mole (brown spot on the skin)
mole (small underground animal)

mortar (cement mixture)
mortar (short cannon)

mount (high hill)
mount (go up)

mule (cross between donkey and horse)
mule (type of slipper)

mum (silent)
mum (chrysanthemum)

nag (scold)
nag (old horse)

nap (short sleep)
nap (rug fuzz)

net (open-weave fabric)
net (remaining after deductions)

nip (small drink)
nip (pinch)

number (numeral)
number (comparative of numb)

*__object__ (a thing)
object (to protest)

pad (cushion)
pad (walk softly)

page (one side of a sheet of paper)
page (youth who runs errands)

palm (inside of hand)
palm (kind of tree)

patent (right or privilege)
patent (type of leather)

patter (rapid taps)
patter (light, easy walk)

pawn (leave as security for loan)
pawn (chess piece)

*__peaked__ (having a point)
peaked (looking ill)

peck (dry measure)
peck (strike at)

pen (instrument for writing)
pen (enclosed yard)

pile (heap or stack)
pile (nap on fabrics)

HOMOGRAPHS AND HETERONYMS CONTINUED

pine (type of evergreen)
pine (yearn or long for)

pitch (throw)
pitch (tar)

pitcher (container for pouring liquid)
pitcher (baseball player)

poach (trespass)
poach (cook an egg)

poker (card game)
poker (rod for stirring a fire)

pole (long piece of wood)
pole (either end of the earth's axis)

policy (plan of action)
policy (written agreement)

*****Polish** (country)
polish (shine)

pool (tank with water)
pool (game played with balls on a table)

pop (short, quick sound)
pop (dad)
pop (popular)

post (support)
post (job or position)
post (system for mail delivery)

pound (unit of weight)
pound (hit hard again and again)
pound (pen)

*****present** (not absent)
present (gift)
present (to introduce formally)

press (squeeze)
press (force into service)

*****primer** (first book)
primer (something used to prepare another)

*****produce** (vegetables)
produce (make something)

prune (fruit)
prune (cut; trim)

pry (look with curiosity)
pry (lift with force)

pump (type of shoe)
pump (machine that forces liquid out)

punch (hit)
punch (beverage)

pupil (student)
pupil (part of the eye)

quack (sound of a duck)
quack (phony doctor)

racket (noise)
racket (paddle used in tennis)

rail (bar of wood or metal)
rail (complain bitterly)

rank (row or line)
rank (having a bad odor)

rare (unusual)
rare (not cooked much)

rash (hasty)
rash (small red spots on the skin)

ream (500 sheets of paper)
ream (clean a hole)

rear (the back part)
rear (bring up)

*****record** (music disk)
record (write down)

*****recount** (count again)
recount (tell in detail)

reel (spool for winding)
reel (sway under a blow)
reel (lively dance)

refrain (hold back)
refrain (part repeated)

*****refuse** (say no)
refuse (waste; trash)

rest (sleep)
rest (what is left)

rifle (gun with a long barrel)
rifle (ransack; search through)

ring (circle)
ring (bell sound)

root (underground part of a plant)
root (cheer for someone)

The Reading Teacher's Book of Lists, Fifth Edition, © 2006 by John Wiley & Sons, Inc.

*row (line)
row (use oars to move a boat)
row (noisy fight)

sage (wise person)
sage (herb)

sap (liquid in a plant)
sap (weaken)

sash (cloth worn around the waist)
sash (frame of a window)

saw (did see)
saw (tool for cutting)
saw (wise saying)

scale (balance)
scale (outer layer of fish and snakes)
scale (series of steps)

school (place for learning)
school (group of fish)

scour (clean)
scour (move quickly over)

scrap (small bits)
scrap (quarrel)

seal (mark of ownership)
seal (sea mammal)

second (after the first)
second (one-sixtieth of a minute)

*sewer (one who sews)
sewer (underground pipe for wastes)

shark (large meat-eating fish)
shark (dishonest person)

shed (small shelter)
shed (get rid of)

shingles (roofing materials)
shingles (viral disease)

shock (sudden violent disturbance)
shock (thick bushy mass)

shore (land near water's edge)
shore (support)

shot (fired a gun)
shot (worn out)

size (amount)
size (preparation of glue)

*slaver (dealer in slaves)
slaver (salivate)

sledge (heavy sled)
sledge (large hammer)

slip (go easily)
slip (small strip of paper)
slip (undergarment)

*slough (swamp)
slough (shed old skin)

slug (small slow-moving animal)
slug (hit hard)

smack (slight taste)
smack (open lips quickly)
smack (small boat)

snare (trap)
snare (string on bottom of a drum)

snarl (growl)
snarl (tangle)

sock (covering for foot)
sock (hit hard)

soil (ground; dirt)
soil (make dirty)

sole (type of fish)
sole (only)

*sow (scatter seeds)
sow (female pig)

spar (mast of a ship)
spar (argue)
spar (mineral)

spell (say the letters of a word)
spell (magic influences)
spell (period of work)

spray (sprinkle liquid)
spray (small branch with leaves and flowers)

spruce (type of evergreen)
spruce (neat or trim)

squash (press flat)
squash (vegetable)

stable (building for horses)
stable (unchanging)

HOMOGRAPHS AND HETERONYMS CONTINUED

stake (stick or post)
stake (risk or prize)

stalk (main stem of a plant)
stalk (follow secretly)

stall (place in a stable for one animal)
stall (delay)

staple (metal fastener for paper)
staple (principal element)

stay (remain)
stay (support)

steep (having a sharp slope)
steep (soak)

steer (guide)
steer (young male cattle)

stem (part of a plant)
stem (stop, dam up)

stern (rear part of a ship)
stern (harsh, strict)

stick (thin piece of wood)
stick (pierce)

still (not moving)
still (apparatus for making alcohol)

stoop (bend down)
stoop (porch)

story (account of a happening)
story (floor of a building)

strain (pull tight)
strain (group with an inherited quality)

strand (leave helpless)
strand (thread or string)

strip (narrow piece of cloth)
strip (remove)

stroke (hit)
stroke (pet, soothe)
stroke (an illness)

stunt (stop growth)
stunt (bold action)

sty (pen for pigs)
sty (swelling on eyelid)

*subject (topic)
subject (put under)

suit (clothing)
suit (court case)

swallow (take in)
swallow (small bird)

tap (strike lightly)
tap (faucet)

*tarry (delay)
tarry (covered with tar)

tart (sour but agreeable)
tart (small fruit-filled pie)

*tear (drop of liquid from the eye)
tear (pull apart)

temple (building for worship)
temple (side of forehead)

tend (incline to)
tend (take care of)

tender (not tough)
tender (offer)
tender (one who cares for)

tick (sound of a clock)
tick (small insect)
tick (pillow covering)

till (until)
till (plow the land)
till (drawer for money)

tip (end point)
tip (slant)
tip (present of money for services)

tire (become weary)
tire (rubber around a wheel)

toast (browned bread slices)
toast (wish for good luck)

toll (sound of a bell)
toll (fee paid for a privilege)

top (highest point)
top (toy that spins)

troll (ugly dwarf)
troll (method of fishing)

unaffected (not influenced)
unaffected (innocent)

vault (storehouse for valuables)
vault (jump over)

wake (stop sleeping)
wake (trail left behind a ship)

wax (substance made by trees)
wax (grow bigger)

well (satisfactory)
well (hole dug for water)

whale (large sea mammal)
whale (whip)

will (statement of desire for distribution
of property after one's death)
will (is going to)
will (deliberate intention or wish)

*__wind__ (air in motion)
wind (turn)

*__wound__ (hurt)
wound (wrapped around)

yak (long-haired ox)
yak (talk endlessly)

yard (enclosed space around a house)
yard (thirty-six inches)

yen (strong desire)
yen (unit of money in Japan)

See also List 19, Homophones; List 23, Easily Confused Words; List 42,
Words with Multiple Meanings.

LIST 23. EASILY CONFUSED WORDS

The following groups of words are frequently used incorrectly. Some are confused because they sound the same but have different meanings; others look and sound different from each other but have meanings that are related. To teach them effectively will require many different strategies and frequent repetitions. Even those of us who understand these words make mistakes when we are in a hurry. These words make tricky but useful spelling lessons.

accede (v.)—to comply with
exceed (v.)—to surpass

accent (n.)—stress in speech or writing
ascent (n.)—act of going up
assent (v., n.)—consent

accept (v.)—to agree or take what is offered
except (prep.)—leaving out or excluding

access (n.)—admittance
excess (n., adj.)—surplus

adapt (v.)—to adjust
adept (adj.)—proficient
adopt (v.)—to take by choice

adverse (adj.)—opposing
averse (adj.)—disinclined

affect (v.)—feeling
effect (n.)—consequence or result

alley (n.)—narrow street
ally (n.)—supporter

allusion (n.)—indirect reference
delusion (n.)—mistaken belief
illusion (n.)—mistaken vision

all ready (adj.)—completely ready
already (adv.)—even now or by this time

all together (pron., adj.)—everything or everyone in one place
altogether (adv.)—entirely

anecdote (n.)—short amusing story
antidote (n.)—something to counter the effect of poison

angel (n.)—heavenly body
angle (n.)—space between two lines that meet in a point

annul (v.)—to make void
annual (adj.)—yearly

ante—prefix meaning before
anti—prefix meaning against

any way (adj., n.)—in whatever manner
anyway (adv.)—regardless

appraise (v.)—to set a value on
apprise (v.)—to inform

area (n.)—surface
aria (n.)—melody

biannual (adj.)—occurring twice per year
biennial (adj.)—occurring every other year

bibliography (n.)—list of writings on a particular topic, references
biography (n.)—written history of a person's life

bizarre (adj.)—odd
bazaar (n.)—market, fair

breadth (n.)—width
breath (n.)—respiration
breathe (v.)—to inhale and exhale

calendar (n.)—a chart of days and months
colander (n.)—a strainer

casual (adj.)—informal
causal (adj.)—relating to cause

catch (v.)—to grab
ketch (n.)—type of boat

cease (v.)—to stop
seize (v.)—to grasp

click (n.)—short, sharp sound
clique (n.)—small exclusive subgroup

collision (n.)—a clashing
collusion (n.)—a scheme to cheat

coma (n.)—an unconscious state
comma (n.)—a punctuation mark

The Reading Teacher's Book of Lists, Fifth Edition, © 2006 by John Wiley & Sons, Inc.

The Reading Teacher's Book of Lists, Fifth Edition, © 2006 by John Wiley & Sons, Inc.

command (n.,v.)—an order, to order
commend (v.)—to praise, to entrust

comprehensible (adj.)—understandable
comprehensive (adj.)—extensive

confidant (n.)—friend or advisor
confident (adj.)—sure

confidentially (adv.)—privately
confidently (adv.)—certainly

conscience (n.)—sense of right and wrong
conscious (adj.)—aware

contagious (adj.)—spread by contact
contiguous (adj.)—touching or nearby

continual (adj.)—repeated, happening again and again
continuous (adj.)—uninterrupted, without stopping

cooperation (n.)—the art of working together
corporation (n.)—a business organization

costume (n.)—special way of dressing
custom (n.)—usual practice of habit

council (n.)—an official group
counsel (v.)—to give advice
counsel (n.)—advice

credible (adj.)—believable
creditable (adj.)—deserving praise

deceased (adj.)—dead
diseased (adj.)—ill

decent (adj.)—proper
descent (n.)—way down
dissent (n., v)—disagreement, to disagree

deference (n.)—respect
difference (n.)—dissimilarity

deposition (n.)—a formal written document
disposition (n.)—temperament

depraved (adj.)—morally corrupt
deprived (adj.)—taken away from

deprecate (v.)—to disapprove
depreciate (v.)—to lessen in value

desert (n.)—arid land
desert (v.)—to abandon
dessert (n.)—course served at the end of a meal

desolate (adj.)—lonely, sad
dissolute (adj.)—loose in morals

detract (v.)—to take away from
distract (v.)—to divert attention away from

device (n.)—a contrivance
devise (v.)—to plan

disapprove (v.)—to withhold approval
disprove (v.)—to prove something to be false

disassemble (v.)—to take something apart
dissemble (v.)—to disguise

disburse (v.)—to pay out
disperse (v.)—to scatter

discomfort (n.)—distress
discomfit (v.)—to frustrate or embarrass

disinterested (adj.)—impartial
uninterested (adj.)—not interested

effect (n.)—result of a cause
effect (v.)—to make happen

elapse (v.)—to pass
lapse (v.)—to become void
relapse (v.)—to fall back to previous condition

elicit (v.)—to draw out
illicit (adj.)—unlawful

eligible (adj.)—ready
illegible (adj.)—can't be read

elusive (adj.)—hard to catch
illusive (adj.)—misleading

eminent (adj.)—well known
imminent (adj.)—impending

emerge (v.)—rise out of
immerge (v.)—plunge into

emigrate (v.)—to leave a country and take up residence elsewhere
immigrate (v.)—to enter a country for the purpose of taking up residence

EASILY CONFUSED WORDS CONTINUED

envelop (v.)—to surround
envelope (n.)—a wrapper for a letter

erasable (adj.)—capable of being erased
irascible (adj.)—easily provoked to anger

expand (v.)—to increase in size
expend (v.)—to spend

expect (v.)—to suppose; to look forward
suspect (v.)—to mistrust

extant (adj.)—still existing
extent (n.)—amount

facility (n.)—ease
felicity (n.)—happiness

farther (adj.)—more distant (refers to space)
further (adj.)—extending beyond a point (refers to time, quantity, or degree)

finale (n.)—the end
finally (adv.)—at the end
finely (adv.)—in a fine manner

fiscal (adj.)—relating to finance
physical (adj.)—relating to the body

formally (adv.)—with rigid ceremony
formerly (adv.)—previously

human (adj.)—relating to mankind
humane (adv.)—kind

hypercritical (adj.)—very critical
hypocritical (adj.)—pretending to be virtuous

imitate (v.)—to mimic
intimate (v.)—to hint or make known; familiar, close

incredible (adj.)—too extraordinary to be believed
incredulous (adj.)—unbelieving, skeptical

indigenous (adj.)—native
indigent (adj.)—needy
indignant (adj.)—angry

infer (v.)—to arrive at by reason
imply (v.)—to suggest meaning indirectly

ingenious (adj.)—clever
ingenuous (adj.)—straightforward

later (adj.)—more late
latter (adj.)—second in a series of two

lay (v.)—to set something down or place something
lie (v.)—to recline

least (adj.)—at the minimum
lest (conj.)—for fear that

lend (v.)—to give for a time
loan (n.)—received to use for a time

loose (adj.)—not tight
lose (v.)—not win; misplace

magnet (n.)—iron bar with power to attract iron
magnate (n.)—person in prominent position in large industry

message (n.)—communication
massage (v.)—rub body

moral (n., adj.)—lesson; ethic
morale (n.)—mental condition

morality (n.)—virtue
mortality (n.)—the state of being mortal; death rate

of (prep.)—having to do with; indicating possession
off (adv.)—not on

official (adj.)—authorized
officious (adj.)—offering services where they are neither wanted nor needed

oral (adj.)—verbal
aural (adj.)—listening

pasture (n.)—grass field
pastor (n.)—minister

perfect (adj.)—without fault
prefect (n.)—an official

perpetrate (v.)—to be guilty of; to commit
perpetuate (v.)—to make perpetual

perquisite (n.)—a privilege or profit in addition to salary
prerequisite (n.)—a preliminary requirement

persecute (v.)—to harass, annoy, or injure
prosecute (v.)—to press for punishment of crime

The Reading Teacher's Book of Lists, Fifth Edition, © 2006 by John Wiley & Sons, Inc.

personal (adj.)—private
personnel (n.)—people employed in an organization

peruse (v.)—to read
pursue (v.)—to follow in order to overtake

picture (n.)—drawing or photograph
pitcher (n.)—container for liquid; baseball player

precede (v.)—to go before
proceed (v.)—to advance

preposition (n.)—a part of speech
proposition (n.)—a proposal or suggestion

pretend (v.)—to make believe
portend (v.)—to give a sign of something that will happen

quiet (adj.)—not noisy
quit (v.)—to stop
quite (adv.)—very

recent (adj.)—not long ago
resent (v.)—to feel indignant

respectably (adv.)—in a respectable manner
respectively (adv.)—in order indicated
respectfully (adv.)—in a respectful manner

restless (adj.)—constantly moving, uneasy
restive (adj.)—contrary, resisting control

suppose (v.)—assume or imagine
supposed (adj.)—expected

than (conj.)—used in comparison
then (adv.)—at that time; next in order of time

through (prep.)—by means of; from beginning to end
thorough (adj.)—complete

use (v.)—employ something
used (adj.)—secondhand

veracious (adj.)—truthful
voracious (adj.)—greedy

See also List 19, Homophones; List 22, Homographs and Heteronyms.

LIST 24. COLLECTIVE NOUNS

The word that names groups or collections of people, animals, and things is called a collective noun. Some collective nouns are very familiar (like a **deck** of cards); others are much less so. These words are often substituted for the person, animal, or object they name. For example: The Marines were on parade; the corps marched with the drumbeat.

academy of scholars
agenda of meeting topics
armada of ships
army of ants (caterpillars, frogs, soldiers)
array of numbers
association of professionals
assortment of items
audience of listeners
aurora of polar bears
bale of cotton (turtles)
band of gorillas (jays, musicians, robbers)
bank of monitors
barren of mules
bask of crocodiles
batch of biscuits (cookies, bread)
bed of clams (flowers, oysters, snakes, vegetables)
belt of asteroids
bevy of ladies (quail, swans)
block of houses (stamps)
brood of children (hens)
bundle of clothes (money, sticks)
cast of actors
cavalcade of horsemen
chain of islands
chapter of a book (verse)
chest of drawers
chorus of singers
class of students
club of members
clump of dirt (earth, grass)
cluster of diamonds (grapes, stars)
clutch of chicks
collection of stamps (books, coins, art)
colony of ants (artists, writers)
committee of people
company of firefighters (soldiers, workers)
conglomeration of businesses
congregation of worshipers
congress of delegates
constellation of stars
convention of professionals

convocation of eagles
corps of marines
council of advisors (chiefs)
couple of people
coven of witches
covey of doves (partridges)
crew of sailors (workers)
crowd of people
culture of bacteria
deck of cards
draught of fish
drove of cattle
exultation of larks
faculty of teachers
family of colors (languages, people)
field of racehorses
fleet of ships
flock of believers (birds, sheep, tourists)
flood of complaints (emotion, money)
flotilla of ships
flush of ducks
gaggle of geese
galaxy of stars
gang of hoodlums (workmen, friends)
group of things
grove of trees
herd of buffalo (cows, reindeer)
hive of bees
horde of enemies (gnats)
host of angels
huddle of lawyers
jury of citizens
knot of toads
league of nations (teams)
line of people
litter of kittens (pigs, puppies)
mob of kangaroos (people, radicals)
mound of dirt (earth)
multitude of followers
murder of crows
nest of bowls (mice, snakes, spies, vipers)
network of computers

pack of dogs (gum, hounds, lies, wolves)
panel of experts
parliament of owls
party of diners (fishermen)
patch of flowers
peep of chickens
people of a city (nation)
pile of things
plague of locusts
pod of whales
portfolio of pictures (stocks, work)
posse of deputies
pride of lions
rag of colts
range of mountains
rookery of penguins
school of fish (porpoises)
set of dishes (teeth)

shelf of books
shock of hair (wheat)
slew of homework
spread of cattle (food, horses)
squad of police (cheerleaders)
stack of pancakes (paper)
staff of employees
string of ponies
swarm of bees (flies, reporters)
team of athletes (horses)
tribe of Indians (natives, peoples)
troop of baboons (kangaroos, police, scouts, soldiers)
troupe of performers
union of workers
wave of emotion (insects, water)
wealth of information
wing of aircraft

LIST 25. MASS NOUNS OR UNCOUNTABLE NOUNS

Mass nouns (sometimes called uncountable nouns) are not countable in the usual sense. That is, while we can have "one book" or "two books," "one pen" or "two pens," we do not usually have "one bread" or "two breads," "one money" or "two moneys." Bread and money are mass nouns. There are many such nouns in the English language and most can be grouped into categories. Some of these categories are listed below along with examples.

Teaching Information

Liquids
blood
gasoline
juice
milk
oil
shampoo
soup
syrup
water

Gases
air
hydrogen
oxygen
pollution
smog
smoke

Solids and Semi-Solids
beef
bread
butter
chicken
cotton
gold
jelly
machinery
paper
peanut butter
rayon
silk
silver
soap
toast
toothpaste

Items with Small Parts
barley
corn
grass
hay
pollen
rice
rye
salt
sand
sugar
water

Collections of Diverse Things
clothing
equipment
furniture
garbage
hardware
jewelry
luggage
machinery
mail
money
silverware
software

Abstract Nouns
advice
beauty
good
happiness
honesty
intelligence
knowledge
literacy
love
peace
sadness
stuff
wealth

Miscellaneous
chess
dissent
history
information
land
momentum
news
psychology
research
scenery
slang
traffic
weather

Actions
homework
housework

Animals
cod
deer
fish
moose
salmon
sheep

The Reading Teacher's Book of Lists, Fifth Edition, © 2006 by John Wiley & Sons, Inc.

Note the following characteristics. Readers and writers usually learn these uses by practice and familiarity.

Plurals of Nouns

- Mass nouns usually do not have a plural (-s) form.
  Example: You say *some furniture*, not *some furnitures*.

- Mass nouns can stand alone (without an article).
  Example: You say *chess is fun*, not *the chess is fun*.

- A few mass nouns **look like plurals but are not**. They end in *-s* but they are really singular.
  Example: You say *the subject of physics is hard*, not *the subject of physics are hard*.

Articles

- Countable nouns (the most common nouns) cannot stand alone in singular form; they need an article.
  Example: You say *the desk is big*, not *desk is big*.

- You do not use *a*, *an*, or *another* or words such as *many*, *these*, or *numbers* (like three) with mass nouns.
  Example: You say *a book*, not *a furniture*. You say *many books*, not *many furnitures*.

- Some nouns can be either a mass noun or a countable noun depending on their use or meaning.
  Example: You say *cake is good*; *two cakes are better*.

Verbs

- A verb that follows a mass noun is always singular.
  Example: You say *the music was good*, not *the music were good*.

Adjectives

- The adjectives *much* and *a little* can be used only with mass nouns, whereas *a few*, *several*, and *many* can be used only with countable nouns.
  Example: You say *a little shampoo*, not *a few shampoo*.

LIST 26. NONREVERSIBLE WORD PAIRS

The following are examples of pairs of words that always appear in the same order. Native speakers of English will probably use the correct order automatically; nonnative speakers, however, will need to learn these through practice. These are also collocations (words commonly used together).

Adam and Eve
bacon and eggs
back and forth
bed and breakfast
black and white
birds and bees
bread and water
bride and groom
business and pleasure
cause and effect
coat and tie
coffee and doughnuts
cream and sugar
crime and punishment
cup and saucer
dead or alive
fish and chips
front and center
fun and games
ham and eggs
hammer and nail
high and dry
husband and wife
in and out
Jack and Jill
knife and fork
ladies and gentlemen
law and order
life or death
lock and key
lost and found

man and wife
name and address
nice and easy
peaches and cream
pen and pencil
pork and beans
pots and pans
profit and loss (profit or loss)
rain or shine
read and write
right and wrong (right or wrong)
rise and fall
salt and pepper
shirt and tie
shoes and socks
short and fat
slip and slide
soap and water
sooner or later
stars and stripes
suit and tie
supply and demand
sweet and sour
tall and thin
touch and go
thick and thin
trial and error
up and down (up or down)
war and peace
wine and cheese

The Reading Teacher's Book of Lists, Fifth Edition, © 2006 by John Wiley & Sons, Inc.

See also List 27, Collocations; List 184, Idiomatic Expressions.

LIST 27. COLLOCATIONS

Collocations are words that are frequently used together. For example, you "take (or have) a bath"; you usually don't say "do a bath." Native English speakers learn collocations along with learning to talk, but English Language Learners (ELL or ESL) often need explicit instruction to learn common collocations. Here are some collocations related to the words *make*, *do*, *catch*, *have*, and *take*.

Make

make preparations
make a decision
make a discovery
make a phone call
make a noise
make a promise
make a complaint
make progress
make an effort
make a comment
make a suggestion
make a list

Do

do damage
do research
do justice
do harm

Catch

catch a ball
catch a cold
catch a movie
catch a train
catch a crook

Have

have a headache
have lessons
have an operation
have a baby
have a party
have breakfast
have fun
have a break

Take

take a bath
take lessons
take a test
take a look
take a picture
take an exam
take a break

See also List 26, Nonreversible Word Pairs.

3

VOCABULARY BUILDERS

LIST 28. THE 20 MOST COMMON PREFIXES

This is a research-based list for those who wish to see the data. These 20 prefixes account for 97 percent of occurences.

Rank	Prefix	Meaning	%	Example
1	**un**	not, opposite of	26	*unhappy*
2	**re**	again, back	14	*return*
3	**in, im, ir, ill**	not, opposite of	11	*indirect*
4	**dis**	not, opposite of	7	*discover*
5	**en, em**	cause to	4	*enjoy*
6	**non**	not, opposite of	4	*nonfiction*
7	**in, im**	in or into	4	*inside*
8	**over**	too much, above	3	*overgrown*
9	**mis**	wrongly	3	*mistake*
10	**sub**	under, lower	3	*submarine*
11	**pre**	before	3	*prepared*
12	**inter**	between, among	3	*international*
13	**fore**	before	3	*foresee*
14	**de**	opposite of, down	2	*descent*
15	**trans**	across	2	*transport*
16	**super**	above, beyond	1	*supermarket*
17	**semi**	half	1	*semicircle*
18	**anti**	against	1	*antiwar*
19	**mid**	middle	1	*midsemester*
20	**under**	too little, below	1	*underfed*

All other prefixes accounted for only 3% of the words. See List 29 for a more complete list of prefixes.

Source: White, T. G., Sowell, V., and Yanagihara, A. (1999). Teaching elementary students to use word-part clues. *The Reading Teacher, 42*, 302–308.

LIST 29. MORE PREFIXES

Prefixes are small but meaningful letter groups added in front of a base word or root that contribute to the meaning of a word. There is some confusion between **prefixes** and **roots.** Linguists solve the problem by calling both **combining forms.** We have chosen to call all combining forms commonly found at the beginning of a word **prefixes.**

Knowing the meaning of these prefixes—together with the meaning of common base words and Greek and Latin roots—will give students the tools for unlocking the meanings of hundreds of words. In addition to teaching these prefixes directly, it is a good idea to explain prefixes and their meanings when students encounter them in new vocabulary words throughout the year.

You may wish to use the special list of prefixes expressing numbers (many of which also appear in the Intermediate to Advanced sublist) to form the basis of a lesson on number words.

BEGINNING PREFIXES

Prefix	Meaning	Examples
anti-	against	antiwar, antisocial, antislavery, antifreeze
dis-	not, opposite	disappear, disagree, disarm, dishonest, discontinue
ex-	former	ex-president, ex-student, ex-athlete, ex-teacher, ex-king
im-, in-	not	impossible, impassable, immobilize, immature, imbalance
		inaccurate, invisible, inactive, indecisive, independent
inter-	among, between	Internet, international, intermission, intervene, interrupt
intra-	within	intramural, intrastate, intravenous, intranet, intramuscular
micro-	small, short	microphone, microscope, microwave, microbe, microfilm
mis-	wrong, not	misbehave, misconduct, misfortune, mistake, miscount
multi-	many, much	multiply, multicolored, multimillionaire, multitude
non-	not	nonsense, nonfiction, nonresistant, nonstop, nonviolent
over-	too much	overdue, overdo, overpriced, overbearing, overactive
post-	after	postpone, postdate, postscript, postmeridian, postwar
pre-	before	prefix, precaution, preamble, prenatal, prelude
pro-	favor	pro-war, Pro-American, pro-education, pro-trade, pro-union
pro-	forward	proceed, produce, progress, project, prognosis, prophet
re-	again	redo, rewrite, reappear, repaint, reheat, relive
re-	back	recall, recede, repay, reflect, retract, rebate

The Reading Teacher's Book of Lists, Fifth Edition, © 2006 by John Wiley & Sons, Inc.

Prefix	Meaning	Examples
sub-	under, below	submarine, subzero, submerge, subordinate, subhuman
super-	above, beyond	superman, supernatural, superior, superpower, supervise
tele-	distant	telephone, telescope, television, telegram, telepathy
trans-	across	transport, transfer, translate, transatlantic, transcribe
un-	not	unhappy, unable, uncomfortable, uncertain, unbeaten
under-	below, less than	underpaid, undercover, underground, underneath, underage

INTERMEDIATE TO ADVANCED PREFIXES

Prefix	Meaning	Examples
after-	after	afternoon, afterward, aftershock, aftereffect, afterthought
ambi-, amphi-	both, around	ambidextrous, ambiguous, ambivalent, ambience amphibian, amphitheater, amphora
auto-	self	automobile, automatic, autograph, autobiography, autonomy
be-	make	befriend, bewitch, beguile, bejewel, becalm
bene-	good	benefit, benefactor, benediction, beneficial, benevolent
bi-, bin-	two	bicycle, binocular, bifocal, biannual, bimonthly
cent-, centi-	hundred, hundredth	century, centigrade, centimeter, centennial
circu-	around	circulate, circumference, circus, circumspect, circumstance
co-	together	cooperate, collaborate, coordinate, coincide, co-chair
com-, con-	with	combine, commune, combat, compare, command concert, concur, connect, confer, concede, confident
contra-	against, opposite	contrary, contradict, contrast, contraband, contraception
counter-	against, opposite	counteract, countermand, counterproposal, counteroffensive
de-	down, away	deduct, descend, decrease, degrade, depart
de-	not, opposite	deform, deplete, deactivate, defuse, dehumidify
dec-	ten	decade, decathlon, December, decennial
deci-	tenth	decimeter, decimate, decibel, decile, decimal

MORE PREFIXES CONTINUED

Prefix	Meaning	Examples
di-	two, double	dilemma, dioxide, dichotomy, diploma, digraph
dia-	through, across	diameter, dialogue, diagonal, diagnose, dialect
du-, duo-	two	duo, duet, dual, duplex, duplicate
dys-	bad	dysfunctional, dysentery, dysphasia, dystrophy
e-	out, away	evict, eject, erupt, emigrate, edict, emancipate
equi-	equal	equator, equation, equilibrium, equidistant, equinox
eu-	good	eulogy, euphoria, euphemism, Eucharist, euthanasia
giga-	billion	gigawatt, gigahertz, gigabyte
hemi-	half	hemisphere, hemistich, hemiplegia, hemicycle
hept-	seven	heptagon, heptameter, heptarchy
hetero-	different	heteronym, heterodoz, heterogenous, heterosexual
hex-	six	hexagon, hexameter, hexagram, hexadecimal
homo-	same	homogeneous, homogenize, homosexual, homophone
hyper-	excessive	hyperactive, hypersensitive, hyperbole, hypercritical
hypo-	under, too little	hypodermic, hypothesis, hypothermia, hypoxia
il-	not	illegal, illegible, illiterate, illogical, illegitimate
ir-	not	irregular, irreconcilable, irrevocable, irresponsible
kilo-	thousand	kilometer, kilogram, kilobyte, kilowatt, kiloliter
macro-	large, long	macroeconomics, macron, macrobiotic, macrocosm
magni-	great, large	magnify, magnificent, magnitude, magnanimous
mal-	bad	maladjusted, malfunction, malice, malevolent
mega-	large, million	megaphone, megalith, megacycle, megawatt, megaton, megabuck, megahertz
meta-	change	metamorphosis, metaphor, metastasis
mid-	middle	midnight, midway, midsummer, midyear, midshipman
milli-	thousand	million, milligram, millimeter, millennium, millibar
mon-, mono-	one	monk, monarch, monocular, monorail, monogamy
neo-	new	neoclassical, neologism, neonatal, neophyte, neon
omni-	all	omnibus, omnificent, omnipotent, omnivorous, omniscient
pan-	all	panorama, panacea, pandemonium, pandemic, Pan-American
para-	almost	paramedic, paralegal, paraprofessional, parasail
per-	through	perennial, permeate, permit, pervade, percolate
peri-	around	perimeter, periscope, peripatetic, periphery, periodontist

The Reading Teacher's Book of Lists, Fifth Edition, © 2006 by John Wiley & Sons, Inc.

Prefix	Meaning	Examples
poly-	many	polysyllabic, polyglot, polyester, polyandry, polygamy
prot-	first, chief	protagonist, proton, prototype, protocol, protoplasm
pseudo-	false	pseudonym, pseudoclassical, pseudointellectual
quadr-	four	quadrangle, quadrant, quadriplegic, quadruple
quint-	five	quintuplet, quintet, quintessential, quintuple
self-	self	selfish, self-denial, self-respect, self-taught
semi-	half	semiannual, semicircle, semiconscious, semiautomatic
sept-	seven	September, septet, septuagenarian
syn-	together	synchronize, syndrome, synergy, synonym, synthesis
tri-	three	triangle, tricycle, trillion, triplet, tripartite, triumvirate
ultra-	beyond	ultramodern, ultraconservative, ultranationalist
uni-	one	unicorn, uniform, unite, universe, unique, unison

PREFIXES EXPRESSING NUMBER

Prefix	Meaning	Examples
deci-	tenth	decimeter
centi-	hundredth	centimeter
milli-	thousandth	millimeter
micro-	millionth	micrometer
nano-	billionth	nanometer
pico-	trillionth	picometer
femto-	quadrillionth	femtometer
atto-	quintillionth	attometer
demi-	half	demigod, demitasse
hemi-	half	hemisphere, hemicycle
semi-	half	semiannual, semicircle, semiclassic
prot-	first	protagonist, protein, proton, prototype
mon-, mono-	one	monk, monarch, monocular, monogamy
uni-	one	unicorn, unicycle, uniform, unify, unite
di-	two	digraph, dioxide, diphthong
tri-	three	triangle, tricycle, trillion, triplet
quadr-	four	quadrangle, quadrant, quadruple
tetra-	four	tetrahedron, tetrameter
pent-	five	pentagon, pentathalon, Pentecost
quint-	five	quintet, quintuplets, quintile
hex-	six	hexagon, hexameter
sex-	six	sextant, sextet, sextuple
hept-	seven	heptagon, heptameter
sept-	seven	September, septuagenarian

MORE PREFIXES CONTINUED

Prefix	Meaning	Examples
oct-	eight	October, octagon, octane, octopus
ennea-	nine	enneagon, enneahedron, ennead
non-	nine	nonagenarian
nove-	nine	November, novena
deca-, dec-	ten	December, decade, decathlon, decameter
cent-	hundred	century (*note:* cent- is a shortened form of centi, which usually means one hundredth)
hect-	hundred	hectogram, hectometer, hectare
milli-	thousand	million, millipede (*note:* in metric system, milli- means thousandth)
kilo-	thousand	kilometer, kilogram, kilowatt, kiloliter
myria-	ten thousand	myriameter, myriad
mega-	million	megawatt, megabyte
giga-	billion	gigabyte
tera-	trillion	terameter
peta-	quadrillion	petameter
exa-	quintillion	exameter

PREFIXES THAT DESCRIBE SIZE

Prefix	Meaning	Examples
macro-	large, long	macrocosm, macron, macroscopic
magni-	great	magnify, magnitude, magnificent
mega-	large	megacycle, megalith, megalomania
micro-	small, short	microbe, microphone, microcosm
mini-	small	miniature, minute, minimall

PREFIXES THAT DESCRIBE WHEN

Prefix	Meaning	Examples
after-	after	afterglow, afternoon, aftertaste, afterward
ante-	before	antebellum, antecedent, antedate, antediluvian
epi-	after	epilogue, epitaph, epidermis
post-	after	postdate, postdoctoral, posterior, postpone, postscript
pre-	before	preamble, precaution, prefix, prejudice
pro-	before	prognosis, progeny, program, prologue

PREFIXES THAT DESCRIBE WHERE

Prefix	Meaning	Examples
a-	on	aboard, afire, afoot, ashore, atop
ab-	from	abnormal, abhor, abolish, abstain
ac-	to	accent, accept, access, accident, acquire
ad-	to	adapt, add, addict, adhere, admit
af-	to	affair, affect, affiliate, affirm, afflict

The Reading Teacher's Book of Lists, Fifth Edition, © 2006 by John Wiley & Sons, Inc.

Prefix	Meaning	Examples
ag-	to	agglomeration, aggrandize, aggravate
an-	to	annex, annihilate, annotate, announce
as-	to	ascend, ascertain, aspect, aspire, assert
by-	near, side	bypass, byplay, bystander, byway
circu-	around	circulate, circumference, circumspect
de-	from, down	debate, decay, deceive, decide, deform
dia-	through, across	diagnose, diagonal, dialogue, diameter
e-	out, away	effect, effort, eject, emigrate, erupt
em-	in	embalm, embed, embezzle, embrace
en-	in	enchant, enclose, encounter, encourage
enter-	among, between	enterprise, entertain
epi-	upon	epicenter, epidemic, epidermis, epithet
ex-	out	excel, exalt, exceed, exhaust, exit
extra-	outside	extracurricular, extraordinary
hypo-	under	hypochondria, hypodermic, hypothesis
im-	into	immediate, immerse, immigrate, implant
in-	into	incision, include, induce, inhale, infect
inter-	among, between	intercede, interpret, interrupt
intra-	within	intramural, intrastate, intravenous
intro-	inside	introduce, introspect, introject, introvert
mid-	middle	midriff, midshipman, midsummer
off-	from	offset, offshoot, offshore, offspring
on-	on	oncoming, ongoing, onrush, onshore
para-	beside	paradigm, paragraph, parallel, paraphrase
per-	throughout	perceive, percolate, perfect, perform
peri-	all around	perimeter, periscope, peripatetic
pro-	forward	proceed, produce, proficient, progress
pro-	in front of	proclaim, profane, profess
re-	back	recall, recede, reflect, repay, retract
retro-	back	retroactive, retrogress, retro-rocket
sub-	under	subcontract, subject, submerge
super-	over	superimpose, superscript, supersede
tele-	distant	telegram, telekinesis, telephone
through-	through	thoroughbred, thoroughfare
trans-	across	transatlantic, transcend, transcribe
under-	below	undercover, underground, underneath
with-	back, away	withdraw, withhold, within, without

PREFIXES THAT DESCRIBE AMOUNT OR EXTENT OF

Prefix	Meaning	Examples
equi-	equal	equal, equilibrium, equidistant, equator
extra-	beyond	extraordinary, extravagant
hyper-	excessive	hyperactive, hyperbole, hypercritical
hypo-	too little	hypoactive, hypoglycemic
is-	equal	isometric, isomorph, isosceles, isotope
multi-	many, much	multicolored, multifarious, multiply
olig-	few	oligarchy, oligopoly, oligophagous

MORE PREFIXES CONTINUED

Prefix	Meaning	Examples
omni-	all	omnibus, omnificent, omnipotent
out-	surpassing	outbid, outclass, outdo, outlive
over-	too much	overactive, overbearing, overblown
pan-	all	panacea, pandemonium, Pandora
pene-	almost	peneplain, peninsula, penultimate
poly-	many	polyandry, polyester, polygamy, polyglot
super-	more than	superfine, superhuman, supernatural
ultra-	beyond	ultraconservative, ultramodern
under-	less than	underage, underdone, underripe

PREFIXES THAT EXPRESS TOGETHERNESS AND SEPARATENESS

Prefix	Meaning	Examples
ab-	away from	abdicate, abduct, aberrant, absent
co-	together	coauthor, cognate, coincide, cooperate
col-	with	collaborate, collateral, colleague, collect
com-	with	combat, combine, comfort, commune
con-	with	concede, concur, concert, confident
syl-	together	syllable, syllogism
sym-	together	symbiosis, symbol, symmetry, sympathy
syn-	together	synchronize, syndrome, synergy

PREFIXES THAT EXPRESS NEGATION

Prefix	Meaning	Examples
a-	not	apathy, atheist, atrophy, atypical
an-	not	anemia, anarchy, anesthesia, anorexia
counter-	opposite	counteract, countermand
de-	opposite	deactivate, deform, degrade, deplete
for-	prohibit	forbid, forget, forgo, forsake, forswear
il-	not	illegal, illegible, illegitimate, illiterate
im-	not	imbalance, immaculate, immature
in-	not	inaccurate, inactive, inadvertent
ir-	not	irrational, irreconcilable, irredeemable
ne-	not	nefarious, never
neg-	not	negative, neglect, negotiate
non-	not	nonchalant, nonconformist, nondescript
un-	opposite	unable, undo, unbeaten, uncertain

PREFIXES THAT MAKE A JUDGMENT

Prefix	Meaning	Examples
anti-	against	antinuclear, antisocial, antislavery
bene-	good	benediction, benefactor, beneficial
contra-	against	contraband, contraception, contradict
dys-	bad	dysentery, dysfunction, dyspepsia
eu-	good	Eucharist, eugenic, euphoria, eulogy
mal-	bad	maladjusted, malaise, malevolent

The Reading Teacher's Book of Lists, Fifth Edition, © 2006 by John Wiley & Sons, Inc.

The Reading Teacher's Book of Lists, Fifth Edition, © 2006 by John Wiley & Sons, Inc.

| mis- | bad | misanthrope, misbehave, miscarriage |
| mis-
pro- | for | pro-American, pro-education |

MISCELLANEOUS PREFIXES

Prefix	Meaning	Examples
ambi-	both, around	ambidextrous, ambience, ambiguous
amphi-	both, around	amphibian, amphitheater, amphora
auto-	self	autobiography, autocratic, autograph
be-	make	becalm, befriend, beguile, bewitch
hetero-	different	heterodox, heteronym, heterosexual
homo-	same	homogeneous, homogenize, homograph
meta-	change	metabolism, metamorphosis, metaphor
neo-	new	neoclassic, neologism, neon, neonatal
para-	almost	paralegal, paramedic
pseudo-	false	pseudoclassic, pseudonym, pseudopod
re-	again	reappear, reclassify, recopy, redo, repaint
self-	self	self-denial, self-respect, selfish

PREFIXES WITH TWO MEANINGS

Prefix	Meaning	Examples
un-	not	unhappy
un-	reversal	undress
a-	not	amoral
a-	on	aboard
in-	not	incomplete
in-	within	inhouse

See also List 28, The 20 Most Common Prefixes; List 30, The 20 Most Common Suffixes; List 31, More Suffixes; List 34, Greek and Latin Roots; List 36, -Ology Word Family; List 37, -Phobia and -Philia Word Families; List 156, Double-Letter Spelling Patterns.

LIST 30. THE 20 MOST COMMON SUFFIXES

This is a research-based list for those who wish to see the data. These 20 suffixes account for 93 percent of occurences.

Rank	Suffix	Meaning	%	Example
1	s, es	plurals	31	*boys*
2	ed	past-tense verbs	20	*wanted*
3	ing	verb form/present participle	14	*playing*
4	ly	characteristic of	7	*friendly*
5	er, or	person connected with	4	*teacher*
6	ion, tion, ation, ition	act, process	4	*action*
7	ible, able	can be done	2	*likeable*
8	al, ial	having characteristics of	1	*final*
9	y	characterized by	1	*funny*
10	ness	state of, condition of	1	*happiness*
11	ity, ty	state of	1	*activity*
12	ment	action or process	1	*enjoyment*
13	ic	having characteristics of	1	*comic*
14	ous, eous, ious	possessing the qualities of	1	*serious*
15	en	made of	1	*enliven*
16	er	comparative	1	*bigger*
17	ive, ative, itive	adjective form of a noun	1	*attentive*
18	ful	full of	1	*sorrowful*
19	less	without	1	*hopeless*
20	est	comparative	1	*biggest*

All other suffixes accounted for only 7% of the words. See List 31 for a more complete list of suffixes.

The Reading Teacher's Book of Lists, Fifth Edition, © 2006 by John Wiley & Sons, Inc.

Source: White, T. G., Sowell, V., and Yanagihara, A. (1999). Teaching elementary students to use word-part clues. *The Reading Teacher, 42,* 302–308.

LIST 31. MORE SUFFIXES

Suffixes are letter groups that are added to the end of a base word or root. They frequently signify the part of speech and sometimes add meaning. There are two types of suffixes: derivational and inflectional.

Derivational suffixes are more numerous. When added to a base word, this type of suffix creates a new word that is "derived" from the base word but has a different meaning. For example, the addition of *-less* to *hope* creates *hopeless*, a word related to *hope* but different in meaning. The following is a list of derivational suffixes. The most frequently occurring suffixes are listed at the beginning level. Suffixes that are somewhat less frequent but still quite common are listed in Intermediate to Advanced.

BEGINNING SUFFIXES

Suffix	Meaning	Examples
-able, -ible	is, can be	comfortable, learnable, walkable, climbable, perishable, durable, gullible, combustible
-ar, -er, -or	one who	beggar, liar, teacher, painter, seller, shipper, doctor, actor, editor
-en	to make	strengthen, fasten, lengthen, frighten, weaken
-er	more	smarter, closer, lighter, quicker, softer, luckier
-ess	one who (female)	princess, waitress, countess, hostess, actress
-est	most	smartest, closest, lightest, quickest, softest, luckiest
-ette	small	dinette, diskette, majorette, barrette
-ful	full of	joyful, fearful, careful, thoughtful, cheerful
-ish	relating to	childish, fiftyish, bookish, selfish
-less	without	thoughtless, tireless, joyless, ageless, careless
-like	resembling	lifelike, homelike, childlike, computerlike
-ly	resembling	fatherly, scholarly, motherly, sisterly, brotherly
-ment	action or process	government, development, experiment
-ness	state or quality of	kindness, happiness, goodness, darkness, fullness
-ship	state or quality of	friendship, hardship, citizenship, internship

INTERMEDIATE TO ADVANCED SUFFIXES

Suffix	Meaning	Examples
-a, -ae	plural	data, criteria, memoranda, alumnae, algae, formulae
-acious	inclined to	loquacious, mendacious, audacious, fallacious
-ade	action or process	blockade, promenade, escapade
-age	action or process	marriage, voyage, pilgrimage, blockage, rummage
-an	relating to	urban, American, veteran, Hawaiian, metropolitan
-ance, -ence	state or quality of	repentance, annoyance, resistance, violence, absence, reticence
-ancy, -ency	state or quality of	buoyance, truancy, vacancy, vagrancy, frequency, clemency, expediency, consistency
-ant, -ent	one who	servant, immigrant, assistant, merchant, regent, superintendent, resident
-ant	inclined to	vigilant, pleasant, defiant, buoyant, observant
-arian	one who	librarian, humanitarian, libertarian

The Reading Teacher's Book of Lists, Fifth Edition, © 2006 by John Wiley & Sons, Inc.

More Suffixes Continued

Suffix	Meaning	Examples
-arium, -orium	place for	aquarium, planetarium, solarium, auditorium
-ary, -ory	place for	library, mortuary, infirmary, laboratory, conservatory
-ation, -ion, -sion, -tion	state or quality of	desperation, starvation, inspiration, tension, caution, suspicion, attention, fascination, companion
-ative	inclined to	demonstrative, pejorative, talkative
-ble	repeated action	stumble, squabble, mumble, tumble, fumble
-dom	state or quality of	freedom, boredom, martyrdom, wisdom
-ectomy	surgical removal of	tonsillectomy, appendectomy, mastectomy
-ee	object of action	payee, lessee, employee
-ence	state or quality of	violence, absence, reticence, abstinence
-ency	state or quality of	frequency, clemency, expediency, consistency
-enne	female	comedienne, equestrienne, tragedienne
-er	action or process	murder, plunder, waiver, flounder, thunder
-ern	direction	eastern, western, northern, postern
-ery	state or quality of	bravery, savagery, forgery, slavery
-ese	state or quality of	Japanese, Chinese, Portuguese, Siamese
-esque	relating to	statuesque, picturesque, Romanesque
-etic	relating to	alphabetic, dietetic, frenetic, athletic, sympathetic
-hood	state or quality of	childhood, adulthood, falsehood, nationhood
-ial, -ian	relating to	filial, commercial, remedial, barbarian, Christian
-ic, -ical	relating to	comic, historic, poetic, public, rhetorical, economical
-ics	scientific or social system	physics, economics, politics, statistics, demographics
-ide, -ine	chemical compound	fluoride, peroxide, sulfide, iodine, chlorine, quinine
-ina, -ine	female	czarina, ballerina, Wilhelmina, heroine, Josephine
-ify	to make	satisfy, terrify, falsify, beautify, villify
-ious	state or quality of	gracious, ambitious, religious, nutritious, delicious
-ism	doctrine of	capitalism, socialism, communism, patriotism
-ist	one who practices	biologist, capitalist, communist, philanthropist
-itis	inflammation of	laryngitis, arthritis, bronchitis, appendicitis
-ity, -ty	state or quality of	necessity, civility, parity, loyalty, honesty, amnesty, unity
-ive	inclined to	active, passive, negative, restive, positive
-ization	state or quality of	civilization, standardization, organization
-ize	to make	standardize, computerize, popularize, pulverize
-ling	small	duckling, yearling, suckling, fledgling
-most	most	utmost, westernmost, innermost, foremost
-oid	resembling	humanoid, asteroid, paranoid, planetoid
-ose	sugars	glucose, sucrose, fructose, dextrose
-ous	full of	joyous, virtuous, nervous, wondrous
-phobia	fear of	claustrophobia, acrophobia (see List 37, -Phobia and -Philia Word Families)
-some	inclined to	meddlesome, awesome, tiresome, fulsome
-th, -eth	numbers	fifth, twelfth, twentieth, fiftieth
-ulent	full of	turbulent, corpulent, fraudulent, truculent

The Reading Teacher's Book of Lists, Fifth Edition, © 2006 by John Wiley & Sons, Inc.

Suffix	Meaning	Examples
-und	state or quality of	rotund, fecund, moribund, jocund
-uous	state or quality of	contemptuous, tempestuous, sensuous, vacuous
-ure	action or process	censure, procure, endure, inure, secure
-ward	direction	forward, backward, eastward, upward, onward
-ways	manner	sideways, longways, crossways
-wise	manner, direction	clockwise, lengthwise, counterclockwise
-y	being or having	fruity, sunny, rainy, funny, gooey, chewy

Inflectional suffixes indicate the grammatical form of words such as the tense or case of verbs, whether a word is an adjective or adverb, and whether a noun is plural or singular. While this sounds complicated, most native speakers of English are already using most of these suffixes in their speech prior to the beginning of formal reading instruction. Therefore, your primary task is to help them translate endings they already know into sounds. If students are reading for meaning, this may happen almost automatically.

NOUN SUFFIX

-s indicates that a noun is plural: books, boys, pencils, dogs, shoes, hands, desks, teachers, students

ADJECTIVE SUFFIXES

Many nouns and/or verbs are changed to adjectives using suffixes. Here are some examples:
 -y (milk—milky; trick—tricky; boss—bossy)
 -like (child—childlike; boy—boylike; life—lifelike)
 -ful (care—careful; thought—thoughtful; fear—fearful)
 -ish (tickle—ticklish; child—childish; Scot—Scottish)
 -ic (scene—scenic; history—historic; metal—metallic)
 -ese (Japan—Japanese; Siam—Siamese; China—Chinese)
 -ward (east—eastward; west—westward; south—southward)
 -en (stole—stolen; chose—chosen; write—written)

These suffixes are used to compare adjectives:
 -er (fatter, shorter, crazier, smarter, faster)
 -est (fattest, shortest, craziest, smartest, fastest)

VERB SUFFIXES

 -ed indicates past tense: walked, cooked, studied, dressed, jumped, cried, typed, tried
 -ing indicates a present participle: eating, singing, freezing, studying, dressing, going
 -en indicates past participle: eaten, frozen, stolen, written, hidden, forgotten, spoken
 -s indicates third-person singular: walks, cooks, studies, dresses, plays, runs, teaches

ADVERB SUFFIX

-ly (or *-ily* if the base word ends in y) indicates an adverb. Many adjectives can be changed to adverbs by adding **ly.** Examples: quick—quickly, clear—clearly, beautiful—beautifully, slow—slowly, skillful—skillfully, neat—neatly, plain—plainly, loud—loudly, soft—softly, clumsy—clumsily, hungry—hungrily, greedy—greedily

See also List 157, Spelling Rules for Adding Suffixes.

MORE SUFFIXES CONTINUED

NOUN SUFFIXES

Suffix	Meaning	Examples
-a	plural	data, criteria, memoranda
-ade	action or process	blockage, escapade, parade, promenade
-ade	product or thing	lemonade, marmalade
-ae	plural (feminine)	alumnae, formulae, larvae, algae
-age	action or process	marriage, voyage, pilgrimage
-al	action or process	refusal, revival
-ance	state or quality of	repentance, annoyance, resistance
-ancy	state or quality of	buoyancy, truancy, vacancy, vagrancy
-ant	one who	servant, immigrant, assistant, merchant
-ar	one who	beggar, liar
-ard	one who	drunkard, steward, coward, wizard
-arian	one who	librarian, humanitarian, libertarian
-arium	place for	aquarium, planetarium, solarium
-ary	place for	library, mortuary, sanctuary, infirmary
-ation	state or quality of	desperation, starvation, inspiration
-ation	action or process	emancipation, narration, computation
-cle	small	corpuscle, particle, icicle, cubicle
-cule	small	minuscule, molecule
-crat	person of power	democrat, autocrat
-cy	state or quality of	accuracy, bankruptcy, conspiracy
-cy	action or process	truancy, diplomacy, vagrancy, piracy
-dom	state or quality of	freedom, boredom, martyrdom, wisdom
-ectomy	surgical removal of	tonsillectomy, appendectomy, mastectomy
-ee	object of action	payee, lessee, employee
-eer	person	engineer, puppeteer, auctioneer
-ence	state or quality of	violence, absence, reticence, abstinence
-ency	state or quality of	frequency, clemency, expediency, consistency
-enne	female	comedienne, equestrienne, tragedienne
-ent	one who	superintendent, resident, regent
-er	one who	teacher, painter, seller, shipper
-er	action or process	murder, thunder, plunder, waiver
-ery, -ry	trade or occupation	surgery, archery, sorcery, dentistry
-ery	establishment	bakery, grocery, fishery, nunnery
-ery, -ry	goods or products	pottery, jewelry, cutlery
-ery, -ry	state or quality of	bravery, savagery, forgery, butchery
-ese	person	chinese, portuguese
-ess	one who (female)	waitress, actress, countess, hostess
-et	small	midget, sonnet, bassinet, cygnet
-ette	small (female)	dinette, cigarette, majorette
-eur	one who	chauffeur, connoisseur, masseur
-eur	state or quality of	hauteur, grandeur
-ful	full	cupful, spoonful
-fy	cause to be	solidify, beautify

The Reading Teacher's Book of Lists, Fifth Edition, © 2006 by John Wiley & Sons, Inc.

Suffix	Meaning	Examples
-hood	state or quality of	childhood, adulthood, falsehood
-i	plural	alumni, foci
-ian	person	musician, Parisian
-ics	scientific or social system	physics, economics, politics, statistics
-ier, -yer	one who	cashier, financier, gondolier, lawyer
-ide	chemical	fluoride, bromide, peroxide compound
-ina	female	czarina, Wilhelmina, ballerina
-ine	chemical or basic substance	iodine, chlorine, caffeine, quinine
-ine	female	heroine, Josephine, Pauline
-ing	material	bedding, roofing, frosting, stuffing
-ion	state or quality of	champion, companion, ambition, suspicion
-ish	near, like, almost	pinkish, sevenish
-ism	state or quality of	baptism, heroism, racism, despotism
-ism	doctrine of	capitalism, socialism, hedonism
-ist	one who practices	biologist, capitalist, communist
-ite	mineral or rock	granite, anthracite, bauxite
-ite	person	socialite, Luddite
-itis	inflammation of	laryngitis, arthritis, bronchitis
-ity, -ty	state or quality of	necessity, felicity, civility, parity
-ization	state or quality of	civilization, standardization, organization
-kin	small	lambkin, napkin, manikin, Munchkin
-let	small	owlet, rivulet, starlet, leaflet, islet
-ling	small	duckling, yearling, suckling, fledgling
-man	one who works with	cameraman, mailman, doorman
-mat	automatic machine	laundromat, vendomat
-ment	action or process	embezzlement, development, government
-ment	state or quality of	amusement, predicament, amazement
-ment	product or thing	instrument, ornament, fragment
-mony	product or thing	testimony, matrimony, ceremony, alimony
-ness	state or quality of	happiness, kindness, goodness, darkness
-ol	alcohols	methanol, ethanol, glycol
-ology	study or science of	biology, psychology (see List 36, -Ology Word Family)
-or	one who	actor, doctor, donor, auditor
-or	state or quality of	error, stupor, candor, fervor, pallor
-orium	place for	auditorium, emporium
-ory	place for	laboratory, conservatory, purgatory
-ose	sugars	glucose, sucrose, fructose, dextrose
-osis	abnormal increase	tuberculosis, fibrosis
-ostracy	rule	aristocracy, demostracy
-phobia	fear of	claustrophobia, acrophobia (see List 37, -Phobia and -Philia Word Families)
-s, -es	plural	pens, books, boxes, parentheses
-'s	possession	John's, dog's

MORE SUFFIXES CONTINUED

Suffix	Meaning	Examples
-ship	skill or art of	penmanship, showmanship, horsemanship
-ship	state or quality of	friendship, hardship, citizenship
-sion	state or quality of	tension, compulsion
-ster	person	gangster, gamester
-th	state or quality of	strength, warmth, filth, depth, length
-tion	state or quality of	attention, caution, fascination
-trix	female	aviatrix, executrix
-tude	state or quality of	gratitude, fortitude, beatitude
-ty	state or quality of	loyalty, honesty, amnesty, unity
-ure	action or process	censure, failure, enclosure, exposure
-wright	one who works with	playwright, shipwright, wheelwright

ADJECTIVE SUFFIXES

Suffix	Meaning	Examples
-able	state or quality of	drinkable, washable
-acious	inclined to	loquacious, mendacious, audacious, fallacious
-al	relating to	natural, royal, maternal, suicidal
-an	relating to	urban, American, Alaskan, veteran
-ant	inclined to	vigilant, pleasant, defiant, buoyant
-ary	relating to	honorary, military, literary, ordinary
-ate	state or quality of	fortunate, desperate, passionate
-ative	inclined to	demonstrative, pejorative, talkative
-ble	inclined to	gullible, perishable, voluble, durable
-en	relating to	golden, ashen, wooden, earthen
-ent	inclined to	competent, different, excellent
-er	more (comparative)	fatter, smaller, crazier, smarter
-ern	direction	eastern, western, northern, postern
-ese	state or quality of	Japanese, Portuguese, Chinese, Siamese
-esque	relating to	statuesque, picturesque, Romanesque
-est	most (comparative)	fattest, smallest, smartest, fastest
-etic	relating to	alphabetic, dietetic, frenetic
-ful	full of	thoughtful, joyful, careful, fearful
-ial	relating to	filial, commercial, remedial
-ian	relating to	barbarian, physician, Christian
-ic	relating to	comic, historic, poetic, public
-ical	relating to	comical, rhetorical, economical
-ide	state or quality of	candid, sordid, lucid, splendid, rigid
-ile	state or quality of	virile, agile, volatile, docile, fragile
-ine	relating to	feminine, bovine, feline, marine
-ious	state or quality of	gracious, ambitious, religious
-ish	relating to	childish, whitish, fiftyish, Scottish
-ive	inclined to	active, passive, negative, affirmative
-less	without	thoughtless, tireless, ageless, careless
-like	resembling	childlike, homelike, lifelike, boylike

The Reading Teacher's Book of Lists, Fifth Edition, © 2006 by John Wiley & Sons, Inc.

Suffix	Meaning	Examples
-ly	resembling	fatherly, motherly, scholarly
-ly	every	daily, weekly, monthly, yearly
-most	most	utmost, westernmost, innermost
-oid	resembling	humanoid, asteroid, paranoid, planetoid
-ose	full of	verbose, morose, bellicose, comatose
-ous	full of	joyous, virtuous, nervous, wondrous
-some	inclined to	meddlesome, awesome, tiresome
-th, -eth	numbers	fifth, twelfth, twentieth, fiftieth
-ular	relating to	granular, cellular, circular, popular
-ulent	full of	turbulent, corpulent, fraudulent
-und	state or quality of	rotund, fecund, moribund, jocund
-uous	state or quality of	contemptuous, tempestuous, sensuous
-ward	direction	forward, backward, eastward, upward
-y	state or quality of	fruity, sunny, rainy, funny, gooey

VERB SUFFIXES

Suffix	Meaning	Examples
-ade	action or process	blockade, promenade, parade
-age	action or process	ravage, pillage
-ate	to make	activate, fascinate, annihilate, liberate
-ble	repeated action	stumble, squabble, mumble, tumble, fumble
-ed, -d	past tense	talked, walked, baked, raised
-en	past completed action	taken, eaten, proven, stolen
-en	to make	strengthen, fasten, lengthen, frighten, weaken
-er	action or process	discover, murder, conquer, deliver
-fy	to make	satisfy, terrify, falsify, beautify
-ing	continuous action	singing, talking, jumping, eating
-ise	to make	advertise, merchandise
-ish	action or process	finish, flourish, nourish, punish
-ize	to make	standardize, computerize, popularize
-s, -es	form third person	runs, finishes
-ure	action or process	censure, procure, endure, inure

ADVERB SUFFIXES

Suffix	Meaning	Examples
-ly	forms adverb from adjective	slowly, beautifully, happily, largely
-ways	manner	sideways, always, longways, crossways
-wise	manner, direction	clockwise, lengthwise
-ward(s)	direction	onwards, northward

See also List 28, The 20 Most Common Prefixes; List 29, More Prefixes; List 30, The 20 Most Common Suffixes; List 34, Greek and Latin Roots; List 157, Spelling Rules for Adding Suffixes; List 158, Plurals; List 180, Parts of Speech.

LIST 32. SYNONYMS

Synonyms are words that have similar meanings. Dictionaries often use synonyms in their definitions. There are whole books of synonyms and special reference works, such as the thesaurus, that have clusters of words or phrases, all with similar meanings. These are particularly useful in finding just the right word when writing. **Caution:** A synonym may be for only one meaning of a word with several meanings. Synonyms are often used in analogies; see List 143.

able—capable—competent
abrupt—sudden—hasty
achieve—accomplish—attain
add—total—sum up
after—following—subsequent
aim—purpose—goal
all—every—entire
allow—permit—grant
anger—rage—fury
answer—response—reply
arrive—reach—get to
ask—question—interrogate
astonish—surprise—amaze

back—rear—behind
bear—endure—tolerate
before—prior to—in front of
begin—start—initiate
below—under—beneath
birth—origin—genesis
border—edge—margin
bother—annoy—pester
boy—lad—youth
brave—courageous—daring
bulge—swell—protrude
busy—occupied—engaged

call—shout—yell
calm—composed—serene
car—auto—vehicle
carry—tote—lug
careful—cautious—prudent
change—vary—alter
charm—fascinate—enchant
cheat—deceive—swindle
children—youngsters—tots
city—borough—town
close—shut—seal
consent—agree—acquiesce
continue—persevere—persist
country—nation—state
cure—heal—restore

danger—peril—hazard
decrease—lessen—diminish
defect—flaw—blemish
delay—postpone—procrastinate
different—varied—diverse
disaster—calamity—catastrophe
divide—separate—split
during—while—at the same time
dwell—live—reside

eat—consume—devour
effort—exertion—endeavor
end—finish—complete
energy—power—strength
enough—adequate—sufficient
error—mistake—fallacy
explain—expound—elucidate

faith—trust—reliance
fat—plump—stout
fetch—bring—retrieve
find—locate—discover
fix—repair—mend
flat—level—flush
food—nourishment—sustenance
form—shape—make up
fragile—delicate—breakable
freedom—independence—liberty
frequent—often—many times

gay—lively—vivacious
gift—present—donation
give—grant—hand over
glum—morose—sullen
go—leave—depart
grateful—appreciative—thankful
great—grand—large
grow—mature—develop

happy—glad—joyous
hard—difficult—troublesome
hate—detest—despise

The Reading Teacher's Book of Lists, Fifth Edition, © 2006 by John Wiley & Sons, Inc.

The Reading Teacher's Book of Lists, Fifth Edition, © 2006 by John Wiley & Sons, Inc.

have—own—possess
heal—mend—cure
help—aid—assist
hide—conceal—secrete
high—tall—lofty
hold—grasp—clutch
hurry—rush—accelerate

idea—thought—concept
ill—sick—indisposed
income—revenue—earnings
injure—wound—hurt

job—work—occupation
junk—rubbish—waste
just—fair—right

keep—hold—retain
key—answer—solution
kind—considerate—helpful
kill—slaughter—murder

large—big—enormous
last—endure—persist
late—tardy—delayed
learn—acquire—understand
leave—depart—go away
like—enjoy—be fond of
listen—hear—attend
little—small—petite
long—lengthy—drawn out
look—glance—see

mad—crazy—insane
make—build—construct
many—multitudinous—numerous
marvelous—wonderful—extraordinary
mean—stand for—denote
mend—repair—restore
method—way—manner
might—may—perhaps
mistake—error—blunder
move—transport—propel

name—title—designation
near—close by—in the vicinity
need—require—want
new—fresh—recent

noise—uproar—clamor
novice—beginner—learner

occur—happen—take place
often—frequently—repeatedly
old—aged—ancient
omit—delete—remove
one—single—unit
open—unlock—unseal
ornament—decoration—adornment
outlive—survive—outlast

page—sheet—leaf
pain—ache—hurt
pair—couple—duo
pardon—forgive—excuse
part—portion—piece
peak—summit—top
people—public—populace
play—frolic—romp
praise—acclaim—applaud
primary—chief—principal
prohibit—forbid—restrict
put—place—locate

raid—attack—invade
reckless—careless—rash
remote—distant—secluded
renew—restore—revive
respect—honor—revive
revise—alter—correct
right—correct—proper

say—state—remark
seem—appear—look
sell—vend—market
shame—humiliation—mortification
show—demonstrate—display
sorry—regretful—penitent
speed—haste—hurry
start—begin—commence
still—unmoving—silent
stop—halt—end
story—tale—account
strength—power—energy
supply—provide—furnish
surpass—exceed—outdo

SYNONYMS CONTINUED

take—grab—seize
tense—taut—rigid
terrify—frighten—alarm
thanks—gratitude—appreciation
thaw—melt—dissolve
thief—robber—crook
thin—slender—slim
think—reflect—comtemplate
time—period—season
timid—fearful—cowardly
tiny—small—diminutive
trial—test—experiment
true—faithful—loyal
try—attempt—endeavor
turn—revolve—pivot

ugly—homely—plain
understand—comprehend—discern
unify—consolidate—combine

uproar—tumult—pandemonium
urge—press—exhort
use—operate—employ
vacant—empty—unoccupied
value—worth—price
vast—huge—immense
verify—confirm—substantiate
victor—winner—champion

walk—stroll—saunter
want—desire—crave
waver—fluctuate—vaccillate
weak—feeble—impotent
wealth—riches—fortune
word—term—expression
work—labor—toil
world—globe—earth
write—record—draft

The Reading Teacher's Book of Lists, Fifth Edition, © 2006 by John Wiley & Sons, Inc.

See also List 33, Antonyms; List 80, Descriptive Words; List 84, He Said/She Said; List 85, Similes; List 86, Metaphors; List 143, Analogies.

LIST 33. ANTONYMS

Antonyms are words that mean the opposite or nearly the opposite of each other. Both synonyms and antonyms are often used in tests and language drills. **Caution:** An antonym may be for only one meaning of a word with several meanings. Antonyms are often used in analogies; see List 143.

above—below
absent—present
accident—intent
accomplishment—failure
achieve—fail
add—subtract
adjacent—distant
admire—detest
admit—reject
adore—hate
advance—retreat
affirm—deny
afraid—confident
after—before
aid—hinder
alarm—comfort
alert—asleep
alive—dead
allow—forbid
alone—together
amateur—professional
amuse—bore
ancient—modern
annoy—soothe
answer—question
apparent—obscure
argue—agree
arrive—depart
arrogant—humble
ascend—descend
attack—defend
attract—repel
awake—asleep
awkward—graceful

back—front
bad—good
bare—covered
beautiful—ugly
before—after
bent—straight
better—worse
big—little

birth—death
bitter—sweet
black—white
blunt—sharp
body—soul
bold—timid
bottom—top
boy—girl
brave—cowardly
break—repair
brief—long
bright—dull
bring—remove
busy—idle
buy—sell

capture—release
cause—effect
cautious—careless
center—edge
change—remain
cheap—expensive
child—adult
chilly—warm
clean—dirty
close—open
cold—hot
command—obey
complex—simple
compliment—insult
constant—variable
continue—interrupt
cool—warm
copy—original
countrymen—foreigner
crazy—sane
crooked—straight
cruel—kind
cry—laugh
curse—bless

damage—improve
dark—light
dawn—sunset

day—night
deep—shallow
destroy—create
difficult—easy
dim—bright
divide—unite
doubt—trust
drunk—sober
dull—sharp
dumb—smart

earth—sky
east—west
easy—hard
elementary—advanced
end—begin
even—odd
evening—morning
evil—good
exceptional—common
expand—shrink

fail—pass
failure—success
false—true
famous—unknown
fancy—plain
fast—slow
fat—thin
fiction—fact
find—lose
finish—start
firm—flabby
fix—break
follow—lead
forgive—blame
forward—backward
free—restricted
fresh—stale
friend—enemy
funny—sad
full—empty

gain—lose
generous—stingy

ANTONYMS CONTINUED

gentle—harsh
get—give
give—receive
glad—sad
gloomy—cheerful
glossy—dull
go—come
gorgeous—ugly
great—small
greed—generous
grief—joy
ground—sky
guard—attack
guess—know

handsome—ugly
happy—sad
hard—soft
hate—love
he—she
head—foot
heal—infect
healthy—sick
heaven—hell
heavy—light
height—depth
help—hinder
hero—coward
high—low
hill—valley
him—her
hire—fire
his—hers
hot—cold
horrible—pleasant
huge—tiny
hurry—slow
hurt—help

idle—active
in—out
individual—group
innocent—guilty
inside—outside
intelligent—stupid

jolly—serious
joy—sadness

keep—lose
kind—cruel
knowledge—ignorance

large—small
last—first
laugh—cry
leading—following
leave—arrive
left—right
less—more
let—prevent
level—uneven
lie—truth
life—death
like—dislike
likely—unlikely
liquid—solid
little—big
lively—inactive
lonely—crowded
long—short
loose—tight
lost—found
loud—soft
love—hate

maintain—discontinue
major—minor
make—destroy
male—female
man—woman
many—few
marvelous—terrible
mature—immature
melt—freeze
mess—tidiness
miscellaneous—specific
mistake—accuracy
mix—separate
moist—dry
more—less
most—least
mother—father
move—stay

naive—sophisticated
nasty—nice
near—far

never—always
new—old
no—yes
nobody—everybody
noise—quiet
none—all
north—south
nothing—something
now—then

obese—thin
obvious—hidden
odd—even
offend—please
offer—refuse
often—seldom
old—young
on—off
one—several
ordinary—uncommon
other—same
over—under

pacify—agitate
pain—pleasure
panic—calm
part—whole
partial—complete
particular—general
pass—fail
passive—active
peace—disturbance
perceive—ignore
permanent—unstable
permit—refuse
pessimistic—optimistic
physical—spiritual
place—misplace
plain—fancy
play—work
plentiful—sparse
plump—thin
polish—dull
polite—rude
pollute—purify
poor—rich
positive—negative
powerful—weak
praise—criticism

The Reading Teacher's Book of Lists, Fifth Edition, © 2006 by John Wiley & Sons, Inc.

The Reading Teacher's Book of Lists, Fifth Edition, © 2006 by John Wiley & Sons, Inc.

preceding—following
present—absent
pretty—ugly
prevent—encourage
pride—modesty
private—public
problem—solution
profit—loss
prohibit—allow
pupil—teacher
push—pull

quality—inferiority
quick—slow
quiet—noise
quit—start

raise—lower
random—specific
rapid—slow
rare—common
raw—cooked
ready—unprepared
rear—front
reduce—increase
regret—rejoice
relax—tighten
remember—forget
repair—destroy
retain—lose
revenge—forgiveness
ridiculous—sensible
right—wrong
rigid—flexible
rise—sink
rough—smooth
rude—polite

sad—happy
same—different
satisfy—displease
secluded—public
segregate—integrate
seldom—often
sell—buy
send—receive
sensational—dull
servant—master
shack—palace

shade—light
shame—honor
sharp—dull
she—he
short—long
show—hide
shy—trusting
sick—healthy
silence—sound
single—married
single—plural
sit—stand
slave—master
slender—fat
slow—fast
small—large
soak—dry
sober—drunk
some—none
something—nothing
sorrow—gladness
sour—sweet
speechless—talkative
spend—earn
stale—fresh
start—stop
started—finished
stay—leave
steal—provide
sterile—fertile
stiff—flexible
still—moving
stingy—generous
stop—go
stranger—friend
strength—weakness
student—teacher
sturdy—weak
sunrise—sunset
superb—inferior
supple—rigid
survive—die
suspect—trust

take—give
tall—short
tame—wild
teach—learn

temporary—permanent
thaw—freeze
there—here
thin—thick
thorough—incomplete
thrifty—wasteful
tidy—messy
tie—loosen
timid—bold
to—from
together—apart
told—asked
top—bottom
toward—away
tragic—comic
transform—retain
transparent—opaque
triumph—defeat
true—false
truth—lie

ultimate—primary
union—separation
unique—common
up—down
upset—stabilize
urge—deter

vacant—full
vague—definite
vanish—appear
vast—limited
vertical—horizontal
villain—hero
visitor—host/hostess

waive—require
wake—sleep
wealth—poverty
weep—laugh
well—badly
wet—dry
white—black
wild—tame
win—lose
with—without
worship—detest
worth—uselessness
wreck—create

See also List 32, Synonyms.

LIST 34. GREEK AND LATIN ROOTS

Most modern English words originated in other languages. The study of word origins, or etymology, is a fascinating subject. The Greek and Latin roots in this list can form the basis for a number of vocabulary-building lessons. Roots are taught successfully in families such as *microscope, telescope, periscope,* to illustrate that *scope* means "see." In the following list, Greek roots are indicated with "G" and Latin roots with "L." Roots have been divided into two categories: more common and less common roots. Most of these "roots" can also be called "combining forms" or "morphemes" (meaning units).

MORE COMMON ROOTS

Root	Meaning	Examples
act (L)	do	action, actor, react, transact, enact
aero (G)	air	aerobics, aerodynamics, aeronautics, aerate
agr (L)	field	agriculture, agrarian, agronomy, agribusiness
alter (L)	other	alter, alternate, alternative, altercation, alterego
anim (L)	life, spirit	animate, animosity, animal, inanimate
ann, enn (L)	year	annual, anniversary, annuity, biennial, millennium
aqua (L)	water	aquarium, aquatic, aqueous, aquamarine, aquifer
ast (G)	star	astronaut, astronomy, disaster, asterisk, asteroid
aud (L)	hear	audience, auditorium, audible, audition, audiovisual
biblio (G)	book	bibliography, Bible, bibliophile, bibliotherapy
bio (G)	life	biology, biography, biochemistry, biopsy, biosphere
card, cord (L)	heart	cardiac, cardiology, cardiogram, cardiovascular, cordial, accord, concord, discord
chron (G)	time	chronological, synchronize, chronicle, chronic
claim, clam (L)	shout	proclaim, exclaim, acclaim, clamor, exclamation
cogn (L)	know	recognize, incognito, cognition, cognizant
corp (L)	body	corporation, corpse, corps, corpuscle, corpus
cosm (G)	universe	cosmonaut, cosmos, cosmopolitan, microcosm
cred (L)	believe	credit, discredit, incredible, credential, credulous
cycl (G)	circle, ring	bicycle, cyclone, cycle, encyclopedia, recycle
dic (L)	speak	dictate, predict, contradict, verdict, diction
doc (L)	teach	doctrine, document, doctor, indoctrinate, docile
don, donat (L)	give	donation, donor, pardon, donate
duc (L)	lead	duct, conduct, educate, induct, aquaduct
fac, fic (L)	make, do	factory, manufacture, benefactor, facsimile efficient, proficient, sufficient, beneficial
flect, flex (L)	bend	reflect, deflect, reflection, inflection, genuflect, reflex, flexible
form (L)	shape	form, uniform, transform, reform, formal
gen (G)	birth, race	generation, generate, genocide, progeny, genealogy
geo (G)	earth	geography, geometry, geology, geophysics
gram (G)	letter, written	telegram, diagram, grammar, epigram, monogram

The Reading Teacher's Book of Lists, Fifth Edition, © 2006 by John Wiley & Sons, Inc.

<u>Root</u>	<u>Meaning</u>	<u>Examples</u>
graph (G)	write	photograph, phonograph, autograph, biography, graphite
homo, hom (L)	man	homicide, hombre, homage, Homo sapiens
inner (L)	within	innermost, innerspring
inter (L)	among, between, shared by	interchange, intercom, interface
intro (L)	into, inward, within	introduce, introject, introspection
junct (L)	join	juncture, conjunction, adjunct, injunction
jud, jur, jus (L)	law	judge, judicial, jury, jurisdiction, justice, justify
lab (L)	work	labor, laboratory, collaborate, elaborate
liber (L)	free	liberty, liberal, liberate, libertine
loc (L)	place	location, locate, dislocate, allocate, local
man (L)	hand	manual, manufacture, manuscript, manipulate
mar (L)	sea	marine, submarine, mariner, maritime
mater, matr (L)	mother	maternal, maternity, matricide, matrimony, matron
meter (G)	measure	thermometer, centimeter, diameter, barometer
migr (L)	change, move	migrate, immigrant, emigrate, migratory
miss, mit (L)	send	missile, dismiss, mission, remiss, submit, remit, admit, transmit
mob, mot, mov (L)	move	mobile, automobile, mobilize, motion, motor, promote, demote, motile, remove, movement
morph (G)	shape	amorphous, metamorphoses, morphology, polymorphous, anthropomorphic
mort (L)	death	mortician, mortuary, mortal, immortal, mortify
nat (L)	born	natal, native, nation, nativity, innate
ordin, ord (L)	row, rank	order, ordinary, ordinal, extraordinary, ordinance
ortho (G)	straight, right	orthodontist, orthodox, orthopedist, orthography
pater, patr (L)	father	paternity, paternal, patricide, patriarch
path (G)	disease, feeling	pathology, sympathy, empathy, antipathy, pathos
ped (G)	child	pedagogy, pediatrician, encyclopedia
ped (L)	foot	pedal, pedestrian, biped, pedestal
phil (G)	love	philosophy, philanthropist, philharmonic, Anglophile, philology
phon (G)	sound	phonograph, symphony, telephone, microphone, phonics
photo (G)	light	photograph, telephoto, photosynthesis, photogenic
pod (G)	foot	podiatrist, podium, tripod
poli (G)	city	metropolis, cosmopolitan, police, political
port (L)	carry	portable, transport, import, export, porter
psych (G)	mind, soul	psychology, psyche, psychopath, psychiatrist
ques, quer, quis (L)	ask, seek	question, inquest, request, query, inquisitive
rad (L)	ray, spoke	radius, radio, radiation, radium, radiator, radiology

GREEK AND LATIN ROOTS CONTINUED

Root	Meaning	Examples
rect (L)	straight	erect, rectangle, rectify, direction, correct
rupt (L)	break	rupture, erupt, interrupt, abrupt, bankrupt
san (L)	health	sanitary, sanitation, sane, insanity, sanitarium
saur (G)	lizard	dinosaur, brontosaurus, stegosaurus
sci (G)	know	science, conscience, conscious, omniscient
scop (G)	see	microscope, telescope, periscope, stethoscope
scribe, script (L)	write	inscribe, describe, prescribe, script, transcript, scripture
sign (L)	mark	signal, signature, significant, insignia
spec (L)	see	inspect, suspect, respect, spectator, spectacle
struct (L)	build	structure, construct, instruct, destruction
tact (L)	touch	tactile, intact, contact, tact
terr (L)	land	territory, terrain, terrestrial, terrace
therm (G)	heat	thermometer, thermal, thermostat, Thermos
tract (L)	pull, drag	tractor, attract, subtract, traction, extract, contract
trib (L)	give	contribute, tribute, tributary, attribute
urb (L)	city	urban, suburb, urbane, suburban
vac (L)	empty	vacant, vacation, vacuum, evacuate, vacate
var (L)	different	vary, invariable, variant, variety, various
vid, vis (L)	see	video, evidence, provide, providence, visible
voc (L)	voice	vocal, advocate, evocation, convocation
void (L)	empty	void, devoid, avoid, voided, unavoidable
vol (L)	wish, will	volition, volunteer, voluntary, benevolent
volv (L)	turn	revolve, involve, evolve, revolver, revolution

LESS COMMON ROOTS

Root	Meaning	Examples
aesthet, esthet (G)	sense, perception	aesthetic, aesthete, anesthesia, anesthetist
alt (L)	high	altitude, altimeter, alto, altocumulus
ambul, amb (L)	walk, go	ambulance, circumambulate, somnambulate, amble, preamble
amo, ami (L)	love	amiable, amorous, amateur, amity
ang (L)	bend	angle, triangle, rectangle, angular, quadrangle
anthr (G)	man	anthropology, philanthropist, misanthrope
arch (G)	ruler, leader	monarch, archbishop, matriarch, oligarchy
archi, arch (G)	primitive, original	archaeology, archaic, archetype, archive
belli (L)	war	bellicose, antebellum, belligerent, rebellion
brev (L)	short	abbreviation, brevity, breve
cad, cas (L)	fall	cadence, cadaver, decadence, cascade
cam (L)	field	camp, campus, encamp, campaign
cand (L)	shine, white	candle, incandescent, candid, candidate
cap (L)	head	cap, captain, capital, decapitate, caput
cede, ceed, cess (L)	go, yield	concede, secede, proceed, exceed, succeed, process, recess, access, concession, cessation
ceive, cept (L)	take, receive	receive, reception, accept, conception, intercept

The Reading Teacher's Book of Lists, Fifth Edition, © 2006 by John Wiley & Sons, Inc.

Root	Meaning	Examples
centr (L)	center	central, centrifugal, egocentric, eccentric, geocentric
cert (L)	sure	certain, certify, ascertain, certificate
cide, cise (L)	cut, kill	suicide, insecticide, genocide, scissors, incision
clar (L)	clear	clarity, declare, clarify, declaration
cline (L)	lean	incline, recline, decline, inclination
clud (L)	shut	include, conclude, exclude, preclude, seclude
commun (L)	common	community, communicate, communism, communion, communal
cum (L)	heap	cumulative, accumulate, cumulus
cur (L)	care	cure, manicure, pedicure, curator, curette
cur (L)	run	current, occur, excursion, concur, recur
dem (G)	people	democracy, demography, endemic, epidemic
dent (L)	tooth	dentist, trident, dentifrice, indent, denture
div (L)	divide	divide, divorce, division, dividend, indivisible
domin (L)	master	dominate, predominate, dominion, A.D. (*Anno Domini*)
dox (G)	belief, praise	orthodox, heterodox, paradox, doxology
fer (L)	bear, carry	ferry, transfer, infer, refer, conifer
fid (L)	faith	fidelity, confidence, infidel, bona fide
fig (L)	form	figure, figment, configuration, disfigure, effigy
firm (L)	securely fixed	firm, confirm, infirm, affirm, firmament
fract, frag (L)	break	fracture, fraction, infraction, fractious, fragment, fragile, fragmentary
frater (L)	brother	fraternal, fraternity, fratricide, fraternize
fric (L)	rub	friction, dentifrice, fricative
funct (L)	perform	function, malfunction, dysfunctional, perfunctory
gam (G)	marriage	polygamy, monogamy, bigamy, gamete, exogamy
gnos (G)	know	diagnose, prognosis, agnostic
gon (G)	angle	pentagon, diagonal, trigonometry, orthogonal
grad, gress (L)	step, go	gradual, grade, gradation, centigrade, graduation, progress, egress, regress, aggression, congress
grat (L)	pleasing	gratitude, gradify, congratulate, ungrateful, ingrate
greg (L)	gather	gregarious, congregation, segregation, aggregate
gyn (G)	woman	gynecologist, misogynist, monogyny, androgyny
hab, hib (L)	hold	habit, habitual, habitat, prohibit, inhibit, exhibit
hosp, host (L)	guest, host	hospitality, hospital, hospice, hostess, host
hydr (G)	water	hydroelectric, hydrogen, hydrant, dehydrate
iatr (G)	medical care	psychiatry, podiatry, pediatrician, geriatrics
imag (L)	likeness	image, imagine, imaginative, imagery
init (L)	beginning	initial, initiate, initiative
integ (L)	whole	integrate, integral, integrity, integer
ject (L)	throw	project, inject, reject, subject, eject, conjecture
kine, cine (G)	movement	kinetic, kinesiology, telekinesis, cinema, cinematic

GREEK AND LATIN ROOTS CONTINUED

Root	Meaning	Examples
laps (L)	slip	elapse, collapse, relapse, prolapse
lith (L)	stone	lithograph, monolith, neolithic, paleolithic, megalith
log (G)	word	prologue, apology, dialogue, eulogy, monologue
luc, lum (L)	light	lucid, elucidate, translucent, illuminate, luminous
luna (L)	moon	lunar, lunatic, lunette
lust (L)	shine	luster, illustrate, lackluster, illustrious
lys (G)	break down	analysis, paralysis, electrolysis, catalyst
mand (L)	order	command, demand, mandate, remand
mania (G)	madness	maniac, pyromania, cleptomania, megalomania
max (L)	greatest	maximum, maxim, maximize
mech (G)	machine	mechanic, mechanism, mechanize
mem, ment (L)	mind	memory, remember, memorial, commemorate, mental, mention, demented
merge, mers (L)	dive	submerge, emerge, merge, merger, submerse, immerse
mim (L)	same	mimic, pantomime, mimeograph, mime
min (L)	small, less	mini, minimum, minor, minus, minimize
minist (L)	serve	minister, administer, administration
mon (L)	advise	admonish, premonition, monitor, admonition
mut (L)	change	mutation, immutable, mutual, commute
nav (L)	ship	navy, naval, navigate, circumnavigate
neg (L)	no	negation, abnegation, negative, renege
neo (L)	new	neophyte, neoclassical, neonatal, neologism
not (L)	mark	notation, notable, denote, notice, notify
noun, nun (L)	declare	announce, pronounce, denounce, enunciate
nov (L)	new	novel, novelty, novice, innovate, nova
numer (L)	number	numeral, enumerate, numerous, enumerable
ocu (L)	eye	oculist, binocular, monocular
onym (G)	name	synonym, antonym, pseudonym, anonymous
opt (G)	eye	optician, optometrist, optic, optical
opt (L)	best	optimum, optimist, optimal, optimize
orig (L)	beginning	origin, original, originate, aborigine
pel (L)	drive	propel, compel, expel, repel, repellant
pend (L)	hang	pendulum, suspend, append, appendix
phob (G)	fear	claustrophobia, xenophobia (See List 37, -Phobia and -Philia Word Families)
plur (L)	more	plural, plurality, pluralism
pop (L)	people	population, popular, pop, populace
pug (L)	fight	pugnacious, pugilist, repugnant, impugn
reg (L)	rule, guide	regal, regent, reign, regulate, regime
rid (L)	laugh	ridiculous, deride, derisive, ridicule
scend (L)	climb	ascend, descend, transcend, descent
sect (L)	cut	section, dissect, intersect, sect, bisect
sed (L)	settle	sedative, sediment, sedentary, sedate

The Reading Teacher's Book of Lists, Fifth Edition, © 2006 by John Wiley & Sons, Inc.

Root	Meaning	Examples
sens, sent (L)	feel	sensation, sense, sensitive, sensible, sensory sentimental, assent, dissent, consent
serv (L)	watch over	conserve, preserve, reserve, reservoir
serv (L)	slave	serve, servant, service, servile
sim (L)	like	similar, simultaneous, simulate, simile
sist (L)	stand	consist, resist, subsist, assist
sol (L)	alone	solo, solitary, desolate, soliloquy
solv (L)	loosen	dissolve, solve, solvent, resolve
son (L)	sound	sonar, sonata, sonnet, unison, sonorous
soph (G)	wise	philosopher, sophomore, sophisticated, sophist
spir (L)	breathe	respiration, inspire, spirit, perspire, conspire
sta (L)	stand	station, status, stabile, stagnant, statue
strict (L)	draw tight	strict, restrict, constrict, stricture
sum (L)	highest	summit, summary, sum, summons
surg, surr (L)	rise	surge, insurgent, resurgent, resurrect, insurrection, resurrection
tain, ten (L)	hold	retain, contain, detain, attain, maintain, sustain, tenacious, tenure, tenant, retentive, tenable
ten (L)	stretch	tendon, tendency, tension, tent, tense
term (L)	end	terminal, terminate, determine, exterminate
tex (L)	weave	textile, texture, text, context
tort (L)	twist	torture, contort, retort, tort, contortion
trud, trus (L)	push	intrude, protrude, intruder, intrusive, obtrusive
turb (L)	confusion	disturb, turbulent, perturb, turbid
ven (L)	come	convene, convention, advent, invent, venue
ver (L)	truth	verify, verity, verdict, aver, veracity
ver (L)	turn	convert, reverse, versatile, introvert, convertible
vict, vinc (L)	conquer	victory, conviction, convince, invincible, vincible
vor (L)	eat	voracious, carnivore, herbivore, omnivorous

See also List 29, More Prefixes; List 31, More Suffixes; List 36, -Ology Word Family; List 37, -Phobia and -Philia Word Families.

LIST 35. WORD STUDY WORKSHEET

(For Instant Words, Subject Words, Any Word)

Name _____   **Date** _____

The word we are studying today is:

_____

1.   Write the word without vowels: _____

2.   Now write the word with vowels: _____

3.   Write the word in variant forms; for example, plural or past tense:

_____

4.   Use the word in a phrase:_____

5.   Write a meaning or synonym for the word:

_____

✳   ✳   ✳   ✳

The word we are studying today is:

_____

1.   Write the word without vowels: _____

2.   Now write the word with vowels: _____

3.   Write the word in variant forms; for example, plural or past tense:

_____

4.   Use the word in a phrase: _____

5.   Write a meaning or synonym for the word:

_____

LIST 36. -OLOGY WORD FAMILY

Many subjects studied in schools and colleges have *-ology* in their names. The suffix *-ology* comes from Greek and means "science of" or "the study of." For example, since *cardia* means "heart," cardiology means "science of the heart." Moreover, since the suffix *-ist* means "one who practices" (see Lists 30 and 31), a cardiologist is "one who practices science of the heart."

WORD	STUDY OF	WORD	STUDY OF
anthropology	people, culture	hematology	blood
archaeology	antiquities	herpetology	reptiles
astrology	stars (supposed influence of stars and planets on human affairs—study of stars is astronomy)	histology	living tissue
		hydrology	water
		ideology	doctrine of a group
		immunology	immunity to disease
audiology	hearing	meteorology	weather
bacteriology	bacteria	microbiology	microbes
biology	life	mineralogy	minerals
biotechnology	using living organisms to make or improve things	morphology	structure of animals and plants
cardiology	heart	musicology	music
chronology	measuring time	mythology	myths
climatology	climate	neurology	nerves
cosmetology	cosmetics	oncology	tumors
cosmology	universe	ornithology	birds
criminology	crime	ophthalmology	eyes
cryptology	codes and ciphers	paleontology	fossils
cytology	cells	pathology	diseases
dermatology	skin	pharmacology	drugs
ecology	relationship of organisms to their environment	physiology	life processes
		pomology	fruit
embryology	embryo	psychology	mind
entomology	insects	radiology	radiation
epidemiology	widespread disease among people	seismology	earthquakes
		sociology	society
epistemology	knowledge	technology	applied science
ethnology	historical development of cultures	theology	God
		toxicology	poisons
etymology	word origins	typology	classification based on type
genealogy	ancestors		
geology	earth	zoology	animals
gerontology	old age		
gynecology	women		

See also List 34, Greek and Latin Roots; List 37, -Phobia and -Philia Word Families.

LIST 37. -PHOBIA AND -PHILIA WORD FAMILIES

The Greek word *phobos,* meaning "fear," is combined with a variety of roots to form an interesting group of phobias. Some of these, such as claustrophobia (fear of closed spaces) or acrophobia (fear of high places), are quite common; others may be new to you. Use the root words of List 34 to coin a few of your own. How about "bibliophobia"? The root *philia* comes from Latin and means "love". You can take almost any -phobia (fear) word and change it to a -philia (love) word. For example: *aerophobia* can become *aerophilia.*

PHOBIA WORD	MEANING	PHOBIA WORD	MEANING
acrophobia	fear of heights (edges)	optophobia	fear of opening your eyes
aerophobia	fear of flying	ornithophobia	fear of birds
agoraphobia	fear of open spaces	phonophobia	fear of speaking aloud
ailurophobia	fear of cats	pyrophobia	fear of fire
amaxophia	fear of vehicles, driving	thaasophobia	fear of being bored
		trichophobia	fear of hair
androphobia	fear of men	triskaidekaphobia	fear of the number thirteen
anthophobia	fear of flowers		
anthropophobia	fear of people	xenophobia	fear of strangers
arachnophobia	fear of spiders		
aquaphobia	fear of water	**PHILIA WORD**	**MEANING**
arachibutyrophobia	fear of peanut butter sticking to the roof of your mouth	acustiophilia	love of noise
		aerophilia	love of air, flying
		aleurophilia	love of cats
astraphobia	fear of lightning	anthophilia	love of plants, flowers
brontophobia	fear of thunder		
claustrophobia	fear of closed spaces	anthropophilia	love of people
chromophobia	fear of color	astraphilia	love of lightning, thunder
cynophobia	fear of dogs		
dementophobia	fear of insanity	astrophilia	love of stars
gephyrophobia	fear of bridges	bibliophilia	love of books
gerontophobia	fear of old age	brontophilia	love of thunderstorms
gynophobia	fear of women		
hemophobia	fear of blood	chionophilia	love of snow
herpetophobia	fear of reptiles	chromophilia	love of colors
ideophobia	fear of ideas	cynophilia	love of dogs
mikrophobia	fear of germs	dendrophilia	love of trees
murophobia	fear of mice	graphophilia	love of writing
nebulaphobia	fear of clouds	hippophilia	love of horses
necrophobia	fear of death	lacanophilia	love of vegetables
numerophobia	fear of numbers	meterophilia	love of weather
nyctophobia	fear of darkness	metrophilia	love of poetry
ochlophobia	fear of crowds	ornithophilia	love of birds
ophidiophobia	fear of snakes	soleciphilia	love of worms

See also List 34, Greek and Latin Roots; List 36, -Ology Word Family

The Reading Teacher's Book of Lists, Fifth Edition, © 2006 by John Wiley & Sons, Inc.

LIST 38. WORDS BORROWED FROM OTHER LANGUAGES

These lists contain a collection of words of foreign origin that have been adopted into the English language. Many are so common we forget where they came from. Words of Greek and Latin origin are not included here because many of them can be found in the example words in List 34, Greek and Latin Roots. In English, borrowed words come from over 120 languages.

African Words
apartheid
banana
cola
gnu
impala
marimba
mumbo jumbo
raffia
safari
samba
yam
zombie

Arabic Words
admiral
alcohol
alfalfa
algebra
artichoke
assassin
bazaar
carafe
caravan
coffee
cotton
harem
kebab
magazine
monsoon
sherbet
sofa
tariff
zero

Australian (Aboriginal) Words
boomerang
dingo
kangaroo
koala

Chinese Words
china (porcelain)
chow
chow mein
gung ho
kowtow
mahjong
shantung
soy
tea
tofu
typhoon
yen

Czech Word
robot

Dutch Words
bush
cole slaw
cookie
drill
maelstrom
pickle
Santa Claus
skate
sketch
skipper
sled
sleight
slim
sloop
split
stoop
stove
wagon
yacht

East Indian (Hindi) Words
bungalow
cashmere

catamaran
cheetah
curry
dinghy
juggernaut
jungle
khaki
loot
pajamas
shampoo
shawl
teak
thug
veranda

French Words
ambiance
attorney
authority
bail
ballet
bizarre
blond
boulevard
bouquet
brochure
cadet
caprice
carousel
chagrin
charade
charity
chef
clergy
clientele
coroner
crime
debris
depot
detour
entourage

WORDS BORROWED FROM OTHER LANGUAGES CONTINUED

essay
expose
fiancé
fiancée
garage
gourmet
government
impromptu
judge
jury
justice
liberty
lingerie
malapropos
mayor
migraine
minister
morale
morgue
motif
naive
nee
noel
nocturne
nuance
pastor
penchant
pension
progress
protégé
public
raconteur
rebel
religion
résumé
sabotage
suede
suite
ticket
traitor
treasurer
troop
trophy
vague
verdict
viola
vis-à-vis

German Words
angst
automat
delicatessen
diesel
ecology
Fahrenheit
flak
frankfurter
gestalt
gestapo
gesundheit
hamburger
kaput
liverwurst
loaf
polka
pumpernickel
sauerkraut
schema
spiel
strudel
torte
wanderlust

Hungarian Word
goulash

Indian (American Words)
chipmunk
pow wow
skunk
totem
wigwam
(and many state names, such as Iowa and Utah)

Irish Words
blarney
brat
whiskey

Italian Words
alfresco
attitude
balcony

ballot
bandit
banister
bologna
brigade
bronze
cannon
carnival
casino
cavalry
cello
colonel
confetti
duel
fiasco
finale
ghetto
gondola
incognito
infantry
influenza
jean
macaroni
malaria
mascara
pasta
pastel
piano
prima donna
relief
sentinel
spaghetti
stiletto
stucco
torso
trio
virtuoso
vista
volcano
wig

Hebrew Words
bar mitzvah
kosher
menorah
shalom
shekel

The Reading Teacher's Book of Lists, Fifth Edition, © 2006 by John Wiley & Sons, Inc.

Japanese Words
banzai
bonsai
hibachi
honcho
judo
jujitsu
kamikaze
karate
origami
sayonara
tycoon

Javanese Words
batik
gong

Lap Word
tundra

Philippine Word
boondocks

Polynesian Words
aloha
hula
taboo

Portuguese Words
commando
marmalade
pagoda
peon
samba

Russian Words
commissar
cosmonaut

czar
dacha
intelligentsia
Kremlin
mammoth
parka
politburo
sputnik

Sanskrit Words
karma
mantra
nirvana
yoga

Spanish Words
adios
adobe
albino
alfalfa
amigo
avocado
armada
bronco
burro
cafeteria
canoe
canyon
chocolate
corral
coyote
fiesta
flotilla
hurricane
junta
loco

maõana
mesa
Montana
mosquito
palomino
patio
pinto
plaza
poncho
potato
ranch
rodeo
rumba
sierra
silo
tobacco
tomato
tornado
tortilla

Turkish Words
kiosk
sherbet
shish kebab
yogurt

Yiddish Words
bagel
kibbutz
klutz
nosh
pastrami
schmaltz
schlep

See also List 34, Greek and Latin Roots; List 39, French and Latin Phrases; List 41, Words Based on People's Names (Eponyms).

LIST 39. FRENCH AND LATIN PHRASES

French and Latin phrases are used in many novels, magazines, and newspapers; in academic and legal writing; and sometimes even in speech. Your students might enjoy learning some of the more common ones. They may well demonstrate a *penchant* for picking up foreign phrases *tout de suite* and using them to impress their friends. *N'est-ce pas*?

FRENCH PHRASES

à la carte—according to the menu, i.e., ordering individual items off the menu as opposed to complete dinners

à la mode—in fashion; frequently used to indicate desserts served with ice cream

à votre santé—to your health; a toast used in drinking

au contraire—on the contrary

au courant—well informed

au revoir—until we meet again

bon appétit—good appetite

bonjour—good day, hello

bon vivant—lover of good living

bon voyage—have a good trip

carte blanche—full discretionary authority

coup d'état—sudden overthrow of a government

cul de sac—dead end

de rigeur—required

double entendre—double meaning

en masse—in a large group

en route—on the way

esprit de corps—group spirit

fait accompli—a thing accomplished; done with

faux pas—mistake

hors d'oeuvre—appetizer

je ne sais quoi—I don't know what

laissez-faire—noninterference

n'est-ce pas?—isn't that so?

noblesse oblige—rank imposes obligations

nom de plume—pen name

objet d'art—article of artistic value

pardonnez moi—excuse me

pièce de résistance—irresistible item or event

raison d'etre—reason or justification for existence

savoir faire—social know-how

tout de suite—immediately

vis-à-vis—in relation to

LATIN PHRASES

ad hoc—with respect to the particular case at hand

ad infinitum—to infinity

ad nauseam—to the point of disgust

bona fide—in good faith

caveat emptor—let the buyer beware

cogito ergo sum—I think, therefore I am

e pluribus unum—one from many

et cetera—and others

in memoriam—in memory of

in toto—totally

mea culpa—my fault

modus operandi—manner of working

non sequitur—it does not follow

nota bene—note well

persona non grata—person not accepted

pro forma—done as a matter of formality

pro rata—according to rate or proportion

quid pro quo—one thing for another

sine qua non—indispensable

status quo—the way things are

sub rosa—secret or confidential

tempus fugit—time flies

vice versa—conversely

The Reading Teacher's Book of Lists, Fifth Edition, © 2006 by John Wiley & Sons, Inc.

LIST 40. BRITISH AND AMERICAN WORDS

Even though our languages are more alike than different, there are certain British words that are very foreign to Americans and vice versa. You and your students can have some fun with the following.

British Words	American Words
anorak	parka, ski jacket
aubergine	eggplant
autumn	fall
bank holiday	legal holiday
bathing costume	bathing suit
bill (resturant)	check (restaurant)
billion (one million million)	billion (thousand million)
biscuit (sweet)	cookie
biscuit (unsweetened)	cracker, biscuit
block of flats	apartment house/building
bonnet	automobile hood
book (v.)	make reservation
boot	automobile trunk
braces	suspenders
break (school)	recess
caravan	trailer
caretaker/porter	janitor
carriage, wagon	car (train)
catapult	slingshot
centre (city/business)	downtown
center reservation	median strip/divider
chemist's shop	pharmacy/drugstore
chips	fried pieces of potato, French fries
class/form (school)	grade (level)
cooker	stove
corporation	city/municipal government
crisps	chips (potato)
dale	river valley
diversion	detour
draughts	checkers
dress circle	mezzanine/loge
dressing-gown	bathrobe
dustbin/bin	garbage can, ash can, trash can
estate agent	realtor
face flannel	wash cloth
Father Christmas	Santa Claus
first floor	second floor
flat	apartment
frock	dress
full stop (punc.)	period

BRITISH AND AMERICAN WORDS CONTINUED

British Words	American Words
gallery (theatre)	balcony
geyser (gas)	water heater
Girl Guide	Girl Scout
grill (v.)	to broil
hair grip	bobby pin
headmaster/mistress	principal
hire purchase	time payment/installment
holiday	vacation
hoover (n.)	vacuum cleaner
housing estate	subdivision
ice	ice cream
ironmonger	hardware store
jab (injection)	shot
joint (meat)	roast
jumper	sweater, pullover
lead (dog)	leash
left luggage office	baggage room
let/lettings	lease, rent/rentals
lift	elevator
lorry	truck
lounge suit	business suit
mackintosh	raincoat
marks	grades
maize, sweet corn	corn
mince	hamburger meat
moor	tract of rough wilderness
motorway	freeway/throughway/super highway
mum	mom
nappy	diaper
nought	zero
oven cloth	pot holders
overtake (vehicle)	pass
pack (of cards)	deck
pants	shorts (underwear)
paraffin	kerosene
pence	penny
personal call	person-to-person
petrol	gasoline
phone-in (programme)	call-in (program)
pillar box	mail box/mail drop
post	mail
pram	baby carriage/baby buggy

The Reading Teacher's Book of Lists, Fifth Edition, © 2006 by John Wiley & Sons, Inc.

British Words	American Words
primary school	elementary school
public school	fee-charging school, private school
put through (telephone)	connect
queue	line (to form a line)
rates/ratings	taxes
read	studied
reception (hotel)	front desk
return ticket	round-trip ticket
revising	reviewing
roundabout (road)	traffic circle
saloon (car)	sedan
scent	perfume
school leavers	graduates
shire	a county
shop assistant	sales clerk/sales girl
single ticket	one-way ticket
sister	nurse
sitting room/living room/lounge	living room
smalls	underclothing
solicitor	lawyer/attorney
spanner	monkey wrench
spirits (drink)	liquor
staff (academic)	faculty
stalls (theatre)	orchestra seats
stand (for public office)	run
state school	public school
sweet shop/confectioner	candy store
take-away food	take-out food
tap	faucet
telly	television
term (academics—three in a year)	semester (two in a year)
torch	flashlight
trainers	sneakers
trunk call	long distance
tube/underground	subway
turn-ups (trousers)	cuffs (pants)
unit trust	mutual fund
vest	undershirt
wash up	do the dishes
windscreen	windshield
wind/mudguard	fender
zed	zee (last letter)

LIST 41. WORDS BASED ON PEOPLE'S NAMES (EPONYMS)

Did you know that the popular *cardigan* sweater was named after the Earl of Cardigan? Or that the word *maverick* came into use after Samuel Maverick, a Texan, refused to brand his cattle? These and other eponyms, words borrowed from names, can be used to stimulate an interest in word origins.

WORDS COINED FROM PEOPLE'S NAMES

Adam's apple	Adam, the first man, who tradition says ate the forbidden fruit, an apple, in the Garden of Eden
America	Amerigo Vespucci, an Italian merchant–explorer who came to the New World shortly after Columbus
baud	Jean Baudot, a French inventor who worked on telegraphic communications
Beaufort scale	Sir Francis Beaufort, an English naval officer, who developed it to describe wind speed
bloomers	Amelia Bloomer, a pioneer feminist who made them popular
bowie knife	James Bowie, an American frontiersman who made this type of knife famous
boycott	Charles Boycott, a British army officer and first victim
braille	Louis Braille, a French teacher of the blind
bunsen burner	Robert Bunsen in 1855, as a heat source for his laboratory experiments
cardigan	Earl of Cardigan, a British officer whose soldiers wore the knitted sweaters during the Crimean War
chauvinist	Nicholas Chauvin, a soldier who worshipped France and Napoleon uncritically
Colt revolver	One of the best-known handguns, named for Samuel Colt, an American firearms designer in the 1800s
Columbia	The country and U.S. District are named after Christopher Columbus
diesel	Rudolf Diesel, a German automotive engineer
dunce	Johannes Duns Scotus, a theologian whose followers were called Dunsmen
Ferris wheel	G. M. Ferris, an American engineer
Frisbee	William Frisbie, a pie company owner in Connecticut in 1871; Yale students played catch with the pie tins
fudge	Supposedly named after Captain Fudge, a seventeenth-century seaman who had a reputation for not telling the truth
gerrymander	Elbridge Gerry, a Massachusetts governor in 1810
graham crackers	Sylvester Graham, an American reformer in dietetics and a vegetarian
guillotine	Joseph Guillotin, a French physician who urged its use
Leninism	Nikolai Lenin, Russian communist revolutionary
leotard	Jules Leotard, a French acrobat who designed it as a costume for his trapeze act
loganberry	J.H. Logan, a judge and a gardener
lynch	William Lynch, an American vigilante
macadam	John Loudon McAdam, a Scottish engineer who invented this road-building material

The Reading Teacher's Book of Lists, Fifth Edition, © 2006 by John Wiley & Sons, Inc.

mackintosh	Charles MacIntosh, inventor of rainproof material
malapropism	Mrs. Malaprop, a character in Sheridan's *The Rivals*
martinet	Jean Martinet, a seventeenth-century French army drill master
Marxism	Karl Marx, a German communist philosopher
maverick	Samuel Maverick, a Texan who didn't brand his cattle
mesmerize	Frederich Mesmer, an Austrian physician who practiced hypnotism
Morse code	Communication code using dots and dashes invented by Samuel Morse
nicotine	Jean Nicot, a French diplomat who introduced the tobacco plant to France about 1561
pasteurize	Louis Pasteur, a French bacteriologist
platonic	Plato, the Greek philosopher
praline	A nut and sugar candy named for Marshal Duplessis-Praslin, whose cook invented it
pullman	George M. Pullman, railroad designer
sandwich	John Montagu, fourth Earl of Sandwich, who invented it so he could gamble without stopping for a regular meal
saxophone	Anton Sax, Belgian instrument maker who combined a clarinet's reed with oboe fingering
sequoia	A Cherokee Indian chief who invented an alphabet; the trees were named for him by a Hungarian botanist
shrapnel	Henry Shrapnel, an English artillery officer
sideburns	Ambrose Burnside, a Civil War general and governor of Rhode Island who had thick side whiskers
silhouette	Etienne de Silhouette, a French finance minister of Louis XV whose fiscal policies and amateurish portraits (by him) were regarded as inept
Stalinism	The political beliefs of Joseph Stalin, Russian political leader
stetson	John Stetson, an American who owned a hat factory in Philadelphia that featured western styles
tawdry	St. Audrey, queen of Northumbria; used to describe lace sold at her fair
teddy bear	Teddy Roosevelt, president of the United States, who spared the life of a bear cub on a hunting trip in Mississippi
valentine	St. Valentine, a Christian martyr whose feast day is February 14—the same date, according to Roman tradition, that birds pair off to nest
vandal	Vandals, the Germanic tribe that sacked Rome
Winchester rifle	Oliver F. Winchester, American manufacturer
zeppelin	German Count von Zeppelin

SCIENCE WORDS COINED FROM PEOPLE'S NAMES

ampere	Andre Ampere, a French physicist
celsius	Anders Celsius, a Swedish astronomer and inventor
decibel	Alexander Bell, a Scottish–American inventor of the telephone
fahrenheit	Gabriel Fahrenheit, a German physicist
mach number	Ernst Mach, an Austrian philosopher and physicist
ohm	Georg Simon Ohm, a German physicist
Richter scale	Charles Richter, an American seismologist

Words Based on People's Names (Eponyms) Continued

volt	Alessandro Volata, an Italian physicist
watt	James Watt, a Scottish engineer and inventor

FLOWER NAMES COINED FROM PEOPLE'S NAMES

begonia	Michel Begon, French governor of Santo Domingo and a patron of science
camellia	George Kamel, European Jesuit missionary to the Far East
dahlia	Andreas Dahl, a Swedish botanist
gardenia	Alexander Garden, a Scottish–American botanist
magnolia	Pierre Magnol, a French botanist
poinsettia	Joel Poinsettia, U.S. ambassador to Mexico
wisteria	Caspar Wistar, an American anatomist
zinnia	J. G. Zinn, a German botanist

WORDS COINED FROM PLACE NAMES (TOPONYMS)

academy	Academeia, a garden where Plato taught his students
bikini	Bikini Atoll (Pacific)
calico	Calicut, India
cashmere	Kashmir, India
cologne	Cologne, Germany
damask	Damascus, Syria
denim	Nimes, France—serge de Nimes (fabric of Nimes)
frankfurter	Frankfurt, Germany
gauze	Gaza, Palestine
hamburger	Hamburg, Germany
jeans	Genoa, Italy
labrador	Labrador, Canada
laconic	Laconia (Sparta, Greece)
Leyden jar	Leyden, Holland
limousine	Limousin, an old French province
mackinaw	Mackinac City, Michigan
manila paper	Manila, the Philippines
marathon	Marathon, Greece
muslin	Mosul, Iraq
panama hat	Panama, Central America
rhinestone	Rhine, river that flows from Switzerland through Germany and the Netherlands
Roquefort cheese	Roquefort, a French town
Suede	Sweden
Tabasco sauce	Tabasco, Mexico
tangerine	Tangier, Morocco
turquoise	Turkey
worsted wool	Worsted, England

BORROWED CALENDAR WORDS

Sunday	The sun's day
Monday	The moon's day

The Reading Teacher's Book of Lists, Fifth Edition, © 2006 by John Wiley & Sons, Inc.

The Reading Teacher's Book of Lists, Fifth Edition, © 2006 by John Wiley & Sons, Inc.

Tuesday	Tiw's day; Tiw was the Teutonic god of war
Wednesday	Woden's day; Woden was the Norse god of the hunt
Thursday	Thor's day; Thor was the Norse god of the sky
Friday	Fria's day; Fria, the wife of Thor, was the Norse goddess of love and beauty
Saturday	Saturn's day; Saturn was the Roman god of agriculture
January	In honor of Janus, the Roman god with two faces, one looking forward and one looking backward
February	In honor of *februa*, the Roman feast of purification
March	In honor of Mars, the Roman god of war
April	A reference to spring, *aprilis*, the Latin word for opening
May	In honor of Maia, a Roman goddess and mother of Mercury
June	In honor of Juno, the Roman goddess of marriage
July	In honor of the Roman general and statesman Julius Caesar
August	In honor of the Roman emperor Augustus Caesar
September	In reference to *septem*, the Latin word for seven; September was the seventh month of the Roman calendar
October	In reference to *octo*, the Latin word for eight; October was the eighth Roman month
November	In reference to *novem*, the Latin word for nine; November was the ninth Roman month
December	In reference to *decem*, the Latin word for ten; December was the tenth Roman month

WORDS FROM ROMAN AND GREEK MYTHOLOGY

Achilles heel	Greek warrior and leader in the Trojan War whose only vulnerable spot was his heel
amazon	Amazons, in Greek mythology, were a tribe of female warriors
aphrodisiac	Aphrodite, Greek goddess of love and beauty
atlas	Atlas, in Greek mythology, was forced to hold the heavens on his shoulders
cereal	Ceres, a Roman goddess of agriculture
echo	Echo, in Greek mythology, was a wood nymph cursed with repeating the last words anyone said to her
electricity	Electra, daughter of Agamemnon
erotic	Eros, Greek god of love and son of Aphrodite
hygiene	Hygeia, the Greek goddess of health
mentor	Mentor, in Greek mythology, was a loyal friend and advisor to Odysseus and teacher to his son, Telemachus
morphine	Morpheus, the Greek god of dreams
oedipus complex	King Oedipus, in Greek mythology, unwittingly murdered his father and married his mother
ogre	Orcus, the Roman god of the underworld
panacea	Panacea, the Roman goddess of health
volcano	Volcan, Roman god of fire

See also List 34, Greek and Latin Roots.

LIST 42. WORDS WITH MULTIPLE MEANINGS

Many words have several meanings. Here are some of the more common ones.

arms
He placed the child in her mother's *arms*.
The rebels needed to buy *arms* to fight the war.

ball
The *ball* rolled under the table.
The women wore their prettiest dresses to the *ball*.

bank
You can cash your check at the *bank*.
We had a picnic on the *bank* of the river.

bark
Did you hear the dog *bark*?
The *bark* on the old tree is dry and brittle.

bat
A *bat* flew from the barn and frightened me.
The children played with the *bat* and ball.

bit
Jenn checked the *bit* in the horse's mouth.
I *bit* into the apple.
It will take just a *bit* longer.

blow
The wind began to *blow*, and the leaves fell.
The *blow* to his head knocked the fighter out.

bridge
We crossed the *bridge* over the Raritan River.
Bridge is a card game for four people.

case
She put her eyeglasses in their *case*.
The lawyer won her first *case*.

compound
The soldiers surrounded the enemy *compound*.
A *compound* sentence is made of two clauses.

count
The duke, *count*, and earl received awards.
The child is learning to *count* from one to ten.

cue
The actor missed his *cue* and did not say his line.
He held the *cue* steady and aimed at the eight-ball.

date
Bill asked Sally for a *date*.
Today's *date* is March 28.

fair
The weather was *fair* on the day of the race.
The judge's decision was *fair*.
We went on the rides at the *fair*.

fan
David is a baseball *fan*; he never misses a game.
It's very warm; please, turn on the *fan*.

file
Put your papers in the *file*.
The children marched in a single *file*.
The prisoner used a *file* to cut the metal bar.

firm
When he finished college, he joined a law *firm*.
Apples should be *firm*, not soft.

fold
Fold your paper in half.
The girl took care of the sheep in the *fold*.

game
It sounded exciting, so I was *game* to try it.
Poker is his favorite card *game*.

The Reading Teacher's Book of Lists, Fifth Edition, © 2006 by John Wiley & Sons, Inc.

The Reading Teacher's Book of Lists, Fifth Edition, © 2006 by John Wiley & Sons, Inc.

hide	The belts were made from the *hide* of a cow.
	I usually *hide* the gifts for the children's birthdays.
grave	There was no laughter on the *grave* occasion.
	The coffin was lowered into the *grave*.
hold	The sailors put their supplies into the ship's *hold*.
	Hold the string or the balloon will drift away.
jam	I tried to *jam* one more coat into the full closet.
	We put strawberry *jam* on our toast.
	We were stuck in a traffic *jam* for an hour.
kind	What *kind* of ice cream do you like?
	She was always *kind* and gentle.
last	I hope this will *last* until Tuesday.
	The *last* time I saw her she was very thin.
like	A briefcase is *like* a bookbag.
	I *like* fudge cookies.
line	We stood in *line* to get tickets.
	Write your name on the *line*.
long	I *long* to go to a quiet beach.
	How *long* is the story?
mean	What did you *mean* when you said that?
	He was *mean* and unkind.
	We calculated the *mean* score for the two teams.
mine	The silver ore is brought out of the *mine* in carts.
	Put you chair next to *mine*.
miss	*Miss* Polk is the new chemistry teacher.
	I will *miss* you when you move to the city.
net	The fish were caught in the *net*, not on hooks.
	After we paid the taxes, our *net* pay was $300.
pen	The pigs live in a *pen*.
	Sign your name with this *pen*.
present	John was absent on Friday, not *present*.
	For her birthday, Jill received a *present* from Kaneesha.
press	The editor and other members of the *press* took notes.
	Ask the tailor to *press* this skirt.
	Press the button to start the machine.
rare	I like my steak *rare*, not well done.
	Only three people have ever owned this *rare* coin.
rest	Anna will do the *rest* of the shopping.
	After the long walk up the hill, I wanted to *rest*.
second	There are sixty *seconds* in a minute.
	I was *second* today, but tomorrow I might be first.
sole	I ordered the *sole* for lunch because I like fish.
	He was the *sole* survivor of the crash.
	There was a hole in the *sole* of his shoe.

WORDS WITH MULTIPLE MEANINGS CONTINUED

spell
The child learned to *spell* his name.
The witch put a magic *spell* on the tree.

stable
Put the horses in the *stable*.
He may leave the hospital if his breathing is *stable*.

stick
The glue was dried, and the stamp would not *stick*.
We collected *sticks* and leaves for the fire.

story
This is a five-*story* building.
Tell the children a bedtime *story*.

temple
He took two aspirin for the pain in his *temple*.
The men walked to the *temple* to pray.

tick
Ticks are insects that spread Lyme's disease.
Can you hear the clock *tick*?

tire
I never *tire* of hearing my favorite music.
I had a flat *tire* on my new car.

vault
The athlete *vaulted* the six-foot barrier with ease.
The actress put her diamond jewelry in the *vault*.

wake
Be quiet or you will *wake* the baby.
The waves in the *wake* of the speedboat were very high.

well
I feel very *well* today.
The boy put the bucket into the *well* to get water.

will
The lawyer wrote a *will* for the old man before he died.
I *will* see the man tomorrow, not today.

yard
A *yard* is equal to thirty-six inches.
We had a picnic in the *yard*.

The Reading Teacher's Book of Lists, Fifth Edition, © 2006 by John Wiley & Sons, Inc.

See also List 19, Homophones; List 22, Homographs and Heteronyms.

LIST 43. OXYMORONS

An oxymoron is the use of words with contradictory or clashing ideas next to one another. Oxymorons are fun to collect and appear frequently in newspapers and advertising. These are some of our favorites.

The Reading Teacher's Book of Lists, Fifth Edition, © 2006 by John Wiley & Sons, Inc.

accidentally on purpose	freezer burn	organized mess
accurate estimate	fresh frozen	original copy
act naturally	genuine imitation	passive aggressive
adult child	global village	plastic glasses
advanced beginner	graduate student	plastic silverware
alone together	honest crook	plastic straw
approximately equal	hopelessly optimistic	poor little rich girl
awfully good	increasing declines	pretty ugly
bankrupt millionaire	inside out	random order
bittersweet	jumbo shrimp	real-life fairy tale
black gold	larger half	resident alien
clearly confused	liquid crystal	same difference
clearly misunderstood	literal interpretation	science fiction
clever fool	little giant	serious fun
completely unfinished	live recording	sleepwalk
constant change	living dead	steel wool
constant variable	living death	student teacher
curved line	loud whisper	sun shade
deafening silence	love–hate relationship	sweet sorrow
definite maybe	make haste slowly	sweet tart
deliberate mistake	minor disaster	synthetic natural gas
even odds	musical comedy	wordless book
exact estimate	never again	work party
expert amateur	new antiques	working vacation
first annual	new routine	young old person
found missing	now then	
free slave	old news	

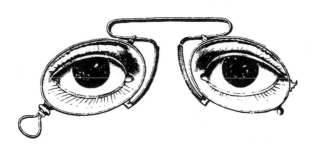

See also List 184, Idiomatic Expressions.

LIST 44. DAILY LIVING WORDS

Words are all around us. Those listed below are part of the American daily living experience. Use these words in literacy education for new and native speakers of English, students with special educational needs, and young students. Check students' comprehension of key survival words like "flammable," "acid," and "combustible."

accident	danger	follow signs
acid	day care	food
admission	delicatessen	fragile
alarm	delivery	free
ambulance	dentist	fuel
apartment	deposit	garage
ATM	destination	gas
bakery	diner	gentlemen
bank	dinner	glass
beauty shop	directions	grocery store
breakfast	discount	hair salon
bus	do not bend	handle with care
bus stop	do not drink	hardware
cab	do not place near heat	harmful if swallowed
cable	do not swallow	help
cafeteria	doctor	help wanted
cancel	don't walk	hospital
car	down	hot
cash	driver	hotel
caution	drug store	husband
cell phone	drugs	information
charge	dryer	insert coins
check	due	job
child	east	keep off
children	electric	keep out
church	elevator	keep refrigerated
cigarettes	emergency	ladies
clean	employer	laundry
cleaners	enter	lease
close door	entrance	license number
closed	exist	lights
closet	explosives	local
clothes	fast food	lost
cold	female	lunch
cold drinks	fire	M.D.
collect	fire escape	male
combustible	fire exit	manager
confidential	fire hose	map
computer	firefighter	married
coupon	first aid	medicine
credit cards	first class	Miss
customer service	flammable	money

The Reading Teacher's Book of Lists, Fifth Edition, © 2006 by John Wiley & Sons, Inc.

money order	private	stop
Mr.	public parking	store
Mrs.	pull	straight ahead
Ms.	push	subway
newspapers	quiet	supermarket
no admittance	radio	supper
no smoking	railroad	swim at your own risk
no trespassing	receipt	tax
north	refund	telephone
northbound	rent	television
notice	repair service	this way
nurse	reservations	ticket
one way	reserved	timetable
open	rest rooms	toll
operator	restaurant	total
order	rinse	train
out	sale	train station
out of order	sales tax	use other door
oxygen	schedule	walk
parking	school	warm
passengers	self-service	warning
payment	sick	wash
pedestrians	size	watch your step
perishable	skills	water
phone	smoking prohibited	weekday
pick-up	south	west
poison	southbound	wife
police	spouse	withdrawal
post office	stairs	women
press	stairway	work
price	state	

See also List 184, Idiomatic Expressions.

LIST 45. SESQUIPEDALIAN SUPERSTARS

The word *sesquipedalian* literally means "a foot and a half." Sesquipedialian words are—simply put—long. Long words are not a modern invention. The word itself was coined in the 1600s referring to the lengthy words used by some poets. The words in this list can be used for spelling bees, middle and high school word study, and vocabulary development. Students enjoy learning to use these words, so pick three to five a week for an interesting word study program. The shortest word on the list has *only* twelve letters!

abovementioned – noted earlier in text
abracadabra – words used by magicians
absentminded – forgetful
acculturation – gaining the habits and ideas of a culture
acetaminophen – nonaspirin medicine used to reduce fevers and pain
acknowledgement – state of being recognized
aforementioned – noted earlier
aggrandizement – to make greater
alphanumeric – using numbers or letters
anagrammatically – related to changing the order of letters in one word to form another
analphabetic – not alphabetic order
anesthesiologist – a doctor who gives pain and sensation medication prior to treatment
anthropocentric – centering views around humans
anthropomorphism – attributing human characteristics to animals or objects
atherosclerosis – condition of having fatty deposits in one's arteries
authoritarianism – governance with strict obedience

biodegradability – can be broken down naturally to return to elements
bougainvillea – a type of flowering vine
bureaucratization – to organize like a government with rules and procedures

characterization – a description of qualities or appearance
cinematography – shooting of a film
circumambulate – to walk around something
circumlocution – indirect or roundabout way of speaking
circumnavigate – to go around the earth
claustrophobia – fear of enclosed places
colloquialism – part of informal way of speaking
committeewoman – woman who is a member of a committee
compartmentalization – to put into separate sections
consequentially – as a result of
contemporaneous – two things happening at the same time
counterclockwise – going from right to left in a circular motion
counterproductive – outcomes that are opposite of what was intended
cruciverbalist – person who does crossword puzzles

dermatological – having to do with the skin
disadvantageous – harmful
disappointment – not as expected
disciplinarian – one who insists on strict rules of behavior
discontinuation – not continuing

disenfranchisement – to take away rights or eligibility
disproportionate – not equal

eavesdropping – listening in secret
electrocardiogram – visual record of electrical activity in the heart
electroencephalogram – visual record of electrical activity in the brain
electromagnetically – caused by the use of an electromagnet
encyclopedia – book containing information on many topics
epidemiological – related to the study of the causes of diseases in populations
euphemistically – using mild or indirect language to refer to something harsh or sensitive
experimentation – to do something and note its outcome
extemporaneous – not rehearsed; without preparation

floccinaucinihilipilification – estimating something as useless
fossilization – process of turning into a fossil

geochronological – relating to the periods in the history of the world

heterogeneous – having different parts or elements
hippopotomonstrosesquipedaliophobia – fear of long words
honorificabilitudinitatibus – honorableness (used by Shakespeare in *Love's Labor's Lost*)
humanitarianism – concern for other people
hyperpolysyllabicsesquipedalianist – person who enjoys using really long words
hypersensitivity – overly sensitive
hyperventilation – rapid shallow breathing
hypochondriac – person who is preoccupied with health issues

iconographer – person who draws illustrations or symbols
idiosyncratic – behavior or characteristic related to an individual
immensurable – not able to be measured; a very large quantity
impenetrability – not able to be penetrated
incomprehensible – impossible to understand
incrimination – appear accused or guilty of a wrong
indistinguishable – impossible to tell apart
interconnectivity – a connection between two or more things
interdepartmental – between two or more departments
interdisciplinary – involving two or more subject areas or disciplines
interscholastic – between schools

kindergartner – child who is in kindergarten

lexicographer – person who writes or edits a dictionary

mathematician – person who works with mathematics
megalomaniacal – obsessed with actions or ideas on a grand scale
metamorphosis – the process of changing from one thing into another
meteorologist – person who studies the weather
microbiologist – person who studies the smallest organisms or living things
mispronunciation – the saying of a word incorrectly
monochromatically – seeming to be of one color
multidimensional – having more than one dimension

Sesquipedalian Superstars Continued

neurotransmitter – chemical substance that aids or hinders transmission of nerve impulses
nonconformance – not acting according to accepted practices or rules
nondiscriminatory – does not show difference in behavior toward something or someone

oceanographer – person who studies the oceans
octogenarian – person who is between 80 and 89 years of age
omnivorousness – eating plant and animal foods
orthography – study of spelling
overemphasize – to make too much of

pachydermal – relating to elephants
pandemonium – chaos, noisy, and out of control
parallelogram – a closed figure with parallel sides
parenthetical – explanatory information contained within parentheses
peacekeeping – the preserving of peace through enforcement and supervision
perpendicular – at a right angle to
perspicacious – clear thinking and wise
phantasmagorical – dreamlike rapid images
pharmaceutical – relating to drugs or medicines prescribed to treat illness
philosophunculist – person who pretends to know more than he or she actually does
phosphorescence – giving off light after exposure to energy; can "glow in the dark"
polyunsaturated – types of fat or oils like corn oil and sunflower oil
pomegranate – a red-skinned fruit with many seeds and juicy pulp
prestidigitation – sleight-of-hand magic
primatologist – person who studies apes, monkeys, and other primates
prognosticator – person who makes predictions
pseudonymous – use of a false name, like a pen name
pseudosophisticated – give the appearance of being worldly
psychodynamic – interaction of mental and emotional processes in behavior
psychosomatic – symptoms of illness caused by emotional or mental stress
pusillanimous – cowardly
pyrotechnist – person who sets off fireworks

quadricentennial – 400th anniversary
quinquennium – a five-year period

rambunctious – loud, unruly
reconceptualization – a rethinking of an idea
refurbishment – to restore or renew
reinforcement – to strengthen
reminiscence – a memory
replenishment – replacing or refilling
representative – person, thing, or idea that takes the place of others or serves as an example
responsibilities – duties or obligations
revolutionary – bringing about a major change

septuagenarian – person who is between 70 and 79 years of age
sesquicentennial – 150th anniversary

The Reading Teacher's Book of Lists, Fifth Edition, © 2006 by John Wiley & Sons, Inc.

simplification – to make more simple or reduce the number of parts
somnambulist – person who walks in his or her sleep
sportsmanship – fair play
stomachache – pain in the abdomen
subterranean – underground
supercilious – prideful, haughty
superfluous – more than needed
syllabication – breaking words into pronouncible parts

tantalizingly – tempting but out of reach
thousandfold – a thousand times
tintinnabulation – bell ringing
transcontinental – crossing the continent
transcription – a written record of a speech or music
transportation – carrying goods or people from one place to another
trustworthiness – deserves to be trusted

underdevelopment – not as developed as expected
understatement – low key
unexceptionable – not exceptional
unidirectional – coming from one direction
uninformative – not providing information
unperturbed – not worried

vaccination – injection of a vaccine to prevent disease
ventriloquist – person who projects his or her voice to seem that it comes from a puppet or another direction
verbalization – something spoken
verisimilitude – truth
vernacularism – pertaining to common language
vicissitudes – small annoyances
vinaigrette – a salad dressing using vinegar as a main ingredient
volunteerism – act of offering to do something
vulnerability – able to be hurt

warmhearted – kindly
weatherproof – treated so as to be unharmed by water
whatchamacallit – substitute name for almost anything

xerographic – relating to a photocopy
zenzizenzizenic – the 8th power of a number

See also List 152, Spelling Demons—Elementary; List 153, Spelling Demons—Intermediate; List 154, Spelling Demons—National Spelling Bee List.

The Reading Teacher's Book of Lists, Fifth Edition, © 2006 by John Wiley & Sons, Inc.

4

CONTENT WORDS

LIST 46. MATH VOCABULARY—ELEMENTARY

Beginning math is challenging for many young students. They must learn concepts like equal, number, and zero as well as the names and symbols for numbers. They also need to learn the specialized vocabulary of math, rules of computation, and how to write the numeral and name of numbers. This is no small feat for students just learning basic word recognition and comprehension skills! Begin teaching math vocabulary and concepts in pre-kindergarten through counting, games, manipulatives, and other active learning strategies. Use the words in this list for word recognition practice, to review math concepts, and to practice word problem skills.

Common Words

act out	height (h.)	possible outcomes
answer	hundreds place	predict
Arabic numeral	idea	prediction
cardinal numbers	identify	problem
chart	include	problem solving
column	increase	process of elimination
conclusion	inside	real-world situation
contain	investigate	reasonable estimate
data	label	regroup
decimal	length (l.)	round
decimal number	line	rounded number
decrease	line graph	row
denominator	listen	score
design	mass	story problem
diagram	mental math	straight
difference	mixed number	strategy
digit	number	survey
discuss	numeral	tens place
distance	numerator	true
draw	one-digit number	two-digit number
equal	one-fourth	unit price
estimate	one-half	unknown
examine	ones place	whole
explain	one-third	whole number
explore	part	width (w.)
false	period	word problem
fraction	place holder	
half	place value	

Measurement Words

acre (A.)	cubic unit	degrees Celsius
amount	cup (c.)	degrees Fahrenheit
area	customary system	distance
baker's dozen	customary units	dozen
capacity	decimeter (dm)	fluid ounce (fl. oz.)
centimeter (cm)	degree	foot, feet (ft.)

MATH VOCABULARY—ELEMENTARY CONTINUED

gallon (gal.)
graduated scale
gram (g)
half-gallon
inch, inches (in.)
kilogram (kg)
kiloliter (kl)
kilometer (km)
liter (L)
measure
measurement
meter (m)
metric system

metric ton (t)
metric units
mile (mi.)
milligram (mg)
milliliter (ml)
millimeter (mm)
nonstandard measure
nonstandard units
ounce (oz.)
pint (pt.)
pound (lb.)
quart (qt.)
ruler

scale
size
standard measure
standard units
temperature
thermometer
ton (T.)
unit
unit fractions
volume (vol.)
weight (wt.)
yard (yd.)
yardstick

Counting Words

zero
one
two
three
four
five
six
seven
eight
nine
ten
eleven
twelve
thirteen

fourteen
fifteen
sixteen
seventeen
eighteen
nineteen
twenty
twenty-one
thirty
forty
fifty
sixty
seventy
eighty

ninety
hundred
thousand
million
billion

count
count back
count backwards
count on
counting numbers
number line
skip counting

Ordinal Numbers

first
second
third
fourth
fifth
sixth
seventh
eighth

ninth
tenth
twentieth
twenty-first
thirtieth
thirty-second
fortieth
fiftieth

sixtieth
seventieth
eightieth
ninetieth
hundredth
hundred and first
hundred eleventh

Time Words

afternoon
a.m. (A.M.)
analog clock
anniversary
autumn

calendar
century
clock
day
daylight

Daylight Saving Time
days of the week
decade
digital clock
elapsed time

The Reading Teacher's Book of Lists, Fifth Edition, © 2006 by John Wiley & Sons, Inc.

evening
fall
half hour
half past
hour
hour hand
midnight
minute
minute hand

month
morning
night
noon
o'clock
p.m. (P.M.)
quarter hour
Roman numerals
season

second
spring
summer
time
week
winter
wristwatch
year

The Reading Teacher's Book of Lists, Fifth Edition, © 2006 by John Wiley & Sons, Inc.

Geometry Words

2-dimensional shape
3-dimensional shape
angle
center
circle
closed figure
closed shape
cone
congruent
congruent figures
corner
cube
curve
cylinder
diagonal
edge
endpoint
equal to ($=$)
equilateral triangle
face
figure
flip (reflection)
geometric figure

geometric pattern
hexagon
horizontal
intersecting lines
irregular shape
length
less than ($<$)
line of symmetry
line segment
octagon
open figure
open shape
parallel lines
parallelogram
pattern
pattern unit
pentagon
perimeter
plane
plane figure
polygon
prism
pyramid

greater than ($>$)
rectangle
regular shapes
rhombus
right angle
right triangle
rotation
shape
side
similar figures
slide (translation)
solid
space
sphere
square
symmetrical figure
symmetry
trapezoid
triangle
turn (rotation)
vertical

Money Words

ATM
bank
cash
cent (¢)
cents
change
check

coin
cost
credit card
currency
dime
dollar ($)
dollar bill

dollar sign ($)
half-dollar
money
nickel
penny
quarter
silver dollar

MATH VOCABULARY—ELEMENTARY CONTINUED

Relationship Words

about
above
actual
after
alike
all
all together
almost
arrange
array
as long as
attribute
average
bar graph
before
below
beside
between
big
bigger
biggest
both
certain
collection
color
column
combine
compare
connect
contrast
decreasing sequences
doubles
doubles minus one
doubles plus one
doubling
equal parts
equally likely
equivalent
equivalent fractions
estimate
estimation
even
expanded form
fact family
factor
fewer

fewer than
frequency table
graph
greater
greater than (>)
greatest
group
grouping
guess
heavier
higher
horizontal
how many
hundred chart
impossible
increase
increasing sequences
inside
inverse operations
irrelevant information
key
large
larger
largest
last
least
less
less likely
less than (<)
lighter
likely
long
longer
longest
lower
many
match
mean
median
member
middle
missing
mode
more
more likely
more than

most
multiple
multiple representations
negative
net
next
next to
number fact
number line
numeric expression
numeric pattern
odd
odd number
one-to-one
opposite
order
ordered pair
organize
organized list
over
overestimate
pair
part
per
physical models
pictograph
picture graph
pie chart
positive
property
question
range
recognize patterns
related facts
relevant information
represent
round (rounding)
same
sequence
set
set of objects
shaded
share
shorter
shorter than
shortest

show
similar
similarities
simplest form
single
small
smaller
smallest
some
sort
strategy
symbol

table
tall
taller
tallest
tally (tallies)
tally chart
tally mark
time line
together
trial and error
true
under

underestimate
unequal
unequal parts
unlikely
use manipulatives
value
variable
Venn diagram
word form
written representations

Operations Words

add
addend
addition
addition fact
addition sentence
addition sign (+)
amount
apply
argument
associative property
caret
commutative property
construct
distributive property
divide
dividend
division

division sign (÷)
divisor
equal to (=)
equation
factor
identity element
identity property
join
minus
minus sign (−)
multiplication
multiplication sentence
multiplication sign (×)
multiply
number sentence
operation
product

quotient
remainder
repeated addition
repeated subtraction
solution
solve
subtract
subtraction
subtraction fact
subtraction sentence
subtraction sign (−)
sum
take away
times
total
variable
zero property

See also List 48, Measurement System Abbreviations; List 49, Metric System Prefixes and Conversions.

LIST 47. MATH VOCABULARY—INTERMEDIATE

The concepts in this list build on those learned in the primary grades and reflect the curriculum taught, and tested, in grades 4 through 6. Use the elementary math vocabulary list as a review, then highlight the terms as the topics are taught in math class. Structural analysis is helpful to students as they encounter the following new words. Familiarity with the terms will enable students to focus their attention on learning the math instead of on how to decode its lexicon.

Common Words

combination	mirror image	reverse
compound	model	rule
computation	net	satisfies
consecutive	network	scale
element	opposite	scale drawing
experiment	origin	short division
exponent	output	sign
expression	partial	signed number
exterior	pattern	significant digits
integer	permutation	subscript
interior	power	substitute
interpret	precision	successive
interval	prime factor	tessellation
inverse	principle	theorem
key	procedure	topology
label	profit	truncate
lateral	progression	undivided
lower limit	quantity	unlimited
markup	reciprocal	unmatched
maximum	reduce	unnamed
minimum	rename	upper limit

Problem Solving

act out	explain	mathematical relationships
analyze	explore	mathematical statements
approach	formulate	methods of proof
argument	graphical representations	model
collaborate	identify	monitor
concrete representations	identity	numerically
conjecture	interpret	observe patterns
construct	invalid approach	organized chart
counterexample	investigate	organized list
develop formulas	irrelevant information	pictorial representations
differentiate	justify	process of elimination
discuss	logic	real-world situation
elapsed time	logical reasoning (and, or, not)	reasonableness of a solution
examine		
example	manipulative(s)	recognize

The Reading Teacher's Book of Lists, Fifth Edition, © 2006 by John Wiley & Sons, Inc.

reflect
relevant information
solution(s)
solve a simpler problem
strategies

trial and error
true/false
understand
use manipulatives
valid approach

verbally
verify claims
verify results
written representations

Communication

accurate
answer
apply
approximate
chart
clarify
clarifying questions
complex
comprehend
consolidate
construct
convert
decode
describe
determine
diagram
differences
disprove
distinguish

drawing
equation
exact
explain
explore
extend
flow chart
focus, foci
graph
grid
image
interpret
investigate
label
mathematical phenomena
mathematical relationships
nonstandard
　representations
notation

objects
organize
physical models
physical phenomena
prove
questions
rationale
sign
similarities
solution
standard representations
symbols
tables
theorem
tree diagram
verbal language
verbal symbols
written language
written symbols

Applications

application
apply
cluster
coherent
compare
conclusion
conjecture (verb)
connect
connections
contrast
draw conclusions

duplicate
explore
fixed
gap
generalization
given
imply
include
infer
investigate
irrelevant information

mathematical relationships
model
model problems
multiple representations
net
network
real-world math
recognize
relevant information
understand

Numbers and Operations

absolute value
additive inverse
arithmetic expression
associative property of
　addition

associative property of
　multiplication
base (of percent)
base ten number system
calculate

common denominator
common factor
common multiple
commutative property of
　addition

MATH VOCABULARY—INTERMEDIATE CONTINUED

commutative property of
  multiplication
compare numbers
compatible numbers
compose a number
composite number
convert
decimal fraction
decimal point
decompose a number
denominator
digit
distributive property
empty set
equivalent
equivalent decimals
equivalent fractions
equivalent ratios
exponent
exponential form
extremes (of a proportion)
factor (verb)
Fibonacci sequence
finite
front-end estimation
greatest common divisor
  (GCD)
greatest common factor
  (GCF)
gross
identity element
identity property of
  addition
identity property of
  multiplication
improper fraction

inequality
infinite
integer
intersection of sets
inverse element
inverse operation
inverse property
irrational number
least (lowest) common
  denominator (LCD)
least (lowest) common
  multiple (LCM)
like denominators
lowest terms
lowest terms (simplest
  form)
magic square
mathematical statement
means (of a proportion)
mixed number
multiple
multiplicand
multiplicative inverse
  (reciprocal)
multiplier
negative
not equal to ($\neq$)
null set
number system
numeration
numerator
order (verb)
order of operations
percent
percentage
perfect number

perfect square
place value
positive
power
prime number
proper fraction
proportion
rate
rate of interest
ratio
rational number
reasonable estimates
repeating decimal
set
short division
signed number
significant digits
simplest terms
simplify fractions
solution set
square number
square root
square units
string
subset
super set
terminating decimal
union
union of sets
unlike denominators
verbal expression
whole
whole number
zero property of addition
zero property of
  multiplication

The Reading Teacher's Book of Lists, Fifth Edition, © 2006 by John Wiley & Sons, Inc.

Algebra

algebra
algebraic expression
algebraic patterns
algebraic relationship
algebraic solution
cast out
coefficient
compound interest

constant
cross-product
derive
discount
equation
evaluate
exponents
extend a pattern

factor tree
formula
graph of the equation
input values
interest
interest rate
inverse operations
line of best fit

linear
linear equation
linear function
monomial
numeric pattern
open sentence
order of operations
proportion

sale price
sales tax
scientific notation
simple interest
simplify
slope
substitute
substitution

symbols in verbal form
symbols in written form
translate
unit price
variable
verbal expression

Geometry

30-60-90 triangle
45-45-90 triangle
acute angle
acute triangle
adjacent
alternate
altitude
angle ($\angle$)
arc
area
axis (axes)
bisect
bisector
capacity
central angle
chord
circle graph
circumference
circumscribe
classify triangles
compass
complementary angles
concave
concentric
congruent triangles
convex
coordinate
coordinate axis

coordinate geometry
coordinate graph
coordinate plane
corresponding
corresponding angles
corresponding sides
cross-section
cylinder
decagon
depth
diameter
dimension
equiangular triangle
equilateral triangle
formula
geometry
height
hemisphere
heptagon
hexagonal
hypotenuse
interior angles
irregular polygon
isosceles triangle
mass
nonagon
obtuse angle
obtuse triangle

perpendicular lines
perspective drawing
pi (π)
plane
plot
point
polyhedron
Pythagorean theorem
quadrant
quadrilateral
radius (radii)
ray
rectangular prism
reflection
regular polygon
scalene triangle
sector
similar triangles
spatial relationships
square
straight angle
surface area
triangular prism
triangular pyramid
vertex (vertices)
x-axis
y-axis

Statistics and Probability

at random
average
bar graph
benchmark
biased sample
box plot
box-and-whisker plot

circle graph
compound events
correlation
cumulative frequency
data
dependent events
deviation

dot graph
event
experimental probability
experimental results
favorable outcomes
formulate
frequency

MATH VOCABULARY—INTERMEDIATE CONTINUED

The Reading Teacher's Book of Lists, Fifth Edition, © 2006 by John Wiley & Sons, Inc.

frequency table	mode	quartile
fundamental counting principle	mutually exclusive	random sample
graph	negative correlation	range
histogram	organized chart	ranking
impossible outcomes	organized list	record data
independent event	outcome	representative sample
interpret graphs	outlier	sampling
justify	percentile	set of data
line graph	poll	single event
line plot	population	statistics
mean	positive correlation	stem-and-leaf plot
median	possible outcomes	survey
midpoint	predict	trial
midway	probability	Venn diagram
	probable	

Prefixes for Super-Small Numbers

Prefix		Meaning	Example
deci-	d	tenth, 10^{-1}	decimeter
centi-	c	hundredth, 10^{-2}	centimeter
milli-	m	thousandth, 10^{-3}	millimeter
micro-	u	millionth, 10^{-6}	micrometer (micron)
nano-	n	billionth, 10^{-9}	nanometer
pico-	p	trillionth, 10^{-12}	picometer
femto-	f	quadrillionth, 10^{-15}	femtometer (fermi)
atto-	a	quintillionth, 10^{-18}	attometer

Prefixes for Super-Large Numbers

Prefix		Meaning	Example
kilo-	(K)	thousand, 10^3	kilometer
mega-	(M)	million, 10^6	megameter
giga-	(G)	billion, 10^9	gigameter
tera-	(T)	trillion, 10^{12}	tetrameter
peta-	(P)	quadrillion, 10^{15}	pentameter
exa-	(E)	quintillion, 10^{18}	exameter

See also List 46, Math Vocabulary—Elementary; List 48, Measurement System Abbreviations; List 49, Metric System Prefixes and Conversions.

LIST 48. MEASUREMENT SYSTEM ABBREVIATIONS

U.S. CUSTOMARY MEASUREMENT SYSTEM

In the customary system of measurement, the reference unit used for length is the **inch;** the reference unit used for liquid capacity is the **ounce.** Inch rulers and yard sticks are used to measure length in the customary system.

Length

12 inches (12 in.)	equal	1 foot (1 ft.)
3 feet (3 ft.)	equal	1 yard (1 yd.)
220 yards (220 yds.)	equal	1 furlong (1 fur.)
8 furlongs (8 fur.)	equal	1 mile (1 mi.)

Liquid Capacity

8 fluid ounces (8 fl. oz)	equal	1 cup (1 c.)
2 cups (2 c.)	equal	1 pint (1 pt.)
16 fluid ounces (16 fl. oz)	equal	1 pint (1 pt.)
2 pints (2 pt.)	equal	1 quart (1 qt.)
32 fluid ounces (32 fl. oz.)	equal	1 quart (1 qt.)
4 quarts (4 qt.)	equal	1 gallon (1 gal.)
128 fluid ounces (128 fl. oz)	equal	1 gallon (1 gal.)

Mass Weight

16 ounces (16 oz.)	equal	1 pound (1 lb.)
2,000 pounds (2,000 lb.)	equal	1 ton (1 T.)

Area

144 square inches (144 sq. in.)	equal	1 square foot (1 sq. ft.)
9 square feet (9 sq. ft.)	equal	1 square yard (1 sq. yd.)
4,840 square yards (4,840 sq. yd.)	equal	1 acre (1 A.)

Volume

1,728 cubic inches (1,728 cu. in.)	equal	1 cubic foot (1 cu. ft.)
27 cubic feet (27 cu. ft.)	equal	1 cubic yard (1 cu. yd.)

METRIC SYSTEM (INTERNATIONAL SYSTEM OF UNITS)

In the metric system of measurement, the reference unit used for length is the **meter;** the reference unit used for capacity is **liter.** Centimeter rulers and meter sticks are used to measure length in the metric system.

Length

10 millimeters (10 mm)	equal	1 centimeter (1 cm)
10 centimeters (10 cm)	equal	1 decimeter (1 dm)
100 millimeters (100 mm)	equal	1 decimeter (1 dm)
10 decimeters (10 dm)	equal	1 meter (1 m)
100 centimeters (100 cm)	equal	1 meter (1 m)
1,000 meters (1000 m)	equal	1 kilometer (1 km)

The Reading Teacher's Book of Lists, Fifth Edition, © 2006 by John Wiley & Sons, Inc.

MEASUREMENT SYSTEM ABBREVIATIONS CONTINUED

Liquid Capacity

10 milliliters (10 ml)	equal	1 centiliter (1 cl)
1,000 milliliters (1000 ml)	equal	1 liter (1 L)

Mass (Weight)

10 milligrams (10 mg)	equal	1 centigram (1 cg)
1,000 milligrams (1000 mg)	equal	1 gram (1 g)
1,000 grams (1000 g)	equal	1 kilogram (1 kg)
1,000 kilograms (1000 kg)	equal	1 metric ton (1 t)

Area

100 square millimeters (100 mm^2)	equal	1 square centimeter (1 cm^2)
10,000 square centimeters (10,000 cm^2)	equal	1 square meter (1 m^2)
10,000 square meters (10,000 m^2)	equal	1 hectare (1 ha)

Volume

1,000 cubic millimeters (1000 mm^3)	equal	1 cubic centimeter (1 cm^3)
1,000 cubic centimeters (1000 cm^3)	equal	1 cubic decimeter (1 dm^3)
1,000,000 cubic centimeters (1,000,000 cm^3)	equal	1 cubic meter (1 m^3)

METRIC CONVERSIONS

Customary System / Metric System

Customary System		Metric System
1 inch	equals	2.5 centimeters
1 foot	equals	30 centimeters
1 yard	equals	0.9 meters
1 mile	equals	1.6 kilometers
1 pound	equals	0.45 kilogram
1 quart	equals	0.95 liter
1 gallon	equals	3.8 liters

Metric System / Customary System

Metric System		Customary System
1 meter	equals	3.3 feet
1 hectare	equals	2.5 acres
1 centimeter	equals	0.4 inch
1 liter	equals	1.06 quarts
2 liter	equals	0.26 gallon
1 gram	equals	0.035 ounce
1 kilogram	equals	2.2 pounds

See also List 46, Math Vocabulary—Elementary; List 52, Reading Math Symbols.

The Reading Teacher's Book of Lists, Fifth Edition, © 2006 by John Wiley & Sons, Inc.

OTHER MEASUREMENT TERMS

acre (ac.)	An area of 43,560 square feet.
Astronomical Unit (A.U.)	93,000,000 miles, the average distance of the earth from the sun.
Board Foot (bd. Ft.)	144 cubic inches (12 in. × 12 in. × 1 in.). Used for lumber.
Bolt (bo.)	40 yards. Used for measuring cloth.
BTU	British thermal unit. Amount of heat.
Carat (c)	200 milligrams. Used for weighing precious stones.
Chain (ch)	A chain 66 feet. Used in surveying.
Decibel (db)	Unit of relative loudness. One decibel is the smallest amount of change detectable by the human ear.
Fathom (fm.)	1 fathom = 6 feet.
Furlong (fur.)	1 furlong = 220 yards.
Gross (gr.)	12 dozen or 144.
Hand (hd.)	4 inches. Used for measuring the height of horses.
Hertz (Hz)	Unit for measurement of electromagnetic wave frequencies (equivalent to "cycles per second").
Horsepower (hp)	The power needed to lift 33,000 pounds a distance of one foot in one minute.
Karat (kt)	A measure of the purity of gold. 24 are pure gold. Sometimes spelled *carat*.
Knot (kn.)	Rate of speed of one nautical mile per hour.
League (L.)	Usually estimated at 3 miles.
Light-Year (ly.)	5,880,000,000,000 miles the distance light travels in a vacuum in a year.
Mach	A ratio; object/speed of sound. Used for airplane speed; about 1,088 ft per second.
Magnum (Mg.)	Two-quart bottle.
Nautical Mile (nm)	1 mile (nautical) = 1.852 kilometers; 1.151 statute miles.
Pi (π)	3.14159265+. The ratio of the circumference of a circle to its diameter. Usually rounded to 3.14.
Pica (pc.)	1/6 inch or 12 points. Used in printing.
Quire (qr.)	Used for measuring paper. Sometimes 24, but more often 25. There are 20 quires to a ream.
Ream (rm.)	Used for measuring paper, often 500 sheets.
Roentgen (R)	International unit of radiation produced by X-rays.
Score (sc)	20 units. fourscore = 80
Sound, Speed of	Usually placed at 1,088 ft. per second.
Span	9 inches or 22.86 cm. End of the thumb and the end of the little finger when both are outstretched.
Township (T)	U.S. land measurement of almost 36 square miles.

See also List 47, Math Vocabulary—Intermediate; List 49, Metric System Prefixes and Conversions.

LIST 49. METRIC SYSTEM PREFIXES AND CONVERSIONS

The metric system was developed by French scientists in 1864. The basic unit is a *meter,* which is one ten-millionth of the distance from the pole to the equator. All units are based on the decimal system of numbers. Hence, a hectometer is 10 meters and a centimeter is 100 meters. See the following tables for other units and for changing the U.S. system into the metric system and vice versa.

Prefix	Symbol	Magnitude	Meaning (multiply by)
Yotta-	Y	10^{24}	1 000 000 000 000 000 000 000 000
Zetta-	Z	10^{21}	1 000 000 000 000 000 000 000
Exa-	E	10^{18}	1 000 000 000 000 000 000
Peta-	P	10^{15}	1 000 000 000 000 000
Tera-	T	10^{12}	1 000 000 000 000
Giga-	G	10^9	1 000 000 000
Mega-	M	10^6	1 000 000
myria-	my	10^4	10 000 (this is now obsolete)
kilo-	k	10^3	1000
hecto-	h	10^2	100
deka-	da	10	10
—	—	—	—
deci-	d	10^{-1}	0.1
centi-	c	10^{-2}	0.01
milli-	m	10^{-3}	0.001
micro-	u (mu)	10^{-6}	0.000 001
nano-	n	10^{-9}	0.000 000 001
pico-	p	10^{-12}	0.000 000 000 001
femto-	f	10^{-15}	0.000 000 000 000 001
atto-	a	10^{-18}	0.000 000 000 000 000 001
zepto-	z	10^{-21}	0.000 000 000 000 000 000 001
yocto-	y	10^{-24}	0.000 000 000 000 000 000 000 001

The Reading Teacher's Book of Lists, Fifth Edition, © 2006 by John Wiley & Sons, Inc.

The Reading Teacher's Book of Lists, Fifth Edition, © 2006 by John Wiley & Sons, Inc.

Conversion Tables

Note: Boldfaced numbers indicate exact values.

U.S. Customary to Metric

	If you have:	Multiply by:	To get:
Length	inches	**25.4**	millimeters
	inches	**2.54**	centimeters
	inches	**0.0254**	meters
	feet	0.3 (0.3048)	meters
	yards	0.9 (**0.9144**)	meters
	miles[1]	1.6 (**1.609344**)	kilometers
Area	sq. inches	6.5 (**6.4516**)	sq. cm.
	sq. feet	0.09 (0.09290341)	sq. meters
	sq. yards	0.84 (0.83612736)	sq. meters
	acres	0.4 (0.4046873)	hectares
	sq. miles	2.6 (2.58998811)	sq. kilometers
Weight	ounces (avdp)	28 (**28.349523125**)	grams
	pounds (avdp)	454 (**453.59237**)	grams
	pounds (avdp)	0.45 (**0.45359237**)	kilograms
	short tons[2]	0.91 (**0.90718474**)	metric tons
	long tons[3]	1 (**1.0160469088**)	metric tons
Liquid meas.	ounces	0.03 (0.02957353)	liters
	cups	0.24 (0.23658824)	liters
	pints	0.47 (0.473176473)	liters
	quarts	0.95 (0.946352948)	liters
	gallons	3.79 (3.785411784)	liters

Metric to U.S. Customary

	If you have:	Multiply by:	To get:
Length	millimeters	0.04 (0.03937)	inches
	centimeters	0.4 (0.3937)	inches
	meters	3.9 (39.37)	inches
	meters	3.3 (3.280840)	feet
	meters	1.1 (1.093613)	yards
	kilometers	0.6 (0.621371)	miles
Area	sq. cm.	0.16 (0.15500)	sq. inches
	sq. meters	10.8 (10.76391)	sq. feet
	sq. meters	1.2 (1.195990)	sq. yards
	hectares	2.5 (2.471044)	acres
	sq. kilometers	0.39 (0.386102)	sq. miles
Weight	grams	0.035 (0.03527396)	ounces (avdp)
	grams	0.002 (0.00220462)	pounds (avdp)
	kilograms	2.2 (2.204623)	pounds (avdp)
	metric tons	1.1 (1.102311)	short tons[2]
	metric tons	0.98 (0.9842065)	long tons[3]
Liquid meas.	liters	33.8 (33.81402)	ounces
	liters	4.2 (4.226752)	cups
	liters	2.1 (2.113376)	pints
	liters	1.1 (1.056688)	quarts
	liters	0.26 (0.264172)	gallons

(1) Statute mile. (2) A short ton is 2,000 pounds. (3) A long ton is 2,240 pounds.

LIST 50. ROMAN NUMERALS

We might have taken our alphabet from the Romans but, thankfully, we did not take their number system. Roman numerals are used for formal or decorative purposes, such as on clocks and cornerstones. For fun and learning, have every student write his or her date of birth in Roman numerals. Write the principal's birthday, too.

Roman	Arabic	Roman	Arabic
I	1	XXI	21
II	2	XXIX	29
III	3	XXX	30
IV	4	XL	40
V	5	XLVIII	48
VI	6	IL	49
VII	7	L	50
VIII	8	LX	60
IX	9	XC	90
X	10	XCVIII	98
XI	11	IC	99
XII	12	C	100
XIII	13	CI	101
XIV	14	CC	200
XV	15	D	500
XVI	16	DC	600
XVII	17	CM	900
XVIII	18	M	1000
XIX	19	MCMLXCIX	1999
XX	20	MMVI	2006

Note: Roman Numerals have the following basic symbols:

I = 1	L = 50	M = 1000
V = 5	C = 100	
X = 10	D = 500	

A smaller symbol *before* a larger symbol means *subtract* the smaller amount, thus:

IX = 9   CM = 900   IL = 49   XXIX = 29

A smaller symbol *after* a larger symbol means *add* the small amount, thus:

XI = 11   LI = 51   XXVIII = 28
MC = 1100   XXXI = 31   LV = 55

The Reading Teacher's Book of Lists, Fifth Edition, © 2006 by John Wiley & Sons, Inc.

LIST 51. OLD MEASUREMENT TERMS

This table gives some interesting insights into the old English measurement system that is the basis of the U.S. "customary" measurement system. These terms crop up in literature and on some tests.

1 inch	=	the distance from the thumb tip to the knuckle
1 hand	=	the width of a closed hand (4 inches) used for horse height
1 span	=	the distance from the thumb tip to the little finger in the outspread hand (approximately 9 inches)
1 foot	=	the length of a man's foot (12 inches)
1 cubit	=	the length of the forearm (17 to 21 inches)
1 yard	=	the distance from the finger tip of the outstretched arm to the chest center (3 feet or 36 inches)
1 fathom	=	the distance of two outstretched arms (2 yards or 6 feet)
1 pace	=	two steps (approximately 2 yards)
1 rod	=	5½ yards (16½ feet)
1 furlong	=	200 paces (220 yards or 1/8th mile or 40 rods)
1 mile	=	1,000 paces (8 furlongs or 1,760 yards or 5280 feet)
1 league	=	3 miles in modern U.S. system, 1.5 old Roman miles
1 bushel	=	64 U.S. pints or 32 quarts
1 peck	=	¼ of a bushel or 8 quarts
1 hogshead	=	63 gallons for wine or 64 gallons for beer

LIST 52. READING MATH SYMBOLS

Students need help to become fluent readers of math's symbolic language. While teaching the concepts and written symbols, provide practice listening to and reading the math expressions. Without skill reading math, students' ability to restate, explain, question, formulate, and apply functions is limited. Being able to "talk math" enables students to "think math."

PRIMARY

See	Say	See	Say
+	and or plus	−	take away or minus
×	times	÷	is divided by
=	is equal to or equals	≠	is not equal to
<	is less than	>	is more than or is greater than
¢	cent or cents	$	dollar or dollars
½	one-half	¼	one-quarter
¾	three-quarters	⅓	one-third
%	percent	#	number or pound

INTERMEDIATE

See	Say	See	Say
+	plus or positive	−	minus or negative
×	is multiplied by	÷	is divided by
=	is equal to or equals	≠	is not equal to
<	is less than	>	is greater than
* and ·	is multiplied by	/	is divided by
?	a missing number	∠	angle
≅	is approximately equal to	⊥	is perpendicular to
≤	is less than or equal to	≥	is greater than or equal to
(	open parenthesis	)	closed parenthesis
[	open bracket	]	closed bracket
@	at	∅	null set, empty set, or zero
:	is to	::	as
∴	therefore	≈	is approximately
R	the set of real numbers	N	the set of natural numbers
∪	in union with or union	∩	intersects or intersection
⊂	contained in or is a subset of	⊄	is not a subset of
∈	is an element of	∉	is not an element of
<=>	equivalent	‖	is parallel to

READING EQUATIONS

See	Say
$a + b = c$	a plus b equals c
$a - b = c$	a minus b equals c
$-a - b$	negative a minus b
$a - (b + c) = d$	a minus the sum of b plus c is equal to d
$a - (b - c) = d$	a minus the difference b minus c is equal to d
$a - (b - c) = d$	a minus the quantity b minus c is equal to d
$a \times b$	a times b (or the product of a and b)
$a * b$	a times b (or the product of a and b)

The Reading Teacher's Book of Lists, Fifth Edition, © 2006 by John Wiley & Sons, Inc.

$a \cdot b$	a times b (or the product of a and b)
ab	a times b (or the product of a and b)
ab	a multiplied by b
$ab + c$	ab plus c
$ab - c$	ab minus c
$a(b - c)$	a times the quantity b minus c
$a + (bc)$	a plus the quantity b times c
$a - (b + c)$	a minus the quantity b plus c
$(a + b) + (c + d)$	the quantity a plus b plus the quantity c plus d
$c \pm 2$	c plus or minus two
$4\overline{)12}$	twelve divided by four (or four goes into twelve)
$\sqrt{9} = 3$	the square root of nine is three
$\sqrt{16}$	the square root of sixteen
$\dfrac{a}{b} * \dfrac{c}{d} = \dfrac{ac}{bd}$	a over b times c over d equals ac over bd
$20\% \text{ of } 100 = 20$	twenty percent of one hundred equals twenty
$1/5 \times 100 = 20$	one-fifth of a hundred equals twenty

READING FORMULAS

Area of a rectangle:
A = lw

The area of the rectangle equals the length times the width.

Perimeter of a rectangle:
P = 2l + 2w

The perimeter of the rectangle is equal to two times the length plus two times the width.

Perimeter:
P = 1l + 2l + 3l + 4l

The perimeter equals the length of the first side, plus the length of the second side, plus the length of the third side, plus the length of the fourth side.
Or
The perimeter is equal to the sum of the lengths of the four sides.

Area of a parallelogram:
A = bh

The area of a parallelogram is equal to the product of the base times the height.

Area of a triangle:
A = ½ bh

The area of a triangle is equal to one-half the product of the base times the height.

Diameter of a circle:
D = 2r

The diameter of a circle is equal to two times the radius.

Circumference of a circle:
πd or 2πr

The circumference of a circle is equal to pi times d or two times pi times r. (r = radius)

Area of a circle:
A = πr^2

The area of a circle is equal to pi times r squared. (r = radius)

Volume of a rectangular solid:
V = lwh

The volume equals the length times the width times the height.

Surface of a rectangle:
S = 2lw + 2lh + 2wh

The surface area equals two times the length times width plus two times the length times height plus two times the width times the height.

LIST 53. SOCIAL STUDIES VOCABULARY—ELEMENTARY

Two central themes of early Social Studies education are the interdependence of people, and the relationship between people and their environment. Beginning with families and communities helps children recognize and appreciate the different roles in society. Learning about Native American history and culture before European influences provides an important context for learning about the discovery of the New World and the history of the United States. This list includes key words from Social Studies texts for grades 1 through 3.

adobe
amendment
American Revolution
ancestor
anthem
architecture
artifact
assembly line
barter
Bill of Rights
biography
black gold
broadcast
budget
calendar
candidate
capital
capital resource
cause
cause and effect
celebrations
century
Cherokee
Christopher Columbus
chronological order
citizen
citizenship
city
city hall
civil rights movement
Civil War
coal
colonist
colony
Comanche
commerce
communication
community
Congress
consent

Constitution
consumer
council
courage
Cree
Declaration of
   Independence
Delaware
demand
diagram
direct democracy
earn
earth lodges
effect
Election Day
Ellis Island
executive branch
explore
explorer
firefighter
fleet
founded
free market
freedom
George Washington
government
governor
history
hogans
holiday
Hopi
House of Representatives
igloos
illegal
immigrant
independence
international trade
Internet search
invention
Iroquois

Jamestown, Virginia
judicial branch
keyword search
laws
leader
lean-tos
legal
legislative branch
letter carrier
Lincoln Highway
longhouses
machine
Magna Carta
mail delivery
Mayflower Compact
mayor
museum
Native Americans
Navajo
opportunity
opportunity cost
oral history
Oregon Trail
Pilgrims
pioneer
Pledge of Allegiance
Plymouth Rock
police officer
Pony Express
Post Road
postal service
Powhatan
president
primary sources
pueblos
Puritans
railroads
religion
representative
   democracy

The Reading Teacher's Book of Lists, Fifth Edition, © 2006 by John Wiley & Sons, Inc.

representative government
republic
responsibility
Seminole
Senate
sequence
settle
settlers
Shawnee
shelter
Sioux
slaves
specialize
spending

St. Augustine, Florida
Star Spangled Banner
state
state capital
state government
Statue of Liberty
supply
tax
technology
tepees
Thanksgiving
town hall
trade
tradition
Transcontinental Railroad

treaty
tribes
United Kingdom
United States
veto
volunteer
vote
voyage
wagon train
Wampanoag
Washington, D.C.
westward movement
wigwams

LIST 54. SOCIAL STUDIES VOCABULARY—INTERMEDIATE

Social Studies—the story of the relationships between people and nations—can come alive through historical fiction, biography, travel books, and histories told through memoirs and artifacts. Events take on greater meaning when students are able to imagine and identify with people. Details will be remembered more easily if the storytelling is superb. Documentaries, videos, and videoconferencing are also excellent ways to teach Social Studies. This list is based on words in Social Studies texts and tests for grades 4 through 6. Be sure to teach related words and spellings, such as *ally, allies, allied,* and *alliance.*

abolitionist
adobe
agriculture
alliance
Allied Powers
ally
almanac
amendment
amnesty
annex
apartheid
archaeologist
arid
aristocracy
arms control
arms race
Articles of Confederation
assassination
Assembly
assembly line
atomic bomb
automation
Axis Powers
badlands
balance of power
bar graph
barge
barter
bay
Bill of Rights
blockade
Boston Massacre
Boston Tea Party
boundary
boycott
bureaucracy
cabinet
canal
canyon

capitalism
captains of industry
carpetbaggers
cash crop
caucus
census
Central Powers
charter
checks and balances
Civil War
civilization
cliff dwellings
cold war
collective bargaining
Committees of
   Correspondence
communism
compromise
concentration camps
Confederacy
conquest
conquistador
consensus
conservation
conservative
Constitution
Constitutional
   Convention
consumer
convention
convert
crisis
crop rotation
crude oil
Cuban missile crisis
currency
customs
debt
declaration

Declaration of
   Independence
defense
degree
delegate
democrat
desegregation
desert
dictatorship
diplomat
disarmament
discrimination
dissent
distribution map
diverse
divine right
domestic
draft
dust bowl
duty
dynasty
economy
elastic clause
electoral college
electoral vote
emancipation
Emancipation
   Proclamation
embargo
emperor
empire
endangered species
enforce
environment
equality
Era of Good Feelings
erosion
ethnic group
evaluate

The Reading Teacher's Book of Lists, Fifth Edition, © 2006 by John Wiley & Sons, Inc.

excise
executive branch
exile
exploration
export
extinct
federal
Federal Reserve
Federalist
filibuster
First Continental
   Congress
foreign
foreign policy
fossil fuels
free enterprise system
free state
Free World
frontier
generalization
Gettysburg Address
glacier
globalization
gold rush
graduated tax
great compromise
Great Depression
Great Famine
holocaust
homestead
Homestead Act
hostage
human resource
humanitarian
hydroelectricity
ice age
ideals
illiteracy
immigration
impeachment
import
inauguration
indentured servant
independence
Industrial Revolution
inflation
initiative
inset map
integration

interdependent
international trade
interstate highway
invasion
Iron Curtain
irrigation
isolationism
Jim Crow laws
judicial branch
justice
Korean War
labor union
laissez-faire
large-scale map
Latin America
league
League of Nations
legend
legislative branch
legislature
liberal
literacy
lodge
longhouse
Louisiana Purchase
loyalists
magnetic compass
majority
mandate
Manifest Destiny
manufacturing
martial law
mass production
Mayflower Compact
mechanical reaper
megalopolis
mercantilism
mercenaries
merchant
meridian
metropolitan area
middle class
Middle East
migrate
migratory farming
militia
minority
minority groups
minutemen

missile
mission
missionary
Missouri Compromise
moderates
monarchy
monopoly
Monroe Doctrine
national anthem
nationalism
navigation
Nazism
negotiate
neutral
New Deal
nominate
nonviolence
nuclear weapons
null and void
occupied
opinion
oppression
pacifists
Parliament
patriotism
per capita
persecution
Persian Gulf War
petition
physical map
pioneer
plain
plantation
plateau
point of view
polar climate
policy
political map
political party
political process
politics
poll tax
pollution
population density map
prairie
precipitation
prejudice
primary
primary source

SOCIAL STUDIES VOCABULARY—INTERMEDIATE CONTINUED

prime minister
private property
process
proclamation
profit
progressive
prohibit
propaganda
prospector
protectorate
protest
Protestant
province
provision
public domain
public opinion
public transportation
public works
radicals
ratify
raw materials
reapportionment
rebellion
recession
Reconstruction
recycle
referendum
refinery
reform
Reformation
refugee
regulation
Renaissance
repeal
representative
republic
republican
reservation
reserves
resign
resolution
resources
retreat
revenue

revolt
revolution
riots
road map
royalist
sabotage
saga
savanna
scale
scandal
sea level
search engine
secede
secession
secondary source
sectionalism
segregation
self-sufficient
senator
Seneca Falls Convention
seniority
separation of powers
sharecropper
siege
slave state
slave trade
small-scale map
smuggling
social security
socialist
society
sociology
sovereignty
space race
spoils system
Stamp Act
standard of living
stock market
strategy
strike
suffrage
supply
Supreme Court
surplus

sweatshops
system
tariff
taxation
technology
temperance
temperate climate
temperature
terrorism
terrorists
textile
The Long Walk
theory
time zone
tolerance
totalitarian
Trail of Tears
traitor
Transcontinental
    Railroad
treason
Treaty of Paris
trend
tropical climate
tundra
tyranny
tyrant
unanimous
unconstitutional
underdeveloped
underground railroad
union
United Nations
unskilled worker
veto
Vietnam war
war hawks
War of 1812
Watergate scandal
waterway
welfare
wetland
World War I
World War II

The Reading Teacher's Book of Lists, Fifth Edition, © 2006 by John Wiley & Sons, Inc.

LIST 55. GEOGRAPHY VOCABULARY—ELEMENTARY

Early positive experiences with geography can lead to a lifelong fascination with people, places, cultures, and environments around the globe. In the elementary grades, students learn about communities, interdependence, and land and water forms, and begin to develop research and map skills. This is a list of key words found in geography units for grades 1 to 3.

adapt	county	globe
address	crop	goods
Africa	crossroads	grain
alike	crust	grasslands
arid	cultivation	Greece
Asia	culture	grid
Atlantic Ocean	custom	group
atlas	data	gulf
atmosphere	desert	Gulf of Mexico
Australia	diagram	habitat
axis	different	harbor
bar graph	directions	harvest
barren	discover	hemisphere
bay	diversity	highlands
border	drought	hill
boundary	earth	history
Canada	east	holiday
canyons	eastern	horizon
capital	eastern hemisphere	human resource
cardinal directions	ecology	ice cap
Caribbean Sea	economy	iceberg
cartographer	ecosystem	import
census	endangered	income
central	England	industry
Central America	environment	interdependence
chart	equator	invention
citizen	ethnic group	inventor
city	Europe	island
classify	evaporation	job
climate	export	jungle
coast	factory	lake
colony	farm	landform
communicate	farming	landmark
community	fertile	latitude
compass	flag	lava
compass rose	forest	law
conservation	fossil	leader
conserve	freedom	legend
continent	fuel	line graphs
contour	geography	livestock
country	glacier	location

GEOGRAPHY VOCABULARY—ELEMENTARY CONTINUED

locator map
longitude
map
map key
map scale
market
mass
meridian
mesa
Mexico
migration
miner
mineral
moderate
money
monument
motto
mountain
nation
native
natural resource
needleleaf forest climate
needs
neighborhood
nomad
nonrenewable resource
north
North America
North Pole
northern
northern hemisphere
oasis
ocean
oil
Pacific Ocean
peak
peninsula

Phoenicians
physical environment
pie chart
plain
planet
plateau
population
port
prairie
precipitation
president
prime meridian
producer
products
profit
rainfall
rainforest climate
range
recreation
recycle
reduce
region
religion
renewable resource
reuse
river
Rome
route
rule
rural
saving
scale of miles
scarcity
school
sea
season
services

soil
south
South America
South Pole
southern
southern hemisphere
Spain
sphere
state
suburb
swamp
symbol
table
temperate climate
temperature
tide
time line
tools
town
trade
transportation
tropical
tundra climate
urban
valley
vast
vegetation
volcano
volunteer
wants
weather
west
western
western hemisphere
wilderness
world
zone

The Reading Teacher's Book of Lists, Fifth Edition, © 2006 by John Wiley & Sons, Inc.

LIST 56. GEOGRAPHY VOCABULARY—INTERMEDIATE

The world in which we live is a fascinating place. Information technology and changing political structures have brought us into a global village. Growing cultural, economic, and political ties to countries around the world increase the importance of students' knowledge of world geography and cultures. This list includes key vocabulary from intermediate-grade geography texts. It builds on concepts presented in the elementary grade list.

absolute power	coalition government	eclipse
agriculture	coast	ecology
alluvial	cold war	economic indicators
altitude	collective farm	economy
Antarctic Circle	colonialism	elevation
anthropology	commercial	empire
apartheid	community	environment
arable	competition	environmentalist
archaeology	condensation	equal area map
archipelago	coniferous	equal opportunity
Arctic Circle	continental divide	equator
arid	contour	equinox
aristocracy	cottage industry	erosion
artisan	country	ethnic
assembly line	coup d'etat	ethnic cleansing
autonomy	crater	European Union
axis	crop rotation	evaporation
barren	crusades	evergreen
basin	cultivation	export
belt	cultural region	fascism
bilingual	cultural revolution	fault
Bill of Rights	culture	fertile
Buddhism	current	feudalism
bureaucracy	dam	flash flood
caliph	data	flood plain
canal	death rate	foliage
canyons	deciduous	fossil
cape	deforestation	free trade zone
capital	degree	frontier
capitalism	delta	fuel
cartographer	democracy	geologist
cash crop	density	geyser
caste	desert	glacier
census	developing nation	globalization
Christianity	dew point	goods
circumnavigate	dictator	grasslands
city-state	diversity	gravity
civilization	domestic	Great Wall of China
clan	drought	greenhouse effect
class system	dust storm	grid
cliff	dynasty	gross national
climate	earthquake	growing season

GEOGRAPHY VOCABULARY—INTERMEDIATE CONTINUED

gulf
gulf stream
harbor
harvest
hemisphere
heritage
highlands
Hinduism
hinterlands
homogeneous
horizon
human rights
humidity
hurricane
hydroelectric
imperialism
import
income
industry
information technology
inland
international date line
international waters
irrigation
Islam
island
isolated
jet stream
labor force
landlocked
latitude
lava
levee
life expectancy
line
literacy
longitude
lowlands
mainland
manufacture
map projection
marine climate
marsh
martial law
meadow
medieval
megalopolis
Mercator map

meridian
mesa
metropolitan area
migrate
millennium
monsoon
mountain
multiculturalism
nationalism
nationality
NATO
natural resources
navigable
navigation
navigator
neighborhood
neutral
nomad
nonrenewable resource
oasis
ocean current
oceanography
oral tradition
orbit
parallel
pasture
peninsula
petroleum
physical map
plain
plateau
polar
pollution
population density
port
prairie
precipice
precipitation
prime meridian
product
propaganda
racism
rain forest
rainfall
range
raw materials
reef
refinery

refugee
region
relief map
religion
renewable resource
reservoir
resources
rotation
scale
scale of miles
scientific revolution
sea level
sediment
sediment
seismograph
semiarid
silt
single product economy
smog
space station
standard of living
steppe
strait
subsistence farming
subtropical
supply
surplus
survey
swamp
temperate
temperature
theocracy
tidal wave
timberline
time line
topography
topsoil
tourism
trade
tributary
tropic
tundra
typhoon
universal
vegetation
vital statistics
water power

The Reading Teacher's Book of Lists, Fifth Edition, © 2006 by John Wiley & Sons, Inc.

CONTINENTS (in size order)

Continent	Square Miles	% Land	Population*	% Population
Asia	11,980,000	21.4	3,866,000,000	60.6
Africa	11,508,000	20.6	874,000,000	13.7
Europe	8,813,000	15.7	729,000,000	11.4
North America	8,260,000	14.8	509,000,000	8.0
South America	6,800,000	12.1	336,7000,000	5.8
Antarctica	5,400,000	9.7	0.0	
Australia	3,254,000	5.8	32,000,000	0.5

*2004 estimates, U.S. Census, International Programs Center, U.S. Dept. of Commerce

The Reading Teacher's Book of Lists, Fifth Edition, © 2006 by John Wiley & Sons, Inc.

WORLD OCEANS

Ocean	Square Miles
Pacific Ocean	**63,800,000**

- South China Sea • Sea of Okhotsk •
- Bering Sea • Sea of Japan •
- East China Sea • Yellow Sea

Atlantic Ocean	**31,800,000**

- Caribbean Sea • Mediterranean Sea •
- Norwegian Sea • Gulf of Mexico •
- Hudson Bay • Greenland Sea •
- North Sea • Black Sea •
- Baltic Sea • Arctic Ocean

Indian Ocean	**28,300,000**

- Arabian Sea • Bay of Bengal •
- Red Sea

MAJOR RIVERS OF THE WORLD

Name	Length (mi)	Continent	Name	Length (mi)	Continent
Nile	4,180	Africa	Zaire	2,716	Africa
Amazon	3,912	So. America	Amur	2,794	Asia
Yangtze	3,602	Asia	Lena	2,652	Asia
Ob	3,459	Asia	Mackenzie	2,635	No. America
Huang Ho	2,900	Asia	Niger	2,600	Africa
Yenisei	2,800	Asia	Mekong	2,500	Asia
Parana	2,795	So. America	Mississippi	2,348	No. America
Irtish	2,758	Asia	Missouri	2,313	No. America

GEOGRAPHY VOCABULARY—INTERMEDIATE CONTINUED

WORLD POPULATION CENTERS (2005 *World Gazetteer*)

Rank	City, Country	Population in Millions	Rank	City, Country	Population in Millions
1	Shanghai, China	14.6	11	Lagos, Nigeria	8.8
2	Bombay, India	12.7	12	Mexico City, Mexico	8.7
3	Karachi, Pakistan	11.6	13	Jakarta, Indonesia	8.5
4	Buenos Aires, Argentina	11.6	14	Tokyo, Japan	8.3
5	Delhi, India	10.9	15	New York, USA	8.1
6	Manila, Philippines	10.4	16	Kinshasa, Congo	7.8
7	Moscow, Russia	10.3	17	Lima, Peru	7.7
8	Seoul, South Korea	10.3	18	Cairo, Egypt	7.7
9	São Paulo, Brazil	10.0	19	Peking, China	7.4
10	Istanbul, Turkey	9.8	20	London, UK	7.4

LARGEST U.S. CITIES (2003 U.S. Census Estimate)

Rank, City, State	Rank, City, State	Rank, City, State
1 New York, N.Y.	11 San Jose, Calif.	21 Charlotte, N.C.
2 Los Angeles, Calif.	12 Indianapolis, Ind.	22 El Paso, Tex.
3 Chicago, Ill.	13 Jacksonville, Fla.	23 Boston, Mass.
4 Houston, Tex.	14 San Francisco, Calif.	24 Seattle, Wash.
5 Philadelphia, Pa.	15 Columbus, Ohio	25 Washington, D.C.
6 Phoenix, Ariz.	16 Austin, Tex.	26 Denver, Colo.
7 San Diego, Calif.	17 Memphis, Tenn.	27 Nashville, Tenn.
8 San Antonio, Tex.	18 Baltimore, Md.	28 Portland, Oreg.
9 Dallas, Tex.	19 Milwaukee, Wis.	29 Oklahoma City, Okla.
10 Detroit, Mich.	20 Fort Worth, Tex.	30 Las Vegas, Nev.

Religions of the World

Religion	# Members	% Worshipers
Christianity	2,069,883,000	33.0
Islam	1,254,222,000	20.0
Nonreligious/Atheist	932,929,000	14.9
Hinduism	837,262,000	13.3
Regional/Tribal	799,481,000	12.7
Buddhism	372,974,000	5.9
Judaism	14,551,000	0.2

The Reading Teacher's Book of Lists, Fifth Edition, © 2006 by John Wiley & Sons, Inc.

LIST 57. U.S. STATES, ABBREVIATIONS, NAME MEANINGS, AND CAPITALS

The official postal abbreviation for each state is listed below. Some are easy to remember, such as NY and FL. Others will take a bit of concentration to get straight, such as MI, MO, MS, MA, MT, and ME. The postal abbreviations generally are not followed by periods. Students need to know them just as they need to know how to spell the state names.

The meanings of state names are interesting and give some historical insights.

Full Name/Abbreviation		Capital	Meaning of State Name
Alabama	AL	Montgomery	Choctaw—"thicket-clearers"
Alaska	AK	Juneau	Inuit—"great land"
Arizona	AZ	Phoenix	Papago—"place of the small spring"
Arkansas	AR	Little Rock	Quapaw—"south wind"
California	CA	Sacramento	Spanish—"earthly paradise"
Colorado	CO	Denver	Spanish—"red" (color of the earth)
Connecticut	CT	Hartford	Mohican—"at the long tidal river"
Delaware	DE	Dover	Named for English governor Lord De La Warr
Florida	FL	Tallahassee	Spanish—"feast of flowers"
Georgia	GA	Atlanta	Named for George II of England
Hawaii	HI	Honolulu	Hawaiian—"homeland"
Idaho	ID	Boise	Shoshone—"light on the mountain"
Illinois	IL	Springfield	Algonquin—"warriors" (French, *illini*)
Indiana	IN	Indianapolis	English—"land of the Indians"
Iowa	IA	Des Moines	Dakota—"the sleepy one"
Kansas	KS	Topeka	Sioux—"land of the south wind people"
Kentucky	KY	Frankfort	Iroquois—"meadow land"
Louisiana	LA	Baton Rouge	Named for Louis XIV of France
Maine	ME	Augusta	Named after a French province
Maryland	MD	Annapolis	Named for Henrietta Maria, queen of Charles I of England
Massachusetts	MA	Boston	Algonquin—"place of the big hill"
Michigan	MI	Lansing	Chippewa—"big water"
Minnesota	MN	St. Paul	Dakota Sioux—"sky-colored water"
Mississippi	MS	Jackson	Chippewa—"big river"
Missouri	MO	Jefferson City	Algonquin—"river of the big canoes"
Montana	MT	Helena	Spanish—"mountains"
Nebraska	NE	Lincoln	Omaha—"river in the flatness"
Nevada	NV	Carson City	Spanish—"snowy"

U.S. STATES, ABBREVIATIONS, NAME MEANINGS, AND CAPITALS CONTINUED

New Hampshire	NH	Concord	Named after an English county
New Jersey	NJ	Trenton	Name after Isle of Jersey in England
New Mexico	NM	Santa Fe	Named after Mexico (Aztec war god, *Mextli*)
New York	NY	Albany	Named for the Duke of York and Albany
North Carolina	NC	Raleigh	Named for Charles I and Charles II of England
North Dakota	ND	Bismarck	Sioux—"friend"
Ohio	OH	Columbus	Iroquois—"fine or good river"
Oklahoma	OK	Oklahoma City	Choctaw—"red people"
Oregon	OR	Salem	Spanish—"land of wild sage"
Pennsylvania	PA	Harrisburg	Named for William Penn and Latin "woodland"
Rhode Island	RI	Providence	Dutch—"red clay"
South Carolina	SC	Columbia	Named for Charles I and Charles II of England
South Dakota	SD	Pierre	Sioux—"friend"
Tennessee	TN	Nashville	Cherokee settlement name, *Tanasi*
Texas	TX	Austin	Spanish—"allies"
Utah	UT	Salt Lake City	Ute—"people of the mountains"
Vermont	VT	Montpelier	French—"green mountain"
Virginia	VA	Richmond	Named for Elizabeth I, the Virgin Queen of England
Washington	WA	Olympia	Named for George Washington
West Virginia	WV	Charleston	So named when Virginia's western counties refused to secede from U.S. in 1863
Wisconsin	WI	Madison	Chippewa—"grassy place"
Wyoming	WY	Cheyenne	Algonquin—"place of the big flats"
District of Columbia	DC	Washington	Named for Christopher Colombus
Puerto Rico	PR	San Juan	Spanish—"rich port"
Virgin Islands	VI	St. Thomas	Biblical—the Virgin Mary

LIST 58. PROVINCES OF CANADA

Province or Territory	Capital	Postal Code
Alberta	Edmonton	AB
British Columbia	Victoria	BC
Manitoba	Winnipeg	MB
New Brunswick	Fredericton	NB
Newfoundland/Labrador	St. John's	NF
Northwest Territories	Yellowknife	NT
Nova Scotia	Halifax	NS
Ontario	Toronto	ON
Prince Edward Island	Charlottetown	PE
Quebec	Quebec	QC or PQ
Saskatchewan	Regina	SK
Yukon Territory	Whitehorse	YT

LIST 59. STATES OF MEXICO

State	Capital	Postal Code
Aguascalientes	Aguascalientes	AGS
Baja California	Mexicali	BCN
Baja California Sur	La Paz	BCS
Campeche	Campeche	CAM
Chiapas	Tuxtla Gutierrez	CHIS
Chihuahua	Chihuahua	CHIH
Coahuila	Saltillo	COAH
Colima	Colima	COL
Distrito Federal (Federal District)	Mexico City	DFJ
Durango	Victoria de Durango	DGO
Guanajuato	Guanajuato	GTO
Guerrero	Chilpancingo	GRO
Hidalgo	Pachuca de Soto	HGO
Jalisco	Guadalajara	JAL
Mexico	Toluca de Lerdo	MEX
Michoacan	Morelia	MICH
Morelos	Cuernavaca	MOR
Nayarit	Tepic	NAY
Nuevo Leon	Monterrey	NL
Oaxaca	Oaxaca de Juarez	OAX
Puebla	Puebla de Zaragoza	PUE
Queretaro	Queretaro	QRO
Quintana Roo	Chetumal	QROO
San Luis Potosi	San Luis Potosf	SLP
Sinaloa	Culiacan Rosales	SIN
Sonora	Hermosillo	SON
Tabasco	Villahermosa	TAB
Tamaulipas	Ciudad Victoria	TAMPS
Tlaxcala	Tlaxcala	TLAX
Veracruz	Jalapa Enriquez	VER
Yucatan	Merida	YUC
Zacatecas	Zacatecas	ZAC

The Reading Teacher's Book of Lists, Fifth Edition, © 2006 by John Wiley & Sons, Inc.

LIST 60. SCIENCE VOCABULARY—ELEMENTARY

Children are naturally curious about life and the world they see, hear, touch, smell, and taste. Elementary science introduces them to the life cycle, the earth, the solar system, simple machines, weather, and natural systems. They learn science through their senses and by using observation, measurement, classification, data collection, and hypothesis testing.

This vocabulary list is drawn from texts for grades 1 through 3. Keep in mind that science words are generally beyond students' instructional reading level and pose pronunciation and spelling challenges. Comprehension is made difficult by the use of common words like "crust" and "pole" for scientific concepts that are beyond their ability to sense and difficult to imagine. Post key terms on a science word wall, include them in language experience charts, and use visual representations and labels to help students master them.

The Reading Teacher's Book of Lists, Fifth Edition, © 2006 by John Wiley & Sons, Inc.

absorb	community	eclipse	freshwater
accurate	compare	ecosystem	friction
adaptation	compass	effect	frost
algae	competition	electric current	fuel
amber	compound	electricity	fulcrum
amoeba	compound machine	element	full moon
amphibian	concave	endangered	fungus (fungi)
ancestor	conclusion	energy	gas
anemometer	condense	environment	germinate
arctic	conductor	equator	gills
astronaut	conifer	erosion	glacier
astronomer	conserve	evaporate	grain
atmosphere	constant	evidence	grassland
atom	constellation	examine	gravity
attract	consumer	expand	habitat
axis	contain	experiment	hail
backbone	continent	extinct	hemisphere
bacteria	contract	Fahrenheit	herbivore
balance	control	fall	heredity
barometer	convex	fern	hibernate
battery	core	fertile	horizon
behavior	crater	fertilizer	host
biology	crust	filament	humus
boil	current	first quarter	hurricane
carbon dioxide	data	float	hypothesis
carnivore	decay	flood	iceberg
cell	decompose	flow	igneous rock
Celsius	degree	flowering plant	image
centimeter	density	flowers	imaginary
chemical	desert	focus	imprint
chemical change	development	fog	inclined plane
chemical symbol	dew	food chain	infection
chemistry	digestion	food web	infer
chlorophyll	dinosaur	force	inherited trait
circuit	direction	forest	insect
circulation	dissolve	form	instinct
classify	distance	forward	interpret
climate	earth	fossil	investigate
communicate	earthquake	freeze	key

SCIENCE VOCABULARY—ELEMENTARY CONTINUED

landform	niche	producer	skin
landslide	nonliving thing	property	smog
larva	nonrenewable	prove	solar system
lava	resource	pull	solid
leaf (leaves)	North Pole	pulley	solution
learned trait	northern	pupa	South Pole
lens	nucleus	pupil	southern
lever	observation	pure	space
life cycle	observe	push	sphere
liquid	ocean	radiant	stem
liter	omnivore	rain forest	stimulus
living thing	opaque	rain gauge	stream
load	optical	rainfall	survive
lungs	orbit	ramp	system
machine	order	range	telescope
magnet	oxygen	rate	temperature
magnetism	paleontologist	recycle	terrarium
mammal	parasite	reduce	texture
mantle	pendulum	reflect	thermometer
marine life	periodic	refract	thunder
mass	perish	relocate	tides
matter	phase	renewable resource	tissue
measure	physical	repel	tornado
measuring cup	physical change	reproduction	transparent
melting point	pitch	reptile	treatment
mercury	plain	reservoir	trunk
metal	plane	response	tundra
metamorphic rock	planet	retina	valley
metamorphosis	plankton	reuse	variable
meteor	poles	revolve	vibrate
microscope	pollen	ridge	volume
migrate	pollute	rotate	waning moon
mineral	pollution	rust	waste
mixture	pond	satellite	water cycle
model	population	scale	water vapor
moisture	position	scavenger	wave
mold	power	screw	weather
molecule	precipitation	season	weather vane
moon	predator	sedimentary rock	weathering
motion	predict	seedling	wedge
mountain	prescribe	senses	weight
natural resource	preserve	separate	wheel and axle
nectar	prey	series	woodland forest
new moon	prism	simple machine	
Newton	produce	skeleton	

See also List 48, Measurement System Abbreviations; List 49, Metric System Prefixes and Conversions.

LIST 61. SCIENCE VOCABULARY—INTERMEDIATE

Understanding ourselves and the world around us requires a solid foundation of basic concepts in science. As the frontiers of science expand and affect our daily lives, every person will need to be familiar with concepts in biology, ecology, chemistry, and physics. The list below was drawn from vocabulary in science texts grades 4 through 6 and builds on the list for the elementary grades.

Students need practice in order to recognize multiword science idioms like **chain reaction** or **circuit breaker** and instruction on how to read multisyllabic words and understand the meaning of science-related prefixes, suffixes, and root words. Be sure to teach the variant forms when introducing new terms; for example, when teaching the concept of **class**, also teach **classify** and **classification**.

The Reading Teacher's Book of Lists, Fifth Edition, © 2006 by John Wiley & Sons, Inc.

abiotic factor	bench mark	compression	dominant factor
absolute zero	Bernoulli	concave lens	Doppler effect
absorption	big bang	concentrate	dormant
acceleration	biodiversity	condensation	drought
acid	biome	conservation	dry cell
acid rain	biotechnology	consumer	
acoustics	biotic factor	contract	echinoderm
action	black hole	convection	echo
air mass	boiling point	conversion factor	ecosystem
air pressure	buoyancy	convex lens	efficiency
alkaline		corrosion	effort
alloy	calorimeter	cross-pollination	effort force
alternating	camouflage	crystal	electric motor
current (AC)	carbohydrate	cumulus cloud	electrochemical cell
alternative energy	carbon cycle	current electricity	electrode
ampere	carrier	cytoplasm	electromagnetic
amplify	catalyst		electron
amplitude	cell cycle	deceleration	elevation
anatomy	cell membrane	decibel (db)	embryo
aneroid	chain reaction	deciduous	endangered species
barometer	chemical bonding	decomposition	endocrine system
antibiotic	chemical equation	delta	endoskeleton
aquifer	chemical formula	dependence	endothermic
Archimedes	chemical reaction	depletion	epicenter
asexual	chromosome	deposition	epidermis
reproduction	circuit breaker	desalination	equilibrium
asteroid	circulatory system	diffraction	era
astronomy	classification	diffusion	erosion
atomic mass	cleavage	digestive system	erratic
atomic number	climate zone	dilute solution	evaporation
aurora	clone	direct current (DC)	evolution
autonomic nervous	coefficient	discharge	excretory system
system	cold front	distillation	exoskeleton
	cold-blooded	diversity	exothermic
barometer	collision theory	DNA	experiment
base	combustion	dominant	extinct

SCIENCE VOCABULARY—INTERMEDIATE CONTINUED

fault
fluorescent
formula
fossil fuel
frame of reference
freeze
freezing point
frequency
friction
front
fulcrum

galaxy
gears
generation
generator
genetic engineering
genetics
genus
geology
geothermal energy
germination
gneiss
gravity
grounded

hazardous waste
heat transfer
hertz (Hz)
heterogeneous
high pressure
  system
homeostasis
homologous
horsepower
host
hybrid
hydrocarbon
hydroelectric
hypothesis

igneous rock
illuminate
imprint
inborn
incandescent
induction
inert

inertia
inexhaustible
  resource
infectious
inflammation
infrared ray
ingestion
inherited
  behavior
inorganic
insoluble
insulate
interference
international date
  line
intrusive
inversion
invertebrate
invisible spectrum
ionic bond
irrigation

jet stream
joule

Kelvin scale
kilogram
kinetic energy
kingdom

larva
laser
lava
law of reflection
leaching
learned behavior
life span
lift
light ray
light-year
lightning
liquid
load
low pressure
  system

magma
magnetic field

malignant
malleable
mammal
marsupial
mechanical
mechanical
  advantage
meiosis
melting point
membrane
meniscus
metabolism
metallic bond
metamorphic rock
metamorphosis
meteor
microbiology
microorganism
milky way
mimicry
mineral
mitosis
mixture
model
modulation
mollusk
momentum
moraine
multicellular
muscular system
mutation

neon
nervous system
neutralization
neutron
Newton
niche
noble gas
node
nomenclature
nonmetal
nonrenewable
  resource
nuclear energy
nuclear fission
nuclear fusion
nuclear waste

nucleic acid
nucleus
nutrient

ohm
orbit
order
ore
organ
organic
organism
osmosis
ossification
output
outwash plain
ovary
oxidation number
ozone

Pangaea
parallel circuit
parasite
pasteurization
periodic
periodic law
peripheral
peristalsis
permafrost
permanent magnet
permeable
petrified
petroleum
pH
phase
pheromone
photoelectric effect
photon
photosynthesis
phylum
physical change
physics
pistil
piston
pitch
pituitary
plasma
plate
plate tectonics

The Reading Teacher's Book of Lists, Fifth Edition, © 2006 by John Wiley & Sons, Inc.

plateau
platelet
polarity
polarized light
pollen
potential energy
prescription drug
pressure
prey
primary color
primate
probability
projectile
property
prophase
protein
proton
protoplasm
psychological
pulley

quark

radar
radiation
radioactive dating
radioactivity
raw material
reactant
reaction
receptor
recessive factor
reflection
reflex
refraction
regeneration
relative humidity
renewable resource
replication
reproduction
resistance

resonance
respiration
respiratory system
retina
reverberation
revolution
rock cycle
root
rotation
runoff

saturate
savanna
scale
scavenger
scientific method
scientific name
secondary color
seed
seismic wave
seismograph
self-pollination
semiconductor
sensory neuron
series circuit
sex-linked trait
sexual reproduction
short circuit
skeletal system
slope
smog
soil water
solar cell
solar energy
soluble
solvent
sonar
sound wave
species
specific gravity
spectrum

sperm
spore
stamen
standard unit
state of matter
static electricity
stationary front
stimulant
stoma (stomata)
stratosphere
stratus cloud
sublimation
subscript
subsoil
supernova
supersaturated
surface current
suspension
switch
symbiosis
symmetry
symptom
synapse
synthesis reaction
synthetic element

taxonomy
temperate
terminal velocity
terminus
theory
thermal expansion
thermostat
thrust
time zone
tissue
tolerance
topsoil
trade wind
transfusion
transistor

translucent
transmutation
transparent
transpiration
transverse wave
tropical rain forest
trough
tsunami
tumor

ultrasonic
ultraviolet ray
unicellular
universe

valence electron
valley glacier
valve
vapor
velocity
vertebrate
vibration
virus
viscosity
visible spectrum
vocal cord
volt
voltage
volume

warm front
warm-blooded
water cycle
water table
watt
wavelength
wet cell

zoology
zygote

See also List 48, Measurement System Abbreviations; List 49, Metric System Prefixes and Conversions.

5

BOOKS

LIST 62. BOOK WORDS

Good readers know how to talk about parts of a book. Here are some terms that can help you in discussing a book, its parts, and some book types. For book contents, see the Library Classifications, List 138 (Library of Congress and Dewey Decimal classifications systems). Your school or neighborhood librarian can also help you with book parts and book classification lessons.

BOOK PARTS

Jacket
Cover—soft
        hard
Spine
Endpapers
Binding—sewn
        perfect
        spiral
Title page—title
        author
        publisher
        (date)
Copyright—date
        L.C. Number
        Dewey Number
        ISBN
        Copying Limits
Dedication
Acknowledgments
Preface
Introduction
Table of Contents
List of Figures
List of Tables
Chapters
Subheadings
Divisions
Index—subject
        author
        (mixed together)
Glossary
Bibliography
References
Appendices
Series
Volume

BOOK TYPES

Reference
Trade
Text
Picture
Coffee table
Juveniles
Fiction

REFERENCE BOOKS

Dictionary
Encyclopedia
Thesaurus
Atlas
Reader's Guide
Almanac
*Reading Teacher's Book
  of Lists*

TYPE FONTS (examples)

Bookman (serif type)
*Contemporary Brush
(sans serif type)*
Baskerville (a serif
  typeface)
Helvetica (a sans serif
  typeface)

TYPE SIZES (examples)

8 point
9 point
10 point
12 point
14 point

THE PAGE

Footnotes (Footer)
Running head (Header)
Subtitles
Paragraph
Indentation
Single space
Double space
Leading (space
  between lines)
Margins (left and right)

PAPER

Newsprint
Bond
Coated
Rag
Weight (thickness)
Tint (color)
Special purpose (photocopy,
  ditto)

LIST 63. GENRE

There are many different kinds of writing to read. Genre (pronounced "zhan rah") refers to the categories of written material. Some categories are very broad with many subcategories, like prose and poetry or fiction and nonfiction. Others are very specific, like historic speeches. This is a partial list of the ways written materials can be grouped.

action	ghost/angels	play
adventure	gothic romance	poetry
animals	historical fiction	political satire
autobiography	horror	prose
ballad	how-to	reference
biography	humor	religious
book review	inspirational	report
character sketch	interview	research report
comedy	joke	romance
coming of age	journal	saga
contemporary realistic fiction	juvenile	satire
diary	letter	self improvement
drama	literary criticism	serial
editorial	man against man	sermon
e-mail	man against nature	short story
epic	man against society	song
essay	multicultural	speech
ethnic	mystery	sports
expository	news article	suspense
fable	nonfiction	technical
fairy tale	novel	textbook
fantasy	novella	tragedy
fiction	occult	verse
folk tale	ode	western
futuristic	picture book	young adult

The Reading Teacher's Book of Lists, Fifth Edition, © 2006 by John Wiley & Sons, Inc.

List **64**. Literary Terms

Every area of knowledge, literature included, has its own specialized vocabulary. Knowing the following terms and their meanings will help students recognize the use of these elements in literature. These terms are basic to discussions about an author's skilled use of language. Many of them can also be used to help beginning writers improve or add interest to their writing.

Accented. A part of a word, phrase, or sentence spoken with greater force or a stronger tone.

Act. Part or section of a play, similar to a book chapter. Acts are usually made up of groups of scenes.

Allegory. Links the objects, characters, and events of a story with meanings beyond the literal meaning of the story.

Alliteration. Occurs when two or more words have the same beginning sound. Example: *Mike mixed some malt in his milk.*

Anadiplosis. The use of the ending word of a phrase or clause as the beginning or base word for the next one. Example: *Pleasure might cause her to read, reading might cause her to know, knowledge might win piety, and piety might grace obtain.*

Analysis. Occurs when we look at and try to understand the parts of something so that we can better understand the whole thing.

Antithesis. Contrasting words or ideas by asserting something and then denying by parallel or balanced phrases. Example: *This soup should be eaten cold, not hot.*

Apophasis. A positive statement made by a negation. Example: *I will not bring up my opponent's ignorance of the fact that . . .*

Assonance. Occurs when an internal vowel sound is repeated in two or more words. Example: *He feeds the deer.*

Author's purpose. Authors write for four main purposes: to entertain, to inform, to express their opinions, and to persuade.

Ballad. A long poem that tells a story. Ballads usually have strong rhythm and rhyme.

Biography. Gives a factual account of someone's life. If the writer tells of his or her own life, it is called an ***autobiography***.

Cast of characters. List of names of all the characters in a play.

Cause and effect. Sometimes an event or circumstance makes another event or circumstance happen. The first one is called the cause or reason for the second one. The second one is called the effect or result.

Characters. People or animals in a story or other writing.

Chiasmus. Change of word order to get the reader's attention and to highlight something. Example: *Down he fell.*

Chronological order. The telling of a group of events in the time order in which they happened.

Cliché. An overused phrase. Examples: *busy as a bee; gala occasion.*

Comparison. Points out the ways in which two or more things are alike or similar.

Conclusions. A decision made after considering several pieces of information. The information may include facts from the reading and ideas that the reader already had.

LITERARY TERMS CONTINUED

Conflict. The problem the characters face in the plot. The conflict can be a problem between two characters or between a character and something in nature or society. Sometimes the conflict makes a character choose between two important ideas.

Connotative. A secondary or more emotional meaning for a word. For example: *a* weed *is an undesirable* plant.

Contrast. Points out the ways in which two or more things are different.

Denotative. A factual, primary, or less emotional description or word. For example: *a plant is a denotative name for a* weed. *Botanists classify* plants, *gardeners pull out* weeds.

Description. A group of details the writer gives that helps the reader imagine a person, place, object, or event. The details help create a picture in the reader's mind.

Dialogue. A conversation between characters in a story or play.

Drama. A story written to be acted out in front of an audience. Another word for drama is play.

Epic. A long narrative poem about the deeds of a hero.

Fact. A statement that can be proven.

Fairy tale. An imaginary story about fairies, elves, magical deeds, giants, etc.

Fantasy. A story that has imagined characters, settings, or other elements that could never really exist.

Fiction. A form of literature that tells stories about characters, settings, and events that the writer invents. Fiction may be based on some real places, people, or events, but it is not a true, factual story about them.

Figure of speech. Words or phrases that have meaning different from the literal meaning, such as idioms, metaphors, and similes. Example: *It's raining cats and dogs.*

Folk tale. A story about people or animals that has been handed down from one generation to the next. Folk tales often explain something that exists in nature or they tell about a hero.

Form. The structure or arrangement of elements in literature. Example: *The form of traditional poetry is lines of poetry in groups called stanzas.*

Generalization. A statement about a whole group that is made based on information about part of the group.

Genre. A category or type of writing, such as fiction and nonfiction, biography, adventure, and science fiction.

Historical fiction. Uses details about real places, events, and times from history as the setting for an imagined story.

Hyperbole. An exaggeration. Example: *He must have been nine feet tall.*

Idiom. An expression that cannot be understood from the literal meaning of its words. Example: *Tom is barking up the wrong tree.*

Imagery. The author's use of description and words to create vivid pictures or images in the reader's mind. Example: *A blanket of soft snow covered the sleeping tractors.*

Inference. A guess or conclusion based on known facts and hints or evidence. Sometimes readers use information from experience to help make inferences about what they are reading.

Irony. The use of tone, exaggeration, or understatement to suggest the opposite of the literal meaning of the words used. Example: *I didn't mind waiting two hours; it was restful.*

Kenning. A short metaphor for a thing that is not actually named. Example: Sky candle *is a kenning for the word* sun.

Litote. An understatement or assertion made by denying or negating its opposite. Example: *He wasn't unhappy about winning the bet.*

Main idea. The one idea that all the sentences in a paragraph tell about. Sometimes the main idea is stated in a topic sentence; sometimes it is not stated but is implied.

Metaphor. The comparison of two things without using the words "like" or "as." Example: *Habits are first cobwebs, then cables.*

> **Abstract metaphor:** Links an abstract concept with an object. Example: *Death is the pits.*
>
> **Animal metaphor:** Associates the characteristics of an animal with human beings, animate or inanimate objects, or abstractions. Example: *What a teddy bear he is!*
>
> **Animistic metaphor:** Attributes life to inanimate objects. Example: *The broom was a dancing machine.*
>
> **Frozen metaphor:** So frequently used that it has become an idiom or an expression with understood but not literal meaning. Example: *head of the class.*
>
> **Humanistic metaphor:** Gives an inanimate object human qualities or humans inanimate qualities. Example: *a user-friendly computer; her porcelain skin.*
>
> **Inanimate metaphor:** Pairs the quality of an inanimate object with another inanimate object. Example: *The walls were paper.*
>
> **Incarnation metaphor:** Links the attributes of a deceased person to another person or entity. Example: *He is a modern George Washington.*
>
> **Sense metaphor:** Relates one of the five senses to an object or situation. Example: *a cool reception.*

Metonymy. The use of a related word in place of what is really being talked about. Example: *"pen"* instead of *"writing."*

Moral. The lesson that a story or fable teaches. Sometimes the moral of a fable is stated at the end of the story.

Motive. A reason a character does something.

Narrative poetry. Poetry that tells a story.

Narrator. The teller of a story.

Nonfiction. Writing that tells about real people, places, and events.

Novel. A long work of fiction.

Ode. A poem written in praise of someone or something.

Onomatopoeia. Words in which the sounds suggest the meaning of the words. Example: *Ouch.*

Opinion. A statement of someone's idea or feelings. An opinion cannot be proven. An opinion can be based on facts.

Oxymoron. The use of words with contradictory or clashing ideas next to one another. Example: *free slaves.*

Personification. The linking of a human quality or ability to an animal, object, or idea. Example: *The wind whispered through the night.*

The Reading Teacher's Book of Lists, Fifth Edition, © 2006 by John Wiley & Sons, Inc.

LITERARY TERMS CONTINUED

Plot. Or storyline. The group of events that happen in order to solve the problem or conflict in the story.

Poetry. An expression of ideas or feeling in words. Poetry usually has form, rhythm, and rhyme.

Point of view. Refers to how a story is narrated. If a story is narrated from the first-person point of view, the narrator is a character in the story and uses the first-person pronouns *I, me, mine, we,* and *our.* If the story is narrated from the third-person point of view, the narrator is not part of the story and uses the third-person pronouns *he, him, she, her,* and *them.*

Predictions. The use of facts in the story and other information you know about the world to guess what will happen.

Rhyme. Two or more words that have the same ending sound.

Rhythm. A pattern of accented and unaccented syllables.

Science fiction. A type of story that is based on science-related ideas. Some of the scientific "facts" and developments in science fiction are not real and may never be possible.

Sequence. The order in which events occur or ideas are presented.

Setting. The time and place in which the story happens.

Simile. A comparison of two things using the words "like" or "as." Example: *She felt as limp as a rag doll.*

Solution. The turning point in a storyline or plot. It is the part in which a decision or important discovery is made or an important event happens that will solve the story's problem or end the conflict. The solution is also called the resolution or the climax of the plot.

Stage directions. What tells actors how to perform their parts of a play. They describe movements, tone, use of props, lighting, and other details.

Stanza. A group of related lines in a poem.

Theme. The message about life or nature that the author wants the reader to get from the story, play, or poem.

Topic sentence. A sentence, often at the beginning of a paragraph, that presents the main idea, theme, mood, or summary.

Voice. The usually unmentioned person who is telling the story. Example: *from a child's perspective.*

The Reading Teacher's Book of Lists, Fifth Edition, © 2006 by John Wiley & Sons, Inc.

LIST 65. OLD AND NEW FAVORITE BOOKS TO READ ALOUD

Reading aloud to children of all ages pays extraordinary, well-documented dividends. It instills a love of books and reading, models fluent reading and inflection, aids understanding story patterns, develops vocabulary, and is a very enjoyable experience. Children's listening levels are higher than their independent reading levels, particularly in the elementary grades. Books for reading aloud may be as much as three years above students' reading level and still be "just right" for comprehension and enjoyment. The following books include some recently published gems that are destined to become classics. Add them to your classroom library collections.

Kindergarten

Alligators All Around, Maurice Sendak
Allison's Zinnia, Anita Lobel
Animals Should Definitely Not Wear Clothing, Judi and Ron Barrett
Bridget and the Gray Wolves, Pija Lindenbaum
Dinorella: A Prehistoric Fairy Tale, Pamela Duncan Edwards
Elmer, David McKee
Gathering the Sun: An Alphabet in Spanish and English, Alma Flor Ada
Growing Vegetable Soup, Lois Ehlert
I Do Not Want to Get Up Today, Dr. Seuss
If You Give a Moose a Muffin, Laura Numeroff
In a Cabin in a Wood, Darcy McNally
Lon Po Po: A Red-Riding Hood Story from China, Ed Young
Madeline, Ludwig Bemelmans
Man on the Moon, Simon Bartram
Mirabelle, Astrid Lindgren; Pija Lindenbaum (Illus.)
Nana Upstairs, Nana Downstairs, Tomie dePaola
Nonsense! He Yelled, Roger Eschbacher
Over in the Garden, Jennifer Ward and Kenneth J. Spengler
The Enormous Crocodile, Roald Dahl
The Grey Lady and the Strawberry Snatcher, Molly Bang
The Gunniwolf, Wilhelmina Harper
The Mitten, Jan Brett
The Napping House, Don and Audrey Wood
The Relatives Came, Cynthia Rylant
The Three Little Javelinas, Susan Lowell

Grade One

Abuela, A. Dorros
Araminta's Paint Box, Karen Ackerman
Biscuit Finds a Friend, Alyssa Capuccilli
Bunny Money, Rosemary Wells
Chicken Man, Michelle Edwards
Chicken Sunday, Patricia Polacco
Elizabeth and Larry, Marilyn Sadler
Everybody Needs a Rock, Byrd Baylor
Feathers for Lunch, Lois Ehlert
Harry and the Terrible Whatzit, Dick Gackenback

The Reading Teacher's Book of Lists, Fifth Edition, © 2006 by John Wiley & Sons, Inc.

OLD AND NEW FAVORITE BOOKS
TO READ ALOUD CONTINUED

Little Red Riding Hood—A Newfangled Prairie Tale, Lisa C. Ernst
Ma Dear's Apron, Patricia McKissack; Floyd Cooper (Illus.)
Once Upon a Springtime, Jean Marzollo
Recess Mess, Grace Maccarone
The Adventures of Taxi Dog, Debra and Sal Barracca; Mark Buehner (Illus.)
The Cow in the House, Harriet Ziefert
The Dinosaurs of Waterhouse Hawkins, Barbara Kerleyl; Brian Selznick (Illus.)
The Mixed-Up Chameleon, Eric Carle
The Mud Flat Olympics, James Stevenson
The Polar Express, Chris Van Allsburg
The Sky Is Falling, Betty Miles
The Sword and the Stone, Grace Maccarone
The World That Jack Built, Ruth Brown
Why Mosquitoes Buzz in People's Ears, Verna Aardema

Grade Two
A River Ran Wild, Lynne Cherry
Amazing Grace, Mary Hoffman
Amelia's Road, Linda Altman
Chickens Aren't the Only Ones, Ruth Heller
Dandelions, Eve and Greg Shed Bunting
Ella Enchanted, Gail Carson Levine
Emma, Wendy Kesselman
Fanny's Dream, Mark and Caralyn Buehner
Hailstones and Halibut Bones, Mary O'Neill; John Wallner (Illus.)
I Invited a Dragon to Dinner & Other Poems to Make You Laugh Out Loud, Chris. L. Demarest
In a Messy, Messy Room, J. Gorog
Juan Bobo: Four Folktales from Puerto Rico, Carmen Bernier-Grand
Lily's Purple Plastic Purse, Kevin Henkes
Many Nations, An Alphabet of Native America, Joseph Bruchac
Max Malone Makes a Million, Charlotte Herman
Miss Rumphius, Barbara Cooney
My Father's Dragon, R. Gannet
One Duck Stuck, Phyllis Root
Shoeless Joe & Black Betsy, Phil Bildner; C. F. Payne (Illus.)
Song and Dance Man, Karen Ackerman; Stephen Gammell (Illus.)
Summer of the Monkeys, Wilson Rawls
The Dragons of Blueland, Ruth Stiles Gannett
The Table Where Rich People Sit, Byrd Baylor
The Widow's Broom, Chris Van Allsburg
Uncle Andy's, James Warhola

Grade Three
Aani and the Tree Huggers, Jeannine Atkins
Amber Brown Is Not a Crayon, Paula Danziger
Borreguita and the Coyote, Vera Aardema
Castle in the Attic, Elizabeth Winthrop
Don't Know Much About the Pioneers, Kenneth C. Davis; Renee Andriani (Illus.)

Goonie Bird Greene, Lois Lowry
Hachiko: The True Story of a Loyal Dog, Pamela Turner
Knights of the Kitchen Table, Jon Scieszka
Maniac Magee, Jerry Spinelli
Marvin Redpost: Kidnapped at Birth?, Louis Sachar
My Great-Aunt Arizona, Gloria Houston
Rebel, Allan Baillie
Sami and the Time of the Troubles, Florence Parry Heide
Seedfolks, Paul Fleischman
The Ghost Belonged to Me, Richard Peck
The Great Frog Race and Other Poems, Kristine O'Connell George
The Stories Julian Tells, Ann Cameron
The Wolf Who Cried Boy, Rob Hartman; Tim Raglin (Illus.)
Tooter Pepperday, Jerry Spinelli
Passage to Freedom: The Sugihara Story, Ken Mochizuki
Twenty-One-Mile Swim, Matt Christopher
Wan Hu Is in the Stars, Jennifer Armstrong
Water Dance, Thomas Locker
Where the Red Fern Grows, Wilson Rawls
Witch Week, Dianna Wynne Jones

Grade Four
A Crack in the Clouds and Other Poems, Constance Levy
A Dog Called Kitty, Bill Wallace
A Light in the Attic, Shel Silverstein
Be a Perfect Person in Just Three Days!, Stephen Manes
Beezus and Ramona, Beverly Cleary
Cockroach Cooties, Laurence Yep
Granny Torrelli Makes Soup, Sharon Creech
Harry Potter and the Sorcerer's Stone, J. K. Rowling; Mary GrandPré (Illus.)
Homecoming, Cynthia Voigt
Kite Fighters, Linda Sue Park
Kokopelli's Flute, Will Hobbs
My Brother Martin: A Sister Remembers Growing Up with the Rev. Dr. Martin Luther King Jr.,
    Christine King Farris; Chris Soentpiet (Illus.)
No Mirrors in My Nana's House, Ysaye M. Barnwell
Poems Have Roots, Lilian Moore
Redwall, Brian Jacques
Remember the Bridge, Carole Boston Weatherford
Saffy's Angel, Hilary McKay
Sideways Stories from Wayside School, Louis Sachar
The Bones in the Cliff, James Stevenson
The Chocolate Touch, Patrick S. Catling
The Night Journey, Kathryn Lasky
The Robber Baby: Stories from the Greek Myths, Anne Rockwell
The Village That Disappeared, Ann Grifalconi; Kadir Nelson (Illus.)
Tom's Midnight Garden, Philippa Pearce

Grade Five
A Taste of Salt, Frances Temple
A Wrinkle in Time, Madeleine L'Engle
America's Great Disasters, Martin W. Sandler

OLD AND NEW FAVORITE BOOKS
TO READ ALOUD CONTINUED

Chasing Vermeer, Blue Balliett
Cousins in the Attic, Gary Paulsen
Harry Potter and the Goblet of Fire, J. K. Rowling; Mary GrandPré (Illus.)
Harry Potter and the Prisoner of Azkaban, J. K. Rowling; Mary GrandPré (Illus.)
Insectlopedia, Douglas Florian
Mary on Horseback: Three Mountain Stories, Rosemary Wells
Mississippi Mud: Three Prairie Journals, Ann Turner
Nothing but the Truth, Avi
Once Upon a Dark November, Carol Beach York
Paul Revere's Ride, Henry Wadsworth Longfellow; Charles Santore (Illus.)
Regarding the Fountain: A Tale in Letters of Liars and Leaks, Kate Klise
Shadow Spinner, Susan Fletcher
The Boy Who Saved Baseball, John Ritter
The Indian in the Cupboard, Lynn Reid Banks
The Secret of Platform 13, Eva Ibbotson
The Spell of the Sorcerer's Skull, John Bellairs
The Westing Game, Ellen Raskin
The Widow's Broom, Chris Van Allsburg
The Wreckers, Iain Lawrence
Where the Sidewalk Ends, Shel Silverstein
White Wash, Ntozake Shange

Grade Six
A Girl Named Disaster, Nancy Farmer
Bud, Not Buddy, Christopher P. Curtis
Casey at the Bat: A Ballad of the Republic, Ernest L. Thayer; Christopher Bing (Illus.)
Cool Melons—Turn to Frogs! The Life and Poems of Issa, Matthew Gollub
Dealing with Dragons, Patricia Wrede
Harry Potter and the Half-Blood Prince, J. K. Rowling; Mary GrandPré (Illus.)
Holes, Louis Sachar
I Know What You Did Last Summer, Lois Duncan
Letters from Rifka, Karen Hesse
Moaning Bones: African American Ghost Stories, retold by Jim Haskins
Radiance Descending, Paula Fox
Shiloh, Phyllis R. Naylor
Surviving the Applewhites, Stephanie Tolan
The First Two Lives of Lukas-Kasha, Lloyd Alexander
The Hatmaker's Sign: A Story by Benjamin Franklin, retold by Candace Fleming
The Shakespeare Stealer, Gary Blackwood
The Slave Dancer, Paula Fox
The Teacher's Funeral, Richard Peck
The Upstairs Room, Johanna Reiss
Tintin: The Complete Companion, Michael Farr
Treasures in the Dust, Tracey Porter
Tuck Everlasting, Natalie Babbitt
Twin in the Tavern, Gary Paulsen
We Were There, Philip Hoose
Wringer, Jerry Spinelli

The Reading Teacher's Book of Lists, Fifth Edition, © 2006 by John Wiley & Sons, Inc.

LIST 66. THE MOST COMMON BOOKS IN LIBRARIES

Various editions of the U.S. Census rank as the most-held work among member libraries in the Online Computer Library Center (OCLC). In late 2004, OCLC Research published a list of the top 1,000 titles owned by member libraries—the intellectual works that have been judged to be worth owning by the "purchase vote" of libraries around the globe.

Here are all the titles that rank in OCLC's top 25:

1. *Census*
2. *Bible*
3. *Mother Goose*
4. *The Divine Comedy* by Dante Alighieri
5. *The Odyssey* by Homer
6. *The Iliad* by Homer
7. *The Adventures of Huckleberry Finn* by Mark Twain
8. *Hamlet* by William Shakespeare
9. *Alice's Adventures in Wonderland* by Lewis Carroll
10. *The Lord of the Rings* by J.R.R. Tolkien
11. *Beowulf*
12. *Don Quixote* by Miguel de Cervantes
13. *Koran*
14. *Aesop's Fables* by Aesop
15. *The Night Before Christmas* by Clement Clarke Moore
16. *Arabian Nights*
17. *The Adventures of Tom Sawyer* by Mark Twain
18. *Garfield* by Jim Davis
19. *Macbeth* by William Shakespeare
20. *Gulliver's Travels* by Jonathan Swift
21. *The Bhagavad Gita*
22. *Robinson Crusoe* by Daniel Defoe
23. *The Canterbury Tales* by Geoffrey Chaucer
24. *Romeo and Juliet* by William Shakespeare
25. *A Christmas Carol* by Charles Dickens

To access the full list of titles, visit the following page on the OCLC Web site: http://www.oclc.org/research/top1000.

Fun Facts About the Top 1,000

Here, are a few fun facts about OCLC's top 1,000 list:

- William Shakespeare has the most books on the list (40). He is followed by Charles Dickens (16 works) and John Grisham (13 works).
- If all the Harry Potter books were bundled together, they would have ranked 8th on the list.
- Jim Davis author of *Garfield,* is the highest ranking living author at number 18. Incidentally, four of the five top works by living authors are cartoons.
- Harper Lee's *To Kill a Mockingbird,* is the highest ranking work by a living female author. It came in at number 149.

Some Newer Children's Books

The following titles were the 2004 Teachers' Choices selections. For Teachers' Choices for every year from 1989 to the present, go to the Web site www.reading.org.

Elementary

- *Around One Cactus: Owls, Bats and Leaping Rats* by Anthony D. Fredericks, illustrated by Jennifer DiRubbio
- *Boxes for Katje* by Candace Fleming, illustrated by Stacey Dressen-McQueen
- *The Elves and the Shoemaker* retold and illustrated by Jim LaMarche
- *How Groundhog's Garden Grew* by Lynne Cherry, illustrated by the author
- *My Brother Martin: A Sister Remembers Growing Up With the Rev. Dr. Martin Luther King Jr.* by Christine King Farris, illustrated by Chris Soentpiet

THE MOST COMMON BOOKS IN LIBRARIES CONTINUED

- *My Brothers' Flying Machine: Wilbur, Orville, and Me* by Jane Yolen, illustrated by Jim Burke
- *Suki's Kimono* by Chieri Uegaki, illustrated by Stéphane Jorisch
- *Swing Around the Sun* by Barbara Juster Esbensen, illustrated by Cheng-Khee Chee, Janice Lee Porter, Mary GrandPré, and Stephen Gammell
- *We All Went on Safari: A Counting Journey Through Tanzania* by Laurie Krebs, illustrated by Julia Cairns
- *You Can't See Your Bones With Binoculars: A Guide to Your 206 Bones* by Harriet Ziefert, illustrated by Amanda Haley

Intermediate

- *DK State-by-State Atlas: A Kids' Guide to the People and Places of America* by Justine Ciovacco, Kathleen A. Feeley, and Kristen Behrens
- *First to Fly* by Peter Busby, illustrated by David Craig
- *Harvesting Hope: The Story of Cesar Chavez* by Kathleen Krull, illustrated by Yuyi Morales
- *How Ben Franklin Stole the Lightning* by Rosalyn Schanzer, illustrated by the author
- *Liberty Street* by Candice Ransome, illustrated by Eric Velasquez
- *River Boy: The Story of Mark Twain* by William Anderson, illustrated by the author
- *Sacagawea* by Lise Erdrich, illustrated by Julie Buffalohead
- *A Voice of Her Own: The Story of Phillis Wheatley, Slave Poet* by Kathryn Lasky, illustrated by Paul Lee
- *The Warriors* by Joseph Bruchac
- *Weather! Watch How Weather Works* by Rebecca Rupp, illustrated by Melissa Sweet and Dug Nap

The Reading Teacher's Book of Lists, Fifth Edition, © 2006 by John Wiley & Sons, Inc.

LIST 67. AWARD-WINNING CHILDREN'S BOOKS

Each year distinguished panels recognize the best new books for children. Three of the most prestigious awards are given the same day: the Caldecott Medal, the Newbery Medal, and the Coretta Scott King Award. The Caldecott Medal, named for Randolph Caldecott, an English illustrator of children's books, has been awarded since 1938 to the artist of the most distinguished American picture book published in the preceding year. The Newbery Medal, in honor of John Newbery, an eighteenth-century publisher of children's books, has been awarded since 1922 to the author of the most distinguished contribution to American children's literature. The Coretta Scott King Award recognizes African American authors and illustrators for outstanding contributions to children's and young adult literature that promotes multicultural understanding and appreciation. It has been awarded since 1969.

The following lists give winners from 1990–2005. For complete lists of winners, visit their respective Web sites.

Caldecott Medal Winners

http://www.ala.org/alsc/caldecott.html

2005   *Kitten's First Full Moon* by Kevin Henkes

2004   *The Man Who Walked Between the Towers* by Mordicai Gerstein

2003   *My Friend Rabbit* by Eric Rohmann

2002   *The Three Pigs* by David Wiesner

2001   *So You Want to Be President?* by Judith St. George and David Small

2000   *Joseph Had a Little Overcoat* by Simms Taback

1999   *Snowflake Bentley* by Mary Azarian and Jacqueline B. Martin

1998   *Rapunzel* by Paul O. Zelinsky

1997   *Golem* by David Wisneiwski

1996   *Officer Buckle and Gloria* by Peggy Rathmann

1995   *Smoky Night* by Eve Bunting, illustrated by David Diaz

1994   *Grandfather's Journey* by Allen Say; Walter Lorraine, text editor

1993   *Mirette on the High Wire* by Emily Arnold McCully

1992   *Tuesday* by David Weisner

1991   *Black and White* by David Macaulay

1990   *Lon Po Po: A Red-Riding Hood Story from China* by Ed Young

AWARD-WINNING CHILDREN'S BOOKS CONTINUED

Newbery Medal Winners

http://www.ala.org/alsc/newbery.html

2005 *Kira-Kira* by Cynthia Kadohata

2004 *The Tale of Despereaux: Being the Story of a Mouse, a Princess, Some Soup, and a Spool of Thread* by Kate DiCamillo and Timothy Basil Ering

2003 *Crispin: The Cross of Lead* by Avi

2002 *A Single Shard* by Linda Sue Park

2001 *A Year Down Yonder* by Richard Peck

2000 *Bud, Not Buddy* by Christopher Paul Curtis

1999 *Holes* by Louis Sachar

1998 *Out of the Dust* by Karen Hesse

1997 *The View from Saturday* by E. L. Koningsburg

1996 *The Midwife's Apprentice* by Karen Cushman

1995 *Walk Two Moons* by Sharon Creech

1994 *The Giver* by Lois Lowry

1993 *Missing May* by Cynthia Rylant

1992 *Shiloh* by Phyllis Reynolds Naylor

1991 *Maniac Magee* by Jerry Spinelli

1990 *Number the Stars* by Lois Lowry

Coretta Scott King Awards

http://www.ala.org/ala/emiert/corettascottkingbookawards/abouttheawarda/cskabout.htm

2005 *Remember the Journey to School Integration* by Toni Morrison. **(author)**
Ellington Was Not a Street by Ntozake Shange, illustrations by Kadir A. Nelson. **(illustrator)**

2004 *The First Part Last* by Angela Johnson. **(author)**
Beautiful Blackbird by Ashley Bryan. **(illustrator)**

2003 *Bronx Masquerade* by Nikki Grimes. **(author)**
Talkin' About Bessie: The Story of Aviator Elizabeth Coleman by Nikki Grimes, illustrations by E. B. Lewis. **(illustrator)**

The Reading Teacher's Book of Lists, Fifth Edition, © 2006 by John Wiley & Sons, Inc.

2002 *The Land* by Mildred Taylor. **(author)**
Goin' Someplace Special by Patricia C. McKissack, illustrations by Jerry Pinkney. **(illustrator)**

2001 *Miracle's Boys* by Jacqueline Woodson. **(author)**
Uptown by Bryan Collier. **(illustrator)**

2000 *Bud, Not Buddy* by Christopher Paul Curtis. **(author)**
In the Time of the Drums by Kim Siegelson, illustrations by Brian Pinkney. **(illustrator)**

1999 *Heaven* by Angela Johnson. **(author)**
I See the Rhythm by Toyomi Igus, illustrations by Michelle Wood. **(illustrator)**

1998 *Forged by Fire* by Sharon M. Draper. **(author)**
In Daddy's Arms I Am Tall, illustrations by Javaka Steptoe. **(illustrator)**

1997 *Slam!* by Walter Dean Myers. **(author)**
Minty: A Story of Young Harriet Tubman by Alan Schroeder, illustrations by Jerry Pinkney. **(illustrator)**

1996 *Her Stories: African American Folktales, Fairy Tales and True Tales* by Virginia Hamilton, illustrations by Leo Dillon and Diane Dillon. **(author)**
The Middle Passage: White Ships/Black Cargo, illustrations by Tom Feelings, introduction by John Henrik Clarke. **(illustrator)**

1995 *Christmas in the Big House, Christmas in the Quarters* by Patricia C. McKissack and Frederick L. McKissack, illustrations by John Thompson. **(author)**
The Creation by James Weldon Johnson, illustrations by James Ransome. **(illustrator)**

1994 *Toning the Sweep* by Angela Johnson. **(author)**
Soul Looks Back in Wonder: Collection of African-American Poets edited by Phyllis Fogelman, illustrations by Tom Feelings. **(illustrator)**

1993 *The Dark-Thirty: Southern Tales of the Supernatural* by Patricia C. McKissack. **(author)**
The Origin of Life on Earth: An African Creation Myth retold by David A. Anderson, illustrations by Kathleen Atkins Wilson. **(illustrator)**

1992 *Now Is Your Time! The African American Struggle for Freedom* by Walter Dean Myers. **(author)**
Tar Beach illustrated by Faith Ringgold. **(illustrator)**

1991 *The Road to Memphis* by Mildred D. Taylor. **(author)**
Aida by Leontyne Price, illustrations by Leo Dillon and Diane Dillon. **(illustrator)**

1990 *A Long Hard Journey: The Story of the Pullman Porter* by Patricia C. McKissack and Frederick L. McKissack. **(author)**
Nathaniel Talking by Eloise Greenfield, illustrations by Jan Spivey Gilchrist. **(illustrator)**

LIST 68. BOOKS WITHOUT WORDS

Wordless picture books allow even very young children to enjoy the stories. With some guidance they can learn to "read" the pictures and develop a host of emergent literacy skills including vocabulary, sequencing, prediction, story line comprehension, characterization, setting, and more. Wordless books can also be used to introduce young English language learners to common vocabulary in context. Early positive reading experiences through picture books motivate children to learn to read. Here are some for your class or library collection.

Alborough, Jez. *Hug*
Anno Mitsumasa. *Anno's Spain*
_____. *Anno's Flea Market*
Baker, Jeannie. *Home*
_____. *Window*
Bang, Molly. *The Grey Lady and the Strawberry Snatcher*
Banyai, Istavan. *Re-Zoom*
_____. *Zoom*
Briggs, Raymond. *The Snowman*
Bruna, Dick. *Another Story to Tell*
Burlson, Joe. *Space Colony*
Carle, Eric. *Do You Want to Be My Friend?*
Collington, Peter. *The Angel and the Soldier Boy*
Day, Alexandra. *Carl Goes Shopping*
_____. *Carl's Birthday*
_____. *Good Dog, Carl*
De Groat, Diane. *Alligator's Toothache*
Demantons, Charlotte. *The Yellow Balloon*
dePaola, Tomie. *Pancakes for Breakfast*
Fleischman, Paul and Hawkes, Kevin. *Sidewalk Circus*
Goodall, John. *Creepy Castle*
_____. *The Midnight Adventures of Kelly, Dot and Esmeralda*
_____. *Paddy Pork's Holiday*
_____. *The Surprise Picnic*
Goodale, Rebecca. *Island Dog*
Gorey, Edward. *The Tunnel Calamity*
Henterly, Jamichael. *Good Night, Garden Gnome*
Hoban, Tana. *Big Ones, Little Ones*
_____. *I Read Signs*
_____. *I Read Symbols*
_____. *Is It Red? Is It Yellow? Is It Blue?*
_____. *Over, Under, Through, and Other Spatial Concepts*
Hutchins, Pat. *1 Hunter*
_____. *Changes, Changes*
_____. *Rosie's Walk*
Jenkins, Steve. *Looking Down*
Keats, Ezra Jack. *Skates!*
_____. *Clementina's Cactus*
Kitchen, Bert. *Animal Alphabet*

The Reading Teacher's Book of Lists, Fifth Edition, © 2006 by John Wiley & Sons, Inc.

Krahn, Fernando. *April Fools*
_____. *The Creepy Thing*
_____. *The Secret in the Dungeon*
Liu, Jae-Soo. *Yellow Umbrella*
Louchard, Antonin. *Little Star*
Martin, Rafe. *Will's Mammoth*
Mayer, Mercer. *A Boy, a Dog, a Frog and a Friend*
_____. *Frog Goes to Dinner*
_____. *Frog, Where Are You?*
_____. *The Great Cat Chase*
_____. *Hiccup*
McCully, Emily Arnold. *Picnic*
Ormerod, Jan. *Moonlight*
Pilkey, Dav. *The Paperboy*
Rogers, Gregory. *The Boy, the Bear, the Baron, the Bard*
Rohmann, Eric. *Time Flies*
Sasaki, Isao. *Snow*
Spier, Peter. *Noah's Ark*
_____. *People*
_____. *Peter Spier's Rain*
Tafuri, Nancy. *Follow Me!*
_____. *Have You Seen My Duckling?*
_____. *Junglewalk*
Turk, Hanne. *Happy Birthday, Max*
_____. *Max Packs*
_____. *Snapshot Max*
Turkle, Brinton. *Deep in the Forest*
Ward, Lynd. *The Silver Pony*
Weisner, David. *Free Fall*
_____. *Tuesday*
Winter, Paula. *The Bear and the Fly*

LIST 69. PREDICTABLE BOOKS

Predictable books use lots of repetition and rhyme to help young readers follow along and enjoy participating in the story. Some predicable books use a strong rhyme scheme; others repeat a refrain, accumulate events as the story moves on, use choral call and respond parts, or use familiar sequences like numbers, days, seasons. These books engage young children and are often part of a beginning reading program.

Aardema, Verna. *Bringing the Rain to Kapiti Plain*

_____. *Why Mosquitoes Buzz in People's Ears*

Becker, John. *Seven Little Rabbits*

Bonne, Rose and Mills, Alan. *I Know an Old Lady*

Brown, Marcia. *The Three Billy Goats Gruff*

Burningham, John. *Hey! Get Off Our Train*

_____. *Mr. Gumpy's Outing*

Carle, Eric. *The Very Busy Spider*

_____. *The Very Hungry Caterpillar*

Chandra, Deborah. *Miss Mabel's Table*

Charlip, Remy. *Fortunately*

Domanska, Janina. *Busy Monday Morning*

Galdone, Paul. *The Gingerbread Boy*

_____. *The Three Little Bears*

Gelman, Rita. *More Spaghetti I Say!*

Ginsburg, Mirra. *The Chick and the Duckling*

Guarino, Deborah. *Is Your Momma a Llama?*

Kellogg, Steven. *Can I Keep Him?*

Kraus, Robert. *Where Are You Going, Little Mouse?*

Langstaff, John. *Oh, A-Hunting We Will Go*

Lobel, Arnold. *A Treeful of Pigs*

Mars, W. *The Old Woman and Her Pig*

Martin Jr., Bill. *Brown Bear, Brown Bear, What Do You See?*

_____. *Polar Bear, Polar Bear, What Do You Hear?*

McGovern, Ann. *Too Much*

Numeroff, Laura, J. *If You Give a Moose a Muffin*

_____. *If You Give a Mouse a Cookie*

Peppe, Rodney. *The House That Jack Built*

Sendak, Maurice. *Chicken Soup with Rice*

_____. *Where the Wild Things Are*

Seuling, Barbara, *The Teeny Tiny Woman*

Shulevitz, Uri, *One Monday Morning*

West, Colin. *Have You Seen the Crocodile?*

Williams, Sue. *I Went Walking*

Wylie, Joanne and David. *A Funny Fish Story*

Zemach, Margot. *The Little Red Hen*

The Reading Teacher's Book of Lists, Fifth Edition, © 2006 by John Wiley & Sons, Inc.

LIST 70. SOUND AWARENESS BOOKS

Sound awareness books help emergent readers focus on sound recognition, discrimination, and production—all important early reading skills. The books use repetition of the sound in initial or ending positions to reinforce sound/symbol relationships. A comprehensive list by sound is included in Joanna Sullivan's *Children's Literature Lover's Book of Lists* (San Francisco: Wiley, 2004).

Aliki. *Digging up Dinosaurs*
Allen, Pamela. *Bertie and the Bear*
Antle, Nancy. *The Good Bad Cat*
Arnold, Marsha. *Quick, Quack, Quick!*
Bang, Molly. *The Paper Crane*
Barrett, Jan. *Animals Should Definitely Not Wear Clothing*
Blocksma, Mary. *Yoo Hoo, Moon!*
Boegehold, Betty. *You Are Much Too Small*
Cameron, Alice. *The Cat Sat on the Mat*
Capucilli, Alyssa. *Biscuit*
Carle, Eric. *Have You Seen My Cat?*
Carratello, Patty. *Duke the Blue Mule*
Coxe, Molly. *Big Egg*
Degen, Bruce. *Jamberry*
dePaola, Tomie. *The Popcorn Book*
Hazen, Barbara. *Tight Times*
Hoberman, Maryann. *A House Is a House for Me*
Hoff, Sid. *Mrs. Brice's Mice*
Hutchins, Pat. *Don't Forget the Bacon!*
Kent, Jack. *The Fat Cat*
Kovalski, Maryann. *The Wheels on the Bus*
Leedy, Loreen. *Pingo the Plaid Panda*
Maccarone, Grace. *Itchy, Itchy Chicken Pox*
Marshall, James. *Fox Be Nimble*
Monsell, Mary. *Underwear*
Oppenheim, Joanne. *Uh, Oh, Said the Crow*
Peet, Bill. *Zella, Zack, and Zodiac*
Petrie, Catherine. *Joshua James Likes Trucks*
Pomerantz, Charlotte. *How Many Trucks Can a Tow Truck Tow?*
Raffi. *Shake My Sillies Out*
Schade, Susan and Buller, Jon. *Toad on the Road*
Seuss, Dr. *Hop on Pop*
_____. *I Am Not Going to Get Up Today!*
Shaw, Nancy. *Sheep in a Jeep*
_____. *Sheep on a Ship*
Shecter, Ben. *Hester the Jester*
Siracusa, Catherine. *Bingo, the Best Dog in the World*
Terban, Marvin. *I Think I Thought*
Wadsworth, Olive. *Over in the Meadow*
Zieffert, Harriet. *Oh, What a Noisy Farm!*
Zolotow, Charlotte. *A Tiger Called Thomas*

LIST 71. RHYMING BOOKS

These books are especially good sources for enjoyable lessons that increase children's attention to rhythm and rhyme in language.

Sheep, Sheep, Sheep, Help Me Fall Asleep, Alan Alda (1992)

I Can't Said the Ant, Polly Cameron (1961)

All About Arthur, Eric Carle (1974)

Anna Banana: 101 Jump Rope Rhymes, Joanne Cole (1989)

Sing a Song of Popcorn, selected by Beatrice de Regniers, illustrated by nine Caldecott Medal artists (1988)

Jamberry, Bruce Degen (1983)

Barnyard Banter, Denise Fleming (1994)

The Beast Feast, Douglas Florian (1994)

Time for Bed, Mem Fox (1993)

Is Your Mama a Llama?, Deborah Guarino (1989)

Alphabears, Kathleen Hague (1984)

Teddy Bear, Teddy Bear: A Classic Action Rhyme, Michael Hague (1993)

Pat the Cat, Colin Hawkins & Jacqui Hawkins (1983)

Mig the Pig, Colin Hawkins & Jacqui Hawkins (1984)

Jen the Hen, Colin Hawkins & Jacqui Hawkins (1985)

Tog the Dog, Colin Hawkins & Jacqui Hawkins (1986)

Seven Silly Eaters, Mary Ann Hoberman (2001)

Don't Forget the Bacon, Pat Hutchins (1976)

Oodles of Noodles, Lucia Hymes & James L. Hymes Jr. (1964)

Annie Bananie, Leah Komaiko (1987)

I Can Fly, Ruth Krauss (1985)

Buzz Said the Bee, Wendy Cheyette Lewison (1992)

The Happy Hippopotami, Bill Martin Jr. (1970)

Barn Dance!, Bill Martin Jr. & John Archambault (1988)

The Reading Teacher's Book of Lists, Fifth Edition, © 2006 by John Wiley & Sons, Inc.

Up and Down the Merry-Go-Round, Bill Martin Jr. & John Archambault (1988)

Chick Chicka Boom Boom, Bill Martin Jr. & John Archambault (1989)

Polar Bear, Polar Bear, What Do You Hear?, Bill Martin Jr. & Eric Carle (1991)

When Dinosaurs Go Visiting, Linda Martin (1993)

Moose on the Loose, Carol P. Ocher (1991)

Not Now! Said the Cow, Joanne Oppenheim (1989)

Moses Supposes His Toeses Are Roses, Nancy Patz (1983)

'Twas the Night Before Thanksgiving, Dav Pilkey (1990)

Down by the Bay, Raffi (1987)

One Fish, Two Fish, Red Fish, Blue Fish, Dr. Seuss (1960)

Fox in Socks, Dr. Seuss (1965)

In a People House, Dr. Seuss (1972)

There's a Wocket in My Pocket, Dr. Seuss (1974)

Sheep in a Jeep, Nancy Shaw (1986)

Sheep on a Ship, Nancy Shaw (1989)

Dance, Ward Schumaker (1996)

A Giraffe and a Half, Shel Silverstein (1964)

Five Little Pumpkins, Iris Van Rynback (1995)

Bunny Days, Rick Walton (2002)

Noisy Nora, Rosemary Wells (1973)

The Lady with the Alligator Purse, Nadine Bernard Westcott (1988)

Silly Sally, Audrey Wood (1992)

The Three Bears Rhyme Book, Jane Yolen (1987)

How Do Dinosaurs Say Goodnight?, Jane Yolen & Mark Teague (2000)

Source: Smith, M., Walker, B. J., & Yellin, D. (2004, November). From phonological awareness to fluency in each lesson. *The Reading Teacher, 58(3),* 302–307. Reprinted with permission of Barbara J. Walker and the International Reading Association.

LIST 72. BOOKS FOR WORD PLAY

Word Play is an excellent way to for children of all ages to learn about language and have a great time. These books provide a range of Word Play from rhyming and alliteration for very young children to puns and linguistic games for older students.

Things That Are the Most in the World, Jan Barrett (1998)

A Mink, a Link, a Skating Rink: What Is a Noun?, Brian P. Cleary (2000)

Hairy, Scary, Ordinary: What Is an Adjective?, Brian P. Cleary (2000)

To Root, to Toot, to Parachute: What Is a Verb?, Brian P. Cleary (2000)

Under, Over, by the Clover: What Is a Preposition?, Brian P. Cleary (2002)

Dearly, Nearly, Insincerely: What Is an Adverb?, Brian P. Cleary (2003)

See the Yak Yak, Charles Ghigna (1999)

The King Who Rained, Fred Gwynne (1970)

A Chocolate Moose for Dinner, Fred Gwynne (1976)

A Little Pigeon Toad, Fred Gwynne (1988)

A Cache of Jewels and Other Collective Nouns, Ruth Heller (1987)

Kites Sail High: A Book About Verbs, Ruth Heller (1988)

Many Luscious Lollipops: A Book About Adjectives, Ruth Heller (1989)

Merry-Go-Round: A Book About Nouns, Ruth Heller (1990)

Up and Away: A Book About Adverbs, Ruth Heller (1990)

Behind the Mask: A Book About Prepositions, Ruth Heller (1995)

Mine, All Mine: A Book About Pronouns, Ruth Heller (1997)

Fantastic! Wow! And Unreal! A Book About Interjections and Conjunctions, Ruth Heller (1998)

Bug Off! A Swarm of Insect Words, Cathie Hepworth (1998)

Carrot/Parrot, Jerome Martin (1991)

Mitten/Kitten, Jerome Martin (1991)

One Sun: A Book of Terse Verse, Bruce McMillan (1990)

C D B!, William Steig (1968)

C D C?, William Steig (1984)

See You Later Alligator . . . A First Book of Rhyming Word Play, Barbara Strauss & Helen Friedland (1987)

Eight Ate: A Feast of Homonym Riddles, Marvin Terban (1982)

In a Pickle and Other Funny Idioms, Marvin Terban (1983)

I Think I Thought, and Other Tricky Verbs, Marvin Terban (1984)

Mad as a Wet Hen! And Other Funny Idioms, Marvin Terban (1987)

The Dove Drove: Funny Homograph Riddles, Marvin Terban (1988)

Guppies in Tuxedos: Funny Eponyms, Marvin Terban (1988)

Superdupers! Really Funny Real Words, Marvin Terban (1989)

Punching the Clock: Funny Action Idioms, Marvin Terban (1990)

Hey, Hay! A Wagonful of Funny Homonym Riddles, Marvin Terban (1991)

It Figures! Fun Figures of Speech, Marvin Terban (1993)

Scholastic Dictionary of Idioms, Marvin Terban (2000)

Punctuation Power! Punctuation and How to Use It, Marvin Terban (2000)

Why the Banana Split, Rick Walton (1998)

Quick as a Cricket, Audrey Wood (1982)

Elbert's Bad Word, Audrey Wood (1988)

Source: Bloodgood, J. W. & Pacifici, L. C. (2004, November). Bringing word study to intermediate classrooms. *The Reading Teacher, 58(3),* 250–263. Reprinted with permission of Janet W. Bloodgood and the International Reading Association.

LIST 73. CHILDREN'S ALL-TIME FAVORITES

What does it take to be an all-time favorite? A great story. Fascinating characters. Superb writing. The following selections have all three characteristics and have been enjoyed by millions of readers since they were first published. Some have been favorites of our parents, grandparents, and even our great-grandparents. Read these and see which ones will be on *your* list of all-time favorites.

Aesop's Fables

Alcott, Louisa May. *Little Women*

Andersen, Hans Christian. *The Complete Fairy Tales and Stories*

Armstrong, William. *Sounder*

Barrie, Sir James. *Peter Pan*

Baum, L. Frank. *The Wizard of Oz*

Bemelmans, Ludwig. *Madeline*

Blume, Judy. *Are You There, God? It's Me, Margaret*

Brown, Margaret Wise. *Goodnight Moon*

Brunhoff, Jean de. *The Story of Babar*

Burnett, Frances Hodgson. *The Secret Garden*

Carle, Eric. *The Very Hungry Caterpillar*

Carroll, Lewis. *Alice in Wonderland and Through the Looking Glass*

Chaucer, Geoffrey. *Chanticleer and the Fox*

Cinderella

Dahl, Roald. *Charlie and the Chocolate Factory*

Dickens, Charles. *A Christmas Carol*

Farley, Walter. *The Black Stallion*

Frank, Anne. *Diary of a Young Girl*

Freeman, Don. *Corduroy*

Goble, Paul. *The Girl Who Loved Wild Horses*

Grahame, Kenneth. *The Wind in the Willows*

Grimm, Jakob and Grimm, Wilhelm. *The Complete Fairy Tales*

Henry, Marguerite. *Album of Horses*

Hutchins, Pat. *Pat the Bunny*

Keats, Ezra Jack. *The Snowy Day*

Kotzwinkle, William. *ET the Extra-Terrestrial Story Book*

The Reading Teacher's Book of Lists, Fifth Edition, © 2006 by John Wiley & Sons, Inc.

L'Engle, Madeleine. *A Wrinkle in Time*

Lang, Andrew (ed.). *The Blue Fairy Book*

McCloskey, Robert. *Make Way for Ducklings*

Milne, A. A. *Winnie-the-Pooh*

Moore, Clement. *The Night Before Christmas*

Potter, Beatrix. *The Tale of Peter Rabbit*

Red Riding Hood

Saint-Exupery, Antoine de. *The Little Prince*

Sendak, Maurice. *Where the Wild Things Are*

Seuss, Dr. *The Cat in the Hat*

Silverstein, Shel. *A Light in the Attic*

————. *Where the Sidewalk Ends*

Stevenson, Robert Louis. *A Children' Garden of Verses*

————. *Treasure Island*

Swift, Jonathan. *Gulliver's Travels*

The Three Bears

Tolkien, J.R.R. *The Hobbit*

Travers, P. L. *Mary Poppins*

Twain, Mark. *The Adventures of Tom Sawyer*

White, E.B. *Charlotte's Web*

————. *The Trumpet of the Swan*

Wilder, Laura Ingalls. *Little House on the Prairie*

————. *Little House in the Big Woods*

Williams, Margery. *The Velveteen Rabbit*

Wright, Blanche F. (illus.). *The Real Mother Goose*

See also List 67, Award-Winning Children's Books.

LIST 74. BOOKS FOR RELUCTANT AND DEVELOPING READERS

The best motivation for reading is a great book. The following books were selected to appeal to even the most reluctant readers. The books on the elementary level (for ages 8–11) are high-interest "easy readers." Many have a great deal of illustrations (a few are advanced picture books) and strong story lines that help struggling readers. The books on the intermediate and older reader list will hold the attention of students in the middle grades and above but are written to be less challenging for the developmental/remedial reader aged 12–16. The lists contain a wide range of poetry, sports, mysteries, biography, historical fiction, adventure, and fiction.

Elementary Level

A Pizza the Size of the Sun. Poems by Jack Prelutsky, Jack Prelutsky
A Swiftly Tilting Planet, Madeleine L'Engle
Awake and Dreaming, Kit Peason
Baseball's Best: Five True Stories, Andrew Gutelle
Blubber, Judy Blume
Crash, Jerry Spinelli
December, Eve Bunting
Driver's Ed, Caroline B. Cooney
Forever Amber Brown, Paula Danziger
Fourth-Grade Celebrity, Patricia Reilly Giff
Ghosts in Fourth Grade, Constance Hiser
Hatchet, Gary Paulsen
I Left My Sneakers in Dimension X, Bruce Coville
Mailing May, Michael O. Tunnel
Maniac Magee, Jerry Spinelli
Mistakes That Worked, Charlotte Jones
My Life in Dog Years, Gary Paulsen
Rapunzel: A Happenin' Rap, David Vozar
Rumble Fish, S. E. Hinton
Secrets of the Shopping Mall, Richard Peck
Skylark, Patricia MacLachlan
Something Upstairs, Avi
Tales from the Brothers Grimm and the Sisters Weird, Vivian Vande Velde
The Good, the Bad, and the Goofy, Jon Scieszka
The Hideout, Eve Bunting
The Pinballs, Betsy Byars
The Sixth-Grade Mutants Meet the Slime, Laura E. Williams
True Lies: 18 Tales for You to Judge, George Shannon
Wayside School Gets a Little Stranger, Louis Sachar
Yours Till Banana Splits, Joanna Cole and Stephanie Calmeson

Intermediate/Older Level

Acceleration, Graham McNamee
Adam Zigzag, Barbara Barrie
America, E. R. Frank
Bar Code Tattoo, Suzanne Weyn
Bronx Masquerade, Nikki Grimes

Chicken Soup for the Teenage Soul, Jack Canfield

Confessions of a Backup Dancer, Tucker Shaw

Draw Your Own Manga: All the Basics, Haruno Nagatomo

Gingerbread, Rachel Cohn

Guitar Girl, Sara Manning

Hey Idiot!: Chronicles of Human Stupidity, Leland Gregory

I Am Not Esther, Fleur Beale

Jason and Kyra, Dana Davidson

Journals: Kurt Cobain, Kurt Cobain

Jump Ball: A Basketball Season in Poems, Mel Glenn

Last Chance Texaco, Brent Hartinger

Oh My Goddess! Wrong Number, Kosuke Fujishima

Planet Hunters: The Search for Other Worlds, Dennis Fradin

Really Useful: Origins of Everyday Things, Joel Levy

Red Scarf Girl: A Memoir of the Cultural Revolution, Ji-li Jiang

Son of the Mob, Gordon Korman

Stupid Crook Book, Leland Gregory

Summer Boys, Hailey Abbott

Technically, It's Not My Fault: Concrete Poems, John Grandits

Ten Days in the Dirt: Spectacle of Off-Road Motorcycling, Russ Rohrer

Ten Sure Signs a Movie Character Is Doomed and Other Surprising Movie Lists,
   Richard Roeper

The A List, Zoey Dean

The Au Pairs, Melissa DeLaCruz

The Hulk: The Incredible Guide, Tom DeFalco

The Last Shot: City Streets, Basketball Dreams, Darcy Frey

The Middle Passage: White Ships/Black Cargo, Tom Feelings

The Music of Dolphins, Karen Hesse

The Official Movie Plot Generator: 27,000 Hilarious Movie Plot Combinations, Jason Heimberg
   and Justin Heimberg

The Samurai's Tale, Erik Haugaard

The Secret Hour, Scott Westerfeld

They Broke the Law; You Be the Judge: True Cases of Teen Crime, Thomas Jacobs

Voices from the Streets: Young Former Gang Members Tell Their Stories, Beth S. Atkin

Wearing of This Garment Does Not Enable You to Fly: 101 Real Dumb Warning Labels,
   Jeff Koon and Andy Powell

LIST 75. KIDS' MAGAZINES FOR READERS AND WRITERS

Children's magazines and their online counterparts—kids' zines (List 169)—are very important for helping students establish lifelong reading habits. Few can ignore the pull of the new weekly or monthly edition of a favorite source of up-to-date information on a hobby, sport, or other interest. Magazines are great sources of high-interest material for reluctant and/or developing readers.

Some kids' magazines are not only written *for* children, but *by* children. These publications are the primary market for children's original writing. Contact them for guidelines for submitting stories, poems, and art. Young writers, whose work is accepted, generally receive copies of the volume instead of monetary rewards. The review and notification time for submissions may take many months, but if published, the wait is well worth it to budding young authors.

American Girl (general interest content for girls; ages 8–12)
http://store.americangirl.com/subscribe_ecomm.html

AppleSeeds (social studies topics; ages 7–9)
http://www.cobblestonepub.com/pages/appmain.htm

Ask: Arts and Sciences for Kids (artists, scientists, thinkers; ages 6–9)
www.cobblestonepub.com/pages/askmain.html

Boys' Life (general interest content for boys; ages 8–13)
http://www.boyslife.org/lo/index.html

Boys' Quest (general interest themes for boys; ages 8–13)
http://www.boysquest.com/

Calliope World History for Young People (world history themes; ages 9–15)
www.cobblestonepub.com/pages/callmain.htm

Chickadee (general interest, activities; ages 5–9)
www.owlkids.com/chickadee/

Click (science and exploration; ages 3–7)
http://www.clickmag.com

Cobblestone American History for Kids (American history topics; ages 8–14)
http://www.cobblestonepub.com/pages/cobbmain.htm

Cricket (children's literature; ages 8–12)
www.cricketmag.com/

Dig (earth science and archaeology; ages 9–14)
http://www.digonsite.com/

Faces: Peoples, Places and Cultures (cultures, geography, and news; ages 9–14)
http://www.cobblestonepub.com/pages/facemain.htm

FootSteps: African American History (African American history; ages 8–14)
http://www.footstepsmagazine.com

Highlights for Children (general interest content and activities; ages 4–12)
http://www.highlights.com/

Hopscotch (general interest content and activities; ages 8–12)
www.hopscotchmagazine.com/

Jack and Jill (general interest content and activities; ages 7–10)
http://www.jackandjillmag.org/

The Reading Teacher's Book of Lists, Fifth Edition, © 2006 by John Wiley & Sons, Inc.

The Reading Teacher's Book of Lists, Fifth Edition, © 2006 by John Wiley & Sons, Inc.

Kids Discover (nature, science, geography; ages 6–12)
http://www.kidsdiscover.com/

Muse (nature, music, science, literature; ages 9–14)
www.cricketmag.com/

National Geographic Kids (wildlife, adventure, geography, science; ages 8–14)
http://www.nationalgeographic.com/ngkids/

Nickelodeon Magazine (children's pop culture and media; ages 8–14)
http://www.nick.com/all_nick/everything_nick/enter_mag.jhtml

Odyssey (science themes; ages 10–16)
http://www.odysseymagazine.com

Plays (drama activities and plays for elementary through high school; ages 8–16)
http://www.playsmag.com/

Ranger Rick (nature, environment, outdoors; ages 7–10)
http://www.nwf.org/gowild/

Soccer Jr. (soccer stars, strategy, inspiration; ages 8–14)
http://www.soccer-for-parents.com/soccer-magazines.html

Skipping Stones (international, multicultural themes; ages 8–16)
http://www.skippingstones.org

Magazines That Publish Young Writers

Boodle: By Kids, For Kids (fiction, poetry, puzzles, humor; ages 6–12)
P.O. Box 1049, Portland, IN 47371

Creative Kids (fiction, poetry, puzzles, humor, artwork; ages 8–14)
http://www.prufrock.com/client/client_pages/prufrock_jm_createkids.cfm
Prufrock Press, P.O. Box 8813, Waco, TX 76714-8813

Discovery Girls (hot topics for girls; ages 8–12)
http://www.discoverygirls.com/
P.O. Box 110760, Campbell, CA 95011

Highlights for Children (stories, poetry, art, humor; ages 4–12)
http://www.highlights.com/
803 Church Street, Honesdale, PA 18431

New Moon (international general content for girls; ages 8–14)
http://www.newmoon.org
P.O. Box 3620, Duluth, MN 55803-3620

Skipping Stones (fiction, poetry, plays, humor; ages 7–18)
http://www.skippingstones.org
P.O. Box 3939, Eugene, OR 97403

Stone Soup (fiction, poetry, plays, artwork; ages 8–16)
http://www.stonesoup.com/main2/printmagazines.html
Submissions Dept., P.O. Box 83, Santa Cruz, CA 95063

The Acorn (fiction, nonfiction, poetry; ages 6–17)
1530 Seventh Street, Rock Island, IL 61201

Young Voices (fiction, poetry, plays, artwork; ages 8–16)
P.O. Box 2321, Olympia, WA 98507

LIST 76. BOOK LIST COLLECTIONS

There are many sources of lists that help identify and locate books on special subjects or grade levels, new and notable books, classic books, and reference books. Public libraries have anthologies, collections, and series on many topics. Some sponsoring organizations publish lists annually; others develop lists as special curriculum or research projects. Use the following list as a reference as you select books for your classroom and school libraries.

American Library Association

http://www.ala.org/booklist
Editors' Choice

American Library Association–Association of Library Services for Children

http://www.ala.org/ala/librariesandyou/recomreading/recomreading.htm
Notable Children's Books; Harry-a-Like Books; Batchelder Awards; Theodor Seuss Geisel Award; Andrew Carnegie Medal; Laura Ingalls Wilder Award; Coretta Scott King Awards; Belpré Awards; Diversity: Great Middle School Reads, Growing Up Latino, Books to Grow On, American Experience, Bilingual Books, Sharing Cultures—Asian American Children's Authors; Books for Boys and Girls Clubs; Reading Is Fundamental

American Library Association–Young Adult Library Services Association

http://www.ala.org/yalsa/
Best Books for Young Adults; Quick Picks for the Reluctant Young Reader; Popular Paperbacks for Young Adults

Caldecott Medal and Honor Books

http://www.ala.org/alsc/caldpast.html
Caldecott Award winners (see List 67, Award-Winning Children's Books)

Center for Children's Books

http://edfu.lis.uicu.edu/puboff/bccb/
Blue Ribbon Book Lists

Children's Literature Web Guide

www.ucalgary.ca/~dkbrown/index.html
Lists according to themes, grade levels, and more

Fairrosa Cyber Library of Children's Books

http://www.fairrosa.info/lists
Thematic lists and links to other lists

Gander Academy

http://www.cdli.ca/CITE/langbr.htm
Book lists on many topics with links to other lists

International Reading Association & Children's Book Council

http://www.reading.org/
Children's Choices; Teachers' Choices; Young Adult Choices

Jim Trelease on Reading

http://www.trelease-on-reading.com/video_biblio.html
Books to read aloud

The Reading Teacher's Book of Lists, Fifth Edition, © 2006 by John Wiley & Sons, Inc.

KidsReads

http://www.kidsreads.com
Book lists by age from 1–12

Monroe County (Indiana) Public Library

http://www.monroe.lib.in.us/childrens/booklists/children_booklists.html
Specialized book lists on 50 topics from adventure to time travel

National Child Care Center

www.nccic.org/poptopics/booklist.pdf
Book lists for emergent reading, bilingual education, creativity

National Council for the Social Studies & Children's Book Council

www.ncss.org/home.html
Notable Trade Books in the Field of Social Studies

National Library Service for the Blind and Physically Handicapped

http://www.loc.gov/nls/
Books and other materials in Braille

National Science Teachers Association & Children's Book Council

http://www.nsta.org/
Outstanding Science Trade Books for Children

Newbery Medal and Honor Books

http://www.ala.org/alsc/newbpast.html
Newbery Award winners (see List 65, Award-Winning Children's Books)

New York Public Library

http://kids.nypl.org/
100 Picture Books Everyone Should Know; 100 Favorite Children's Books

Online Computer Library Center

http://www.oclc.org
1,000 books most widely available in libraries

Publisher's Weekly

www.bookwire.com/pw/
Best Children's Books

School Library Journal

http://www.slj.com/
Best Books of the Year

Smithsonian Magazine

http://smithsonianmag.com/
Notable Books for Children

LIST 77. BOOK INTEREST AROUSERS

Here are some tried and true ways to interest students in independent reading. Research suggests that children who grow up in homes with adult readers and many books, become readers themselves. Classrooms with lots of interesting books at students' independent reading level and scheduled time for "free reading" also encourage students to develop strong reading-for-pleasure habits.

1. **Library corner in your classroom.** Change frequently. Add a bulletin board with rotating themes, such as horses, history, science, favorite authors, mysteries, and so forth.

2. **New-book advertisements.** Have a teacher or student make brief reviews, oral reports, posters, or a contest with a competing book.

3. **Book fair.** Exchange an exhibit of books with another class. Show off award winners. Specialize in some types of new books, old books, picture books, Native American books, joke books, novels, and so forth.

4. **Oral reading** by the teacher or a child. Read a whole book, read interesting parts, read just the first chapter, read about a specific character. Especially read to upper-grade children. They love it.

5. **Poetry reading** by a teacher or a student. Have students memorize classic poems. Read new poems by published authors or read students' poems. Read winners from a schoolwide poetry contest.

6. **Hold individual reading conferences** regularly with every student. Discuss books being read. Suggest similar books. Suggest other types of books.

7. **Visit libraries** both in school and in other classes, as well as your public library. Make sure every parent gets every student a public library card.

8. **Keep a books-read chart** for your class and for each student. Encourage progress and sometimes competition.

9. **Have book-related activities.** In art, design new book jackets or illustrations of book scenes. In drama, act out parts of a book. Discuss different endings.

10. **Tie in book with other subjects.** What was happening in history at the same time? Was the radio invented then? What causes volcanos? Are sports upsets really happening today?

11. **Tell a friend** about a book you really liked. Word-of-mouth is a great motivator.

12. **Visit bookstores.** Stores often display new books in a most interesting fashion.

The Reading Teacher's Book of Lists, Fifth Edition, © 2006 by John Wiley & Sons, Inc.

LIST 78. BOOK REPORT FORM

This form can be duplicated and distributed for reports on short stories, plays, and books.

TITLE _____

AUTHOR _____

ILLUSTRATOR _____

PUBLISHER _____

COPYRIGHT DATE _____

THEME:

MAIN CHARACTERS:

SETTING:

SUMMARY:

REACTION:

See also List 79, Book Report Alternatives.

LIST 79. BOOK REPORT ALTERNATIVES

Once you have enticed your students to read, consult this list of alternatives for fifty exciting things to do in place of writing a book report.

1. Rework an exciting chapter of the book for Readers' Theater—or see if you can find it already scripted online. Have students highlight their speaking parts, practice reading them with expression, then bring students together in a circle for a "reading." A student codirector may be used to help encourage appropriate expression, timing, etc.

2. Have a talk show with one to four "hosts." The hosts interview the main characters in front of a live audience (the rest of the class). They also moderate questions from the audience. Everyone should dress for their character parts.

3. Using a graphics or drawing program, create a new book jacket, complete with related illustrations and blurbs from classmates.

4. Using the table function in your word processor, prepare a chart showing the characters, their relationships, and a few biographical facts about each.

5. Using a variety of art media, design poster-sized ads for the book.

6. Have a "news program" with a panel of reporters giving their reports on various aspects of the story.

7. Dramatize an incident or an important character through a student-written soliloquy.

8. Digitally record students doing "radio" announcements to "publicize" the book. Keep this in an audio file at a computer near the class library so others can listen to the ads and use them to help choose a book to read.

9. Meet individually with students for a book conference to delve into their comprehension of the book and for their personal reactions.

10. Appoint a committee to conduct peer discussion and seminars on books.

11. Illustrate the story, take digital pictures, coordinate music and narration, and assemble it in a multimedia presentation.

12. Write a play based on the continuation of the story or a new adventure for the characters.

13. Demonstrate what was learned from a "how-to" book.

14. Write a text message about the book, limited to twenty words. Use txt wrds.

15. Read aloud a section of the book to the class to get the rest of the students "hooked" on it.

16. Keep diaries for the characters in the story, using first person. Write about the events from the characters' perspective. Encourage expression of personality traits exhibited in the book.

17. Write a letter to the author telling why you liked the book, your favorite parts, what you would have done with the plot. Mail it to the author in care of the book publisher.

18. Be a newspaper columnist; write a review for the book section.

19. Spin the wheel of fortune! Create a wheel with ten events or character-related details. Spin the wheel to pick the element, then write an explanation of how the story might have ended if the new element had been part of it.

20. Write a letter to the key character to tell him or her how to solve the problem.

21. Write a newspaper article based on an incident from the book.

22. Write a biography of the leading character, using information from the book.

23. Write an obituary about a key character, giving an account of what he or she was best known for.

The Reading Teacher's Book of Lists, Fifth Edition, © 2006 by John Wiley & Sons, Inc.

24. Give a testimonial speech citing the character for special distinctions noted in the book.

25. Watch the movie version of the book, and compare and contrast the movie and book. Use the table function of your word processor to set up the class response.

26. Design and illustrate a time line to depict the events in the story.

27. Have a panel discussion if several students read the same book.

28. Construct a story map to show the plot and setting.

29. Make a 3-dimensional model of the story setting.

30. Have a character day. Students dress up as their favorite character in the story and relive some of the story. Adopt language patterns and mannerisms, if appropriate.

31. Journal about the effect the book had on you. What specific part of the book triggered those feelings?

32. Rewrite the story as a TV movie, including staging directions.

33. Examine the story for the author's craft and try to write a story of your own, imitating the use of tone, setting, style, and so on.

34. *Quotable lines:* Select memorable lines that you may want to quote and write them in your reading journals.

35. Make sketches of some of the action sequences. Bind them as a book of illustrations.

36. Make your own audio-book. Read the story and digitally record it so that others may listen to it.

37. *Context clues:* Do research on the period of history in which the story is set. Gather and share the information about key elements of life at the time.

38. Make a word wall list of similes, metaphors, or succinct descriptions used in the book.

39. Make puppets and present a show based on the book.

40. Build a clay or papier-mâché bust of a key character.

41. Paint a mural that shows the key incidents in the story.

42. Rewrite the story for students in a lower grade. Keep it interesting.

43. Imagine a magazine cover story on the book you've just read. What are several scenes you think ought to be photographed? Describe the photographs and write captions for them.

44. Journal about any new, interesting, or challenging ideas you gained through reading the book.

45. Letter the title of the book vertically; then write a brief phrase applicable to the book for each letter. Or, describe the main characters using words that start with the letters in their names.

46. Explain why you think this book will/will not be read a hundred years from now. Support your viewpoint by making specific references to plot, setting, characters, and author's style.

47. Make a list of five to ten significant questions about this book that you think anyone else who reads this book should be able to answer.

48. Write a résumé for one of the characters in the book based on information in the book.

49. Create travel brochures or posters advertising the location in the book. Use your imagination to fill in details from the past or future.

50. Create a 4- or 6-panel comic strip that shows what happens in the book.

6

WRITING

LIST 80. DESCRIPTIVE WORDS

What do telling tales and writing poetry or reports have in common? They depend on descriptive words to create vivid and accurate images in the reader's mind. A good stock of descriptive words will bolster the quality of your students' writing exercises. Use these lists of adjectives and adverbs to nudge reluctant writers into developing characters and setting, or to help students "retire" overused words.

The Reading Teacher's Book of Lists, Fifth Edition, © 2006 by John Wiley & Sons, Inc.

Ability—Condition

able	confident	gentle	lucky	smooth
adequate	courageous	hardy	manly	spirited
alive	curious	healthy	mighty	stable
assured	daring	heavy	modern	steady
authoritative	determined	heroic	open	stouthearted
bold	durable	important	outstanding	strong
brainy	dynamic	influential	powerful	super
brave	eager	innocent	real	sure
busy	easy	intense	relaxed	tame
careful	effective	inquisitive	rich	tough
cautious	energetic	jerky	robust	victorious
clever	firm	light	sharp	zealous
competent	forceful	lively	shy	
concerned	gallant	loose	skillful	

Anger—Hostility

agitated	combative	evil	irritated	rude
aggravated	contrary	fierce	mad	savage
aggressive	cool	furious	mean	severe
angry	cranky	hard	nasty	spiteful
annoyed	creepy	harsh	obnoxious	tense
arrogant	cross	hateful	obstinate	terse
belligerent	cruel	hostile	outraged	vicious
biting	defiant	impatient	perturbed	vindictive
blunt	disagreeable	inconsiderate	repulsive	violent
bullying	enraged	insensitive	resentful	wicked
callous	envious	intolerant	rough	wrathful

Depression—Sadness—Gloom

abandoned	debased	discarded	forsaken	jilted
alien	defeated	discouraged	gloomy	kaput
alienated	degraded	dismal	glum	loathed
alone	dejected	downcast	grief	lonely
awful	demolished	downhearted	grim	lonesome
battered	depressed	downtrodden	hated	lousy
blue	desolate	dreadful	homeless	low
bored	despairing	empty	hopeless	miserable
burned	despised	estranged	horrible	mishandled
cheapened	despondent	excluded	humiliated	mistreated
crushed	destroyed	forlorn	hurt	moody

DESCRIPTIVE WORDS CONTINUED

mournful	rebuked	ruined	stranded	unhappy
obsolete	regretful	rundown	sullen	unloved
ostracized	rejected	sad	tearful	whipped
overlooked	reprimanded	scornful	terrible	worthless
pathetic	rotten	sore	tired	wrecked
pitiful				

Distress

afflicted	displeased	hindered	puzzled	tormented
anguished	dissatisfied	impaired	ridiculous	touchy
awkward	distrustful	impatient	sickened	troubled
baffled	disturbed	imprisoned	silly	ungainly
bewildered	doubtful	lost	skeptical	unlucky
clumsy	foolish	nauseated	speechless	unpopular
confused	futile	offended	strained	unsatisfied
constrained	grief	pained	suspicious	unsure
disgusted	helpless	perplexed	swamped	weary
disliked				

Fear—Anxiety

afraid	dreading	insecure	overwhelmed	tense
agitated	eerie	intimidated	panicky	terrified
alarmed	embarrassed	jealous	restless	timid
anxious	fearful	jittery	scared	uncomfortable
apprehensive	frantic	jumpy	shaky	uneasy
bashful	frightened	nervous	shy	upset
dangerous	hesitant	on edge	strained	worrying
desperate	horrified			

Inability—Inadequacy

anemic	disabled	incapable	powerless	unable
ashamed	exhausted	incompetent	puny	uncertain
broken	exposed	ineffective	shaken	unfit
catatonic	fragile	inept	shaky	unimportant
cowardly	frail	inferior	shivering	unqualified
crippled	harmless	insecure	sickly	unsound
defeated	helpless	meek	small	useless
defective	impotent	mummified	strengthless	vulnerable
deficient	inadequate	naughty	trivial	weak
demoralized				

Joy—Elation

amused	comical	elevated	excited	gay
blissful	contented	enchanted	exuberant	glad
brilliant	delighted	enthusiastic	fantastic	glorious
calm	ecstatic	exalted	fit	good
cheerful	elated	excellent	funny	grand

The Reading Teacher's Book of Lists, Fifth Edition, © 2006 by John Wiley & Sons, Inc.

gratified	jolly	marvelous	satisfied	tremendous
great	jovial	overjoyed	smiling	triumphant
happy	joyful	pleasant	splendid	vivacious
hilarious	jubilant	pleased	superb	witty
humorous	magnificent	proud	terrific	wonderful
inspired	majestic	relieved	thrilled	

Love—Affection—Concern

admired	conscientious	giving	mellow	reliable
adorable	considerate	good	mild	respectful
affectionate	cooperative	helpful	moral	sensitive
agreeable	cordial	honest	neighborly	sweet
altruistic	courteous	honorable	nice	sympathetic
amiable	dedicated	hospitable	obliging	tender
benevolent	devoted	humane	open	thoughtful
benign	empathetic	interested	optimistic	tolerant
brotherly	fair	just	patient	trustworthy
caring	faithful	kind	peaceful	truthful
charitable	forgiving	kindly	pleasant	understanding
comfortable	generous	lovable	reasonable	warm
congenial	genuine	loving	receptive	worthy

Miscellaneous Emotions

confused	exhausted	pained	serious	
curious	hysterical	perplexed	thoughtful	
excited	mischievous	puzzled	undecided	

Quantity

ample	few	lots	paucity	scarcity
abundant	heavy	many	plentiful	skimpy
chock-full	lavish	meager	plenty	sparing
copious	liberal	much	profuse	sparse
dearth	light	numerous	scads	sufficient
empty	loads	oodles	scant	well-stocked

Relationships

abandoned	controlled	deserted	ignored	rejected
attacked	criticized	dominated	insulted	shamed
betrayed	crushed	doubted	neglected	unloved
blamed	defensive	hurt	oppressed	wounded

Sad

| depressed | empty | hurt | lovesick | sorry for self |
| disappointed | grieving | lonely | miserable | sullen |

Sight—Appearance

| adorable | beautiful | bright | broad | bloody |
| alert | blinding | brilliant | blonde | blushing |

Descriptive Words Continued

chubby	dim	graceful	narrow	sparkling
clean	distinct	grotesque	obtuse	spotless
clear	dull	hazy	rotund	square
cloudy	elegant	high	round	steep
colorful	fancy	hollow	pale	stormy
contoured	filthy	homely	poised	straight
crinkled	flat	light	quaint	strange
crooked	fluffy	lithe	shadowy	ugly
crowded	foggy	low	shady	unsightly
crystalline	fuzzy	misty	shallow	unusual
curved	glamorous	motionless	sheer	weird
cute	gleaming	muddy	shiny	wide
dark	glistening	murky	skinny	wizened
deep	glowing	nappy	smoggy	

Size

ample	elfin	immense	miniature	stupendous
average	enormous	large	minute	tall
behemoth	fat	little	petite	tiny
big	giant	long	portly	towering
bulky	gigantic	mammoth	prodigious	vast
colossal	great	massive	puny	voluminous
diminutive	huge	microscopic	short	wee
dwarfed	hulking	middle-sized	small	

Smell—Taste

acrid	fragrant	putrid	sour	sweet
antiseptic	fresh	ripe	spicy	tangy
bitter	juicy	rotten	stale	tart
choking	medicinal	salty	sticky	tasteless
clean	nutty	savory	strong	tasty
delicious	peppery	smoky	stuffy	

Sound

bang	groan	melodic	screech	thud
booming	growl	moan	shrill	thump
buzz	harsh	mute	silent	thunderous
clatter	high-pitched	noisy	snarl	tinkle
cooing	hiss	purring	snort	voiceless
crash	hoarse	quiet	soft	wail
crying	hushed	raspy	splash	whine
deafening	husky	resonant	squeak	whispered
faint	loud	screaming	squeal	

Time

ancient	brief	centuries	crawling	daybreak
annual	brisk	continual	dawn	daylight

The Reading Teacher's Book of Lists, Fifth Edition, © 2006 by John Wiley & Sons, Inc.

decade	intermittent	noonday	rapid	swift
dusk	late	old	short	tardy
early	lengthy	old-fashioned	slowly	twilight
eons	long	outdated	speedy	whirlwind
evening	modern	periodic	sporadic	yearly
fast	moments	punctual	sunrise	years
flash	noon	quick	sunset	young

Touch

boiling	dirty	grubby	shaggy	stinging
breezy	dry	hard	sharp	tender
bumpy	dusty	hot	silky	tight
chilly	filthy	icy	slick	uneven
cold	flaky	loose	slimy	waxen
cool	fluffy	melted	slippery	wet
creepy	fluttering	plastic	slushy	wooden
crisp	frosty	prickly	smooth	yielding
cuddly	fuzzy	rainy	soft	
curly	gooey	rough	solid	
damp	greasy	sandpapery	sticky	

Fun Facts About Words

Question:

How many words are there in the English language?

Answer:

The largest English dictionary, the Oxford English Dictionary (OED),

has 17,476 different words.

About half are nouns, a quarter are adjectives,

and a seventh are verbs.

See also List 32, Synonyms; List 97, Activities for Language Development.

LIST 81. STORY STARTERS

Writer's block happens to even the best writers. Use these to ignite students' imaginations and get them started. You can also use these as starters for a group writing project. Post a story starter on newsprint or on the computer at the writing station. During the course of a day (or week) each student reads the story so far and adds another sentence or paragraph. At the end of the period, the story is read aloud and printed. Each student, then, writes a suitable ending for the story as an at home or independent writing assignment. When using these for individual writing experiences, remind students to use the Descriptive Words list for ideas for adding color and detail to their stories.

1. Grandpa's attic is full of old clothes and other stuff from long ago. My sisters and I like to go up there and make believe we are . . .

2. Just as she settled into her favorite chair to read her book, Jessica's cell phone rang. "Who would be calling this late at night?"

3. It was just after noon when Andrew hungrily opened his Justice League lunch box. He couldn't have been more surprised. Right next to the apple he found . . .

4. If you think about it, every season has its good points and its bad points. For me, the best thing about winter is . . .

5. Mom told me to look left and look right before I crossed the street. But she never told me to look up! I was about halfway across when BOOM! It fell from the sky and landed right in front of me. Well, finders, keepers . . .

6. Garret and Clayton were excited as they boarded the plane to visit their grandparents' farm in New York. But they were going to miss all the things they usually saw when their father drove them to the farm.

7. The ball crashed through the window. "Oh, no," Alex said aloud. "Who's in trouble now?"

8. The first one had been perfect. Then the second one, well, near perfect. Could I get three in a row and win? I held my breath and tried not to think of the crowd.

9. The perfectly formed footprint was the biggest one David had ever seen out on the trail. What had long thin toes like that? He bent down to look at it closer. He as studying the footprint when he heard the sound and turned to look behind him.

10. "This will show them," Emily thought as she hammered the last nail into place.

11. My brother Philip is fussy. He doesn't like many foods. So we experimented in the kitchen. That's how we discovered the prize-winning recipe for chocolate-covered . . .

12. The directions on the package said to pour the powder into a large bowl and then briskly stir in a cup of water. As I stirred the mix, a sweet smelling smoke came up out of the bowl and swirled over my head. I looked up. Through the haze I saw two bright eyes. "That's quite enough, now. And, thank you for the water. I was very thirsty."

13. Tiptoeing in the dark, Jenn stepped around the desk. She pushed Professor Dracket's chair against the wall so she could open the center drawer. Freeing Benji may turn out easier than she thought it would be. After class, she had seen Dracket drop the key the drawer. All she had to do now was take the key, sneak into the lab, and open the cube.

14. Taking his cloak from the peg on the wall, Steven looked around the room one last time. "I will miss this place," he said to himself. As he left the Hall of Years he heard a faint reply: "We'll miss you, too." Without looking back, Steven stepped across the threshold and into the mist. He knew his first challenge was to cross the Smoking River. As he started walking toward its shore he had an idea . . .

The Reading Teacher's Book of Lists, Fifth Edition, © 2006 by John Wiley & Sons, Inc.

15. Candi brought the mail into the kitchen and sat down at the table. "Lots of junk mail," she thought as she sorted through the stack throwing most of the envelopes in the trash. Then, she saw it. The trademark gold envelope. She was picked for the new Incredible Journeys show! Where would they send her? She held her breath as she opened it. Of all the places in the world, she was going to . . .

16. For a long time, I thought every day was pretty much the same as the next. I got up, went to school, came home, had supper, did homework, watched TV, and went to bed. Then I did it again. That all changed the day I discovered . . .

17. "Wait right there—don't move! I'm coming to get you! I'm coming!" the voice called urgently. Surprised, Hanna looked down the tree and saw . . .

18. Tomorrow is my Great-Granny's birthday. Everyone is so excited. She's going to be 100! I love to visit with her. She tells me stories about when she was young. Would you believe back then they didn't have . . .

19. Saturday was a very rainy day. The sky was a funny gray, almost white. The rain was coming down hard and straight. Well, it might not be a good day for a bike ride, thought Jared, but it was a perfect day for Jacob and me to . . .

20. The directions on the box said, "Washes off with warm water." Jaime had been trying to wash it off for an hour. But it was still there. How could she explain why her face was . . .

21. Yabbo checked the instruments. Everything was ready. In just a few minutes they would leave the shelter of the space station and venture forth on Terra 34. What would they find?

22. Dad's company gave him a promotion. It's a good thing, I guess. It means they think he is doing a great job. The problem is, we have to move again. This time in March. Right in the middle of the season. I wish I didn't have to go because . . .

23. Chris bent down just enough to see whether the liquid came up to the mark on the measuring glass. Nope. She needed to pour just a bit more to make it perfect. Measuring your ingredients is important. She learned that last year in Potions 101. Tom had put just a pinch too much of toads' tail in his kettle and, "poof." The green smoke rose so quickly they had all breathed in it. It wasn't much fun hopping from place to place. Luckily that problem lasted only a day. But, if she were to mix in too much oil of . . .

24. The absent-minded old man left the door to the car open and his keys inside while he carried his groceries into the house. That was all the time the thief needed to steal the car. As he climbed in, he reached around the wheel and turned the key. The engine sprang to life. He put the car in gear and stepped on the gas just as the old man came from the house. "Nadine! Nadine!" he cried. "Who's Nadine?" the car thief wondered. Just as he had that thought . . .

25. The winds were strong. So strong that you had to hold onto your hat with both hands. I felt silly walking down the street like that. Arms up. Elbows out. Leaves and old newspapers blew passed me. All of a sudden, I felt a claw circle my waist and yank me off the ground and into the air. I screamed as I looked over my shoulder and saw the huge . . .

The Reading Teacher's Book of Lists, Fifth Edition, © 2006 by John Wiley & Sons, Inc.

LIST 82. CHARACTERISTICS OF NARRATIVE AND EXPOSITORY TEXT

Pre-reading and early reading experiences help students develop frameworks for dealing with narratives. Most students, by the time they are learning to read, are sufficiently familiar with "Once upon a time"—they recognize it as the beginning of a fairy tale. But many other characteristics and conventions of text are not so familiar. Use this list to discuss differences between narrative and expository text.

Narrative (Stories)	Expository (Explanations)
Many based on common events from life	Often about topics not known
Familiarity makes prediction easier	New information makes prediction harder
Familiarity makes inferences easier	New information makes inferences harder
Key vocabulary often known	Key vocabulary often new
Simple vocabulary	Multisyllabic vocabulary, roots + affixes
Cause and effect known	Cause and effect not known
Concrete, real concepts	Abstract concepts
People oriented	Thing or subject oriented
Dialogue makes text less concept dense	Facts make text more concept dense
Stories can have personal meaning	Explanations have impersonal meaning
May give insight for own life/interest	May have no relation to own life/interest
Purpose is to entertain or share experience	Purpose is to explain or persuade
Chronological structure	Structure varies: definition/example; cause and effect; sequence of steps; main idea/details; examples/generalization
Simple concepts	Complex concepts
Familiar story types	Presentation varies; few recognizable types

The Reading Teacher's Book of Lists, Fifth Edition, © 2006 by John Wiley & Sons, Inc.

See also List 63, Genre.

LIST 83. PROMPTS FOR EXPOSITORY WRITING

Expository writing to inform or persuade is a skill needed by every student. Expository writing helps reinforce students' content learning, provides opportunities to process new knowledge in students' own words, develops students' ability to communicate clearly, and, enables students to perform well on standardized writing assessments.

Many teachers use a five-step writing process with one step each day: Prepare (think and organize), Draft, Revise content, Edit for grammar and format, and Publish. The prompts below will get your class writing from September to June. Create others from your content area lessons or other shared experiences in your classroom. Most of the topical prompts can be re-written for lower elementary grades. They can also used for group writing, debates, panel discussions, and oral reports.

1. Emily Post is famous for her books on manners and suggestions for how people of all ages should behave at meals and in other social situations. Write a list of good manners (at least 7) that you believe everyone in your class should follow. Put the most important one first.

2. Playgrounds, beaches, and parks are taken care of by our government. They are paid for with money from taxes. Does your city or town have enough "green spaces" for its citizens health and recreation needs? Write a letter to the mayor telling what you think.

3. Pablo Picasso is a world famous painter. He was born in 1881 and started the art style called *cubism*. It uses strong lines and vivid colors. Talent for art and music must be developed. Do you think art and music lessons should be part of every school day? Write an essay explaining why or why not.

4. Giving gifts is part of many holiday traditions. Interview three people, including one adult, and ask them for advice about how to pick out a gift for someone. Use their suggestions to write a "Tips for buying gifts" article for the school newspaper.

5. Each fall, thousands of people go to New York City to run in the Marathon. Many train for years and run in local races as practice. Use the Internet to find advice for young people who want to begin to run as an exercise or sport. Write an article about how to get started. You may include a weeklong schedule, tips for safety, and recommendations for where to run in your city or town.

6. Some people have unusual pets. Pick an unusual animal you would like to have as a pet. Find out about it and write a paper explaining how to care for it. Include a description of the pet, its size when it is an adult, the kind of habitat it needs, its food, and any other information you or a friend would need to know before you purchased one.

7. On Election Day, adults elect others to serve in important government positions. Through this process citizens pick the people who will make laws, administer them, and decide whether the laws have been followed or broken. This is what makes a democracy. Unfortunately, some people don't bother to vote. Write a letter to an adult and urge him or her to vote in the next election. Use a chart to show the pro's and con's of voting.

8. Everyone knows that smoking is bad for your health. It can cause serious medical problems like cancer. Write a letter to someone you know and ask him or her to pick a "Break the Habit" date to stop smoking. Include reasons why it is important for this particular person and you. Go online and find suggestions to help them quit and include them in your writing.

PROMPTS FOR EXPOSITORY WRITING CONTINUED

9. James Naismith was a physical education teacher. In 1891, he invented a game that could be played indoors during the cold and snowy months. He nailed peach baskets to the gym walls and had his students toss soccer balls into them. To make it more fun, he divided the class into teams and assigned points for each "basket" they made. Now, more than 100 years later, basketball is a major sport played in schools and by professional teams worldwide. Does being on a sports team help students? Write an essay to persuade others that your view is correct.

10. More than a hundred years ago, Alfred Nobel invented dynamite. It was used in mining and for leveling the ground for roads and railways. Later it was used in wars. Nobel was troubled that what he invented for good purposes also resulted in the death of many people. Think of another invention that has been used both to help and to hurt people. List the ways it helps and hurts. Then answer the question: Is this a "good" invention? Write your answer to persuade others of your view.

11. Many things we do every day seem simple but have many steps. Write directions for making toast, putting on a sweater, or tying your sneakers. Include a list of things that are needed and a numbered set of steps that tell what to do. Add drawings or diagrams to help others see what you mean. You may use a digital camera to take pictures of each step in the process.

12. Teams from more than 75 countries participate in the Winter Olympics. There are events in seven sports: biathlon, bobsled, curling, ice hockey, luge, skating, and skiing. Use an almanac or the website www.olympic.org. to find the gold medal winners of the last winter games. Make a table showing the five countries that won the most gold medals and which sport they were in. Think about your data. Write a brief summary of the results.

13. The first CD player went on sale in 1982 for $625 and few people could afford them. Now they cost much less and many people have them. Go online and find how to clean and care for your CDs and DVDs. Write a paper called "Caring for Your CDs and DVDs." Use at least a bulleted or numbered list in your paper.

14. At the end of 2004, an earthquake in the Indian Ocean caused a giant tsunami that caused huge damage and killed many people. What are tsunamis and earthquakes and how are they related? Use two or more sources to find out. Then write a paper explaining what you learned. Add diagrams to show the earthquake and the tsunami.

15. On class trips, you travel and learn. In 2000, an American and Russian team moved into the International Space Station miles above the earth. They proved that people could live in space safely. Imagine you are a travel agent for educational trips. Write an advertising brochure for a class trip to the International Space Station. Include a description of what students might see and learn about.

16. The motto of the Boy Scouts of America is, "Be Prepared." What should you do to prepare for a weather-related emergency like a blizzard, hurricane, flood, dust storm, or tornado? Find out and make a flyer that explains where to go, what to do, what supplies you should have at home, etc. to "be prepared."

17. Thomas Edison invented more than 1000 things including electric lights, the phonograph, moving pictures, and telephone transmitters. Work with two classmates to pick 10 of the most useful inventions. Find out who invented them and when. Next, add your information to the other teams and construct a timeline showing the dates, inventions, and inventors picked for the whole class.

The Reading Teacher's Book of Lists, Fifth Edition, © 2006 by John Wiley & Sons, Inc.

18. We often use directions to travel to new places. Sometimes we give directions to help others. Write the directions for traveling from your home. Include direction words (north, south, east, west, left, right, straight ahead). Include street names and a description of key buildings or other markers that will help travelers know they are on the right street. Draw a map to illustrate your directions.

19. "If at first you don't succeed, try, try, again." Trying again, keeping at it until you are successful is called "perseverance." Work with a classmate to make a list of 5 important things students in your grade need to work at to be successful. Tell why it is important to succeed with these things. Suggest ways to keep from giving up.

20. Most of the energy we have is produced by using fuels like coal and gas. These fuels are being used up. Scientists are working to find new fuels that won't run out. Conservation helps us use less fuel. Visit www.earthday.net or other websites to find out about conserving energy and creating new energy sources. Write a paper that summarizes what you learn about renewable and non-renewable energy sources.

LIST 84. HE SAID/SHE SAID

Dialogue can bring a story to life, or it can put the reader to sleep. Here are lively alternatives to ho-hum "he said/she said" exchanges. Use these vocal verbs in place of "said" or use the vocal adverbs to describe just how "he said/she said." Working with dialogue is a simple but very effective way to improve your storytelling.

Vocal Verbs

added
admitted
advised
agreed
announced
answered
argued
asked
asserted
began
bellowed
blurted
called
cautioned
claimed
commented
complained
conceded
concluded
confessed
continued
cried
demanded
exclaimed
explained
gasped
groaned
insisted
interrupted
joked
lied
mentioned

moaned
mumbled
muttered
noted
objected
observed
ordered
quipped
remarked
replied
reported
responded
said
screamed
shouted
snapped
sobbed
stated
swore
taunted
teased
told
vowed
warned
whined
whispered
yelled

Vocal Adverbs

adamantly
admiringly
adoringly
angrily

anxiously
arrogantly
bashfully
brazenly
casually
cautiously
cheerfully
clearly
cowardly
coyly
curiously
cynically
decisively
defensively
defiantly
dramatically
eerily
energetically
fiendishly
flatly
formally
gaily
gleefully
gloomily
happily
harshly
hysterically
jealously
joyfully
joyously
loudly
lovingly
meanly

meekly
mysteriously
nervously
offensively
off-handedly
pensively
proudly
questioningly
quickly
quizzically
rapidly
sadly
sarcastically
selfishly
serenely
seriously
sheepishly
shyly
sleepily
softly
sternly
stoically
stubbornly
sullenly
tauntingly
teasingly
tenderly
thankfully
thoughtfully
unexpectedly
unhappily
wisely

LIST 85. SIMILES

A simile is a figure of speech that uses the word "as" or "like." Figures of speech are used like adjectives or adverbs. They modify or describe a person, place, thing, or action with a colorful and often visual term or phrase. Creative writers and poets make good use of these. The following are frequently used similes.

Similes Using "As"

as bright as the noonday sun
as blind as a bat
as busy as a bee
as certain as death and taxes
as clear as a bell
as clear as day
as clear as the nose on your face
as cold as ice
as comfortable as an old shoe
as cool as a cucumber
as cuddly as a baby
as cute as a button
as dark as night
as deaf as a doorpost
as deep as the ocean
as dry as a bone
as fat as a pig
as flat as a pancake
as fresh as dew
as green as grass
as happy as a lark
as hard as nails
as hard as rock
as hungry as a bear
as innocent as a newborn baby
as large as life
as light as a feather
as loud as thunder
as lovely as a rose
as mad as a wethen
as meek as a lamb
as old as the hills
as quick as a wink
as quiet as a mouse
as rough as sandpaper
as skinny as a rail
as slow as molasses in January
as sly as a fox

as smart as a whip
as smooth as glass
as soft as old leather
as soft as silk
as stiff as a board
as strong as an ox
as stubborn as a mule
as sweet as honey
as white as new fallen snow

Similes Using "Like"

acts like a bull in a china shop
chatters like a monkey
cheeks like roses
cry like a baby
drinks like a fish
eat like a pig
eat like it's going out of style
eats like a bird
eyes like stars
feel like two cents
fits like a glove
fought like cats and dogs
laugh like a hyena
moves like a snail
run around like a chicken with its head
    cut off
run like a deer
sing like a bird
sit there like a bump on a log
slept like a dog
sparkled like diamonds
spoke like an orator
stood out like a sore thumb
waddle like a duck
walk like an elephant
work like a dog
works like a charm

See also List 80, Descriptive Words; List 86, Metaphors; List 183, Common Word Idioms.

LIST 86. METAPHORS

Metaphors are figures of speech that compare two things, but do not use the words "like" or "as." These colorful phrases are used like adverbs or adjectives to describe persons, places, things, or actions; however, some metaphors are used so often that they lose their appeal. Metaphors do not have literal meanings, so they are sometimes difficult for English language learners. This list will help you familiarize students with how metaphors work and enable them to recognize them in print as well as write their own.

The small boat was a ping-pong ball bouncing around on the waves.

Viewed from the airplane, the rush-hour traffic was an army of ants working its way slowly toward home.

There was no rush, so we sent the letter by snail mail.

Michael clammed up and refused to say anything.

At a flick of a switch, the theater came alive with music.

The car slowed as it approached the hairpin turn.

I work so hard during the day that I become a couch potato at night.

Her eyes lit up when she saw that her friend was safe.

The birch tree danced in the breeze.

The fog was a blanket covering the valley floor.

The stars were diamonds sparkling in the sky.

Her heart was overflowing with kindness.

She was so shy that she kept her ideas bottled up inside her.

Mr. Mather's bark is worse than his bite.

The air conditioning was so strong that the room became an icebox.

That car is a dinosaur. It's time to get a new one.

The toddler was a clinging vine on his mother.

The children grew up near a lake and were fish in the water.

My mother gave me a real tongue lashing when she saw my poor grades.

The branches of the tree were fingernails scratching my bedroom window.

The students were so excited about the new project that they became a fountain of ideas.

The growing boy's stomach was a bottomless pit.

Her porcelain skin contributed to her beauty.

The Reading Teacher's Book of Lists, Fifth Edition, © 2006 by John Wiley & Sons, Inc.

LIST 87. NON-DISCRIMINATORY LANGUAGE GUIDELINES

"Sticks and stones can break my bones, but words can never hurt me." Remember this childhood refrain? We knew, even at the age of five or six, that it wasn't true and that name calling and taunts hurt. Now we know that even subtle, unintended biased or discriminatory words hurt students' self-esteem as well as their relationships with others. The guidelines below address typical problems relating to gender, race, ethnicity, age, and disability encountered in school writing. Make a conscious effort to use and teach inclusive positive language in your classes.

Instead of	Use	Comment/Rule
actor, actress	actor	Accepted term for both men and women.
alumnus/a, alumni/ae	alum(s), graduate(s)	Use gender-neutral word.
anchorman	anchor, news anchor	Use gender-neutral word.
benefactor, benefactress	benefactor	Accepted term for both men and women.
businessman, businessmen, salesman, sales lady, sales girl	business owner, manager, shop owner, executive, company owner, retailer, sales manager, sales representative, salesperson, sales associate, sales clerk	Use gender-neutral word.
chairman	chairperson, chair	Use gender-neutral word.
cleaning lady, maid	housekeeper, house cleaner, room staff, cleaning person	Use gender-neutral word.
clergyman/clergymen	priest(s), rabbi(s), pastor(s), member(s) of the clergy, the clergy	Use gender-neutral word.
congressman/congressmen	member(s) of Congress, legislator(s), representative(s), senator(s)	Use gender-neutral word.
fireman, policeman, mailman, postman	firefighter, police officer, mail carrier, letter carrier, postal worker	Use gender-neutral word.
forefathers	ancestors	Use inclusive group word.
freshman, freshmen	first-year students	Use gender-neutral word.
mankind	human beings, humanity, people, humankind	Use inclusive group word.
housewife	homemaker	Use gender-neutral word.
Man has inhabited . . .	People have inhabited . . ., Humans have inhabited . . .	Use inclusive group words.

NON-DISCRIMINATORY LANGUAGE GUIDELINES CONTINUED

man-made	machine-made, manufactured	Use gender-neutral word.
man-made diamond	synthetic diamond	Use gender-neutral word.
manpower	personnel, staff, workers, employees	Use inclusive group word.
patron, patroness	patron	Accepted term for both men and women
stewardess, steward	flight attendant	Use gender-neutral word.
waiter(s), waitress(es)	server, wait staff	Use gender-neutral word.
weatherman	meteorologist, weathercaster, weather reporter	Use gender-neutral word.
workman, workmen	worker(s)	Use gender-neutral word.
Dear Sir:	Dear Editor: (or Service Manager, Service Representative, Colleague, Members of the Committee, etc.); To Whom It May Concern:	Use gender-neutral word.
A senator appoints his own office staff.	Office staff are appointed by the senator.	Avoid gender-specific pronouns.
The student will choose his or her final project by mid-semester.	Students will choose their final projects by mid-semester.	Use plural forms.
The student will choose his final project by mid-semester.	Final projects will be chosen by mid-semester.	Rewrite to avoid gender reference.
Man's scientific discovery is limited only by his diligence.	Scientific discovery is limited only by our diligence.	Use first-person plural to be inclusive.
Each hiker should bring his own gear.	Hikers should bring their own gear.	Use plural forms.
The nurse will explain it to her patients.	Nurses will explain it to their patients.	Use plural form; avoid stereotype.
The male nurse said . . . The woman dentist said . . .	The nurse said . . . The dentist said . . .	Use inclusive term with no gender-added descriptor.
The child suffers from lack of mothering.	The child suffers from lack of nurturing (parenting).	Use inclusive nonstereo-type words.
The chairman said . . .	The chairperson (moderator, chair, leader, facilitator)	Use inclusive term.
Afro-American, Oriental, Asiatic	African American, black, Asian, Pacific Islander, Chinese American, Japanese American, Korean	Use preferred terms. Use country of origin with "American."

The Reading Teacher's Book of Lists, Fifth Edition, © 2006 by John Wiley & Sons, Inc.

Indians, Eskimos, natives, aborigines	Native Americans, Inuit, Alaska Natives, native peoples, aboriginal peoples, early inhabitants	Use preferred terms. Use tribal name (Navajo, Hopi, etc.), if known.
Hispanic (acceptable)	Hispanic, Latino, Latinos, Latina, Latinas, Puerto Rican, Mexican American, Cuban, Cuban American, Colombian	Use preferred terms. Use country of origin, if known.
the black teacher, the Hispanic math teacher	the teacher, the math teacher	Avoid unnecessary emphasis on race or other differences.
the elderly, the aged, old, geriatric, old folks	seniors, senior citizens, older people, older person, persons over 65 (or specific age)	Use nonstereotype term. Keep emphasis on person, not descriptor.
the disabled, the handicapped	persons with disabilities, persons with mobility (or visual etc.) impairments	Keep emphasis on person, not descriptor.
wheelchair-bound	person who uses a wheelchair	Keep emphasis on person, not descriptor.
AIDS sufferer, person afflicted with AIDS	person living with AIDS (HIV)	Keep emphasis on person, not descriptor.
the deaf, the blind	people who are deaf, child with a hearing loss, child who is hard of hearing, deaf persons, people who are blind, child with low vision, child who is visually impaired, blind persons	Keep emphasis on person, not descriptor.
the retarded children, the slow children, the mentally impaired children, the mentally handicapped children, brain-damaged children	children with developmental disabilities, children with learning disabilities, children with ADHD, children with ADD, children who have had brain injuries, etc.	Use accepted terms. Keep emphasis on person, not descriptor. Developmental disabilities include: autism, epilepsy, seizure disorders, conditions caused by diseases like muscular dystrophy and cerebral palsy, sensory disorder, and congenital disabilities.

Non-discriminatory Language Guidelines Continued

autistic child	child with autism	Keep emphasis on person, not descriptor.
mentally or emotionally disabled	person with schizophrenia, person with a personality disorder	Use accepted terms. Keep emphasis on person, not descriptor.
crazy, psychotic, neurotic	person with a psychiatric disability, person with an emotional disorder, person with a mental disorder, person with a cognitive impairment, etc.	Use accepted terms. Keep emphasis on person, not descriptor.
long-time drug user	person with history of substance abuse	Use accepted terms. Keep emphasis on person, not descriptor.
the special student	student with a disability	Avoid vague or euphemistic terms.
the mother who is a cancer victim	the mother who has cancer	Avoid emotional words like *victim* and *sufferer*.

The Reading Teacher's Book of Lists, Fifth Edition, © 2006 by John Wiley & Sons, Inc.

LIST 88. BUILD-A-SENTENCE

Select one from each column.

Who? (subject noun)	What? (verb predicate)	Why? (prepositional phrase)	When? (adverb)	Where? (object)
A boy	climbed into an airplane	for a vacation	last summer	in New York
The shark	looked everywhere	to find his mother	in 2020	on the moon
A big dump truck	slid		during the game	outside my house
The monster	laughed	to get a million dollars	next year	in a cave
	swam			on a farm
My dad	dove	for fun	today	under a rock
A rattlesnake	swung on a rope	because he was on fire	at midnight	next to a lion
Maria	fell	to fall in love	forever	100 feet beneath the ocean
Mickey Mouse	yelled loudly		before breakfast	in bed
A tiny ant	flew	for an ice cream cone	always	on top of a tree
			500 years ago	at the circus
The train	ran fast	to build a house	right now	in front of the city hall
Iron John	jumped	to fight the enemy	in a month	in a corn field
A beautiful princess	kicked		after school	behind the stove
	couldn't stop	to get to school	in an hour	in space
			yesterday	downtown
A large bird	slithered	to be kissed	during the war	inside an egg
My good friend	crawled			in Africa
	hopped on one foot	for a coat of paint	at dawn	out West
A teacher		because it was made		on a tropical island

Feel free to add more words to make your sentence read better or add interest. You can leave out anything except a subject and a verb. Make your own Build-a-Sentence chart using a theme like a monster, earthquake, or family. Also, try adding adjectives to your sentences (usually between the articles "the," "an," or "a" and the subject/noun).

See also List 182, Basic Sentence Patterns; List 180, Parts of Speech.

LIST 89. PUNCTUATION GUIDELINES

This list will help students review the use of punctuation marks. Refer to it as part of your proofreading practice. Post an enlarged copy on the wall where students can see it during their writing activities. For an interesting lesson, give the students a passage with all capitalization and punctuation removed. Let them put the capitalization and punctuation back in.

Symbol	Name	When used
.	**Period**	1. At the end of a statement or command sentence. *Birds fly.*
		2. At the end of a command sentence. *Go home.*
		3. After most abbreviations. *Mr. Co. Ave.*
		4. To show decimals and money. *$1.95 and 3.1416.*
?	**Question Mark**	1. At the end of a question sentence. *Who is he?*
		2. To express doubt. *He ate 14 doughnuts?*
!	**Exclamation Point**	1. To show strong emotion with a word. *Great!*
		2. To show strong emotion with a sentence. *You're the best!*
" "	**Quotation Marks**	1. To show a direct quote. *She said, "May I help you?"*
		2. To set off a title of a short poem. *He read "A Visit from Saint Nicholas"*
		3. To imply sarcasm or someone else's use of a term. *The "hero" was not at home.*
' '	**Single Quotation**	Used inside quotation marks. *She said, "You call him a 'friend' of yours?"*
'	**Apostrophe**	1. To form the possessive. *Bill's bike*
		2. In contractions, to show missing letters. *Isn't*
		3. To form the plurals of symbols. *Two A's*
,	**Comma**	1. To separate items in a series. *One, two, three*
		2. To separate things in a list. *bread, milk, cheese*
		3. To separate parts of a date. *February 22, 2006*
		4. After the greeting in a friendly letter. *Dear Gerry,*
		5. After the closing in a letter. *Sincerely,*
		6. To separate the city and state in an address. *New York, NY*
		7. To separate a name and a degree title. *Jenn Stock, M.D.*
		8. Between inverted names. *Smith, Joe*
		9. In written dialogue between the quotation and the rest of the sentence. *She said, "Stop it." "Ok," he replied.*
		10. Between more than one adjective or adverb. *the big, bad wolf*

The Reading Teacher's Book of Lists, Fifth Edition, © 2006 by John Wiley & Sons, Inc.

11. To set off a descriptive or parenthetical word or phrase. *Tina, the announcer, read her lines.*
12. Between a dependent and independent clause. *After the game, we went home.*
13. To separate independent clauses. *I like him, and he likes me.*
14. To set off incidental words. *I saw it, too. Naturally, I went along. Oh, I didn't see you.*

( )   **Parentheses**

1. To show supplementary material. *The map (see below) is new.*
2. To set off a word or phrase more strongly than with commas. *Joe (the first actor) was ready.*
3. In numbering or lettering a series. *Choices: (a) a game or (b) a song; two steps: (1) Open the door. (2) Step in.*

:   **Colon**

1. To introduce a series. *He has three things: a pen, a book, and a backpack.*
2. To show a subtitle. *The book: How to read it.*
3. To separate clauses. *The rule is this: Keep it simple.*
4. After a business letter greeting. *Dear Ms. Polk:*
5. To separate hours and minutes or to show ratio. *10:15 A.M. 3:1 ratio*

;   **Semicolon**

1. To separate sentence parts more strongly than a comma. *November was cold; January was freezing.*
2. To separate sentence parts that contain commas. *He was tired; therefore, he took a nap.*

-   **Hyphen**

Used in compound words that are adjectives. *the brick-faced house*

–   **En Dash**

To show period of time or space between. *2000–2005, Chicago–Boston*

—   **Em Dash**

To show the insertion of a word or phrase. *Carla—the tallest student—held the flag.*
This is also called parenthetical material as the same material can be set off by commas or parentheses at the option of the writer. Most writers do not distinguish between an Em Dash and an En Dash; they just use a dash, which is also often the Hyphen key.

PUNCTUATION GUIDELINES CONTINUED

. . .	**Ellipsis**	1. To show that words have been left out. *The boy . . . was not at home . . . but his mom answered the phone.*
		2. To show a pause for suspense or to heighten mood. *The announcer called out, "The winner is . . . Chris."*
•	**Bullet**	To show the items in a list. *Things to do on Saturday* • *Go swimming* • *Visit Uncle Chuck* • *Clean my room.*
/	**Slash, Virgule, Stroke, Diagonal**	1. To show lines of poetry. *Twinkle, twinkle, little star/how I wonder . . .*
		2. To set off numbers or symbols. */a/ first point, /b/ second point*
		3. To indicate phonemes. */b/ is the first phoneme in "boy"*
		4. To show common fractions. *3/4*

See also List 123, Fluency and Punctuation.

The Reading Teacher's Book of Lists, Fifth Edition, © 2006 by John Wiley & Sons, Inc.

LIST 90. WRITEABILITY CHECKLIST

The following is a list of suggestions for writing materials that are on an easy readability level. You can also use this as a readability checklist.

Vocabulary

❏ Avoid large and/or infrequent words. (submit—send)

❏ For high-frequency words use lists such as the Carroll, Davies, Richman word list (*The American Heritage Word Frequency Book,* Boston: Houghton-Mifflin, 1971) or 3000 Instant Words. (See List 16, Instant Words.)

❏ Avoid words with Latin and Greek prefixes. (See List 34.) (implement—carry out)

❏ Avoid jargon. (terms known in only one field)

❏ Okay to use technical words but make sure to define them and, if possible, give an example when you use them for the first time.

Sentences

❏ Keep sentences short on the average. For adults, keep average sentence below fifteen words.

❏ Avoid splitting sentence kernel (embedding).

❏ Keep verb active (avoid nominalizations).

❏ Watch out for too many commas. (See List 89, Punctuation Guidelines.)

❏ Semicolons and colons may indicate need for new sentence.

Paragraphs

❏ Keep paragraphs short on the average.

❏ One-sentence paragraphs are permissible at times.

❏ Indent and line up lists. (Keep lists out of paragraph.)

Organization

❏ Suit organization plan to topic and your purpose.

❏ Try to use SER—Statement, Example, Restatement.

❏ Use subheads.

❏ Use signal words. (See List 118, Signal Words.)

❏ Use summaries.

❏ Watch cohesion.

Personal Words

❏ Use personal pronouns, but not too many. (*Example:* I, you)

❏ Use personal sentences. (*Example:* 1. Sentences directed at reader, "You should . . . " 2. Dialogue sentences, "Dick said, 'Hello.'")

For further information, see the chapter "Writeability: The principles of writing for increased comprehension" in *Readability, Its Past, Present, and Future* 1988. Published by the International Reading Association, Newark, DE.

WRITEABILITY CHECKLIST CONTINUED

Imageability

- ❏ Use more concrete or high imagery words.
- ❏ Avoid abstract or low imagery words.
- ❏ Use vivid examples.
- ❏ Use similes and metaphors. (See List 85, Similes, and List 86, Metaphors.)
- ❏ Use graphs whenever appropriate. (See List 134, Graph Types.)

Referents

- ❏ Avoid too many referents (*Example:* it, them, they). Replace some referents with nouns or verbs.
- ❏ Avoid too much distance between noun and referent.
- ❏ Don't use referent that could refer to two or more nouns or verbs.

Motivation

- ❏ Select interesting topics.
- ❏ Select interesting examples.
- ❏ Write at level that is a little below your audience. (See List 100, Readability Graph.)

The Reading Teacher's Book of Lists, Fifth Edition, © 2006 by John Wiley & Sons, Inc.

LIST 91. PROOFREADING
CHECKLIST—ELEMENTARY

Check

❑   It says what I wanted it to say.

❑   Every sentence is a complete thought. (Contains a subject and a verb.)

❑   No words are missing.

❑   Every sentence begins with a capital letter.

❑   Every sentence has an end mark.

❑   Every word is spelled correctly.

❑   I checked the verb forms I used.

❑   I checked the pronouns I used.

❑   I checked all punctuation marks.

❑   I indented the first line of every paragraph.

❑   My writing is neat and can be read.

❑   I used interesting words instead of the most common ones.

❑   If it is a letter, it has the correct format.

❑   If it is a story, it has an interesting title.

LIST 92. PROOFREADING
CHECKLIST—INTERMEDIATE

Content

Did I:

- ❏ Stick to my topic?
- ❏ Use good sources for information?
- ❏ Use enough sources for information?
- ❏ Organize my information carefully? (sequence, logical order, Q/A, main idea/supporting details, thesis statement/arguments, etc.)
- ❏ Check my facts?
- ❏ Consider/use graphs, tables, charts for data?
- ❏ Consider my readers and select words to catch their interest? to help them understand? to create images in their minds? to help them follow the sequence?
- ❏ Use sufficient detail and description?

Format

Did I:

- ❏ Choose an appropriate title?
- ❏ Use quotations correctly?
- ❏ Use headings and subheadings?
- ❏ Label graphs, charts, and tables?
- ❏ Include a list of resources or bibliography?
- ❏ Number the pages?
- ❏ Include my name, class, and date?

Mechanics

Did I:

- ❏ Check sentences for completeness and sense?
- ❏ Check for consistent verb tense?
- ❏ Check for consistent point of view?
- ❏ Check for subject–verb agreement?
- ❏ Check for proper use of pronouns?
- ❏ Check all spelling?
- ❏ Check for end marks and other punctuation?
- ❏ Check for capital letters and underlining?
- ❏ Check for paragraph indentations?
- ❏ Check legibility?

LIST 93. PROOFREADING MARKS

Helping students develop essays, short stories, term papers, or other writing goes more smoothly when you use proofreading symbols. Introduce these early in the school year and use them throughout. The time and space saved may be devoted to comments on content and encouragement.

Notation in Margin	How Indicated in Copy	Explanation
¶	true. The best rule to follow	New paragraph
⌒	living room	Close up
#	Mary hada	Insert space
∿	Mary had a lamb little	Transpose
sp	There were 5 children.	Spell out
cap	mary had a little lamb.	Capitalize
lc	Mary had a little Lamb.	Lower case
ℒ	The correct procedure	Delete or take out
stet	Mary had a little lamb.	Restore crossed-out word(s) (let stand as before corrected)
little	Mary had a lamb.	Insert word(s) in margin
⊙	Birds fly	Insert a period
⸴	Next the main	Insert a comma
BF	Mary had a little lamb.	Boldface
ital	Mary had a _little_ lamb.	Italicize
u.s.	Mary had a little lamb.	Underline (or underscore)

See also List 91, Proofreading Checklist—Elementary; List 92, Proofreading Checklist—Intermediate; List 94, Teacher's Correction Marks.

LIST 94. TEACHER'S CORRECTION MARKS

ab	abbreviation problem	**pass**	misuse of passive voice
agr	agreement problem	**pr ref**	pronoun reference problem
amb	ambiguous	**pun**	punctuation needed or missing
awk	awkward expression or construction	**reas**	reasoning needs improvement
cap	capitalize	**rep**	unnecessary repetition
case	error in case	**ro**	run-on
cp	comma problem	**shift**	faulty tense shift
cs	comma splice	**sp**	incorrect spelling
d	inappropriate diction	**thesis**	improve the thesis
det	details are needed	**trans**	improve the transition
dm	dangling modifier	**tx**	topic sentence needed (or improved)
dn	double negative	**u**	usage problem
frag	fragment	**uw**	unclear wording
ital	italics or underline	**v**	variety needed
lc	use lower case	**vag**	vague
mm	misplaced modifier	**ve**	verb error
num	numbers problem	**vt**	verb tense problem
^	insert	**w**	wordy
¶	new paragraph needed	**wc**	better word choice
||	faulty parallelism	**wm**	word missing
,	insert comma	**ww**	wrong word

The Reading Teacher's Book of Lists, Fifth Edition, © 2006 by John Wiley & Sons, Inc.

See also List 91, Proofreading Checklist—Elementary; List 92, Proofreading Checklist—Intermediate; List 93, Proofreading Marks.

7

TEACHING
IDEAS

LIST 95. GOOD IDEAS FOR READING TEACHERS

Teachers get some of the best advice from other teachers. Here are some suggestions from a wide range of reading specialists and researchers.

1. Integrate reading into the curriculum and make it part of social studies and math; integrate the language arts of reading, spelling, and writing.

2. Use a variety of teaching methods and strategies, phonics, comprehension, fluency, etc.

3. Give plenty of reading practice for fluency and automaticity.

4. Use formal and informal assessment and diagnosis.

5. Use good reading materials: literature, expository, and variety.

6. Teach phonics and decoding, especially for beginners.

7. Develop vocabulary, both general and in subject areas.

8. Emphasize comprehension.

9. Pay attention to individual differences; tackle problems early.

10. Theory is important: schema, goals, emergent literacy, text structure, motivation, and success.

11. Have students read a passage and restate it in their own words—a simple, but important technique.

12. Preview difficult vocabulary before asking students to read a passage; discuss the words and related words. Have students keep a log of new words and their meanings.

13. Work on fluency. Have students read a short, not too difficult passage aloud. Count the errors and mark the time in seconds. Point out errors, discuss, and have the student reread and try to improve the time and error rate. Repeat for four or five readings. Gradually move to longer, more difficult passages.

14. Match students' reading material to their reading level using standardized test scores and readability formulas. If neither are available, have the student read aloud a passage from a book. If he or she averages more than one error for every twenty words, the book is too difficult.

15. Encourage and reward practice. Musicians, sports teams, artists, and readers all need practice to improve their skills. Don't worry about students reading materials that are too easy or on unconventional subjects. Worry only if they are not reading.

16. Write every day. Reading and writing are related. Improving one improves the other. Include at least some writing every day and lots of writing some days.

17. Focus on spelling. Improving word knowledge and recognition helps reading. Target high-frequency words, subject vocabulary lists, and words students misspelled in assignments. Use spelling lessons as an opportunity to review phonics.

18. Keep interest high. Nothing works better than interest and motivation. Have fun in reading class with jokes, humorous writing, and word play of all sorts. Find out students' interests and help them find books they'll love to read.

See also List 6, Phonics Awareness; List 102, Teaching with Newspapers; List 103, One Hundred Ways to Praise; List 111, Games and Methods for Teaching.

LIST 96. STUDENTS' SUGGESTIONS FOR APPEALING READING ACTIVITIES

Positive Activities

- Teacher reads aloud whole books
- More time for independent reading
- Teacher tells about good books
- Teacher reads short segments of books
- Teacher is enthusiastic about reading
- Creative dramatics (for example: role playing)
- Teacher/Students read poetry aloud
- Students choose their own materials
- A variety of materials is used:
  Magazines
  Comic books
  Mysteries
  Books with scary themes
  Jokes
  Humorous stories
  Series books
  Sports
  Adventures
- Teacher/Students read easy-to-read books
- Books with relevant themes are used:
  Ethnic problems (for example: race problems)
  Country of origin (for example: family's nationality)
  Personal problems (for example: divorce, death, weight)

Negative Activities/Factors

- Assignments (You have to do it.)
- Worksheets, reports
- Required journal entries
- Journal entries are read aloud
- Nothing but older, dated books are available
- Small school/class libraries

Case Studies

Just about any classroom can show examples of how reading was made more appealing to students. Here are just a few examples:

- A boy who hated reading but was interested in wrestling started on a book on wrestling
- A Mexican-American girl who didn't like to read until she found Mexican-American authors
- A girls' club that read a whole series
- A young teen who memorized a driver's license manual

LIST 97. ACTIVITIES FOR LANGUAGE DEVELOPMENT

Many children love acting. With these activities they can have some fun and learn a few words at the same time. Many of these words will make children write more colorful and interesting stories.

1. In One Place—Make Your Body:

wiggle	collapse	expand	hang
wriggle	shake	contract	slouch
squirm	rock	curl	droop
stretch	sway	uncurl	sink
bend	bounce	rise	tumble
twist	bob	lurch	totter
turn	spin	lean	swing
flop	whirl	sag	

2. From Place to Place—Make Your Body:

creep	hop	meander	stalk
crawl	tramp	limp	race
roll	hustle	hobble	plod
walk	stride	stagger	amble
skip	prance	scramble	sprint
run	strut	march	slink
gallop	stroll	scurry	dodge
leap	saunter	trudge	

3. Make Your Legs and Feet:

kick	stamp	trample	mince
shuffle	tap	tip-toe	stumble
skuff	drag	slip	

4. Make Your Face:

smile	wink	yawn	wince
frown	gape	chew	grimace
sneer	scowl	stare	squint
pout	grin	glare	blink
leer	smile		

5. Make Your Hands:

open	grasp	snatch	pinch
close	clap	pluck	poke
clench	scratch	beckon	point
grab	squeeze	pick	tap
stroke	wring	slap	clasp
poke	knead	pat	rub

6. Make Your Arms and Hands:

pound	reach	thrust	throw
strike	wave	lift	fling
grind	slice	stir	catch
sweep	chop	weave	whip
cut	push	clutch	grope
beat	pull	dig	punch

ACTIVITIES FOR LANGUAGE DEVELOPMENT CONTINUED

7. Pantomime or Dramatize:

yawning	speaking	hiccupping	twittering
sighing	cooling	wheezing	crowing
groaning	calling	murmuring	lowing
moaning	chuckling	muttering	squalling
grunting	rustling	sputtering	neighing
growling	snoring	whistling	shinnying
howling	whimpering	hissing	rattling
roaring	wailing	cackling	clanging
bellowing	shouting	trilling	ringing
screeching	laughing	hooting	honking
screaming	sneezing	creaking	popping
crying	snickering	braying	clicking
sobbing	tittering	whispering	buzzing
gasping	giggling	singing	purring
shrieking	sniffing	humming	ticking
whining	panting	croaking	chirping
mumbling	coughing	barking	squeaking

8. Dramatize These Moods:

fear	boredom	despair	contempt
pain	wonder	hope	reluctance
rage	generosity	pity	admiration
joy	reverence	hate	delight
sorrow	jealousy	love	anticipation
loneliness	envy	compassion	impatience
satisfaction	resentment	horror	happiness
frustation	pride	disgust	doubt
contentment	shame	surprise	greed
discontentment	repentence	gratitude	
anxiety	resignation	gaiety	

9. Dramatize These Activities:

work	destroy	fight	plant
play	harvest	build	
worship	study	celebrate	

10. Represent:

cat	caterpillar	bee	mosquito
dog	apple tree	seagull	any living thing

The Reading Teacher's Book of Lists, Fifth Edition, © 2006 by John Wiley & Sons, Inc.

LIST 98. WAYS TO DEFINE A WORD

Following is a list of traditional and nontraditional ways to define a word. You may want to try some of these the next time you give your students a word definition assignment.

Formal Definition

word = A word is a sound or group of sounds that has meaning and is an independent unit of speech.

Definition by Example

phoneme = An example of a phoneme is the /p/ in "pin."

Definition by Description

rectangle = A rectangle is a geometric shape that has four straight line sides and four right angles.

Definition by Comparison

moon = The moon looks like a lighted disk in the sky (simile).
moon = The moon is a lighted ball in the sky (metaphor—note similes use "like" or "as").

Definition by Contrast

occupation = You might call it just a job, but I call it an occupation.

Definition by Synonym

consent = We want your consent that you agree to everything.

Definition by Antonym

dead = He wasn't dead, he was very much alive.

Definition by Apposition

(a meaning put in parentheses or set off by commas)
plaintiff = The plaintiff (person bringing suit) spoke to the judge first.
mango = The mango, the fruit that tastes something like a blend of peach and pineapple, is his favorite dessert.

Definition by Origin

telescope = The word telescope comes from the root "tele," which means "far," and the root "scope," which means "view."

Denotation and Connotative Meanings

The denotation meaning is the dictionary definition and is similar to most of the definition types listed above. The connotation meaning involves the feeling that surrounds the word. Note the differences in these words:

prison—house of correction
bum—unemployed person
moron—mentally handicapped
fat—overweight, heavy

See also List 32, Synonyms; List 33, Antonyms; List 34, Greek and Latin Roots.

LIST 99. MULTIPLE INTELLIGENCES AND READING

Howard Gardner increased our understanding of the nature of intelligence by arguing that it is not simply a matter of how smart someone is, but more a matter of *how* he or she is smart. Teachers have long respected individual differences in learning and expression and have worked to provide a range of instructional activities that allow students to learn and demonstrate their understanding in a variety of ways. This list provides examples of activities linked to each of Gardner's eight kinds of intelligence.

Verbal/Linguistic (probably the most common teaching and learning strategies; focuses on ability to read, write, and understand through the use of words)

Dictated stories	Journals and logs
Outlines	Sequenced directions
Written summaries or précis writing	Oral reports
Written reports	Essays and reaction papers
Debates	Panel discussions
Daily oral "news reports"	Word-a-day
Poetry	Dramatic reading

Visual/Spatial (ability to think and understand through pictures, diagrams, and the arrangements of objects within a picture, diagram, map, etc.)

Find pictures to represent ideas	Draw pictures to illustrate concept or things
Design a logo or icon	Color, underline, highlight to emphasize
Build a model	Construct a mobile showing interrelations
Sequence pictures to illustrate change	Follow pictograms to construct an object
Design ideographs to tell a story	Make a photo-collage on a topic
Make a video to tell a story/report	Select format, type, materials for purpose

Body/Kinesthetic (ability to use the body for expression, for skilled action, for accomplishing tasks, for creating)

Act out/dramatize an event	Show a process through dance (e.g., growth)
Use papier-mâché, other media to express	Choreograph movement to problem-solve
Grow and observe plant development	Use bodies, movement, materials to weave
"Simon Says"	Perform precision drill routines
Cooking experiences	Dissection
Science experiments	Math manipulatives
Show through pantomime	Make facial expressions to demonstrate emotional states

The Reading Teacher's Book of Lists, Fifth Edition, © 2006 by John Wiley & Sons, Inc.

See also List 97, Activities for Language Development.

Interpersonal (ability to get along with others and work together for common purposes)

Buddy learning

Reciprocal learning

Peer editing

Simulations and role play

Team competitions

Peer tutoring

Team research projects

Interviewing

Games for two or more

Class clubs

Logical/Mathematical (ability to use logic and mathematical processes to represent and manipulate ideas)

Categorize information

Compare and contrast

Create equations/rules for process/concept

Interpret data to support arguments

Use analogies, metaphors to explain

Extrapolate trends from historic data

Recognize anomalies, missing pieces

Develop flow charts, organization charts

Use formulas to compute answers

Distinguish facts from opinions

Use math processes to problem-solve

Recognize cause-and-effect relationships

Musical (ability to recognize and respond to rhythm, rhyme, tone, and other musical elements; to compose, perform, respond to musical compositions)

Listen to and appreciate rap, chants

Represent feelings with music

Create lyrics to tell story/express idea

Select music for multimedia presentation

Perform a set musical composition

Choral reading in parts

Respond to moods created by instruments

Relate musical style to social/historical idea

Sing alone or in groups

Perform an improvised musical composition

Intrapersonal (ability to know the self, to be aware of own thoughts, motivations, goals, principles, strengths and weaknesses)

Make and follow a plan

Diaries/journals/logs

Being aware of/explaining own actions

Appreciating self growth

Track own progress in learning

Create family tree and history

Develop school/personal growth portfolio

Prepare for a long-term goal

Estimate time/effort for personal activity

Metacognitive awareness during learning

Accurate self-evaluation of work/effort

Articulation of reasons for choosing hero

Link career options to personal qualities

Make scrapbook of photos/memorabilia

Environmental (ability to recognize, differentiate, appreciate objects and events in the natural world; attention to and appreciation of environment, including its natural systems)

Care for a pet

Collect and classify leaves

Experiment with simple machines

Observe and track weather for patterns

Keep an ant farm

Photograph/video one location in four seasons

Learn about and join a recycling project

Keep a log of nature's impact on daily life

LIST 100. READABILITY GRAPH

The Readability Graph is included on the next page so you will have it on hand when you need it. Use it to help judge the difficulty level of the materials your students use so that you can better match reading selections to students' reading abilities.

1. Randomly select three sample passages and count out exactly 100 words beginning with the beginning of a sentence. Count proper nouns, initializations, and numerals.

2. Count the number of sentences in the hundred words estimating length of the fraction of the last sentence to the nearest 1/10th.

3. Count the total number of syllables in the 100-word passage. If you don't have a hand counter available, an easy way is to put a mark above every syllable over one in each word, and then when you get to the end of the passage, count the number of marks and add 100. Small calculators also can be used as counters by pushing numeral "1," then push the " + " sign for each word or syllable when counting.

4. Enter graph with *average* sentence length and *average* number of syllables; plot a dot where the two lines intersect. The areas where a dot is plotted will give you the approximate grade level.

5. If a great deal of variability is found in syllable count or sentence count, putting more samples into the average is desirable.

6. A word is defined as a group of symbols with a space on either side; thus, "Joe," "IRA," "1945," and "&" are each one word.

7. A *syllable* is defined as a phonetic syllable. Generally, there are as many syllables as vowel sounds. For example, *stopped* is one syllable and *wanted* is two syllables. When counting syllables for numerals and initializations, count one syllable for each symbol. For example, *1945* is four syllables, and *IRA* is three syllables, and & is one syllable.

Example

	SYLLABLES	SENTENCES
1st hundred words	124	6.6
2nd hundred words	141	5.5
3rd hundred words	<u>158</u>	<u>6.8</u>
AVERAGE	141	6.3

READABILITY 7th GRADE (see dot plotted on graph)

The Reading Teacher's Book of Lists, Fifth Edition, © 2006 by John Wiley & Sons, Inc.

See also List 90, Writeability Checklist; List 101, Readability Score Comparisons.

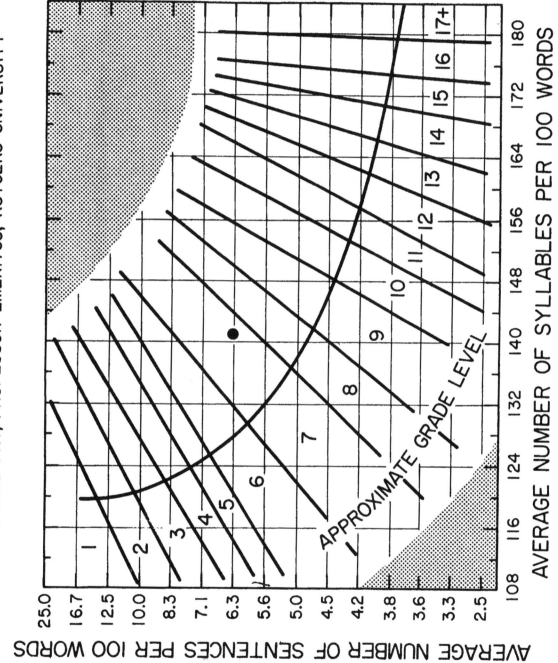

The Reading Teacher's Book of Lists, Fifth Edition, © 2006 by John Wiley & Sons, Inc.

GRAPH FOR ESTIMATING READABILITY–EXTENDED
BY EDWARD FRY, PROFESSOR EMERITUS, RUTGERS UNIVERSITY

AVERAGE NUMBER OF SYLLABLES PER 100 WORDS

AVERAGE NUMBER OF SENTENCES PER 100 WORDS

APPROXIMATE GRADE LEVEL

LIST 101. READABILITY SCORE COMPARISONS

Educators, state departments of education, researchers, and publishers use readability formulas and leveling protocols to grade books by difficulty level. The formulas rely on quantifiable features; leveling considers more subjective ones. All are designed to match their grade scores with mean grade scores on nationally standardized reading tests.

The charts below show the correlations or approximate equivalents across well-known readability and leveling scores to help you find the grade level books you are looking for, no matter which method was used.

Chart One

Readability Scores Correlation Chart Grades 1–13

Grade Level Dale-Chall, Fry, ATOS	Lexile	DRP
1	200–370	32–46
2	370–500	39–49
3	490–670	43–53
4	650–800	46–55
5	800–930	49–57
6	880–1000	51–61
7	960–1030	53–63
8	1000–1100	54–64
9	1030–1120	54–65
10	1120–1200	51–68
11	1130–1210	56–68
12	1210–1300	57–69
13–College	1320–1490	70–76

Chart Two

Leveling Scores Correlation Chart for First Grade

Basal Level	Fountas & Pinnell	Reading Recovery
PP1	C	3 & 4
PP2	D	5 & 6
PP3	E	7 & 8
Primer	F	9 & 10
Primer	G	11 & 12
Grade 1	H	13 & 14
Grade 1	I	15, 16, 17

Chart Three

Leveling Loose Correlations

Basal Level Grade	Wright Group Stage	Wright Group Level 1	Reading Recovery	Fountas & Pinnell
K–1	Early Emergent	A–D	1–4	A–G
1–2	Upper Emergent	E–J	5–17	D–I
1–2	Early Fluency	K–N	18–20	J–M
3–4	Fluency	O–T		N–R

The Reading Teacher's Book of Lists, Fifth Edition, © 2006 by John Wiley & Sons, Inc.

LIST 102. TEACHING WITH NEWSPAPERS

Newspapers—whether delivered to your home in the morning or available 24 hours a day online—are our link to current events, local news, community happenings, and much more. They record history as it happens. One mark of a literate society is the rate of newspaper readership. In reading classrooms, newspapers offer unlimited opportunities for high interest, purposeful, natural reading activities. The list below will get you started.

Primary

- Circle words that begin with the target letter.
- Make an alphabet book—cut out pictures for words that begin with each letter of the alphabet.
- Find words and pictures that belong to a category: food, home, people, community helpers, fun, sports, animals, work, clothing, buildings.
- Compare prices of food or other current sale items.
- Find people from different countries; post the pictures around a world map and connect the photos by colored yarn to the countries.
- Find pictures (comics, ads, or news) that show a feeling (happy, sad, frightened, proud, etc.).
- Find pictures (comics, ads, or news) that show a concept (sharing, learning, teamwork, etc.).
- Find words that have a target ending (-ed, -ing, -ly, -tion, -ment, -ish).
- Find money words and symbols.
- Find long words for the class to divide into syllables.
- Make a pictograph with all the faces in today's newspaper. Which group had more: male/female? young/old?
- Add pictures/headline words to word walls on nouns, verbs, adjectives, adverbs, prepositions.
- Read a suitable comic strip together; "white out" the dialogue, duplicate, and have students create new dialogue for the pictures.
- Glue suitable comic strips to tagboard, cut into frames, and have students put in proper order.
- Read comic strip with a group. Discuss sequence, what changes in language and in the pictures.
- For a month, track the temperature on a graph.
- For a month, track the number of sunny, cloudy, foggy, snowy, rainy days in a table or in a graph.
- For a five-game period, track the number of runs made by the class's favorite baseball teams; add them; compare; make tables; make pictographs; make scatter graphs.
- Using a grocery ad, list all the items that cost less than $1.00; less than $.50.
- Discuss movie ads—what they portray, what appeals and doesn't; adult or kids' movie, topic, genre (mystery, adventure, thriller, war, etc.).

See also List 95, Good Ideas for Reading Teachers.

LIST 103. ONE HUNDRED WAYS TO PRAISE

Everyone needs to be recognized for their efforts and accomplishments. Praise builds confidence, motivates, confirms, shows respect, acknowledges, rewards, and sets standards for accomplishment. Use words of praise often—even for small successes; it will encourage greater ones. Be careful, however, to match your words to the situation. Be genuine about what was praiseworthy, and about how well it was done.

GR 8!

Awesome!

Fantastic!

Great style!

This is very well organized.

Very convincing!

Good use of details.

You've really mastered this.

Excellent beginning!

That's really nice.

★ quality!

That's clever.

You're right on target.

Thank you!

Wow!

You've made my day.

Very creative.

Very interesting.

I like the way you're working.

Good thinking.

A+ work.

That's an interesting way of looking at it.

Now you've figured it out.

Keep up the good work.

Be sure to share this—it's great!

You're a Rising Star!

You're on the right track now.

You showed you're a leader on this!

This is quite an accomplishment.

I like the way you've tackled this.

Way 2 go!

That's coming along nicely.

You've shown a lot of patience with this.

You've really been paying attention.

It looks like you've put a lot of work into this.

You've put in a full day today.

This is prize-winning work.

Bravo!

I like your style.

Pulitzer Prize–winner in training.

Your work has such personality.

That's very perceptive.

Hurray!

This is a moving scene.

Your remark shows a lot of sensitivity.

Clear, concise, and complete!

A well-developed theme!

You are really in touch with the feeling here.

The Reading Teacher's Book of Lists, Fifth Edition, © 2006 by John Wiley & Sons, Inc.

You're on the ball today.

This is something special.

That's the right answer.

Exactly right.

I like your choice of words.

I can tell you were very careful with this.

You made me smile.

1 derful!

You're a great team member.

You're quite an expert.

Very informative.

You really caught on!

You're right on the mark.

Good reasoning.

I can tell you really understand this.

You made an important point here.

Dynamite!

Outstanding!

This is a winner!

Superb!

Superior work.

Super!

Great going!

Where have you been hiding all this talent?

I knew you could do it!

What neat work!

You really outdid yourself today.

That's a good point.

That's a very good observation.

That's certainly one way of looking at it.

This kind of work pleases me very much.

Congratulations! You got ____ correct today.

Terrific!

Your parents will be proud of your work.

That's an interesting point of view.

You've got it now.

You make it look so easy.

This shows you've been thinking.

You're becoming an expert at this.

Beautiful.

I'm very proud of your work today.

Excellent work.

Very good. Why don't you show the class?

The results are worth all your hard work.

You've come a long way with this one.

Marvelous.

Very fine work.

I like the way you've handled this.

This looks like it's going to be a great report.

That's quite an improvement.

What an imagination!

Phenomenal!

LIST **104.** INTEREST INVENTORY—PRIMARY

Whether choosing read-aloud books, interdisciplinary themes, or trying to reach and develop students' special interests and talents, interest inventories are a great help. For students not yet able to write their answers, use the inventories during your individual conference time with students and record their responses.

1. My favorite color is _____.

2. My favorite food is _____.

3. My favorite toy is _____.

4. My favorite game is _____.

5. My favorite story is _____.

6. My favorite sport to play is _____.

7. My favorite TV show to watch is _____.

8. My favorite person to play with is _____.

9. I like to collect _____.

10. I like to go to _____.

11. I like to learn about _____.

12. I like stories about _____.

13. I like to read about _____.

14. I have a pet named _____. It is a _____.

15. Things I like to do at school: _____.

16. Things I like to do at home: _____.

17. Things I like to do by myself: _____.

18. Things I like to do with friends: _____.

19. I go to the library.   Yes   No

20. I have a library card.   Yes   No

21. I like to read.   Yes   No

22. I read books at home.   Yes   No

23. I read magazines at home.   Yes   No

The Reading Teacher's Book of Lists, Fifth Edition, © 2006 by John Wiley & Sons, Inc.

LIST 105. INTEREST INVENTORY—ELEMENTARY/INTERMEDIATE

Knowing students' interests, preferences, and activities helps you plan instruction that builds on strengths, prior knowledge, and natural enthusiasm. This information also helps you suggest research topics, good books, and project themes. Use this inventory as a getting-to-know-you activity the first week of school.

1. What are your two favorite school subjects?_____ and _____

2. What do you like best about school? _____

3. What do you like least about school? _____

4. What do you do after school? _____

5. What do you like to read? (*circle answers*)

Stories about young people	Sports stories	Mysteries
Stories about animals	Fables/Folktales	Biographies
Stories about real people and events	Adventures	How-to-do-it books
Real science stories	Science fiction	Fantasy
Poetry		None

6. What part of the newspaper do you read (at least sometimes)? (*circle answers*)

Headlines	Sports	Comics	News	Letters to Editor
Advertisements	Classified Ads	Advice (like Dear Abby)		Fashion
Movie and Concert Reviews		Feature stories	Editorials	None

7. What magazines do you read? _____

8. What are your hobbies? _____

9. What places have you visited that you liked a lot? _____

10. Circle the things you like:

Working alone	Working with a friend	Reading	Doing projects
Using the library	Using the computer	Explaining things	Writing
Drawing/Art	Listening to music	Playing an instrument	

11. What is your favorite sport to play? _____

12. Have you played on a team?   Yes   No   Sport _____

13. What is your favorite sport to watch? _____

14. TV programs I regularly watch are _____.

15. Computer games I play are _____.

16. Three words that describe you: _____

The Reading Teacher's Book of Lists, Fifth Edition, © 2006 by John Wiley & Sons, Inc.

LIST 106. STUDENT/GROUP PROJECT GUIDE

Name: _____ Today's date: _____

Project topic: _____ Date due: _____

Two things I/we want to learn: (1) _____

(2) _____

Related ideas and words to look up: _____

_____

_____

INFORMATION SOURCES:

❏ almanac
❏ art
❏ biographical dictionary
❏ biographies
❏ CD-ROMs
❏ CDs or audiotapes
❏ Dictionary
❏ e-mail to expert
❏ encyclopedia

❏ experiment
❏ history books
❏ interviews
❏ magazines
❏ maps/atlas
❏ microscopic slides
❏ museum exhibits
❏ music
❏ newspapers

❏ nonfiction books
❏ photographs
❏ posters
❏ reference books
❏ speeches
❏ thesaurus
❏ video clips/tapes
❏ video disks (DVD)
❏ Web sites

WAYS TO ORGANIZE INFORMATION:

Text
❏ order of events
❏ sequence
❏ category/subcategories
❏ comparison/contrast
❏ cause and effect
❏ questions and answers
❏ logical order
❏ main idea/details
❏ before and after

Graphics
❏ time line
❏ flow chart
❏ tables
❏ graphs
❏ cause-and-effect diagram
❏ fact sheet
❏ tree diagram
❏ outline, word web, or story map
❏ photos/drawings or charts

The Reading Teacher's Book of Lists, Fifth Edition, © 2006 by John Wiley & Sons, Inc.

PROJECT PRESENTATION WILL INCLUDE:

❏ demonstration ❏ photocollage

❏ picture essay ❏ diorama

❏ exhibit of artifacts ❏ library display

❏ model ❏ music and/or dance

❏ photo sequence ❏ press release

❏ play ❏ poetry

❏ speech ❏ videotape

❏ audiotape with poster ❏ travel brochure

❏ PowerPoint slides ❏ animation

PROJECT SCHEDULE AND CHECKLIST: DATE

❏ I have planned my project. _____

❏ I have discussed my project with my teacher and we agree. _____

❏ I have located the information and materials I need. _____

❏ I have reviewed the information, and I have selected the best
sources. _____

❏ I have enough information to complete the project I planned. _____

❏ I have read and organized my information in notes and other
ways as planned. _____

❏ I have made a first draft of my report or other presentation
materials. _____

❏ I have edited and revised my first draft. _____

❏ I have completed all the parts of my project. _____

❏ I have proofread all the written materials. _____

❏ I have practiced my oral presentation. _____

See also List 107, Working in Teams.

LIST 107. WORKING IN TEAMS

A person can do and understand many things, but no person has enough knowledge and skill to understand and do everything. Working in teams will help you learn more and solve complex problems in school and out. Before starting to work, decide who will have each of the jobs described below. Change jobs every time you start a new team project so that everyone has an opportunity to try each job.

Team Manager

- Describes the task or problem to the team, including what product or result is required.
- Explains the outcome that the teacher will use to judge whether the team is successful and keeps track of the team's progress toward the goal.
- Monitors the team's work to be sure it stays on target.

Organizer

- Schedules meetings if they are not during class.
- Gets materials the group will need.
- Returns materials after use.
- Organizes and is responsible for clean-up.
- Arranges for computer time, AV equipment, etc.

Researcher

- Checks facts, computations, and other information.
- Locates library, Internet, and other reference materials.
- Skims background materials and makes brief summary presentations to the team.
- Keeps log of sources and bibliographic information.

Member

- Suggests ideas in brainstorming and problem solving.
- Shares knowledge and skills related to the task.
- Criticizes ideas, not people.
- Stays on task.
- Does a fair share of the work.

Charter

- Creates flowcharts, diagrams, time lines, and other visual presentations of the problem and the solution.

The Reading Teacher's Book of Lists, Fifth Edition, © 2006 by John Wiley & Sons, Inc.

Scribe

- Writes down brainstorming ideas, checking that the written statements match the team members' ideas.
- Records steps in the team's process or activities.
- Records the team's discoveries and answers.
- Drafts the report of the team's work.

Editor

- Checks the draft report for accuracy and completeness.
- Does final report and gives copies to team members and the teacher.

Presenter

- Gives an oral presentation of the team's work.
- Prepares video and/or audiotape presentation, if used.

See also List 106, Student/Group Project Guide; List 108, Teamwork Rules.

LIST 108. TEAMWORK RULES

Teamwork means working together to achieve a shared goal. These rules will help your teamwork work:

- Respect all teammates.
- Disagree without being disagreeable.
- Take turns speaking; don't interrupt.
- Be on time and prepared for meetings.
- Offer to share your special skills; for example, artistic talent, computer skills, typing.
- Share ideas; if you find or know something that will help a teammate, pass it on.
- Speak loudly enough to be heard by your group, but not so loudly that you disturb other teams.
- Don't give up or go off on your own project.
- Ask for help if you are stuck or forgot something.
- Don't decide by voting; figure out the right answer.

LIST 109. ACTIVITIES FOR TUTORS

Reading tutors are often volunteers with little or no previous experience in teaching reading. That's okay, there are plenty of good things that they can do to help a child or an adult read better. Here are some of them.

Read to the Student

Students of all ages, even adults, like to listen to stories. Note the success of audiotapes for adults.

- Make it more of a lesson by having students retell the story or part of it in their own words.

- Discuss the story, its setting, similar stories, or similar real-life situations. Get the student to contribute to the discussion.

- Discuss interesting words and those with which the student might not be familiar.

Diagnostic Listening

Have the student read a story and listen very carefully.

- If the student is making a lot of mistakes, get an easier book. As a general rule of thumb, when reading orally the student should make less than one mistake in twenty words.

- Help the student with correct pronunciation. Sometimes just tell the student the difficult word.

- Sometimes help the student to figure out the word by seeing what word would make sense in that sentence, or by sounding it out using the first letter or initial sound as a clue.

- Encourage the student's reading by lots of praise. Sometimes the tutor takes a turn reading.

Silent Reading

Many beginning students will simply not read on their own. It is not a waste of time for the tutor to ask the student to read silently and wait while it is being done. Helping the student to develop silent reading habits is very important.

- Tell the student you are available to help with difficult words or to understand a difficult sentence.

- Check up on comprehension by asking questions. Ask a variety of comprehension questions. (See List 117, Comprehension Questions.)

- Help the student select a variety of different kinds of reading materials: short stories, book-length stories, jokes, comics, poems, factual stories from newspapers, or easy encyclopedias.

Encourage Writing

Reading and writing are often practiced together.

- Have the student write something every day.

- Write a variety of things such as a continuing story or diary, a summary of a story just read, and/or a letter to a relative or friend.

- Write a rough draft first (using any kind of spelling or grammar).

- Check spelling, grammar, and punctuation.

- Sometimes have the story rewritten.

Encouragement

Everybody needs encouragement. Beginning readers need a lot.

- One of the best forms of encouragement is success in learning. Therefore, make your lessons or individual tasks easy enough and short enough that the student really experiences success.

- Use a lot of praise. Praise a correct reading. Praise a good retelling. Praise a good question, etc.

- Show progress over time. Save some writing samples periodically to show the student that stories just written are longer or better. Reread some easier material.

- Select stories or material that is interesting. Use an interest inventory to find student interests. (See Lists 104 and 105.) Assign a fun book to be read at home. Help the student to read something wanted, or write something needed.

- Don't get discouraged yourself. Be patient. It takes a long time to develop good reading and writing skills so don't expect immediate success. But every little bit helps. Every hour is important. Have a set schedule for lessons. Teaching someone how to read is very, very important.

See List 95, Good Ideas for Reading Teachers; List 126, Oral Reading Activities; List 110, Reading Tips for Parents; List 111, Games and Methods for Teaching.

LIST 110. READING TIPS FOR PARENTS

Parents are important partners in the reading life of children. You can instill in your children a love of books and a delight in wordplay. You can help them develop the pre-reading skills they need for kindergarten and first grade. Your impact doesn't stop in the early grades. You can also have a huge positive impact on your child's views and success with reading throughout their school years. Here are 50 ways parents can be partners in reading and literacy education.

1. Read to your child every day. It's never too early to start. Even before children understand words, they respond to the flow and sounds of language. Once your child is a reader, take turns, with each of you reading a paragraph or a page.

2. Recite or sing nursery rhymes and children's songs often, even to very young children.

3. Read and reread books without words, predictable books, rhyming books, and picture books to young children. Rereading helps develop memory for the story line, awareness of rhyme, and many other pre-reading skills.

4. Give your "junk mail" to children to pretend read.

5. Point to the words as you read; after a time, have your child point as you read.

6. Use the pictures in books to help your child understand the story. Have your child point to details in the pictures to highlight them.

7. Let your child "read" you the pictures in a familiar picture book. Ask questions: Why? What happens next? Then what? Where did it go?

8. Help preschoolers make their own books by picking out pictures in discarded magazines to cut-and-paste into "books." Some book ideas: a yellow book (all things yellow), a happy book, a fast book, a sleepy book, a numbers book, a people book, a hungry book.

9. Use the pictures in books to expand your child's vocabulary. Provide synonyms for words he/she knows. (Sometimes we call that a. . . .)

10. Help your child organize knowledge by reviewing related words. (What other train words can you think of? Food words? Feeling words?)

11. Take your child to Story Time at your local library or bookstore—sharing books with other children increases enjoyment and connects children in a different social setting.

12. Encourage your child's personal response to stories. Ask "Do you think that was a good idea? Would you want to do that, too?"

13. Provide paper and pencils and encourage your child to pretend write while you are writing a shopping list, paying bills, writing greeting cards.

14. Introduce your child to different kinds of art through a selection of picture books: photos, line drawings, watercolor impressionism, cartoons, etc.

15. When reading to your child, stop periodically and talk about what has happened so far. Ask the child to tell what he/she thinks will happen next, then read to find out.

16. Help your child get a library card in his/her own name as early as your library allows.

The Reading Teacher's Book of Lists, Fifth Edition, © 2006 by John Wiley & Sons, Inc.

17. Help develop attention and memory using books with lots of repetition by pausing for your child to supply the repeated word.

18. Use a book to begin a conversation about a difficult life topic like a trip to the hospital, the birth of a sibling, divorce, the death of a grandparent.

19. Treat books as though they are special. Your child will also.

20. Offer choices for your read-aloud time: Which would you like today? A story about a family on a trip, or a story about a boy and his new friend?

21. Read with expression to help communicate meaning as well as hold interest.

22. Give books as presents or to commemorate a special event.

23. Start your child's use of reference books early with a picture dictionary.

24. Set an example as an avid reader. Let your child see you reading a book, magazine, the newspaper.

25. Pick a letter for the day. Draw a large one, then have your child find more of them on a page from a discarded magazine. The child can mark it with a highlighter.

26. Make a costume for your child based on his/her favorite book character.

27. Make rebus recipe cards (using small pictures and diagrams) and help your child make a favorite snack by reading the recipe. Some are available on the Web or in bookstores.

28. Talk to your child about the parts of a book. Give them names: front cover, title, spine, table of contents.

29. Encourage response to stories by providing different kinds of art materials and ideas for creating after-reading artwork; for example, fingerpaint, paper-plate masks, sponge paintings, potato stamps.

30. Take favorite books or books on tape in the car, on vacation, to grandparents' homes, wherever you travel. Children's travel restlessness is often easy to overcome with a familiar favorite story.

31. Encourage and respond to children's interests by helping them pick out books on special topics; for example, pets, dinosaurs, bugs, horses, building things, how things work.

32. Use new sights and experiences as teaching tools for new words. Explain new things, tell stories about new places, tell the names of new objects and their uses.

33. Discuss the difference between real and make believe. Can animals talk like people do? Are there really magic stones?

34. Use a book character as the theme for a birthday party.

35. Use similes to help define a new concept. This helps bridge something your child knows to understanding something new. "It's like a train but it has . . . "

36. Tell a humorous story from your childhood and have your child illustrate it.

37. Help your child recognize cereal names and other common food stuff and help read the labels in the supermarket.

READING TIPS FOR PARENTS CONTINUED

38. Show your child how to act out a character's part with a finger puppet. Then both of you take parts and tell the story together through your finger puppets.

39. Show how useful words can be. Label common objects in the child's room. Put his/her name on some belongings, a coat hook, book shelf, etc.

40. Try tongue twisters, hink pinks, and other wordplay games in the car as you travel, even on short trips.

41. Encourage your child to "read" signs for favorite fast-food restaurants, stop signs, stores, etc.

42. Ask your child to tell you a story and then write it (or use a word processor) in large print. Read it back pointing to the words. Have child read it back with you. Ask him/her to pick out key words like names, places, etc., if child is able.

43. Help your child focus on the sounds that begin or end a word. Ask "What other word starts like Sam?" Give two words; one that starts with the sound and one that does not. Have the child pick. Later have the child suggest a word that begins with the same sound.

44. Play "Before and After" for a familiar sequence. For example: "Do you put your shoes on before or after your socks? Do you get a bowl before or after you pour your cereal?" Have the child ask you before and afters also.

45. Ask your child to help write the family shopping list. Together consult the supermarket ads in the newspapers and point out the names of fruit, vegetables, and other items that will be on the list.

46. Play OK/NoWay: Tell your child to listen carefully to what you say, then make up sentences, including some that make no sense. After each sentence, the child says "OK or No Way!" For example: John sleeps in a bed. (OK) Mary put her toys away in the lamp. (No Way!)

47. Keep a weather chart with your child. On a calendar, have child draw a symbol for the day's weather: sun, raindrops, snowflakes, clouds.

48. Record some favorite books so you can "read" to your child, even if you are not home or busy.

49. Show interest and delight in stories and books; tell which are your favorites and why. Ask which are your child's favorites and why.

50. Talk about a story, asking your child to recall facts (What did the bear do?) and to make inferences (Why did he put on his mittens? How can you tell?).

The Reading Teacher's Book of Lists, Fifth Edition, © 2006 by John Wiley & Sons, Inc.

LIST 111. GAMES AND METHODS FOR TEACHING

The games and methods for instruction listed here are suggestions for class activities that will help students learn many of the lists or words presented in this book.

1. Pairs. A card game for two to five players. Five cards are dealt to each player, and the remainder of the deck is placed in the center of the table. The object of the game is to get as many pairs as possible. There are only two cards alike in each deck. To play, the player to the right of the dealer may ask any other player if he or she has a specific card, for example, "Do you have *and*?" The player asking must hold the mate in his or her hand. The player who is asked must give up the card if he or she holds it. If the first player does not get the card asked for, he or she draws one card from the pile. Then the next player has a turn at asking for a card. If a player can't read his or her own card, the player may show the card and ask any other player how to read it.

If the player succeeds in getting the card asked for, either from another player or from the pile, he or she gets another turn. As soon as the player gets a pair he or she puts the pair face down in front of him or her. The player with the most pairs at the end of the game wins. *Note:* A deck of 50 cards (25 pairs) is good for two to five players. This game works well with an Instant Word list of 25 words with each word on two cards (see List 16). It can also work well with homophones (List 19) or any association in this section.

2. Bingo. Played like regular Bingo except that the players' boards have 25 words in place of numbers. Children can use bits of paper for markers, and the caller can randomly call off words from a list. Be certain when making the boards that the words are arranged in a different order on each card. Use with 25 Instant Words or any 25 words. Caller can write each word called on the board to help players learn to read the words.

the	of	it	with	at
a	can	on	are	this
is	will	you	to	and
your	that	we	as	but
be	in	not	for	have

GAMES AND METHODS FOR TEACHING CONTINUED

3. Board Games. Trace a path on posterboard. Mark off one-inch spaces. Write a word in each space. Students advance from Start by tossing dice until one reaches the finish line. Students must correctly pronounce (or give the meaning or sample use) of the word in the square. If you don't have dice, use three pennies; shake and advance number of squares for heads up.

4. Contests. Students, individually or as teams, try to get more words in a category than anyone else. For example, the teacher may start the contest by giving three homographs. The students try to amass the longest list of homographs. There may be a time limit.

5. Spelling. Use the list words in spelling lessons or have an old-fashioned spelling bee. See Lists 152 through 154 or Instant Words (List 16).

6. Use Words in a Sentence. Either orally or written. Award points for the longest, funniest, saddest, or most believable sentence.

7. Word Wheels. To make a word wheel, attach an inner circle to a larger circle with a paper fastener. Turn the inner wheel to match outer parts. This is great for compound words, phonograms, or matching a word to a picture clue. Sliding strips do the same thing.

8. Matching. Make worksheets with two columns of words or word parts. Students draw a line from an item in column A to the item in column B that matches (*prefix* and *root, word* and *meaning,* two synonyms, etc.). Matching also can be done by matching two halves of a card that has been cut to form puzzle pieces. See Association Pairs later in this list for suitable lists of paired words.

9. Flash Cards. The word or word part is written on one side of a card. The teacher or tutor flashes the cards for the student to read instantly. Cards also can be shuffled and read by the student. Cards also can be used in sentence building, finding synonyms and antonyms, and the Concentration game.

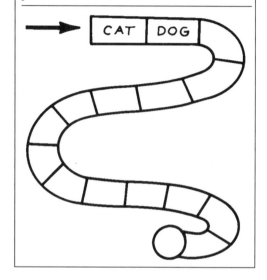

WORD RACE

Toss three pennies, move marker X number of heads. Read the word you land on.

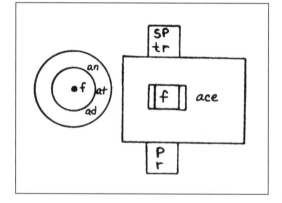

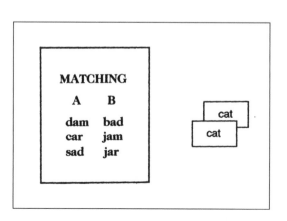

The Reading Teacher's Book of Lists, Fifth Edition, © 2006 by John Wiley & Sons, Inc.

10. Hidden Words (or Word Search Puzzle). To make a word search puzzle, write words horizontally, vertically, or diagonally on a grid (graph paper is fine), one letter per box. Fill in all the other boxes with letters at random. Students try to locate all of the target words. When they find a word, they circle it.

11. Concentration. To play Concentration, use one-sided flash cards or any card with a word or symbol written on one side. Cards must be in pairs (duplicate) such as two identical cards or an association pair. Shuffle four or more pairs (more for older or advanced students) and place cards face down, spread out randomly over a table surface. The player may pick up any two cards and look at them. If they are a pair, he or she keeps them; if they are not, the cards must be put back in exactly the same place from which they came. The trick is to remember where different cards are located while they are sitting on the table face down so that when you pick up one card, you remember where its pair is located. Players take turns, and the object is to accumulate the most cards. Learning is needed to know what cards are pairs, for example, and which definition matches which card or any association pair.

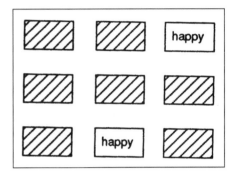

12. TV Show Games. Make your own TV game based on such popular shows as *Jeoprady, Wheel of Fortune,* or *Who Wants to Be a Millionair.* Have committees of students make up the show using some of the Association Pair suggestions in on page 289.

13. Tutoring. A teacher and a student, or a tutor and a student, or even two students can use these double-sided association pair cards in many ways. The tutor holds up one card, and the student calls off the associated definition. Students can take turns, have contests, win prizes, and so on.

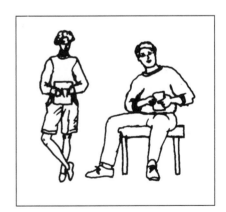

GAMES AND METHODS FOR TEACHING CONTINUED

14. Testing. Although it is often overused, testing is also a powerful learning motivator and teaching device. Done kindly and thoughtfully, testing can cause a lot of learning to occur in a classroom or tutoring situation. A technique of testing is to assign a set of association pairs to be learned (using any game or technique) and then test the results. Some teachers assign short daily tests that accumulate points or cause movement on a big chart. Other teachers give weekly tests and assign numeral or percent grades; these are shown to parents, or the five best papers are posted on a bulletin board. Part of the learning occurs because the students are motivated to study and because the students get feedback or knowledge or the results as to whether they know or don't know something. Hence, the corrected papers should be returned, or the students should trade papers and correct for more immediate and sometimes better knowledge of results.

Testing also gives feedback to the teacher or tutor so that the teacher can regulate the amount of new learning (number of words) to be learned next or the amount needing review. It also can help the student to individualize and to give some students more and other students less to be learned.

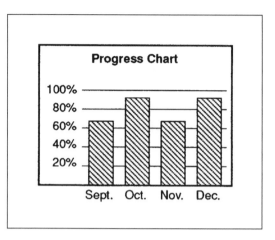

15. Computer Instruction. Use computers to provide instruction, practice, and tests. Programs teach vocabulary both in and out of context, different types of comprehension, and subject content reading. They use many elements of programmed instruction, such as small steps (limited from content), clear objectives, careful sequencing, active student response, immediate feedback on correctness, and often branching and recordkeeping. Most teachers buy programs already made, but it is possible to develop your own with the aid of an authoring program. The *Reading Teacher's Book of Lists* has excellent content for such programs.

The Reading Teacher's Book of Lists, Fifth Edition, © 2006 by John Wiley & Sons, Inc.

16. Humor. Don't overlook the good effects of humor on learning. Both children and adults love word games and jokes. Many jokes use homophones and homographs. For example, "What is an outspoken hot dog? A frank frank." (See List 201, Hink Pinks and Jokes.) Children also like to draw humorous pictures of idiomatic expressions such as "It's raining cats and dogs" or "She's a ball of fire." Try a few Wacky Wordies (List 209).

17. Word Walls. Word walls help students recognize and recall new vocabulary and aid spelling and independent reading and writing skills. When teaching a new topic, make collections of related words and list them on a wall or chalkboard. Have students suggest additional words to add. Here are some categories of words that make good word walls. (Also see List 112, Word Walls Lists.)

Common nouns: bugs, stores, signs, places, drinks, sports, clothing, flowers, animals, oceans, colors, holidays, community helpers, family members, foods, transportation

Language categories: parts of speech, phonograms, phonics rules, suffixes, prefixes, homophones, contractions, spelling demons

Association categories: anger words, happy words, taste words, book words, camping words, adventure words, school words, feeling words

18. Kids' Book of Lists. Kids can categorize and list, too. Have students make booklets of their lists. Make a Kids' Book of Lists as a final project for a theme unit, or just for fun. Here are some categories to use:

Seven salty foods	Seven things most kids do better than most adults
Eight things to take to camp	Six things a nurse needs to know how to do
Six TV shows about families	Six events that could make you late for school
Twelve "strange" words	Eight things you do well
Five uses for a rubber band	Six things you can do after school

19. Honing Homophone Skills. Remember: (1) a computer's spell checking program will not detect homophone errors; (2) you learn to distinguish between homophones by paying attention to them. Here are some ways to hone students' homophone skills:

• Have some fun: Both you and students can develop homophone-based riddles and jokes. "What is a large animal without its fur?" (a bare bear) "An insect relative?" (an ant aunt)

• Proofread and correct sentences. "Please drink sum milk." "Turn write at the end of the street."

• Make flash cards. Put one of a homophone pair on each side. Student sees one side and tries to spell the other. Discuss meaning of both and use in sentences.

• Make playing cards for Go Fish, Concentration, or Rummy-type games.

• Make worksheets for student practice. Complete the homophone pair: sell _____. Select the correct word: Dogs have (for/four) legs.

• Make a Bingo or crossword game in which half of a pair of homophones is provided.

• Make spinner or dice board games based on homophone pairs.

• Have an old-fashioned spelling bee with homophones.

• Find homophones in other materials—social studies, art, math. Have classroom teams compete to see which term finds the most.

GAMES AND METHODS FOR TEACHING CONTINUED

- Make a word wall of homophones. Discuss them for two minutes every day. Add a new one daily.

20. Vocabulary Stretching. Work on building vocabulary every day. Encourage students to use new words in speech and writing. Do not criticize misuse or near misses—praise the attempt. Constantly point out new words in every subject—art, science, social studies. Use the new and important words in your own speech and check students' knowledge in quizzes. Teach word roots and their origins. Put related words on the board or a word wall. Lead from a known word to an unknown word.

For example: *tele*vision ↦ *tele*scope ↦ *tele*metry. Encourage wide reading: stories, newspapers, encyclopedia, directions, poetry, songs. Use a variety of techniques, including the tried and true (like games and flash cards) and the new ones (like computer simulations).

21. Graphing. Make ideas visible using graphic organizers (see List 132) and mostly numerical graph types (List 134).

22. Association Cards. For students who don't want to fool around with games, a useful learning device is to develop a set of association pair cards with the word on one side and its definition on the other side. The student first studies both sides of a set of cards; then the student goes through a stack of cards reading the words and attempting to recall the definition. If correct, he or she puts the card into the "know pile"; if incorrect or the student can't remember, the card is studied and put into the "don't-know pile." Next, the "don't-know pile" is sorted once more into "know" and "don't-know." This process is complete when all cards are in the "know pile"; unfortunately, there is also something called forgetting, so the stack of cards should be reviewed at later intervals, such as a few days later and a few weeks later. Students should not attempt to learn (associate) too many new (unknown) cards at one time, or learning will become boring. But as long as motivation is high and

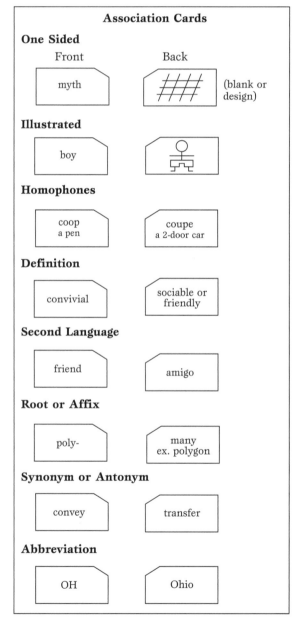

Association Cards

One Sided
Front — myth
Back — ### (blank or design)

Illustrated
boy

Homophones
coop
a pen
coupe
a 2-door car

Definition
convivial
sociable or friendly

Second Language
friend
amigo

Root or Affix
poly-
many
ex. polygon

Synonym or Antonym
convey
transfer

Abbreviation
OH
Ohio

learning is occurring, this is an excellent learning and study technique. Primary students can use picture nouns; older students, List 34, Greek and Latin Roots.

23. Association Pairs. This is a table of items to be associated or learned together. We are calling them association pairs because they are often taught by association learning. The following association pairs can be used in developing games such as Concentration and Association, and in creating programs for computer-aided instruction.

USE THESE PAIRS FOR GAMES AND LESSONS

LIST NUMBER	ASSOCIATION PAIR
19	Word—Homophone (bare–bear)
22	Homograph—Definition (stoop–bend down; stoop–porch)
23	Word look-alike or sound-alike word (coma–comma)
49	Measurement term—Abbreviation (mm–millimeter)
49	Measurement term—Numerical relation (kilometer–1,000 meters)
34	Word—Synonym (see–look)
35	Word—Antonym (back–front)
140	First three words in analogy—Last word (story:read::song:sing)
185	Clipped word—Full word (pop–popular)
203	Portmanteau word—Full words (brunch–breakfast + lunch)
158	Contraction—Full words (she'd–she would)
219	Acronym—Full words (CB–citizens band)
43	Borrowed word—Origin (pasteurize–Louis Pasteur)
40	Foreign word—Translation (origin) (bonjour–good day, French)
38	-Ology word—Definition (cryptology–codes)
170	Computer term—Definition (bug–error)
39	-Phobia word—Definition (agoraphobia–open places)
36	Greek and Latin roots—Meaning (graph–write), (duct–lead)
30/31	Prefix—Meaning (anti–against)
32/33	Suffix—Meaning (-ee–one who, ex. payee), Grammar (-s–plural)
9	Illustrating word or example word—Phoneme (at–short A)
121	Persuasive technique—Example
134	Key object—Number (five–15)
180	Part of speech—Definition (noun–name of person, place)
181	Irregular verb present—Past (am–was), Past participle (am–been)
60	Literary term—Definition (ballad–long narrative poem)
211	State abbreviation—Full name (CA–California)
215	Common abbreviation—Full term (Aug.–August)
192	Alphabet—Manual alphabet or Morse Code (B-. . .)
52	Symbol—Verbal equivalent (+ –plus)
91	Proofreading symbol—Explanation (¶–New paragraph)
222	Arabic number—Roman numeral (12–XII)
24	Collective Nouns—Animal (gaggle–geese)

See also List 95, Good Ideas for Reading Teachers; List 126, Oral Reading Activities; List 198, Jump-Rope Rhymes; List 199, Anagrams.

LIST 112. WORD WALL LISTS

Word walls—lists of target words organized and displayed in the classroom—have become a mainstay teaching and learning tool. They have an integral role in models for teaching reading and writing. They are also indispensable aids in vocabulary building in content areas from kindergarten through high school. Word walls (WW) are an evolution of word "banks" and word "journals." Develop your WWs with your class over the school year and use them frequently every week. Most teachers have students keep a personal copy of the WW of their own and add to it as new words are displayed.

Word Walls Support Learning by:

1. Showing the alphabetic principle

2. Providing exemplars for phonic elements

3. Providing visual scaffolding for new words

4. Supporting students' independent writing efforts

5. Adding visual memory elements to word study and recall

6. Enabling analogy strategies for word recognition

7. Involving students in selecting words for study

8. Recording progress in word mastery through the year

There are three essentially different purposes of word walls: for **reading and writing** instruction; for building **content vocabulary;** and for providing **structure and process reminders.** They should be displayed separately and their purposes explained so students know where to look for the help they need.

To Construct a Word Wall

- *For primary-grade reading and writing:* Post the letters of the alphabet on a large wall. Write the words with bold black marker and cut them out to highlight their unique visual outline. Back the words with colored paper to make them easier to view and distinguish. Post the words under the alphabet letter they begin with.

- *For other word walls:* Post the words alphabetically under a key word, or use an alternate appropriate organizational scheme. For example, in math you might use size order or the order of operations.

Word Wall for Reading and Writing—Primary

For primary-grade **reading and writing**, your WW will display high-frequency words, including those with common rhymes like make (_ake) or sit (_it) and words that are not phonically regular. Also include high-use words from your basal reading selections and words that students misspelled in their weekly writing.

Most teachers begin with the names of the students in the class. They use these familiar words to begin sound-letter pairings. Then they add about five words each week that are the focus of their direct teaching of decoding and spelling skills. Daily work with the new and existing words builds automaticity and fluency in reading, independence in writing, and strategies for applying phonics knowledge to new words. The list below is a typical WW for primary-grade reading and writing. Incorporate Instant Words, phonograms, and irregularly spelled words; as well as words from basal reading texts, language experience charts, and student writing.

I	we	seed	again
the	said	rug	they
and	tip	duck	want
cat	wing	number	old
bag	ink	people	four
say	there	first	answer
hill	Sam	who	are
of	how	down	father
you	word	find	listen
was	hot	did	top
pin	map	come	hide
are	bank	part	sent
with	cake	little	care
bed	Jack	new	came
tell	will	light	jump
cap	up	line	picture
him	out	sock	mother
this	time	year	live
have	two	give	door
from	look	most	country
one	like	very	must
word	has	after	turn
had	more	low	different
but	pail	Bob	page
were	rain	him	kind

WORD WALL LISTS CONTINUED

Word Walls for Content Vocabulary—Elementary

Word walls for **content vocabulary** reinforce key words in themed units and help students enrich their schema for the topic. Words are taken from prior knowledge, brainstorming, and introductory activities such as viewing a video or listening to a story, or they are introduced during a lesson. Drawings or digital photos may be used along with the word to provide additional visual cues, especially in the early grades. Repeated work with the words during content area lessons, in supplemental independent reading materials, and in daily or weekly expository writing builds students' reading/writing vocabulary as well as their conceptual knowledge.

Content vocabulary WWs are often set up on bulletin boards or three-panel display boards at learning centers around the room. Add words from any math, science, social studies, health, music, career, technology, art, or other content subject studied or encountered. Remember to start with the subject, then together with students, select the key words for your WW. The following examples will get you started.

Mathematics

- **Counting numbers:** zero, one, two, three, four, five, six, seven, eight, nine, ten, eleven, twelve, thirteen, fourteen, fifteen, sixteen, seventeen, eighteen, nineteen, twenty, twenty-one, thirty, forty, fifty, sixty, seventy, ninety, hundred, thousand, million, billion

- **Ordinal numbers:** first, second, third, fourth, fifth, sixth, seventh, eighth, ninth, tenth, twentieth, twenty-first, thirtieth, fortieth, fiftieth, sixtieth, hundredth, hundred and first

- **Measurement:** ruler, yardstick, meterstick, unit, inch, inches, foot, feet, yard, mile, millimeter, centimeter, meter, kilometer, cup, pint, quart, gallon, milliliter, liter

- **Time:** clock, second, minute, hour, wristwatch, o'clock, Roman numerals, half hour, day, week, month, year, decade, century, sunrise, morning, noon, midday, afternoon, dusk, sunset, evening, season, summer, fall, autumn, winter, spring, anniversary

- **Geometry:** shape, circle, square, rectangle, triangle, pentagon, hexagon, octagon, cone, cylinder, sphere, length, width, height, intersect, line, side, vertical, horizontal, figure

- **Operations:** + add, addition, total, − subtract, subtraction, difference, × or * or · multiply, multiplication, times, ÷ or / divide, division, group, regroup, increase, decrease, more, fewer, = equals, > greater than, < less than, ones place, tens place, estimate, solve

Science

- **Weather:** temperature, thermometer, degree, Fahrenheit, Celsius, cloud, rain, snow, hail, ice, wind, storm, hurricane, overcast, humidity, frozen, desert, arid, tropics, barometer, wind sock, weather vane, tsunami, earthquake, tornado, blizzard, frost, dew, thunder, winter, summer, autumn, fall, spring, smog, fog

- **Space:** sun, moon, star, planet, Mercury, Venus, Earth, Mars, Jupiter, Saturn, Uranus, Neptune, Pluto, solar system, Milky Way, space, orbit, astronaut, atmosphere, revolve, constellation, space station, NASA, galaxy, light-years, gravity, weightless, eclipse, meteor

- **Life:** biology, cell, cycle, food chain, endangered, decompose, biologist, adaptation, amoeba, amphibian, ancestor, backbone, bacteria, balance, breathe, carnivore, herbivore, chlorophyll, community, ecosystem, digestion, dinosaur, extinct, fish, flower, food web, fossil, gills, habitat, heredity, hibernate, human, inherited trait, leaf, life cycle, living, mammal, marine life, nonliving, omnivore, paleontologist, predator, producer, pollen, pollute, parasite, reptile, recycle, root, seed, seedling, shelter, skeleton, skin, taste, tissue, trunk

- **Physics:** absorb, electric, electron, current, circuit, heat, air current, atom, battery, conductor, energy, filament, light, heat, temperature, force, friction, fulcrum, gravity, inclined plane, lens, lever, load, machine, magnet, magnetic field, magnetism, mass, matter, measure, melting point, motion, Newton, optical, opaque, pendulum, periodic, physical change, pitch, ramp, refraction, reflection, prism, power, position, rotate, screw, simple machine, solid, surface, transparent, vibrate, vibration, volume, wave, wedge, weight, wheel and axle, work

- **Earth Science:** amber, arctic, climate, conifer, continent, core, crater, crust, desert, earth, earthquake, flood, flow, fertile, equator, erosion, forest, glacier, grassland, groundwater, hemisphere, horizon, iceberg, igneous rock, landform, mantle, map, metamorphic rock, mineral, mountain, natural resource, North Pole, northern, ocean, oil, plain, pond, rain forest, range, reservoir, ridge, river, rocks, rotate, scale, sediment, sedimentary rock, soil, South Pole, southern, stream, surface, terrarium, tundra, valley, volcano, weathering, woodland forest

Art

- **Color:** color, hue, shade, dark, light, tint, cool, warm, primary, secondary, red, blue, yellow, orange, green, violet, white, black, palette, color wheel, pigment

- **Media:** paint, crayon, pen, pastels, chalk, watercolor, acrylic, pencil, charcoal, clay, stone, metal, media, medium

- **Product:** portrait, landscape, still life, graphic, print, silkscreen, illustration, collage, assemblage, digital image, ceramics, pottery

- **Element:** style, technique, space, depth, shallowness, scale, perspective, composition, contrast, background, foreground, balance, shape, line, texture, rough, smooth, slick, sandy, grainy, harmony, movement, pattern, contrast

- **Method:** draw, sketch, paint, outline, sculpt, carve, model, construct, print, photograph, illustrate, design

WORD WALL LISTS CONTINUED

Word Walls for Structure and Process—Elementary

Structure and process reminders help students become independent, active learners. Structure WWs help students self-check for things like word usage, spelling, capitalization, and punctuation, and include lists like irregularly spelled words, compound words, rules for plurals, suffixes/prefixes and meanings, root words and meanings, and descriptive words. Process WWs are reminders of steps that need to be completed and include lists like steps for decoding a word, solving a problem, writing a letter, and reading a textbook chapter. Here are some examples of word walls commonly used in elementary grades. They can be revised for younger and older students.

Structure

Irregularly Spelled Words

again	color	island	move	two
although	do	learn	of	was
answer	does	listen	off	were
become	feather	live	said	women
brought	give	most	sign	work

See also List 13, Phonically Irregular Words.

Irregular Plurals

child—children	ox—oxen
man—men	foot—feet
tooth—teeth	woman—women
goose—geese	deer—deer
person—people	mouse—mice

See also List 158, Plurals.

Plurals

1. Add -*s* to the end of the word: *car—cars*
2. Add -*es* if the word ends in -*s*, -*sh*, -*ch*, -*x*, or -*z*: *fox—foxes*
3. Change -*y* to *i* and add –*es*: *city—cities*
4. Add -*s* if the word ends in a vowel and *y*: *key—keys*
5. Change the *f* to *v* and add -*es*: *leaf—leaves*
6. Add -*es* to words that end with a consonant followed by *o*: *hero—heroes*

See also List 158, Plurals.

The Reading Teacher's Book of Lists, Fifth Edition, © 2006 by John Wiley & Sons, Inc.

The Reading Teacher's Book of Lists, Fifth Edition, © 2006 by John Wiley & Sons, Inc.

Overused Words

(Develop a list like this from student writing; then develop replacement words like those under "Editor's Choice Words.")

happy	interesting	bad	kind	like
beautiful	make	big	small	mean
tall	fat	nice	old	part
see	said	fast	think	funny
get	give	go	saw	want

See also List 84, He Said/She Said.

Editor's Choice Words

delighted	fascinating	naughty	variety	enjoy
gorgeous	construct	immense	miniature	intend
statuesque	plump	charming	aged	segment
examine	exclaimed	swift	ponder	comical
obtain	bestow	advance	spied	crave

Process

Steps to Decode a Word:

1. Look again.
2. Look for parts.
3. Is it similar to a word you know?
4. What fits in the sentence?
5. Check the beginning sounds and ending sounds.
6. Sound it out.
7. Try a vowel sound first.
8. Look for picture clues.
9. Check the word wall.
10. Ask a buddy.

Steps to Think and Learn like a Scientist:

1. Pick your subject.
2. Observe and record.
3. Read about it.
4. Form a question.
5. Predict what will happen.
6. Plan an experiment to find out.
7. Do the experiment.
8. Record the results in an organized way.
9. Discuss what you found out.
10. Compare the results to your prediction.
11. Form a new question.

WORD WALL LISTS CONTINUED

Steps to Read to Learn:

1. Look at the pictures.
2. Read the title, headings.
3. Look at key words in **bold** or *italics.*
4. Think about what you know.
5. Do a KWL chart (know, want to learn, learned) or write some questions.
6. Read to find out.
7. Look for main ideas and supporting facts.
8. Notice signal words for lists, comparisons, sequence.
9. Look for cause and effect, and problems and solutions.
10. Think about how the author organized the information.
11. Highlight or underline important words or ideas.
12. Put notes in the margin.
13. Review what you have learned. Complete the KWL.
14. Write the answers to your questions.
15. Talk about what you learned.

See also 130, Study Skills Checklist.

Steps to Solve a Word Problem:

1. Read the problem to find out what it is about.
2. Draw a picture or diagram of the problem.
3. Find the question in the problem. What do you need to find out?
4. Make a list of facts you have.
5. Cross out facts that are not related to the problem.
6. Make a table.
7. Find a pattern.
8. Write a number sentence or equation.
9. Estimate your answer.
10. Solve the number sentence.
11. Check your answer to be sure it is possible.
12. Work backwards.
13. Use logical reasoning.

Parts of a Letter:

1. Date
2. Return Address
3. Inside Address
4. Greeting
5. Message
6. Closing
7. Signature

The Reading Teacher's Book of Lists, Fifth Edition, © 2006 by John Wiley & Sons, Inc.

8

COMPREHENSION

LIST 113. NEW LITERACIES

What are new literacies? They are reading and writing activities different from traditional uses of reading and writing. Traditional uses of literacy are books, letters (correspondence by mail), reports, etc. New literacies include reading and writing e-mail, instant messaging, posting in chat rooms, and manga (words and cartoons).

The reason new literacies are important is because traditional literacies are in steep decline. A Census Bureau survey for the National Endowment for the Arts found that literature reading in the United States went from 57% of the population in 1982 down to 47% in 2002 with no end in sight as younger adults read far less than older adults. However, many adults and students read off of a computer screen many hours a day and magazine sales and proliferation are up, so reading and writing will never really go out of style!

Blogs or Weblogs. Open commentary/reviews written and posted on the Internet by users of items, Web sites, just about anything. Blogs can contain annotated links (to other Web sites), are generally journal-like, and may reference hybrids of products, sites, and services.

E-mail. Written communications to an individual or a group on the Internet, often with a very informal writing style. E-mail may use emoticons like :-) (a happy face turned sideways) to show pleasure or acronyms like IMHO (in my humble opinion).

Gaming. Terminology used in video console games, computer games, and Internet-mediated games.

Manga. Written communications that rely either heavily or partly on pictures. The Sunday comics are manga, but so are more sophisticated adult cartoons, like pages, that contain real or imaginary pictures with written text placed in various parts of the illustration. Some manga can be read in a nonlinear fashion, whereby the reader decides which part to read first. Manga can be fictional or story-like; or realistic like maps or mechanical illustrations.

Meta-zines. Zines about zines.

Webpages. Paging or scrolling through a Web site. When a Websearch results in a lot of information, it may require display on more than one screen. Each screen of information displayed is called a Webpage. Schools, companies, and many individuals and organizations have Web sites.

Zines. Online magazines for children and adults, both professionally written and volunteer written, fiction and nonfiction, illustrated and nonillustrated.

LIST 114. COMPREHENSION SKILLS

Reading comprehension skills refer to a wide range of understandings and abilities competent readers develop over time. This list includes many traditional terms found in scope and sequence charts for reading texts and textbooks about reading instruction.

Identify details	Draw conclusions
Recognize stated main idea	Make generalizations
Follow directions	Recognize paragraph (text) organization
Determine sequence	Predict outcomes
Recall details	Recognize hyperbole and exaggeration
Locate reference	Experience empathy for character
Recall gist of story	Experience emotional reaction to text
Label parts	Judge quality/appeal of text
Summarize	Judge author's qualifications
Recognize anaphoric relationships	Recognize facts and opinions
Identify time sequence	Apply understanding to new situation
Describe a character	Recognize literary style
Retell story in own words	Recognize figurative language
Infer main idea	Identify mood
Infer details	Identify plot and story line
Infer cause and effect	Detect use of propaganda techniques
Infer author's purpose, intent	Appreciate mental imagery
Classify, place into categories	Illustrate using other media
Compare and contrast	Judging usefulness of text

The Reading Teacher's Book of Lists, Fifth Edition, © 2006 by John Wiley & Sons, Inc.

Observable Comprehension Products

Students demonstrate their comprehension in many ways. This is a sample list of observable performance indicators that can be used to evaluate comprehension.

- *Recognizing:* underlining; multiple-choice items; matching; true/false statements
- *Recalling:* writing a short answer; filling in blanks; flash card Q&A
- *Paraphrasing:* retelling in own words; summarizing; providing similes, metaphors
- *Classifying:* grouping components; naming clusters; completing comparison table; ordering components on a scale
- *Following directions:* completing steps in a task; using a recipe; constructing something
- *Visualizing:* graphing; drawing a map; illustrating; making a time line; creating a flow chart
- *Fluent reading:* accurate pronunciation; phrasing; intonation; dramatic qualities

Other Comprehension Factors

These are some factors that affect good or poor comprehension, or any tests involving reading comprehension.

THE READER
Age, IQ
Education
Background, SES
Out-of-school experiences
Fatigue, Health

TYPE OF MATERIAL
Fiction, Stories
Expository articles, Textbooks
Advertisements
Forms, Poetry
Different subjects (for example, social studies, science)

READER'S PURPOSE
Find out content, Learn
Study for test
Get general idea quickly
Recreation
Goals, Rewards

READABILITY
Difficulty level
Clear writing
Personal words
Legibility, Imagery

TIME
Delay, Need to remember
Immediate post test, Action

LENGTH
Sentence, Paragraph
Chapter, Book

ENVIRONMENT
Classroom, Home
Distractions
Light, Noise, Chair

GRAPHS
Comprehend illustrations
Bar charts, Maps, Tables

See also List 117, Comprehension Questions; List 120, Comprehension Thesaurus; and List 130, Study Skills Checklist.

LIST 115. COMPREHENSION STRATEGIES

Students' success in understanding what they read depends on many factors, including the active reading and learning strategies they use before, during, and after reading. During guided reading lessons, build competency in one or more of these strategies until students develop independence in their application to new texts. Help students recognize which strategies work best with narratives or expository material.

BEFORE-READING STRATEGIES

Organize

- Gather everything you need (text, paper, highlighter, pen, Post-its®, dictionary, assignment pad).
- Check the assignment. (Most reading assignments are two parts: read and remember for discussion; read text and prepare for class; read and remember for quiz; read and tell others; read and use the information; read and take notes; read and write a reaction; read and answer questions.)
- Set aside enough time to complete the assignment or a particular part of the assignment.

Tune in to the task

- Think about what you already know about the subject or story.
- Think about the special directions you were given about the assignment.
- Think about what you will need to notice/remember in order to do the post-reading assignment (details, main ideas, summary, story line, characters, your opinion, etc.).
- Check to see how the author organized her/his writing (chapters? headings? dialogue? numbered steps? texts + drawings or pictures?).
- Think about what you expect to find out by reading and why.

Set up for success

- Make a KWL chart.
- Read the questions at the end so you'll recognize the answers when you get to them.
- Start a word web for the reading.

DURING-READING STRATEGIES

Find and mark

- Use a Post-it® to mark the paragraph in which you found an answer to one of your questions.
- Add important words to your word web.
- Write down the page number where you found important information.

The Reading Teacher's Book of Lists, Fifth Edition, © 2006 by John Wiley & Sons, Inc.

If the book is yours:

- Highlight an answer or important information when you see it.
- Put a check mark in the margin next to important information.
- Underline key new words.

Keep track of progress

- "Talk" to the author. (Imagine saying "OK, I got that, I like this part, I wouldn't do it that way," or whatever else you might say if the author was there with you as you read.)
- When you notice that you're telling the author that it doesn't make sense, go back to a part that did and reread.
- Add a Post-it® where you really liked what you read.
- Add a Post-it® where the reading was difficult for you.

AFTER-READING STRATEGIES
Review the reading

- Check back on all marked sections.
- Add to your word web.
- Retell a short version of the story or text in your own words.
- Reread any parts that you marked because they were difficult.
- Think about your feelings for the story or text. (Was it interesting? Did you like it? Was it easy to follow? Did it help you learn?)

Use what you've read

- Use the marked pages or sections to answer questions.
- Fill in the KWL chart.
- Write your reaction to the story/text.
- Create an outline or notes from the important information and key words.
- Make a vocabulary/spelling list of new words.
- Write questions to research later on the same topic.
- Think about how this story/information is like what you have read before.
- Teach part of what you learned to a classmate.
- Rate the reading material's difficulty: too easy, just right, too hard.
- Rate the reading material's interest: very interesting, OK, not very interesting.
- Rate the amount you learned: learned a lot, learned some, learned very little.

See also List 95, Good Ideas for Reading Teachers; List 114, Comprehension Skills; List 116, Comprehension Strategy Initializations.

LIST 116. COMPREHENSION STRATEGY INITIALIZATIONS

There are many ways to teach comprehension, just as there are many elements or aspects of comprehension. (See List 114 for some comprehension elements.) Vocabulary learning is similar to reading comprehension; vocabulary is just comprehension of one word. Teachers will encounter many specific techniques or strategies; those in this list are known by just their initials or a key word.

B-D-A—Before During After (Laverick)

List what you know about the topic before reading, take notes during reading, summarize after reading.

CSSR—Context Structure Sound Reference (Gray)

Learn vocabulary during reading by using context, structure (word parts), sound (pronounce word aloud), reference (dictionary or glossary).

DEJ—Double Entry Journaling (Vaughn)

Student journal writing to a prompt before reading and after reading.

DL–TA—Directed Listening–Thinking Activity (Stauffer)

Teacher reads a story aloud, stops at intervals, and asks for predictions.

DRA—Directed Reading Activity

This is the traditional basal reader lesson with small group:
1. *Preparation:* discussion, new vocabulary, build interest
2. *Silent Reading:* teacher sets purpose, students read
3. *Comprehension:* discussion, questioning
4. *Oral reading:* rereading parts to answer questions
5. *Follow-up activities:* workbook use, vocabulary study, etc.

DR–TA—Directed Reading–Thinking Activity (Stauffer)

Uses predilection, verification, judgment, and extension.

EIR—Early Intervention in Reading (Taylor)

Special instruction for a small group of underachieving first graders.

GMA—Group Mapping Activity (Davidson)

Students create maps of article content. (See List 132, Graphic Organizers.)

InQuest—Investigative Questioning Procedure (Shoop)

Students role-play a reporter and question a story character.

The Reading Teacher's Book of Lists, Fifth Edition, © 2006 by John Wiley & Sons, Inc.

KWL—Know-Want-Learn (Ogle)

What I already know, what I want to know, what I learned.

PreP—PreReading Plan (Langer)

Pre-reading in three steps: Discuss initial associations of topic, reflect on those associations, and re-form in discussion information.

QARs—Quest-Answer Relationship (Raphael)

Focuses on sources of answers such as in text, from prior knowledge.

ReQuest—Reciprocal Questioning (Manzo)

Teacher and students take turns in posing oral questions after silent reading of text segments. Teacher models question types.

SDEI—Semantic Development Enrichment Instruction (Beck)

Extends vocabulary development lessons outside the classroom.

SFA—Semantic Feature Analysis (Johnson & Pearson)

Vocabulary knowledge improved by graphing features. (See List 133, Using Computer-Based Graphic Organizers.)

SQ3R—Survey Question Read Recite Review (F. Robinson)

A study technique using the five steps listed in its name. (See List 131, SQ3R Study Guide.)

SSR—Sustained Silent Reading (McCracken)

General reading improvement by doing lots of silent reading.

TVC—Teaching Vocabulary in Context (Moore)

Introduce new vocabulary words before reading, and show their relevance to the story and children's background.

VSS—Vocabulary Self-Collection Strategy (Haggard)

After reading, student(s) and teacher select a word(s) for examination.

See also List 117, Comprehension Questions.

LIST 117. COMPREHENSION QUESTIONS

Here are some question types to help you add variety to your questioning. These questions can be adapted for use with any prose. Examples of each question type are based on the story of Cinderella.

Vocabulary

1. Questions to help students understand the meaning of a particular word. For example: *What does the word **jealous** mean? What did the stepsisters do that shows they were jealous?*

2. Questions to help students understand words used in the text in terms of their own lives. For example: *Have you ever known someone who was jealous? Have you ever been jealous? Why?*

3. Questions to help students understand multiple meanings of words. For example: *What does **ball** mean in this story? Can you think of any other meaning of the word **ball**?*

Pronoun Referents

4. Questions to help students understand what or who some pronouns refer to and how to figure them out. For example: *In the second sentence of the third paragraph, who does **she** refer to? How do you know?*

Causal Relations

5. Questions to help students recognize causal relations stated directly in the text. For example: *Why were Cinderella's stepsisters jealous of Cinderella?*

6. Questions to help students recognize causal relations not directly stated in the text. For example: *Why did the stepmother give Cinderella extra work to do on the day of the ball?*

Sequence

7. Questions to help students understand that the sequence of some things is unchangeable. For example: *What steps did the Fairy Godmother follow in order to make a coach for Cinderella? Could the order of these steps be changed? Why or why not?*

8. Questions to help students understand that the sequence of some things is changeable. For example: *What chores did Cinderella do on the day of the ball? Could she have done some of them in a different order? Why or why not?*

Comparison

9. Questions to encourage students to compare things within the text. For example: *How did the behavior of the stepsisters differ from the behavior of Cinderella?*

10. Questions to encourage students to compare elements of the story with elements of other stories. For example: *In what ways are the stories of Cinderella and Snow White similar? In what ways are they different?*

11. Questions to encourage students to compare elements of the story with their own experiences. For example: *If you were in Cinderella's place, how would you have acted toward your stepsisters? Is this similar or different from the way Cinderella acted?*

The Reading Teacher's Book of Lists, Fifth Edition, © 2006 by John Wiley & Sons, Inc.

The Reading Teacher's Book of Lists, Fifth Edition, © 2006 by John Wiley & Sons, Inc.

Generalizing

12. Questions to encourage students to generalize from one story to another. For example: *Are most heroines of fairy tales as kind as Cinderella? Give some examples to support your answer.*

13. Questions to encourage students to generalize from what they read to their own experiences. For example: *Can we say that most stepmothers are mean to their stepchildren? Why or why not?*

Predicting Outcomes

14. Questions to encourage students to think ahead to what may happen in the future. For example: *After Cinderella's beautiful dress changes back to rags, what do you think happens?*

Detecting Author's Point of View

15. Questions to help students detect the author's point of view. For example: *What is the author's opinion of the stepsisters and what makes you think this? Support your answer with examples from the story.*

Summarizing

16. Questions to help students restate the important points in their own words. For example: *How might you sum up Cinderella's feelings when the clock struck twelve and she had to leave the ball?*

Question Generating

17. Make up your own set of questions for a passage. Try to have a variety of question types.

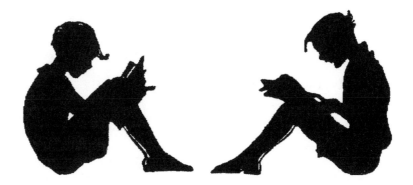

See also List 114, Comprehension Skills; List 115, Comprehension Strategies; List 116, Comprehension Strategy Initializations; List 117, Comprehension Questions; List 120, Comprehension Thesaurus.

LIST 118. SIGNAL WORDS

These are words that the author uses to tell us how to read. Signal words help us to understand how information is organized and provide clues about what is important. Teach signal words one group at a time. Give your students a few examples from category and have them add others as they run across them in their reading. In terms of schema theory, signal words tell the reader about the enabling schema, story grammar, or structure. Note that signal words are independent of the content; they can be used with any kind of article or story. Some writing books might call these *transition words* or *linking expressions*.

1. Continuation Signals (*Warning—there are more ideas to come.*)

and	also	another
again	and finally	first of all
a final reason	furthermore	in addition
last of all	likewise	more
moreover	next	one reason
other	secondly	similarly
too	with	

2. Change-of-Direction Signals (*Watch out—we're doubling back.*)

although	but	conversely
despite	different from	even though
however	in contrast	instead of
in spite of	nevertheless	otherwise
the opposite	on the contrary	on the other hand
rather	still	yet
while	though	

3. Sequence Signals (*There is an order to these ideas.*)

first, second, third	since	while
in the first place	o'clock	until
then	later	during
before	A, B, C	always
after	for one thing	on time
into (*far into the night*)	next	earlier
last	now	

4. Time Signals (*When is it happening?*)

when	immediately	now	before
lately	already	little by little	after
at the same time	final	after awhile	earlier
once	during	later	during
soon	tomorrow	next week	meanwhile

The Reading Teacher's Book of Lists, Fifth Edition, © 2006 by John Wiley & Sons, Inc.

5. Illustration Signals (*Here's what that principle means in reality.*)

for example	specifically	like
for instance	to illustrate	just as
such as	much alike	
in the same way as	similar to	

6. Emphasis Signals (*This is important.*)

a major development	especially relevant	remember that
a significant factor	especially valuable	should be noted
a primary concern	important to note	the most substantial
a key feature	it all boils down to	issue
a major event	most of all	the main value
a vital force	most noteworthy	the basic concept
a central issue	more than anything	the crux of the matter
a distinctive quality	else	the chief outcome
above all	of course	the principal item
by the way	pay particular	
especially important	attention to	

7. Cause, Condition, or Result Signals (*Condition or modification is coming up.*)

because	if	of
for	from	so
while	then	but
that	until	since
as	whether	in order that
so that	therefore	unless
yet	thus	due to
resulting from	consequently	without

8. Spatial Signals (*This answers the "where" question.*)

between	below	about	left	alongside
here	outside	around	close to	far
right	over	away	side	near
near	in	into	beside	inside
middle	next to	beyond	north	outside
east	on	opposite	over	along
south	there	inside	in front of	against
under	these	out	behind	amid
across	this	adjacent	above	behind
toward	west	by	upon	under

SIGNAL WORDS CONTINUED

9. Comparison-Contrast Signals (*We will now compare idea* **A** *with idea* **B.**)

and	or	also	similarly
too	best	most	on the other hand
either	less	less than	instead of
more than	same	better	as opposed to
even	then	half	in contrast to
much as	like	analogous to	also
but	different from	still	as
yet	however	although	conversely
opposite	rather	while	even though
though			

10. Conclusion Signals (*This ends the discussion and may have special importance.*)

as a result	consequently	finally	at last
from this we see	in conclusion	in summary	nevertheless
hence	last of all	therefore	thus
thus	therefore	all in all	in short

11. Fuzzy Signals (*Idea is not exact, or author is not positive and wishes to qualify a statement.*)

almost	if	looks like
maybe	could	some
except	should	alleged
nearly	might	reputed
seems like	was reported	purported
sort of	probably	

12. Nonword Emphasis Signals

exclamation point (!)
<u>underline</u>
italics
bold type
subheads, like *The Conclusion*
  indentation of paragraph
graphic illustrations
numbered points (1, 2, 3)
very short sentence: *Stop war.*
"quotation marks"

The Reading Teacher's Book of Lists, Fifth Edition, © 2006 by John Wiley & Sons, Inc.

See also List 182, Basic Sentence Patterns.

LIST 119. USING LANGUAGE TO SUPPORT COMPREHENSION

Knowledge of grammar and the workings of our language are powerful comprehension tools. But not all students recognize just how useful they are in a learning solution. Use this "story" and list of questions to demonstrate the impact of word order in sentences; noun, adjective and adverb markers; verb forms; and plural spellings, and punctuation.

> For a long time, Haro, the nimp fizbin, was the only fizbin in the zot. Every midsee, he would cond and ren, cond and ren, cond and ren. Then one midsee, Haro was zommed! There, in the middle of the parmon, was the nimpest fizbin and she was conding and renning just like Haro. Haro was so arky! He dagged up to the nimpest fizbin and chared. Soon Haro and the nimpest fizbin, Bindy, were ponted. Then every midsee, they conded and renned abatly in the parmon of the zot.

1. Who was Haro?
2. What did he do every midsee?
3. How do you think Haro felt in the beginning of the story? Why?
4. What words helped show his feelings?
5. Where was Bindy when Haro first saw her?
6. What was she doing?
7. How did Haro act when he saw her?
8. How do you think Haro felt at the end of the story? What changed his feelings?
9. How are Haro and Bindy the same?
10. How are they different?
11. List four things that a fizbin can do.
12. Which is larger, the zoyt or the parmon?
13. Add a new sentence to tell what happened later.
14. If you could rewrite the story, what words would you use instead of:

fizbin	midsee
cond	ren
zommed	arky
abatly	zot

See also List 115, Comprehension Strategies; List 117, Comprehension Questions.

The Reading Teacher's Book of Lists, Fifth Edition, © 2006 by John Wiley & Sons, Inc.

LIST 120. COMPREHENSION THESAURUS

Here is a Comprehension Thesaurus with which you can generate an astounding ten thousand eighty-seven (that's 10,087) different comprehension terms! Impress your principal by using a different one every day for the next 56 years. Although this list is mainly "tongue in cheek," it does make a point about the confusing multiplicity of comprehension terminology and jargon that some educators use. While polishing up your "educationese," remember there are also really good comprehension ideas here.

Directions: Select any term from Part A and link it with any term in Part B to form a Reading Comprehension Skill. (See List 200, Doublespeak, for another phrase generator.)

PART A: THE ACTION

Getting	Organizing	Providing
Identifying	Outlining	Reading (for)
Understanding	Using	Following
Classifying	Locating	Previewing
Recalling	Retelling	Apprehending
Selecting	Reasoning (about)	Determining
Finding	Interpreting	Working (with)
Recognizing	Comprehending	Visualizing
Summarizing	Demonstrating	Thinking (about)
Grasping	Applying	Thinking critically
Drawing	Obtaining	Getting excited (about)
Evaluating	Predicting	Dealing (with)
Relating	Contrasting	Judging
Paraphrasing	Proving	Translating
Comparing	Anticipating	Synthesizing
Transforming	Internalizing	Checking
Clarifying	Sifting	Deriving
Specifying	Inferring	Integrating
Matching	Referring (to)	Actively responding (to)
Criticizing	Drawing	Describing
Analyzing	Making	Questioning
Noting	Concluding	Verbalizing
Perceiving	Forecasting	Processing
Extending	Extrapolating	Encoding
Restating	Foreshadowing	Learning
Reacting (to)	Producing (from memory)	

PART B: THE CONCEPT

Main ideas	Ambiguous statements	Climax
Central thoughts	Mood	Outcome
Author's purpose	Tone	Objective ideas
Author's intent	Inference	Subjective ideas
Point of view	Inference about author	Events
Thought units	Conjecture	Interactions
Story content	Information	Relevancies
Details	Text information	Semantic constraints
Supporting details	Important things	Linguistic constraints
Essential details	Humor	Convictions
Specifics	Directions	Inclinations
Specific facts	Trends	Characterization
Inferences	Goals	Personal reaction
Wholes and parts	Aims	Effects
Conclusions	Principles	Comparisons
Propositions	Generalizations	Time
Propositional relationships	Universals	Event-to-time relationship
Schema	Abstractions	Tense
Schemata	Abstract ideas	Propaganda
Constructs	Structures	Flashbacks
Meanings	Judgments	Repetitive refrain
Scenarios	Literary style	Personification
Scripts	Elements of style	Answers to questions
Sense	Elements	Directly stated answers
Classifications	Imagery	Indirectly stated answers
Categories	Mental imagery	Extended answers
Multiple meanings	Cause and effect	Various purposes
Connotations	Organization	Validity
Denotations	Story line	Antecedents
Causal relations	Story problem	References
Sequence	Plot	Experiences
Sequence of events	Plot structure	Vicarious experiences
Sequence of ideas	Time of action	Concrete experiences
Chronological sequence	Types of literature	Concepts
Trends	Context	Familiar concepts
Seriation	Affective content	Unfamiliar concepts
Anaphora	Answers	Vocabulary
Associations	General idea	Vocabulary in context
Facts	Facts	Word meaning
Deep structure	Concepts	Terminology
Analogies	Relationships	Descriptions
Figurative language	Lexical relationships	Criteria
Metaphors	Textual relationships	Attributes
Similes	Written works	Content

See also List 114, Comprehension Skills.

LIST 121. PERSUASIVE TECHNIQUES

These persuasion devices are often used in advertising and political campaigning. Teach your students to be critical readers and listeners by being alert to these attempts to mold their choices and viewpoints. Viewed negatively they are used for "propaganda." Viewed positively they are "persuasive" devices.

Bandwagon. Using the argument that because everyone is doing it, you should, too. *Last year 30 million winners switched to AIR-POPS athletic shoes. Isn't it time you did, too?*

Card Stacking. Telling only one side of the story as though there is no opposing view. *This tape is especially designed to give the best audio playback money can buy.* (No mention is made that the tape wears out very quickly and is expensive.)

Exigency. Creating the impression that your action is required immediately or your opportunity will be lost forever. *Saturday and Sunday only! It's your last chance to get a really great deal on Camp jeans.*

Flag Waving. Connecting the person, product, or cause with patriotism. *Drink foreign beer? Never! I drink Bot Beer—American all the way.*

Glittering Generality. Using positive or idealistic words based on a detail or minor attribute to create an association in the reader's mind between the person or object and something that is good, valued, and desired. *Ron's been on the varsity team for all four years—you couldn't find a better team player or a more sportsmanlike young man.*

Innuendo. Causing the audience to become wary or suspicious of the product, person, or cause by hinting that negative information may be kept secret. *Other products claim they can handle the big, grimy, once-a-year cleaning jobs like a garage floor. Think what they will do to the no-wax finish on your kitchen floor where your baby plays.*

Name Calling. Using negative or derogatory words to create an association in the reader's mind between the person or object and something that is bad, feared, or distasteful. *Do you really want a mob-linked mayor?*

Overpowering. Saying something LOUD or repeatedly over and over and over again. **Using large or bold type.**

Plain Folks. Using a person who represents the "typical" target of the ad to communicate to the target audience the message that because we are alike and I would use/buy/believe this, you should, too. *If you're a sinus sufferer like I am, take extra-strength Azap. It helps me. It'll help you, too.*

Pleasant Images. Showing association with a smiling pretty girl, beautiful landscape, or cute puppy.

Prestige Identification. Showing a well-known person with the object, person, or cause in order to increase the audience's impression of the importance or prestige of the object, person, or cause. *We treat our hotel guests like stars (the ad shows a celebrity walking into the hotel).*

The Reading Teacher's Book of Lists, Fifth Edition, © 2006 by John Wiley & Sons, Inc.

Red Herring. Highlighting a minor detail as a way to draw attention away from more important details or issues. *The XT399—the only sports car available in 32 "eye-catching" colors.*

Snob Appeal. Associating the product, person, or cause with successful, wealthy, admired people to give the audience the idea that if they buy or support the same things, they will also be one of the "in-crowd." *There really isn't a better racket (man in tennis clothes holding a racket in front of a very elegant country club building).*

Testimonial. Using the testimony or statement of someone to persuade you to think or act as he or she does. *I'm a doctor, and this is what I take when I have a headache.*

Transfer. Linking a known personal goal or ideal with a product or cause in order to transfer the audience's positive feelings to the product or cause. *Buy Pino in the biodegradable box and help end water pollution.*

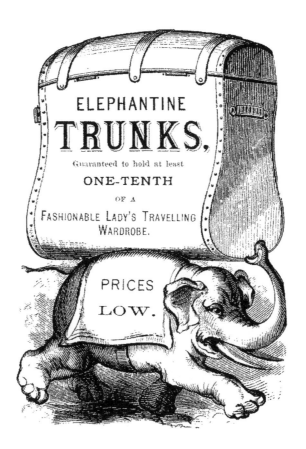

See also List 114, Comprehension Skills.

9
FLUENCY

LIST 122. FLUENCY ELEMENTS

Fluency has three main elements:

Rate—This is reading speed, which is usually measured in words per minute read aloud.

Accuracy—The number of errors made while reading aloud is a useful measure of a student's reading skill.

Prosody—Variation in pitch, loudness, speed, rhythm, and pause, which provide the spoken equivalent of written text.

Prosodic Features:

The following features are also used for stress.
- *Pitch:* high tone or low tone
- *Loudness:* soft or loud voice
- *Speed:* fast or slow
- *Pause:* short or long

Paralinguistic Features:
- *Whisper:* for secrecy
- *Breathiness:* for emotion
- *Huskiness:* for disparagement
- *Nasality:* for anxiety or sarcasm
- *Over articulation:* for exaggeration

Examples of Prosodic and Paralinguistic Features:
- *Clipped:* "No, don't bother me again." (angry, impatiently)
- *Elongated:* "No, but I could change my mind." (hesitant, unsure)
- *Louder:* "No, I will not!" (defiant, definite)
- *Softer:* "No, I'm sorry." (apologetic)
- *Pause:* "No . . . why not?" (questioning)
- *Even pitch:* "Please say 'yes' or 'no'." (informative)
- *High pitch:* "No, you are not getting married." (delight, excitement)
- *Low pitch:* "No, not in this class." (authoritative)
- *Whisper:* "No, don't tell anyone." (secrecy)
- *Nasality:* "No, that's not my sister." (childish, sarcastic)
- *Breathiness:* "No, I can't do that." "I'm sorry." (emotional)
- *Lip rounding:* "No, baby can't have that." (talk to infant or pet)

See also List 123, Fluency and Punctuation; List 125, Sentence Tunes.

LIST 123. FLUENCY AND PUNCTUATION

Readers use punctuation as signposts. Each symbol provides information that helps the reader adjust pace, pauses, and intonation. Consider, for example, your automatic response to the commas before and after the phrase "for example" in this sentence. Or the difference in your reading: *I'm sorry you're right* or *I'm sorry. You're right.* This list will help students learn how to use punctuation to guide their fluent reading.

.   The **period** is the most important punctuation mark for prosody. If students don't give a generous pause for a period at the end of a sentence, they really need help and practice.

,   The **comma's** length of pause is usually less than for a period but more than the pause given by many immature readers.

?   The **question mark** indicates a sentence tune that is most often a rising pitch towards the end of the sentence. It is followed by a major pause.

!   An **exclamation point** indicates a strong and definite thought pattern, so increase the loudness, particularly near the end of the sentence. However, other prosodic features can be used to indicate stress. (See List 122, Fluency Elements.)

;   A **semicolon** is not used nearly as often as a comma or a period, but it falls somewhere in between a comma and a period length of pause and completion of a thought unit. For oral reading, a colon is treated like a semicolon.

" "   **Quotation marks** are usually used in dialogue, which gives the oral reader a chance to change voice and use paralinguistic features like a whisper or breathiness. Quotation marks are also used to call attention to a word, title, or phrase; hence, you can use any of the stressing techniques of prosodic features, like changing pitch or speed.

( )   **Parentheses** are stronger than commas for setting off parenthetical material; hence, they require a longer pause than just a comma, both before and after the word or words they contain. The words within the parentheses can also be spoken differently from the rest of the sentence using prosodic features or paralinguistic features.

-    The **hyphen** between two words joins the words, almost making them a compound word. This sometimes changes the meaning. Note the difference between "a man eating lobster" and "a man-eating lobster." The hyphen can decrease any pause of juncture between words.

—   A **dash** is printed larger than a hyphen and separates parts of a sentence or even makes a separate sentence. Oral readers should treat a dash as a period.

The Reading Teacher's Book of Lists, Fifth Edition, © 2006 by John Wiley & Sons, Inc.

See also List 89, Punctuation Guidelines.

LIST 124. FLUENCY TEACHING METHODS

One of the most direct means of improving students' fluency, is to **model** how to read a selection, then have the students reread it with you while they try to imitate your speed, intonation, and other prosodic features. Here are other activities that can help improve students' fluency.

Repeated Readings: Reread the same short passage several times to try to improve *rate, accuracy,* and *prosody.* Use of a tape recorder can show progress.

Modeling: Students listen to a recorded reading by a fluent reader.

Sight Words: Practice instant recognition of common words. (See List 16, Instant Words.) Use flashcards or rapid reading of a word list.

Phonics: Help the student develop the skill of sounding out common graphemes. (See Section One, Phonics.)

Word Parts: Develop a student's recognition of morphemes (roots, prefixes, and suffixes) and phonograms. (See List 12, The Most Common Phonograms.)

Timed Reading: Time the student's oral and/or silent reading. Encourage the student to try to improve on rereading.

Dramatic Reading: Have students practice oral reading of parts for a play, radio drama, or prose with dialogue.

Vocabulary Improvement: Teach the meaning and pronunciation of words unfamiliar to the student.

Punctuation: Teach the importance of punctuation for prosody. (See List 123, Fluency and Punctuation.)

Instruction Level: Select passages for fluency practice that are at the student's Instructional Level of difficulty (95% first reading accuracy).

Feedback: Keep a record of improvement such as decreasing errors or improving speed. (Either the student or the teacher can keep this record.) Student listens to his or her own voice on a tape recorder or uses an amplification, such as a whisper phone, while reading.

Variety: Change passages frequently. Teachers often start with nonfiction and move to stories, poems, plays, etc.

See also List 122, Fluency Elements.

LIST 125. SENTENCE TUNES

If you have a doubt that changing the way you say something can change the meaning, this example should convince you. Your students will enjoy playing with this sentence and should be able to create their own multi-tuned sentences. The changes in meaning are due to what are called *supersegmental phonemes*. A phoneme is a speech sound that changes the meaning. A supersegmental phoneme is one that has an additional change to the typical phoneme—in this case, inflection/stress—that affects meaning. Besides being interesting, this change in meaning as a result of inflection is an important characteristic of English that needs to be explicitly taught, particularly to students for whom English is a new or developing language.

Directions: Read the sentences below, emphasizing or stressing the bold word to change the meaning of the sentence.

I did not say you stole my red hat.   (Someone else said it.)

I **did** not say you stole my red hat.   (Strong indignant denial of saying it)

I did **not** say you stole my red hat.   (Strong denial of saying it)

I did not **say** you stole my red hat.   (I implied it, but I didn't say it.)

I did not say **you** stole my red hat.   (I wasn't talking about you.)

I did not say you **stole** my red hat.   (You did something else with it.)

I did not say you stole **my** red hat.   (You stole someone else's.)

I did not say you stole my **red** hat.   (You stole one of another color.)

I did not say you stole my red **hat**.   (You stole something else that was red.)

Try the same shifting of emphasis with these sentence and discuss the results.

Tom didn't push George first.

I didn't tell Mom you spent the dollar.

Ana didn't lose the book.

You weren't asked to go to the store.

See also List 126, Oral Reading Activities; List 122, Fluency Elements.

The Reading Teacher's Book of Lists, Fifth Edition, © 2006 by John Wiley & Sons, Inc.

LIST 126. ORAL READING ACTIVITIES

Every opportunity to read aloud is an opportunity to develop students' reading fluency. Here are a several popular activities that you can use.

Choral Reading. Group oral reading. It allows advanced readers to lead and delayed readers to follow. Also excellent for poetry.

Glossing. The teacher reads aloud slowly and accurately with good sentence tunes. Teacher "glosses" by stopping occasionally to explain a word, phrase, or idea. Students just listen or listen and follow along in their books.

Official Announcer. Appoint a student each day to read announcements, bulletins, student writings, short selections, continuing story, and so forth. Announcer may prepare and seek help from teacher or another student.

Radio Program. Small group takes parts and reads play or radio script into tape recorder for class or parent presentation.

Overviewer. Student reads aloud subheads, key words, and/or key sentences in a text before class studies it. Excellent in science or social studies.

Flash Cards. Students try to read word or phrase on flash cards the fastest, most accurate, or in turn.

Play Reading. Like radio program except students read play parts for live performance.

Singing. Read lyrics while learning new song. This is also great for ESL or learning foreign language. Singing may also help students with speech impairments.

Games. A number of board games and other games like Trivial Pursuit™ require players to read a word, set of directions, or questions aloud.

Formal Speech. Student writes a speech for an occasion or learning unit and reads it to a group. May be part of a speech contest.

Find the Answer. Teacher asks a question, student reads aloud just the part of the text that answers the question. This activity aids comprehension improvement and generates good discussions.

Joke of the Day. Read aloud a joke or humorous selection.

Letter. Read a letter sent or received by the class.

Author's Chair. Read aloud a story that is being written to obtain group feedback.

Word Wall. Read aloud known words listed on word walls or on the chalkboard.

See also List 65, Old and New Favorite Books to Read Aloud; List 111, Games and Methods for Teaching; List 125, Sentence Tunes.

LIST 127. SPEECH SOUND DEVELOPMENT

Oral speech sounds (phonemes) develop slowly over five or six years. Here is a chart showing the age at which 75 percent of children have mastered each spoken phoneme.

CONSONANTS

IPA*	Conventional	Initial Age	Medial Age	Final Age
m		2	2	3
n		2	2	3
ŋ	(ng) sing	—	3	nt**
p		2	2	4
b		2	2	3
t		2	5	3
d		2	3	4
k		3	3	4
g		3	3	4
r		5	4	4
l		4	4	4
f		3	3	3
v		5	5	4
θ	(voiceless) thin	5	nt	nt
ɣ	(th voiced) this	5	5	nt
s		5	5	5
z		5	3	3
ʃ	(sh) shoe	5	5	5
ʒ	(zh) measure	nt	5	nt
h		2	nt	—
w		2	nt	—
j	(y) yes	4	4	—
tʃ	(ch) chief	5	5	4
dʒ	(j) just	4	4	6

VOWELS AND DIPHTHONGS

IPA	Conventional	Example	Age
i	Long E	Me	2
ɪ	Short I	Is	4
ɛ	Short E	Met	3
æ	Short A	At	4
ʌ	Short U	Up	2
ə	Schwa	Alone	2
ɑ	Broad A	Father	2
ɔ	Broad O	Off	3
ʊ	Short OO	Look	4
u	Long OO	Moon	2
ju	Long U	Use	3
ou	Long O	Go	2
au	Ou	Out	3
eɪ	Long A	May	4
aɪ	Long I	Ice	3
ɔɪ	OI	Boy	3

CONSONANT BLENDS

Blend	Age	Blend	Age
pr-	5		
br-	5		
tr-	5	sl-	6
dr-	5	sw-	5
kr-	5	tw-	5
gr-	5	kw-	5
fr-	5	-ŋk	4
θr-	6	-ŋg	5
pl-	5	-mp	3
bl-	5	-nt	4
kl-	5	-nd	6
gl-	5	spr-	5
fl-	5	spl-	5
-ld	6	str-	5
-lk	5	skr-	5
-lf	5	skw-	5
-lv	5	-ns	5
-lz	5	-ps	5
sm-	5	-ts	5
sn-	5	-mz	5
sp-	5	-nz	5
st-	5	-ŋz	6
-st	6	-dz	5
sk-	5	-gz	5
-ks	5		

*IPA stands for International Phonetic Alphabet. **Not tested.

See also List 6, Phonics Awareness.

The Reading Teacher's Book of Lists, Fifth Edition, © 2006 by John Wiley & Sons, Inc.

10
STUDY SKILLS

LIST 128. STUDY TECHNIQUES

Here are some techniques that are useful in memorizing. Show your students how to use these techniques when they study for your tests.

1. **Study actively.** You are more likely to remember material if you write it or say it out loud than if you merely read it or hear it.

2. **Make sure you understand.** If you understand what you're trying to learn, you'll find that you can remember it better and for a longer period of time.

3. **Associate new information with old.** When learning something new, try to compare it with something similar that you are already familiar with.

4. **Make up examples.** When learning general principles, try to make up examples of your own. In addition to helping you remember the principle better, this will also help you check your understanding. If you're not sure that your example is correct, check it with your teacher.

5. **Visualize what you're trying to learn.** This can involve creating a mental image or drawing a graph (a time line to help with time sequences, a hierarchical chart for organizations or family trees, etc.) (See List 134, Graph Types, for other ideas.)

6. **Group items into categories.** If you have to learn a long list of things, try to group similar items together. For example, to memorize a shopping list you would want to group vegetables together, meats together, dairy products, and so on.

7. **Be selective.** Most of the time you will not be able to memorize every detail, and if you try you may end up learning almost nothing. Concentrate on general concepts and a few examples to go with each. Pay particular attention to information the teacher indicates is important. Teachers frequently send signals to help you identify what is most important (information written on the chalkboard, or repeated several times orally, or prefaced by statements such as "You should know this.") (See List 118, Signal Words.)

8. **Space your study sessions.** You are more apt to remember material if you study over several days rather than in one crash session.

9. **Use key words.** For example, to learn this list of suggestions for improving your memory, pick out a key word for each suggestion and then learn just the key words. To learn items 1 through 9, you might choose the following key words: active, understand, associate, examples, visualize, group, selective, space, key words.

10. **Learn how many items are on the list.** When learning lists, make sure you learn the number of items on the list. For example, in item 9, it is not enough to learn the key words. You also should learn that there are nine items. This will aid you in recalling all the items.

STUDY TECHNIQUES CONTINUED

11. **Rhymes and sayings can be helpful.** For example, how many of us can remember the number of days in the months without:

> Thirty days have September,
> April, June, and November;
> All the rest have thirty-one,
> Excepting February alone,
> Which has just four and twenty-four,
> And every leap year one day more.

12. **Use alliteration.** Repeating initial sounds can be helpful in remembering information. For example, to remind sailors entering a harbor to keep the red harbor light on their right, they learn:

> Red to right returning

13. **Try acrostics.** Sometimes you can use the first letter of a list of words to form another word or sentence. These are referred to as acrostics and are similar to acronyms (see List 217, Acronyms and Initializations). For example, "ROY G. BIV" can help us remember the colors of the spectrum: Red, Orange, Yellow, Green, Blue, Indigo, and Violet.

14. **Exaggerate.** This is especially helpful when you are using visualization. Try to make your images BIG, colorful, and with lots of details. This will make them interesting and easier to remember.

15. **Have confidence.** Don't go around saying, "I can't remember names." You can if you try.

16. **Use a mnemonic device.** This is very useful when memorizing a list of anything.

17. **Plan your time.** Use a time-planning chart so that you have definite study times and some time for recreation and pleasure reading.

See also List 130, Study Skills Checklist.

The Reading Teacher's Book of Lists, Fifth Edition, © 2006 by John Wiley & Sons, Inc.

LIST 129. TIME-PLANNING CHART

A time-planning chart is a standard study skills tool. This is a practical one, just in case you don't have one readily available for your students. Use it to encourage leisure reading and studying.

The Reading Teacher's Book of Lists, Fifth Edition, © 2006 by John Wiley & Sons, Inc.

STUDY, READING, WORK, RECREATION SCHEDULE

	Mon.	Tues.	Wed.	Thurs.	Fri.	Sat. Sun.
Study Period During School Day						A.M.
After School Afternoon						P.M.
Early Evening						
Late Evening						

Directions: Fill in every square with one or two of the following activities:

1. STUDY: Homework assignments, activity related to courses you are taking.
2. READING: Reading primarily books for your pleasure, or, at most, supplemental or extra-interest material for course you are taking.
3. WORK: Work that you do outside of school for pay, or at home.
4. RECREATION: Talking to friends, watching TV, sports, goofing around.

See also List 130, Study Skills Checklist; List 134, Graph Types.

LIST 130. STUDY SKILLS CHECKLIST

Mastering these study skills will enable students to succeed at any grade level, in any subject. Integrate instruction in these skills during subject matter classes, applying each skill to the texts, resources, and needs of the class. Review them monthly and have students reflect on their progress. Remember, skills develop through practice.

Preparing to study

❑ Writing down assignments and due dates in a calendar/assignment book
❑ Planning and managing time—how much and when
❑ Creating a study space where there are few distractions
❑ Gathering the things needed before starting to study—references, supplies
❑ Monitoring what works: taking notes, outlining, time lines, story maps, word webs, etc.

Reading with a purpose

❑ Using KWL—list of what you know, want to learn, and have learned
❑ Determining a purpose for reading
❑ Fitting the approach—skimming, scanning, careful reading—to the purpose
❑ Fitting reading speed to the purpose
❑ Monitoring understanding while reading
❑ Using strategies to correct misunderstanding/lack of understanding
❑ Recognizing facts and opinions
❑ Recognizing author's bias
❑ Judging author's credentials
❑ Judging relevance of material to assignment
❑ Recognizing the use of propaganda techniques

Using your textbooks and other resources

❑ Using the parts of the book: table of contents; introduction; headings and subheadings; chapter summary; chapter/unit review questions; chapter/unit vocabulary lists; glossary; appendices; index
❑ Recognizing organizational patterns: chronological order; thematic; simple/complex; cause/effect; comparison/contrast
❑ Understanding graphics, tables, graphs, and charts
❑ Using a map, diagram, time line

Learning new vocabulary

❑ Using context
❑ Using the glossary, standard and special dictionaries
❑ Noting special or new meanings for familiar words
❑ Recognizing author's techniques to highlight key words
❑ Using roots and affixes
❑ Using signs and symbols

Gathering and organizing information
❏ Underlining key ideas
❏ Taking notes from text
❏ Outlining text
❏ Summarizing text
❏ Categorizing information
❏ Organizing your information
❏ Making a table, chart, time line, or graph (see List 134, Graph types)
❏ Listening skills
❏ Taking notes from lectures, multimedia presentations
❏ Using the online library catalogs and library classification systems
❏ Doing a basic online search for information on the Internet
❏ Using multimedia reference materials: CD-ROMs, video discs, videotapes, CDs
❏ Identifying your sources (quoting, writing footnotes, listing bibliographic information)

Learning from texts and other resources
❏ Using SQ3R study technique
❏ Using a study guide
❏ Creating a story map, time line, word web, matrix, database
❏ Using mnemonic devices

Preparing written assignments
❏ Organizing research notes
❏ Answering the questions asked
❏ Developing an outline
❏ Writing a first draft
❏ Using tables, graphs, time lines, and other graphics as support
❏ Editing/proofreading the draft and final version

Preparing for and taking tests
❏ Reviewing text, study guides, text notes, and class notes
❏ Creating a list of potential test questions to use as a self-quiz
❏ Knowing key test words
❏ Becoming "test wise"
❏ Pacing yourself during a test
❏ Knowing you know—developing sense of when you know "enough"

See also List 128, Study Techniques; List 131, SQ3R Study Guide.

LIST 131. SQ3R STUDY GUIDE

Name _____ **Date** _____

Title _____

SQ3R stands for Survey, Question, Read, Recite, Review.

Survey (clues from the title, headings, pictures, graphs, charts, tables, captions, and words in bold or italic print)

  This will be about:

  I will probably learn:

My questions (based on headings or at end of each page)

  1.
  2.
  3.
  4.

Read and Recite (These are the answers I found.)

  1.
  2.
  3.
  4.
  5.

Review (Looking at the headings or my questions, I will think about what I read. I will answer my questions silently without rereading.)

See also List 132, Graphic Organizers.

The Reading Teacher's Book of Lists, Fifth Edition, © 2006 by John Wiley & Sons, Inc.

LIST 132. GRAPHIC ORGANIZERS

Graphic organizers are called Semantic Mapping or Webbing. You can often improve a student's comprehension of a story or a subject by having the student draw a graphical representation. This list of story graphs contains only suggestions; most of them can be made larger and more complex. These graphs can be used in many other subjects, such as science or history. They can be used by writers in planning stories or expository articles. They are also excellent for note-taking and studying.

Spider Map

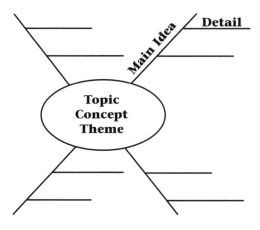

Used to describe a central idea: a thing (a geographic region), process (meiosis), concept (altruism), or proposition with support (experimental drugs should be available to AIDS victims). Key frame questions: What is the central idea? What are its attributes? What are its function?

Chain of Events (Flowchart)

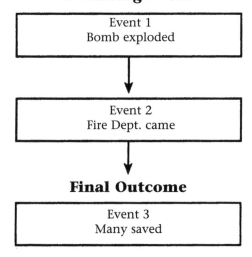

Used to describe the stages of something (the life cycle of a primate); the steps in a

linear procedure (how to neutralize an acid); a sequence of events (how feudalism led to the formation of nation states); or the goals, actions, and outcomes of a historical figure or character in a novel (the rise and fall of Napoleon). Key frame questions: What is the object, procedure, or initiating event? What are the stages or steps? How do they lead to one another? What is the final outcome?

Continuum Scale (Time Line)

1950	1960	1970	1980	1990
Born		Moved to N.Y.	Wrote book	

Low - - - - - - - - - - Mid - - - - - - - - - - High

1   2   3   4   5   6   7   8   9

Used for time lines showing historical events or ages (grade levels in school), degrees of something (weight), shades of meaning (Likert scales), or ratings scales (achievement in school). Key frame questions: What is being scaled? What are the endpoints? Multiple time lines can show relationship of two or more simultaneous events, like one line for Presidents and one line for Wars.

Compare/Contrast Matrix (Spreadsheet)

	Maria	Sally
Attribute 1 Friendliness	Liked everybody	Liked only a few people
Attribute 2 Dependability	Always on time	Missed school often
Attribute 3		

Used to show similarities and differences between two things (people, places, events, ideas, etc.). Key frame questions: What

GRAPHIC ORGANIZERS CONTINUED

things are being compared? How are they similar? How are they different? Spreadsheets can be enlarged to contain many rows and columns.

Semantic Feature Analysis

A Semantic Feature Analysis or grid can also be used to show which features or classes have things in common with a plus sign or not in common with a minus sign.

This is similar to the Compare/Contrast Matrix: both are basically a spreadsheet. They can easily be created in software programs like Microsoft Excel.

Structured Overview

A Structured Overview is another type of map similar to the first simple Semantic Map that shows clusters of ideas, terms, or features.

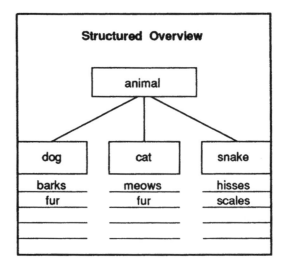

Venn Diagram

A Venn Diagram is often used in mathematics, but can easily be used with words and ideas to show features in common between two different concepts.

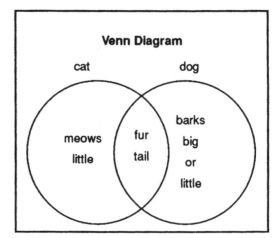

The Reading Teacher's Book of Lists, Fifth Edition, © 2006 by John Wiley & Sons, Inc.

Problem/Solution Outline

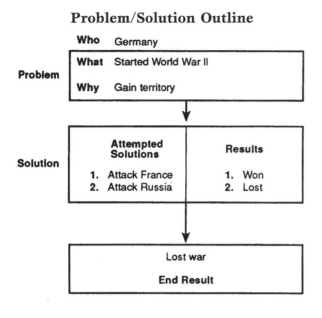

Human Interaction Outline

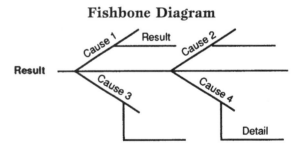

Used to represent a problem, attempted solutions, and results (the national debt). Key frame questions: What was the problem? Who had the problem? What attempts were made to solve the problem? Did those attempts succeed?

This is similar to a Flowchart or Chain of Events.

Network Tree (dendrogram)

Used to show causal information (causes of poverty), a hierarchy (types of insects), or branching procedures (the circulatory system). Key frame questions: What is the superordinate category? What are the subordinate categories? How are they related? How many levels are there?

This is similar to the Structured Overview.

Used to show the nature of an interaction between persons or groups (European settlers and Native Americans). Key frame questions: Who are the persons or groups? What were their goals? Did they conflict or cooperate? What was the outcome for person or group?

This chart compares interactions of two persons, groups, or processes.

Fishbone Diagram

Used to show the causal interaction of a complex event (an election, a nuclear explosion) or complex phenomenon (juvenile delinquency, learning disabilities). Key frame questions: What are the factors that cause X? How do they interrelate? Are the factors that cause X the same as those that cause X to persist?

GRAPHIC ORGANIZERS CONTINUED

Class/Example Map

Another more formal Class/Example Map can show hierarchy relationship plus related features or properties. These Class/Example Maps are useful for teaching vocabulary, "thinking skills," and complex relationships in many subjects.

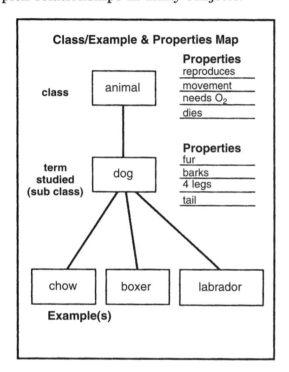

Coordinate Class Example Map

A Coordinate Class Example Map not only shows a hierarchy relationship but contrasts two similar or different terms, both of which belong to the same class and have some features or properties in common and some features that are different. Both contrasted terms have different examples.

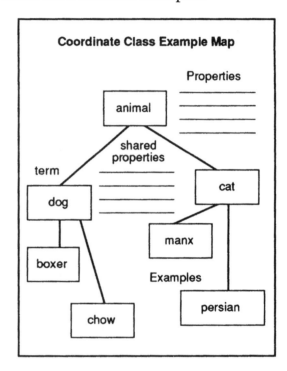

The Reading Teacher's Book of Lists, Fifth Edition, © 2006 by John Wiley & Sons, Inc.

Cycle

Used to show how a series of events interact to produce a set of results again and again (whether phenomena, cycles of achievement and failure, the life cycle). Key frame questions: What are the critical events in the cycle? How are they related? In what ways are they self-reinforcing?

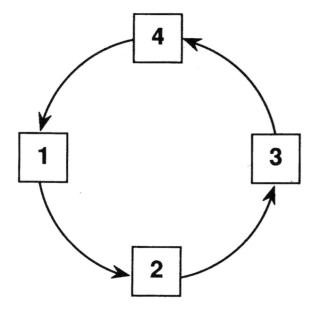

Semantic Mapping

There are a number of ways to make some of the ideas in stories or expository text graphically visible. These are sometimes called Semantic Maps or Cognitive Maps, Webbing, or a number of other terms. They are also excellent for developing or enriching vocabulary.

A simple **Semantic Map** might have a term, title, or vocabulary word in the middle and four clusters or areas of related terms. Or this map could show causes (left side) and effects (right side). This map could also be called a Multi-Flow Map.

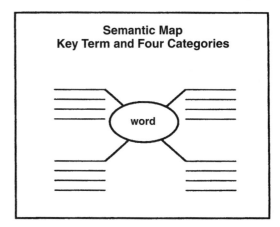

Interactions and Contrast

This is similar to the Compare/Contrast Matrix. Useful in analyzing stories and plays, it can also be used for many science or social science topics.

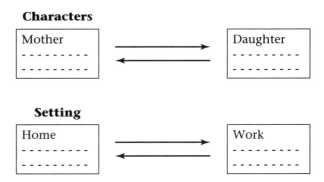

See also List 126, Oral Reading Activities; List 134, Graph Types.

LIST 133. USING COMPUTER-BASED GRAPHIC ORGANIZERS

Most teachers use graphic organizers to help students organize information, see patterns, present findings, and visualize and understand relationships. Software applications make these uses even more powerful teaching and learning tools. For example, Inspiration™ makes creating story maps easy and—with a mouse click—can turn a traditional outline into a concept map. Whether you are using a specialized concept development visualization application, the drawing tools in your word processing program, or markers and paper, the uses of graphic organizers are plentiful. Here are 50 ideas to get you started.

1. Make a class book of each student's photo, nickname, favorites, birthday.
2. Compare the characteristics of two animals.
3. Show prior knowledge using a concept map.
4. Brainstorm ideas.
5. Organize information students already have.
6. Organize information as students collect it doing research.
7. Make a KWL chart.
8. Show a plan for doing an interdisciplinary theme unit.
9. Show similarities and differences for two things.
10. Give directions for a complex activity.
11. Illustrate "what we learned about ____."
12. Create worksheets for matching words and definitions.
13. Create worksheets for matching pictures and words or definitions.
14. Compare and contrast characters in a play.
15. Show cycles of growth.
16. Create Venn or tree diagrams.
17. Outline a persuasive essay showing the main point and supporting details.
18. Show organization of school.
19. Illustrate parts of a plant.
20. Develop study guides for test reviews.
21. Create a student's family tree.
22. Assess student learning by having the class fill in a graphic organizer.
23. Create a zoo book: templates with pictures of animal, name, habitat, food, geographic location, size, name of young.
24. Overview the curriculum plan for a semester showing the interconnectedness of topics.
25. Provide structure for the writing process.
26. Organize ideas before starting to write.
27. Show work flow for a project.
28. Illustrate steps in an experiment.
29. Create story boards for presentations or Web sites.

The Reading Teacher's Book of Lists, Fifth Edition, © 2006 by John Wiley & Sons, Inc.

30. Show sequence of events in a time line.

31. Help visualize and understand the root cause of a problem.

32. Show math process steps.

33. Illustrate artifacts for a historic period.

34. Explain a learning center's relation to a theme unit.

35. Provide visual information as a supplement to text information and/or oral information.

36. Show links between instructional plans and state learning standards.

37. Teach spatial relationships.

38. Create a template for researching other countries: name, flag, language, continent, population, major occupations, capital, government, etc.

39. Make story maps.

40. Show cause and effect.

41. Show hierarchy of knowledge.

42. Show organization of files, areas, etc., by making a color-code chart.

43. Assign roles in a cooperative learning project or team assignment.

44. Support cooperative curriculum mapping.

45. Teach online search skills through visualization of "and," "or," "not."

46. Develop a study guide for content areas.

47. Illustrate and track progress toward independent reading goals.

48. Flowchart stages in a process.

49. Make lab note templates.

50. Display inspirational quotations.

LIST 134. GRAPH TYPES

Here is an organized list (a taxonomy) of graphs. It covers most (perhaps not all) of the types of graphs that students will encounter in their reading. Sometimes graphs just help the student to understand the written text better, while other times graphs are absolutely necessary for good comprehension.

A useful teaching technique is to have students find, copy, or make some graphs of most examples of these graph types.

1. Lineal (nonnumerical)

   a. Simple (*example:* story)

   b. Multiple (*example:* history)

   c. Complex:

      Hierarchy (*example:* organization)

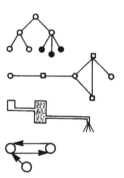

      Flow (*example:* computer)

      Process (*example:* chemicals)

      Sociogram (*example:* friendship)

2. Quantitative (numerical)

   a. Frequency Polygon (*example:* growth)

   b. Bar graph (*example:* production)

   c. Scattergram (*example:* test scores)

   d. Status Graph (*example:* scheduling)

   e. Pie Graph (*example:* percentage)

   f. Dials (*example:* clock)

The Reading Teacher's Book of Lists, Fifth Edition, © 2006 by John Wiley & Sons, Inc.

3. Spatial (maps)

a. Two Dimensions (single plane)
(*examples:* map, floor plan)

b. Three Dimensions (multiplane)
(*examples:* relief map, math shapes)

4. Pictorial

a. Realistic

b. Semipictorial

c. Abstract

d. Menga (mixture of drawing and words)

5. Hypothetical

a. Conceptual

b. Verbal

6. Near Graphs

a. High Verbal Outline

Main Idea

a. Detail

b. Another detail

b. High Numerical (tables)
(spatial placement of number has meaning)

Table	
25	4.2
37	6.1
71	7.3

c. Symbols

d. Decorative Design

LIST 135. MNEMONIC DEVICE

This mnemonic device has actually been known for centuries. It is still impressive as a study technique. Done with a bit of showmanship, it will also provide great entertainment. Your students can impress their parents by memorizing a list of twenty objects in just a few minutes (after they study and learn the mnemonic device).

The Reading Teacher's Book of Lists, Fifth Edition, © 2006 by John Wiley & Sons, Inc.

The following is (1) an interesting trick with which the students can interest and amuse their friends, (2) a serious experiment in psychology that clearly demonstrates the power of associative learning, and (3) a useful skill that can sometimes help the student to remember a long and not necessarily related list of facts (useful in passing some examinations and in going to the market).

First, let us give an example of how the trick might be done in school. The student asks his or her friends to call out slowly a list of objects—any objects. The friends call out "clock–chair–hammer," and so on. Often a friend will write them down on the chalkboard so that the others will not forget them: "1. clock; 2. chair; 3. hammer." The student does not look at the chalkboard. After twenty objects, or however many the students decide, someone calls a halt and immediately announces that he or she has memorized all the objects and can call them out in any order—forward, backward, every other way—in fact, he or she can tell them the number of any object (without looking at the board). The friends say that they do not believe the student; one of them asks, "What is number three?" The student immediately replies, "Hammer." Then after a few such questions, the student demonstrates complete mastery by calling off the whole list either forward or backward.

Now, almost anyone can do this trick, once he or she knows how. The secret lies in memorizing a set of "key objects." You must first take a little time to memorize (make mental associations between) a "key object" and the number. For example, the key object for number one is "sun" and the key object for number two is "shoe," and so on (see list on the following page). You must learn the association between the key object and the number so well that whenever you say "one" to yourself you visualize "sun." You should easily be able to learn the first ten key objects and their numbers in a short learning session on the first day, ten more the next day, and so on. After you have learned the key objects well, you are ready to do the trick. When the first friend calls out the word "clock" as the first item for you to memorize, you must mentally picture a "clock" next to a "sun," which is your key object for number 1. After you have made a clear mental picture of a clock next to a sun, you then allow the next friend to call out a second item to be memorized, such as "chair"; you then mentally picture a chair with your key object, a shoe, sitting on it. You control the rate at which your friends can call out names of objects; at first, you will go rather slowly, but after you have done the trick a few times you can go more rapidly.

KEY OBJECTS

1. Sun	11. Elephant
2. Shoe	12. Twig
3. Tree	13. Throne
4. Door	14. Fort
5. Hive	15. Fire
6. Sticks	16. Silver coin
7. Heaven (an angel)	17. Sea
8. Gate	18. Apron
9. Sign	19. Knife
10. Pen	20. Baby

There are several important learning principles involved in this trick that also apply to other learning. One is the "mental visualization"—it is a powerful factor in memory and can be developed with relatively little practice. Another important factor is self-confidence; if you say beforehand "I can't do it" you probably won't be able to. Self-confidence is also important during the trick, for you must concentrate only on the object to be remembered; you cannot worry about "Did I learn the first three things?" Exaggeration of mental pictures, making them large, brightly colored, or even purposefully distorted, will often aid memory.

This type of memorizing is not a new discovery. It was well known by the ancient people of both Greece and India.

The key objects have been chosen to take advantage of another learning principle—that of rhyming. The first ten objects all have an end-rhyme with the name of the number. The second ten objects all begin with the same sound as the name of the number, except for 20, where a rough rhyme is used to avoid confusion with 12. If you wish to extend the list of objects to 50 or 100, or to change any of the suggested list, you can choose any key objects that you wish. The important thing is that they be easily visualized and never change.

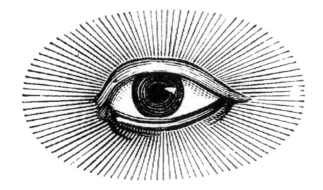

See also List 128, Study Techniques; List 132, Graphic Organizers.

LIST 136. PROBLEM-SOLVING GUIDE

Use this three-step guide to solve problems when working alone or in problem-solving teams.

1. **Understand the problem by:**
   - Stating the problem in your own words.
   - Visualizing the problem.
   - Acting out the problem.
   - Drawing a diagram, flowchart, or picture of the problem.
   - Making a table, Venn diagram, or graph of the problem.
   - Looking for patterns in the problem.
   - Comparing it with another problem you have solved.
   - Listing everything you know about it.
   - Thinking about its parts, one at a time.

2. **Propose and try solutions by:**
   - Using logical reasoning.
   - Brainstorming alternatives.
   - Writing an equation.
   - Choosing an operation and working it through.
   - Estimating and checking the results.
   - Working backward from the product or result.
   - Linking a solution to each part of the problem.
   - Solving problems within the problem.
   - Evaluating and sorting the information you have.
   - Organizing the information in a grid or matrix.
   - Eliminating solutions that don't work.
   - Solving a simpler version of the problem first.

3. **Check the results by:**
   - Filling in an information matrix.
   - Redoing the computation with a calculator.
   - Creating a flowchart or visual of the answer.
   - Dramatizing the result.
   - Comparing the results with the estimates made earlier.
   - Using the results on a trial basis.
   - Monitoring the effects of the results over time.
   - Checking the answer with a reference source.
   - Having another team or the teacher critique the result.

The Reading Teacher's Book of Lists, Fifth Edition, © 2006 by John Wiley & Sons, Inc.

See also List 137, Test-taking Strategies; List 143, Analogies.

LIST 137. TEST-TAKING STRATEGIES

Teaching these strategies should help make your students "test wise" and improve their performance on essay and objective tests. Although a few students may use these strategies on their own, most will need instruction and encouragement.

General

- If you have a choice of seats, try to sit in a place where you will be least disturbed (e.g., not by a door).
- When you first receive the test, glance over it, noting the types of questions and the numbers of points to be awarded for them.
- Budget your time, making sure you allow sufficient time for the questions that are worth the most points.
- Read directions carefully. Underline important direction words, such as *choose one, briefly,* and so on.
- Start with the *easiest questions.*
- Be alert for information in some questions that may provide help with other more difficult questions. If you find such information, be sure to note it before you forget.

Objective Tests

- Before you start, find out if there is a penalty for guessing and if you can choose more than one answer.
- Read the questions and all possible answers carefully.
- Be especially careful about questions with the choices of *all of the above* and *none of the above.*
- Underline key words and qualifiers such as *never, always,* and so on.
- Answer all of the questions you know first.
- Make a mark next to those you can't answer so you can go back to them later.
- After you complete the questions you know, go back and reread the ones you didn't answer the first time.
- If you still can't answer a question the second time through, here are some strategies to try:
  1. For a multiple-choice item, read the question; then stop and try to think of an answer. Look to see if one of the choices is similar to your answer.
  2. Start by eliminating those answers that you know are *not* correct and then choose among the remaining alternatives.
  3. Read through all the answers very carefully and then go back to the question. Sometimes you can pick up clues just by thinking about the different answers you have been given to choose from.
  4. Try paraphrasing the question and then recalling some examples.
  5. For a multiple-choice item, try reading the question separately with each alternative answer.
- If there is no penalty for guessing, make sure you answer all questions, even if you have to guess blindly.
- If there is a penalty for guessing, you usually should guess if you can eliminate one of the choices.

TEST-TAKING STRATEGIES CONTINUED

- If you have time, check over the exam. Change an answer only if you can think of a good reason to do so. Generally, you're better off if you stick with your first choice.

Essay Tests

- Read through all the questions carefully.
- Mark the important direction words that tell you what you're to do: *compare, trace, list,* and so on.
- Number the parts of the question so you don't forget to answer all of them.
- Take time to try to understand what the question is asking. Don't jump to conclusions on the basis of a familiar word or two.
- As you read through the questions, briefly jot down ideas that come into your mind.
- Briefly outline your answers before you begin to write. Refer back to the question to be sure your answer is focused on the question.
- As you write, be careful to stick to your outline.
- If possible, allow generous margins so you can add information later if you need to.
- Don't spend too much time on one question that you don't have time for other questions.
- If you have time, proofread what you have written. This is a good time to double-check to make sure you have answered all parts of the questions.
- If you run short of time, quickly outline answers to the questions that remain. List the information without worrying about complete sentences.

Quantitative Tests

- Read the questions carefully to make sure you understand what is being asked.
- Do the questions you are sure of first.
- Budget your time to allow for questions worth the most points.
- Don't just write answers. Make sure to show your work.
- As you work out answers, try to do it neatly and to write down each step. This helps you avoid careless mistakes and makes it possible for the tester to follow your work. It may make the difference between partial credit and no credit for a wrong answer.
- Check your answer when you finish to make sure it makes sense. If it doesn't seem logical, check again.
- If you are missing information needed to calculate an answer, check to see if it was given in a previous problem or if you can compute it in some way.
- Check to see if you have used all the information provided. You may not always need to, but you should double-check to be sure.
- If you have time, go back and check your calculations.

See also List 116, Comprehension Strategy Initializations; List 131, SQ3R Study Guide.

LIST 138. LIBRARY CLASSIFICATIONS

Most universities, research organizations, large public libraries, and, of course, the Library of Congress, use the Library of Congress classifications for organizing their book collections. Most school libraries and smaller public libraries use the Dewey Decimal System. Students should have at least a modest acquaintance with both systems.

LIBRARY OF CONGRESS CLASSIFICATION

A   General Works
B   Philosophy and Religion
C   History of Civilization
D   General History
E–F   History—Americas
G   Geography and Anthropology
H   Social Sciences
J   Political Science
K   Law
L   Education
M   Music
N   Fine Arts
P   Language and Literature
    PA   Classical Language and Literature
    PB–PH   Modern European Languages
    PJ–PL   Oriental Language and Literature
    PN   General Literature
    PQ   French, Italian, Spanish, Portugeuse Literature
    PR   English Literature
    PS   American Literature
    PT   German, Dutch, Scandinavian Literature
Q   Science
R   Medicine
S   Agriculture
T   Technology
U   Military Science
V   Naval Science
Z   Bibliography

SIMPLIFIED DEWEY DECIMAL SYSTEM

000   General Works
100   Philosophy and Psychology
200   Religion
300   Social Sciences
    310   Statistics
    320   Political Science
    330   Economics
    331   Labor Economics
    331.3   Labor by Age Groups
    331.39   Employed Middle-Aged and Aged
    340   Law
    350   Administration
    360   Welfare and Social Institutions
    370   Education
    380   Public Services and Utilities
    390   Customs and Folklore
400   Philosophy
500   Pure Science
600   Applied Science
700   Fine Arts
800   Literature
900   History

Note: Libraries that use the Dewey Decimal System classify fiction by author's last name and it is usually divided into Adult Fiction and Children's Fiction. All the books in the library are listed in the "Card Catalog." If a "paper" card catalog is still used, most books have 3 cards: an author card, a subject card, and a title card. Most libraries, however, currently have their card catalog online.

LIST 139. DICTIONARY SKILLS

Students need to be taught how to use a dictionary. Here are some of the skills they need.

Alphabetization

You can't find anything without alphabetizing skills.

1. Practice **looking up short words** (3 letters), **then longer words** (4 syllables).

2. Practice **using guidewords.** These are words or 3-letter parts of a word indicating the first and last word alphabetically that appear on that particular page.

3. Practice internal alphabetization where **the first 3 or 4 letters are the same but the fourth or fifth letter determines the order.** For example: Does *luxurious* come before or after *luxuriance*?

Inflected Forms

Most nouns and all verbs have inflected forms that may or may not be a main entry (the word to look up) in a dictionary.

1. For example: The word *lurch* as a noun means "a sudden leaning or roll to one side."

2. The plural is *lurches* (not a main entry).

3. As a verb, *to lurch* has more variant forms: *lurched* and *lurching*.

4. Many other suffixes yield variant forms around the central meaning. (See Lists 30 and 31 on Suffixes.) For example:

kind	*teach*	*joy*	*child*
kinder	*teacher*	*joyful*	*childish*
kindness	*teaching*	*joyless*	*childlike*

5. Many prefixes yield new word forms that alter the meaning. (See Lists 28 and 29 on Prefixes.) For example:

rewrite	*antiwar*	*unhappy*
repaid	*antislavery*	*uncertain*

Dictionary Entry Parts

Different dictionaries vary somewhat in their format, but they usually have the following common parts.

1. The **entry word** gives a correct spelling(s) usually with syllabification given by spaces or dots between syllables. For example:

    a   ban   don   *a • ban • don*

The Reading Teacher's Book of Lists, Fifth Edition, © 2006 by John Wiley & Sons, Inc.

2. The **pronunciation** is given in some type of phonetic spelling. The kind of phonetic spelling varies with the dictionary, but there is always a key. (It helps that you know some phonics.) For example:

(ə ban´ dən)

3. The **definition** is given. There may be several definitions, perhaps followed by a sample usage. For example:

to give up ⟨we *abandon* the idea⟩
to leave without intention to return ⟨to *abandon* the ship⟩

4. **Inflected forms**—and sometimes irregular inflected forms—are given. Here are some irregular inflected forms:

lose—lost	*light—lit*	*give—gave*
sell—sold	*spin—spun*	*fight—fought*

(See List 181 for more irregular verb forms.)

5. **Parts of speech** often give some insight into meaning and usage. They are often abbreviated "v." (verb), "n." (noun), and so on.

Other Information

Different dictionaries give differing amounts of information about the entry word, such as the word history or origin, homographs, idiomatic use, etc. Read the introduction to your dictionary to find out what yours offers.

LIST 140. DICTIONARY PHONETIC SYMBOLS

Dictionaries tell you how to pronounce words by using phonetic symbols. These are based on the Roman alphabet but add diacritical marks and special letter combinations. Although all dictionaries use similar phonetic symbols, they are not all identical. This list shows four of the more widely used sets of symbols.

PHONEMES	COMMON AND UNCOMMON SPELLINGS	PHONEMES	COMMON AND UNCOMMON SPELLINGS
ă	**A Short** hat, plaid, England	ĭ	**I Short** been, bit, sieve, women, busy, build, hymn
ā	**A Long** age, aid, gaol, gauge, say, break, vain, they	ī	**I Long** aisle, aye, height, eye, ice, lie, buy, sky
ā, er, ar, âr	**A** ("air" sound-diphthong) care, air, ear, where, pear, their	j	**J** bridge, gradual, soldier, tragic, exaggerate, jam
ä	**A Broad** father, heart, sergeant	k	**K** coat, account, chemistry, back, acquire, sacque, kind, liquor
b	**B** bad, rabbit		
ch	**CH Digraph** child, watch, righteous, question virtuous	l	**L** land, tell
		m	**M** drachm, paradigm, calm, me, climb, common, solemn
d	**D** did, add, filled		
ě	**E Short** many, aesthetic, said, says, let, bread, heifer, leopard, friend, bury	n	**N** gnaw, knife, no, manner, pneumonia
		ng	**NG Blend** ink, long, tongue
ē	**E Long** Caesar, quay, equal, team, bee, receive, people, key, machine, believe, phoenix	o, ȧ, ŏ	**O Short** watch, hot
		ō	**O Long** beau, yeoman, sew, open, boat, toe, oh, brooch, soul, low
ėr, ə, ûr	**R** (or short u plus R) stern, pearl, first, word, journey, turn, myrtle		
f	**F** fat, effort, laugh, phrase	ô, ȯ	**O Broad** all, Utah, taught, law, order, broad, bought
g	**G** go, egg, ghost, guest, catalogue	oi, ȯi	**OI Diphthong** boil, boy
h	**H** he, who	ou, əu	**OU Diphthong** house, bough, now
hw	**WH Digraph** wheat	p	**P** cup, happy

The Reading Teacher's Book of Lists, Fifth Edition, © 2006 by John Wiley & Sons, Inc.

PHONEMES	COMMON AND UNCOMMON SPELLINGS	PHONEMES	COMMON AND UNCOMMON SPELLINGS
r	**R** run, rhythm, carry	v	**V** of, Stephen, very, flivver
s	**S** cent, say, scent; schism, miss	w	**W** choir, quick, will
sh	**SH Digraph** ocean, machine, special, sure, schist, conscience, nauseous, pshaw, she, tension, issue, mission, nation	y	**Y** (consonant) opinion, hallelujah, you
t	**T** stopped, bought, tell, Thomas, button	z	**Z** has, discern, scissors, Xerxes, zero, buzz
th	**TH (voiceless)** thin	zh	**ZH** garage, measure, division, azure, brazier
TH, th, th	**TH (voiced)** then, breathe	ə	**Schwa** alone, fountain, moment, pencil, complete, cautious, circus
u, ə, ŭ	**U Short** come, does, flood, trouble, cup		
yü, yo͞o	**U Long** beauty, feud, queue, few, adieu, view, use		
u̇, u, o͝o	**U Short** wolf, good, should, full		
ü, o͞o	**OO Long** maneuver, threw, move, shoe, food, you, rule, fruit		

Diacritical Marks

ôrder	(circumflex)
ēqual	(macron)
cañon	(tilde)
naïve	(dieresis)
façade	(cedilla)
pu̇t	(single dot)
attaché	(acute accent)
à la mode	(grave accent)
căt	(breve)

The Reading Teacher's Book of Lists, Fifth Edition, © 2006 by John Wiley & Sons, Inc.

See also List 1, Consonant Sounds; List 2, Vowel Sounds; List 9, Phonics Example Words.

11

ASSESSMENT

LIST 141. ALTERNATE ASSESSMENT TECHNIQUES

Much attention is given to language arts assessment, particularly to standardized language arts tests used by districts and states to monitor yearly progress. Schools also use diagnostic tests and criterion-referenced tests linked to their reading programs. Teachers can use the following assessment techniques to evaluate different components of reading proficiency and to plan instruction and practice.

Running Records

Based on the work of Dr. Marie Clay, a running record uses students' individual oral reading of a selection of text on their developmental level and their retelling of the material to assess word recognition, metacognitive awareness, fluency, and comprehension. As the student reads the selection aloud, the teacher systematically records accuracy, self-corrections, and errors. Errors are classified (omissions, insertions, substitutions, and repetition) to provide and identify skill needs. Fluency traits are also noted. The students' retelling after reading provides data on comprehension. There are many resources available for using running records.

Fluency Lists

One component of fluency is students' ability to immediately recognize and read words without resorting to phonics or other word analysis techniques. Choral practice reading lists of target words help students develop automaticity that, in turn, helps fluency and comprehension. Use key words from content area units, high frequency words, irregularly spelled words, and word wall lists. (See Section 9, Fluency.)

Retellings

After students read a story or have one read to them, ask them to retell as if they were telling someone else who had never heard it before. It is important to let students know in advance that they will be asked to do this. Use minimal cues like "Tell me more." "And then?" Retellings can be scored for fiction and nonfiction readings. There are three parts to evaluating retellings: accuracy, language used, and student response. For *accuracy,* look for restatement of all main ideas, each with some supporting detail; organization that follows the text (chronology, comparison, question and answer, beginning/middle/end, etc.); inclusion of all major characters or topics; and correct use of key vocabulary from text (for example, does not substitute more common words like "the man" when the text referred to "the astronaut"). For *language used,* look for sentence structure, vocabulary, time and sequence signals, and use of idioms. For *student response,* look for indications that the student recognizes the genre, purpose, and audience of the material; makes links between student's background or prior knowledge and the material read; evaluates the material; and makes extensions by relating the material to other ideas or readings.

The Reading Teacher's Book of Lists, Fifth Edition, © 2006 by John Wiley & Sons, Inc.

ALTERNATE ASSESSMENT TECHNIQUES CONTINUED

Dictations

The teacher reads a sentence through once, then again by phrases. Students listen to the first reading, and then begin to write each phrase as it is reread. At early stages, dictations are scored by the number of correct sound-letter correspondences, not accurate spelling. For example, if "sed" was written for "said," and "mil" for "mill," each would receive a score of 3 for correct sound-letter combinations. Later, score 1 point for each correctly scored word in the sentence. For example, "I askt Mary to go to the park with me." would be scored 9. For the most advanced dictation, 1 point is given for each correct word and each correct capitalization and punctuation. For example: "I herd the noise, too." would be scored 7; 4 for correctly spelled words, and 1 point each for capitalizing "I," using the comma correctly, and using the period correctly.

Reading Logs

Have students keep a log of all their independent reading at school and at home. The log should include works completed and works started but not completed. The log should include: title, author, pages read, what I thought (reaction to content, how I felt about the task/difficulty/genre). Periodic discussions of these logs will provide insight on how the students are developing as independent readers and suggest ways in which the teacher can give added encouragement. Student reflections on what they thought and how they felt about a variety of books will help them recognize their reading preferences and strengths. The reading logs can be placed in students' portfolios.

Checklists

Use checklists to monitor progress of individual students and the whole class against a set of defined learning objectives. For example: A checklist for letter writing might include date, return address, salutation, consistency of alignment (block or indented), closing, and signature. For each practice letter, date and check off items each student did well. The checklist for individual students can be part of their portfolios, showing improvement in letter writing. Charting the information for all students in the class shows progress and potential small group needs by letter element.

Portfolios

Portfolios are systematic collections of student work over time. These collections are artifacts of student growth and development. It is essential that students develop a sense of ownership about their portfolios so they can understand how to use them to see their own progress and recognize areas where more work is needed.

Reading portfolios may include a broad range of material depending on the grade level and purposes for which the portfolio will be used. Some portfolios are collections of students' best work in each area showing mastery of the learning objectives. Others are meant to show progress across a range of skills and include first drafts and final versions; pre- and post-tests; beginning-of-year and end-of-year writing samples, etc. The following items are often included in reading portfolios: interest inventories; reading logs; audiotapes of student reading from September, December, and June; journal responses to readings; written retellings; concept maps; time lines or sequence charts; chart of speed and fluency test results; checklists for unit learning objectives; running records; original writing (stories, poems, letters); and student reflection on portfolio components.

The Reading Teacher's Book of Lists, Fifth Edition, © 2006 by John Wiley & Sons, Inc.

LIST 142. ENGLISH LANGUAGE ARTS STANDARDS

Standards for English Language Arts broadly articulate common expectations for the English language arts outcomes of instructional programs. They imply common understanding of what we know about reading and learning and about factors that contribute to developing a full range of literacy skills. The standards below are from the National Council of Teachers of English and the International Reading Association. Most states have developed standards, curriculum frameworks, and related assessment protocols which are available from their state departments of education.

Standards for the English Language Arts

1. Students read a wide range of print and nonprint texts to build an understanding of texts, of themselves, and of the cultures of the United States and the world; to acquire new information; to respond to the needs and demands of society and the workplace; and for personal fulfillment. Among these texts are fiction and nonfiction, classic and contemporary works.

2. Students read a wide range of literature from many periods in many genres to build an understanding of the many dimensions (e.g., philosophical, ethical, aesthetic) of human experience.

3. Students apply a wide range of strategies to comprehend, interpret, evaluate, and appreciate texts. They draw on their prior experience, their interactions with other readers and writers, their knowledge of word meaning and of other texts, their word identification strategies, and their understanding of textual features (e.g., sound–letter correspondence, sentence structure, context, graphics).

4. Students adjust their use of spoken, written, and visual language (e.g., conventions, style, vocabulary) to communicate effectively with a variety of audiences and for different purposes.

5. Students employ a wide range of strategies as they write and use different writing process elements appropriately to communicate with different audiences for a variety of purposes.

6. Students apply knowledge of language structure, language conventions (e.g., spelling and punctuation), media techniques, figurative language, and genre to create, critique, and discuss print and non-print texts.

7. Students conduct research on issues and interests by generating ideas and questions, and by posing problems. They gather, evaluate, and synthesize data from a variety of sources (e.g., print and nonprint texts, artifacts, people) to communicate their discoveries in ways that suit their purpose and audience.

8. Students use a variety of technological and information resources (e.g., libraries, databases, computer networks, video) to gather and synthesize information and to create and communicate knowledge.

9. Students develop an understanding of and respect for diversity in language use, patterns, and dialects across cultures, ethnic groups, geographic regions, and social roles.

10. Students whose first language is not English make use of their first language to develop competency in the English language arts and to develop understanding of content across the curriculum.

11. Students participate as knowledgeable, reflective, creative, and critical members of a variety of literacy communities.

12. Students use spoken, written, and visual language to accomplish their own purposes (e.g., for learning, enjoyment, persuasion, and the exchange of information).

From: National Council of Teachers of English/International Reading Association @ http://www.ncte.org/

The Reading Teacher's Book of Lists, Fifth Edition, © 2006 by John Wiley & Sons, Inc.

LIST 143. ANALOGIES

Analogies are used for teaching and testing. The key is to determine the relationship of the first pair of words and then find a second pair of words that has the same relationship. For example, "in" is to "out" as "hot" is to "_____." (In the notation used below, this is written: "in : out :: hot :   .") Since "out" is the opposite of "in," the answer is "cold," which is the opposite of "hot." Below are some common types of analogies and several examples for each.

Antonyms

open : close :: up : down
serious : comical :: happy : sad
fiction : fact :: love : hate
large : small :: laugh : cry
waive : require :: transparent : opaque

Synonyms

back : rear :: under : below
near : close-by :: thin : slim
find : discover :: danger : peril
divide : separate :: flat : level
right : correct :: terrify : frighten

Cause and Effect

tired : sleep :: hungry : eat
work : success :: study : learn
wash : clean :: fertilize : grow
happy : smile :: sad : cry
earthquake : destruction :: disease : fever

Sequence

breakfast : lunch :: afternoon : evening
pour : drink :: cook : eat
go : arrive :: flower : fruit
sleep : dream :: plant : harvest
cold : snow :: cloudy : rain

Numerical Relationship

three : six :: four : eight
two : three :: seven : eight
one : three :: four : six
four : two :: eight : four
nine : three :: twelve : four

Opposite Characteristic

millionaire : indigent :: bigmouth : mute

Degree (Intensity)

pretty : beautiful :: warm : hot
intelligent : brilliant :: hungry : starving

simmer : boil :: brown : burn
dirty : filthy :: clean : spotless
interesting : fascinating :: nice : wonderful

Grammatical Relationship

she : her :: he : him
eat : ate :: sleep : slept
run : running :: talk : talking
apple : apples :: goose : geese
he : his :: I : mine

Part–Whole Relationship

finger : hand :: page : book
room : house :: branch : tree
handle : cup :: eraser : pencil
hand : clock :: yolk : egg
lens : camera :: wheel : car

Member–Group Relationship

fish : school :: student : class
professor : faculty :: sister : sorority
soldier : regiment :: star : constellation
athlete : team :: state : country
senator : congress :: judge : court

Object–Action

hand : write :: bell : ring
sun : shine :: knife : cut
clock : tick :: foot : kick
lamp : light :: rooster : crow
baby : cry :: airplane : fly

Person–Action

dawdler : lingers :: witness : testifies
doctor : curing :: miser : hoarding
voyeur : seeing :: auditor : hearing

Object–Class

peach : fruit :: fork : silverware
poodle : dog :: chair : furniture
shirt : clothing :: ring : jewelry

The Reading Teacher's Book of Lists, Fifth Edition, © 2006 by John Wiley & Sons, Inc.

arm : limb :: jazz : music
white : color :: triangle : shape

Object–Description
floor : hard :: test : difficult
food : delicious :: sky : blue
flower : fragrant :: child : cute
bed : comfortable :: tree : tall
honey : sticky :: ice : cold

Object–Place
bear : den :: bee : hive
bird : sky :: fish : sea
car : garage :: stove : kitchen
computer : office :: tractor : farm
money : wallet :: hammer : toolbox

Object–Use
book : read :: food : eat
car : travel :: milk : drink
stove : cook :: nose : breathe
piano : music :: ladder : reach
clown : laugh :: coat : warm

Object–User
crib : baby :: guitar : musician
library : student :: oven : baker
register : cashier :: ship : sailor
pool : swimmer :: racquet : tennis player
microscope : scientist :: gun : robber

MORE ANALOGIES
mother : aunt :: father : uncle
car : driver :: plane : pilot
green : color :: cinnamon : spice
coffee : drink :: hamburger : eat
arrow : bow :: bullet : gun
ceiling : room :: lid : pan

page : book :: Ohio : U.S.
glove : hand :: boot : foot
swim : pool :: jog : road
meat : beef :: fruit : apple
date : calendar :: time : clock
carpenter : house :: composer : symphony

soldier : regiment :: star : constellation
duck : drake :: bull : cow
cells : skin :: bricks : wall
paw : dog :: fin : fish
moon : earth :: earth : sun
tree : lumber :: wheat : flour

library : books :: cupboard : dishes
princess : queen :: prince : king
story : read :: song : sing
length : weight :: inches : pounds
one : three :: single : triple
blind : deaf :: see : hear

wrist : hand :: ankle : foot
engine : go :: brake : stop
glass : break :: paper : tear
book : character :: recipe : ingredient
sing : pleased :: shout : angry
penny : dollar :: foot : yard

cabin : build :: well : dig
temperature : humidity :: thermometer : hygrometer
left : right :: top : bottom
easy : simple :: hard : difficult

See also List 32, Synonyms; List 33, Antonyms; List 137, Test-Taking Strategies.

LIST 144. RUBRICS FOR WRITING—PRIMARY

Even very young writers need feedback in order to understand their writing strengths and the areas in which they can improve. "Good job" or "You can do better" do not provide enough information to enable them to focus on important aspects of good writing. Be sure to show students examples of work at each level and discuss them, so they can develop self-monitoring skills.

Name			Date		
	Beginning 1	**Developing 2**	**Accomplished 3**	**Exemplary 4**	**Score**
Topic	Key word(s) near beginning	Main idea or topic in first sentence	Good main idea or topic sentence	Interesting, well-stated main idea/ topic sentence	
Words	Related words or ideas mentioned	Some key words or related ideas included as details with meaning	Key related words and ideas used as details with meaning	Key related words and ideas used correctly; defined for reader; interesting choices of words	
Order	Ideas not ordered	Some order of main idea + details or sequence	Main idea + details or sequential, as appropriate	Good flow of ideas from topic sentence + details or sequence	
Sentences	Sentence fragments	Mostly complete sentences	Complete sentences	Complete sentences; variety	
Punctuation	Some punctuation	Most sentences have punctuation	Correct punctuation	Correct punctuation and variety	
Capital Letters	Upper- and lowercase not distinguished	Uses upper- and lowercase	Begins sentences with uppercase	Correct use of case for beginning of sentence, names, etc.	
Spelling	Many spelling errors	Some spelling errors	Few spelling errors	No spelling errors	
Handwriting	Hard to read; not well formed	Mostly legible	Well-formed letters	Neat, easy to read, well formed	

The Reading Teacher's Book of Lists, Fifth Edition, © 2006 by John Wiley & Sons, Inc.

LIST 145. RUBRICS FOR WRITING—ELEMENTARY/INTERMEDIATE

Good writing is a complex accomplishment involving the organization of ideas, the select use of vocabulary, attention to readers and purpose, and the "mechanics" of grammar, spelling, punctuation, and handwriting. Rubrics provide students information about the qualities and dimensions of good writing and feedback about their progress. Examples of written work at each of the four levels should be available. Develop rubrics with your students for special writing projects such as reports, short stories, or journals.

Name			Date		
	Beginning 1	**Developing 2**	**Accomplished 3**	**Exemplary 4**	**Score**
Topic	Key word(s) near beginning	Main idea or topic in first sentence	Good main idea or topic sentence	Interesting, well-stated main idea/topic sentence	
Organization	Ideas not ordered	Some order of main idea + details or sequence	Main idea + details or sequential, as appropriate	Good flow of ideas from topic sentence + details or sequence	
Paragraphs	One paragraph or text divided but not by content	Supporting details mostly grouped into appropriate paragraphs	Ideas appropriately divided into paragraphs with supporting details	Strong paragraphs ordered to develop story or exposition	
Sentences	Mostly complete sentences; some fragments or run-on	Complete sentences; few run-on sentences	Complete sentences; no run-ons or fragments; some variety in length and type	No sentence errors; variety in length and type; sentence types relate to style of writing	
Vocabulary	Related words or ideas mentioned; limited basic vocabulary	Attempts to use new key words in description; goes beyond basic vocabulary	Uses new key/related words and ideas correctly; varies language	Uses new key/related words/ideas easily; colorful, interesting words suitable for topic and audience	
Grammar	Many errors in agreement, number, tense	Some errors in agreement, number, tense	Few errors in agreement, number, tense	No errors in agreement, number, tense	
Punctuation and Case	Several punctuation and case errors	Few punctuation and case errors	Minor errors in punctuation and case; variety used	Correct punctuation and case throughout; variety used	
Spelling	Many spelling errors	Some spelling errors	Few spelling errors	No spelling errors	
Handwriting	Hard to read; not well formed	Mostly legible	Well-formed letters	Neat, easy to read, well formed	

LIST 146. PRESENTATION RUBRICS

Studies on the exchange of knowledge and research have shown that peer teaching, reciprocal teaching, and even the age-old "show and tell" are valuable teaching and learning activities. Developing students' presentation skills aids knowledge integration, speaking skills, interdisciplinary and creative thinking, self expression, and self confidence. Students need support and instruction throughout the various stages in the development process. The preparation also helps develop time-management skills.

Name			Date		
	Beginning 1	Developing 2	Accomplished 3	Exemplary 4	Score
Preparation	Storyboard or outline incomplete; lacks props or resources	Storyboard or outline doesn't represent whole; resources and props few or inappropriate	Storyboard or outline complete; resources and props appropriate	Storyboard or outline complete and well organized; resources and props outstanding	
Content	Mentions key ideas; little evidence of understanding	Expresses key ideas; not fully at ease with concepts	Expresses key ideas and shows understanding	Key words and ideas correctly used; defined for reader; interesting choices of words	
Order	Ideas not ordered; audience has difficulty following	Some order of ideas; but jumps around	Logical sequence of presentation; audience can follow	Logical sequence, easy to follow; good overview and transitions	
Media, Graphics, and Props	Media, graphics, and props missing or do not add information	Media, graphics, and props tangential to text; minor value	Media, graphics, and props relate to text; add value or information	Media, graphics, and props relate, add information, help explain, keep interest	
Speaking	Hesitates, whispers; many "fillers"; poor eye contact	Some hesitation; some "fillers" but moves along; some eye contact, but reads mostly	Clear, good pace and pronunciation; good eye contact; checks notes	Clear, well paced, well modulated; good eye contact; well rehearsed, little need for notes	
Q&A	Defensive; frequent "don't know" shrugs	Some "I don't know's"; some defensiveness	Answers correctly with little hesitancy	Answers correctly; expands, explains	

The Reading Teacher's Book of Lists, Fifth Edition, © 2006 by John Wiley & Sons, Inc.

LIST 147. TEST WORDS

For students to perform well on tests, end-of-chapter questions, labs and other assessment tasks, they must understand what they are being asked to do. In addition, there are important modifiers that if not noticed, will result in students' providing wrong answers. Teach the meaning of the test words and the difference each modifier makes. Use a variety in your homework assignments and tests.

analyze	directions	mention	relationship
apply	discriminate	missing	repeat
appraise	discuss	name	restate
argue	distinguish	next	review
assess	does not belong	none of these	rhyming
best	draw conclusions	not true	right
blank	effect	opposite	row
categorize	enumerate	organize	same as
cause	error	outline	sample
change	estimate	pairs	section
check your work	evaluate	paragraph	select
choose	example	paraphrase	show how
circle	explain	passage	significance
cite evidence	express	point out	solve
classify	false	predict	specify
column	fill in the blank	print	state
compare	following	probably	subdivide
complete	formulate	propose	suggest
consider	general	prove	summarize
construct	generalize	provide	support
contrast	give an example of	put an X	survey
convince	go on to next page	question	tell
correct	identify	rank	trace
create	illustrate	rate	transform
criticize	interpret	react	translate
cross out	judge	read	true
define	justify	rearrange	underline
definitions	label	reason	utilize
demonstrate	list	recall	wait for directions
describe	locate	recognize	weigh
develop	mark	recommend	why
diagram	match	record	
differentiate	memorize	relate	

See also List 118, Signal Words; List 148, Important Modifiers.

LIST 148. IMPORTANT MODIFIERS

all	less	often
always	many	seldom
best	more	some
equal	most	sometimes
every	never	usually
few	none	worst

See also List 147, Test Words.

The Reading Teacher's Book of Lists, Fifth Edition, © 2006 by John Wiley & Sons, Inc.

LIST 149. CLOZE VARIATIONS

Cloze is a sentence-completion technique in which a word (or part of a word or several words) is omitted and the student fills in the missing part. Cloze can be used as a test or practice of reading comprehension or language ability, as a research tool, or as a measure to estimate readability or passage difficulty.

To estimate the readability or difficulty level appropriate for instruction, one suggested criterion is that a student be able to fill in 35 to 44 percent of the exact missing words when every fifth word is deleted from a 250-word passage.

Cloze passages can be made easily by the teacher on any subject or any type of material. All you need to do is omit parts of the passage and ask the students to fill in the missing parts. Here is a list of some possible variations:

Passage Variations (different kinds of passage to start with)

A. Content of Passage
   (1) Science
   (2) History
   (3) Literature, etc.
B. Difficulty of Passage
   (1) Readability level
   (2) Imageability
   (3) Legibility
C. Length of Passage
   (1) Sentence
   (2) Paragraph
   (3) 500 words, etc.

Deletion Variations (different kinds of deletions or blanks)

A. Mechanical—automatic or no judgment used in deletions
   (1) Delete every *n*th word (5th, 10th, etc.).
   (2) Randomized deletion but average every *n*th word.
B. Selective—judgment used in selected deletions
   (1) Delete structure words or content words only.
   (2) Delete only one part of speech. (For example, nouns omitted.)
   (3) Delete particular letters (blends, bound morphemes, prefixes, vowels, consonants, etc.).
   (4) Delete only words or letters that best fit a particular skill objective.
C. Size of Deletion
   (1) One word, two words, etc.
   (2) One letter, two letters, etc.

Cueing Variation (different prompts or hints)

A. No cues
B. Multiple choice (sometimes referred to as "Maze"). If this is used, distractor words (wrong choices) can be varied as follows:
   (1) Similar to correct answer in length or different.

The Reading Teacher's Book of Lists, Fifth Edition, © 2006 by John Wiley & Sons, Inc.

(2) Similar or different in phonemes.

(3) Similar or different in meaning.

C. One or more letters, depending on how many letters have been deleted.

Administration Variations

A. Preparation

(1) Student reads complete passage (no blanks) before answering.

(2) Student listens to complete passage before answering.

(3) Student is given a brief introduction to passage.

(4) No preparation.

B. Answering

(1) Student reads passage and writes answers.

(2) Teacher reads passage orally and student writes answers.

(3) Teacher reads passage orally and student gives answers orally.

(4) Student told to guess or not to guess.

Scoring Variations

A. Score as correct only exact word, or score synonym as correct.

B. Correct spelling required or not required.

C. Self-correction, teacher correction, other-student correction.

D. Discuss answers or no discussion.

Uses of Cloze

A. *Test student's ability.* All students take the same cloze passage: students are ranked by number correct. Cloze scores can be assigned norms or grade levels.

B. *Measure readability of a passage.* A group of students takes two different cloze passages. The passage with the highest mean score is most readable. Some research indicates that a cloze score of 35 to 45 percent correct on a fifth-word random deletion indicates Independent Reading Level for that student (or group).

C. *Research.* Cloze is used in many types of language research. For example, ESL ability, knowledge or pronoun use, generating wrong answers for Maze, spelling, memory.

D. *Teaching.* Cloze passages are used for reading comprehension drills, subject content knowledge, language use, discussion starters, and much more.

Sample cloze passage. This is a fifth-word deletion often used for comprehension teaching or testing.

Each night Mrs. Darling _____ upstairs, read a story _____ her three children, and put them to bed. _____ was the oldest of _____ Darling children, then John, _____ little Michael. They had _____ dog named Nana.

See also List 182, Basic Sentence Patterns; List 117, Comprehension Questions.

LIST 150. TESTING TERMS

Most school districts give tests. Most teachers get the results of those tests. What do those test scores mean? How do you interpret them? One place to start is with an understanding of the terminology that test makers use. Familiarity with these terms will help you to explain test results to interested and sometimes anxious students and parents.

Achievement tests. Tests that measure how much students have learned in a particular subject area. Weekly spelling tests that teachers give are informal achivement tests. These tests can yield a percent score.

Aptitude tests. Tests that attempt to predict how well students will do in learning new subject matter in the future. Examples of aptitude tests are Art Aptitude or IQ tests.

CEEB test scores. College Entrance Examination Board test scores. This type of score is used by exams such as the Scholastic Aptitude Test. It has a mean of 500 and a standard deviation of 100. SATs use this type of score but the 500 mean changes over time.

Correlation coefficient. A measure of the strength and direction (positive or negative) of the relationship between two things.

Criterion-referenced tests. Tests for which the performance of the test taker is compared with a fixed standard or criterion. The primary purpose is to determine if the test taker has mastered a particular unit sufficiently to proceed to the next unit.

Diagnostic tests. Tests that are used to identify individual students' strengths and weaknesses in a particular subject area.

Grade equivalent scores. The grade level for which a score is the real or estimated average. For example, a grade equivalent score of 3.5 is the average score of students halfway through the third grade.

Mean. The arithmetical average of a group of scores.

Median. The middle score in a group of ranked scores.

Mode. The score that was obtained by the largest number of test takers.

Normal distribution. A bell-shaped distribution of test scores in which scores are distributed symmetrically around the mean and where the mean, median, and mode are the same.

Norming population. The group of people to whom the test was administered in order to establish performance standards for various age or grade levels. When the norming population is composed of students from various sections of the country, the resulting scores are called *national norms*. When the norming population is drawn from a local school or school district, the standards are referred to as *local norms*.

Norm-referenced tests. Tests for which the results of the test taker are compared with the performance of others (the norming population) who have taken the test.

Percent is a slight modification of a raw score. For example, if a student gets 10 words correct on a 20-word spelling test, then that student got a score of 50%.

Percentile rank. A comparison of an individual's raw score with the raw score of others who took the test (usually this is a comparison with the norming population). This comparison tells the test taker the percentage of other test takers whose scores fell below his or her own score.

Raw score. The initial score assigned to test performance. This score usually is the number correct; however, sometimes it may include a correction for guessing.

Reliability. A measure of the extent to which a test is consistent in measuring whatever it purports to measure. For example, does a reading test really measure reading ability consistently? Reliability coefficients range from 0 to 1. In order to be considered highly reliable, a test should have a reliability coefficient of 0.90 or above. There are several types of reliability coefficients: *parallel-form* reliability (the correlation of performance on two different forms of a test), *test–retest* reliability (the correlation of test scores from two different administrations of the same test to the same population), *split-half* reliability (the correlation between two halves of the same test), and *internal consistency* reliability (a reliability coefficient computed using a Kuder–Richardson formula).

Standard deviation. A measure of the variability of test scores. If most scores are close to the mean, the standard deviation will be small. If the scores have a wide range, then the standard deviation will be large.

Standard error of measurement (SEM). An estimate of the amount of measurement error in a test. This provides an estimate of how much a person's actual test score may vary from his or her hypothetical true score. The larger the SEM, the less confidence can be placed in the score as a reflection of an individual's true ability. Some tests give a *band score* which is a range from +1 SEM to −1 SEM.

Standardized tests. Tests that have been given to groups of students under standardized conditions and for which norms have been established.

Standardized tests frequently tell students how their raw scores (the number right) compare with a standardized group, such as all the 8th graders in the district (local norms) or of a random sample of 8th graders in the country (national norms).

Percentile scores indicate how the students rank with one hundred typical students in their norm group. Percentile is not like a *percent;* percentile means "rank placement," not "amount." For example, a student who got a percentile score of 43 would be ahead of 42 out of 100 typical 8th graders. This would place that student in the 4th *decile* (tenth) because that decile covers the range of percentile scores between 40 and 49. It also places that student in the second *quartile* (quarter) of percentile scores between 25 and 49; or in the third *quintile* (fifth) of percentile scores between 40 and 59.

One argument for not using percentile is that most tests are really not accurate enough to say a student who scores 43 is worse than a student who scores 44. So some larger grouping might be more fair, such as saying the student scored in the 4th decile or the middle quintile.

Stanine scores. Whole number scores between 1 and 9 that have a mean of 5 and a standard deviation of 2.

True score. The score that would be obtained on a given test if that test were perfectly reliable. This is a hypothetical score that is what you want but all you can ever get is an *obtained score* (the student's actual score).

Validity. The extent to which a test measures what it is supposed to measure. Two common types of validity are *content validity* (the extent to which the content of the test covers situations and subject matter about which conclusions will be drawn), very important for achivement tests, and *predictive validity* (the extent to which predictions made from the test are confirmed by evidence gathered at some later time), very important for aptitude tests.

See also List 151, The Normal Distribution Curve.

The Reading Teacher's Book of Lists, Fifth Edition, © 2006 by John Wiley & Sons, Inc.

LIST 151. THE NORMAL DISTRIBUTION CURVE

Reading Achievement test scores tend to follow a normal curve for any population. The following curve, for example, is for the ninth grade of a school district or a state.

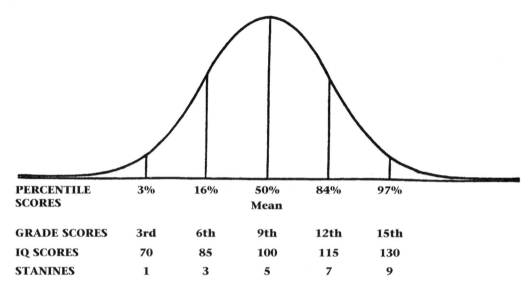

PERCENTILE SCORES	3%	16%	50% Mean	84%	97%
GRADE SCORES	3rd	6th	9th	12th	15th
IQ SCORES	70	85	100	115	130
STANINES	1	3	5	7	9

There is a strong but far from perfect correlation between Reading Achievement scores and IQ. In other words, on average a ninth grader with an IQ of 85 tends to read about at the sixth-grade level. Note that you always have many students below average or "Grade Level." This is not a fault of poor teaching; it's just the way students come. Good teaching can raise the mean a little, but good teaching will not eliminate the Normal Distribution Curve for any large population or even one class.

TYPICAL READING ABILITIES FOUND IN A FOURTH-GRADE CLASS

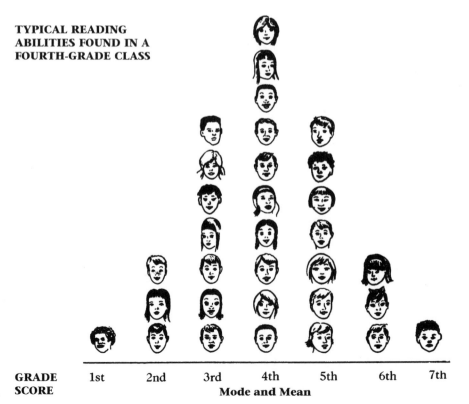

GRADE SCORE	1st	2nd	3rd	4th	5th	6th	7th
				Mode and Mean			

The Reading Teacher's Book of Lists, Fifth Edition, © 2006 by John Wiley & Sons, Inc.

12
SPELLING

LIST 152. SPELLING DEMONS—ELEMENTARY

Those who study children's spelling errors and writing difficulties have repeatedly found that a relatively small number of words make up a large percentage of all spelling errors. Many commonly misspelled words are presented in this Spelling Demons list. Other lists in this book, such as Homophones, Instant Words, and Content Words, can also be used as spelling lists.

about	could	Halloween	off	shoes	tonight
address	couldn't	handkerchief	often	since	too
advise	country	haven't	once	skiing	toys
again	cousin	having	outside	skis	train
all right	cupboard	hear	party	some	traveling
along	dairy	heard	peace	something	trouble
already	dear	height	people	sometime	truly
although	decorate	hello	piece	soon	Tuesday
always	didn't	here	played	store	two
among	doctor	hospital	plays	straight	until
April	does	hour	please	studying	used
arithmetic	early	house	poison	sugar	vacation
aunt	Easter	instead	practice	summer	very
awhile	easy	knew	pretty	Sunday	wear
balloon	enough	know	principal	suppose	weather
because	every	laid	quarter	sure	weigh
been	everybody	latter	quit	surely	were
before	favorite	lessons	quite	surprise	we're
birthday	February	letter	raise	surrounded	when
blue	fierce	little	read	swimming	where
bought	first	loose	receive	teacher	which
built	football	loving	received	tear	white
busy	forty	making	remember	terrible	whole
buy	fourth	many	right	Thanksgiving	women
children	Friday	maybe	rough	their	would
chocolate	friend	minute	route	there	write
choose	fuel	morning	said	they	writing
Christmas	getting	mother	Santa Claus	though	wrote
close	goes	name	Saturday	thought	you
color	grade	neither	says	through	your
come	guard	nice	school	tired	you're
coming	guess	none	schoolhouse	together	
cough	half	o'clock	several	tomorrow	

LIST 153. SPELLING DEMONS—INTERMEDIATE

Intermediate-level students may misspell words on the elementary list of Demons, and as their writing is more advanced than the younger students, they may also have trouble with these Demons. If you use these for spelling lessons, don't assign too many at once—pick and choose some you know students need.

absence	approximately	ceiling	descend
absolutely	arctic	celebrate	describe
acceptable	argue	cemetery	description
accidentally	arguing	certainly	desert
accommodate	argument	character	despair
accompany	around	chief	develop
accurate	arrangement	cite	difference
accustom	assistance	college	dilemma
ache	athlete	comfortable	diligence
achieve	attempt	coming	dining
acknowledgment	attendance	committed	disagreeable
acquaintance	author	committee	disappear
acquire	awful	comparative	disappoint
across	awkward	complete	disastrous
actually	balloon	concede	discipline
adolescent	banquet	conceive	discover
advantageous	bargain	condemn	discussion
advertisement	beautiful	conquer	disease
advice	before	conscience	dissatisfied
against	beginning	conscientious	divided
aisle	belief	conscious	doubt
all right	believe	consider	dropped
almost	beneficial	continually	drowned
although	benefited	control	effect
always	bicycle	controversial	eighth
amateur	biggest	controversy	eleventh
ambition	boundary	council	eligible
among	breathe	courageous	embarrass
amusing	brilliant	courteous	emigrate
analyze	Britain	criticism	endeavor
ancient	built	criticize	enough
announces	bulletin	crowd	environment
annually	buried	dangerous	equipment
answered	bury	deceive	equipped
anticipated	business	decided	especially
anxious	cafeteria	decision	eventually
apology	calendar	defense	evidently
apparent	captain	definitely	exaggerate
appearance	career	definition	exceed
appreciate	carrying	democracy	excellent
approach	category	dependent	except

excitement	humorous	moral	prestige
exercise	hurrying	muscle	prevalent
exhausted	hypocrite	mysterious	principal
exhibit	ignorant	naturally	principle
existence	imaginary	necessary	privilege
expense	immediately	neither	probably
experience	importance	niece	procedure
explanation	impossible	nonsense	profession
extraordinary	incredible	noticeable	professor
extremely	independent	numerous	prominent
familiar	individual	obedience	pursue
fascinate	innocent	occasion	quantity
fascinating	intelligence	occasionally	realize
favorite	interest	occur	receipt
fierce	interrupt	occurred	receive
finally	irrelevant	occurrence	recognize
flies	its	often	recommend
foreign	jealousy	omitted	referred
formerly	judgment	opinion	referring
fortunately	knife	opportunity	renowned
forty	knowledge	ordinary	repetition
forward	laboratory	paid	representative
friend	led	parallel	responsibility
gaiety	leisure	paralyzed	responsible
gauge	library	particular	restaurant
generally	license	performance	rhythm
genuine	lieutenant	permanent	running
government	lightning	permitted	sacrifice
grammar	likely	personal	safety
grateful	listener	personnel	salary
grieve	literature	persuade	sandwich
guarantee	lose	physical	satisfactory
guard	losing	picnicking	saucer
guessed	luxury	planned	scene
guidance	magnificent	pleasant	schedule
guilty	maneuver	pledge	scheme
handkerchief	marriage	politician	science
happened	mathematics	portrayed	seize
having	meant	possess	sense
heard	medicine	practical	sensible
height	mere	precede	separate
heroes	million	prefer	sergeant
hesitate	miniature	preferred	serious
hindrance	miscellaneous	prejudice	shining
honorable	mischief	preparation	shriek
hoping	mischievous	prescription	siege

SPELLING DEMONS—INTERMEDIATE CONTINUED

similar	success	together	vegetable
sincerely	sufficient	toward	vengeance
skiing	suggestion	tragedy	victim
soldier	supersede	transferred	villain
sophomore	suppose	tremendous	visible
source	surprise	tries	waive
special	susceptible	truly	weigh
stationary	swimming	twelfth	weird
stopped	system	unnecessary	woman
straight	technique	until	wrench
strength	temperature	unusual	write
stubborn	terrible	using	writing
studying	therefore	usually	written
substantial	thief	vacant	yacht
subtle	thorough	vacuum	yield
succeed	tired	valuable	

Here are some real challengers:

Antidisestablishmentarianism: State support of the church.

Supercalifragilisticexpialidocious: Mary Poppins says it means "good."

Pheumonoultramicroscopicsilicovolcanoconiosis: Lung disease caused by inhaling silica dust.

Floccinaucinhilipilification: Action of estimating as worthless.

The Reading Teacher's Book of Lists, Fifth Edition, © 2006 by John Wiley & Sons, Inc.

See also List 45, Sesquipedalian Superstars; List 152, Spelling Demons— Elementary; List 154, Spelling Demons—National Spelling Bee List.

LIST 154. SPELLING DEMONS—NATIONAL SPELLING BEE LIST

Every May, the E. W. Scripps Company sponsors the National Spelling Bee in Washington, DC. It is the longest-running educational competition in the US.

Originally started in 1925 by the *Louisville-Courier Journal* in Kentucky to garner interest in a "dull" subject, the competition has grown from a local event to a national one with more than 250 finalists. Local competitions are sponsored by newspapers from all over the nation. Finalists are typically eighth graders, thirteen or fourteen years old. More boys than girls have been finalists in recent years.

The Scripps Spelling Bee web site (www.spellingbee.com) provides many resources. There is a compendium of words that appear frequently, less frequently and rarely, rules for entry and sponsorship, a history of the national spelling bee, and complete lists of the 80 national champions and their winning words. An additional resource of note is the audio paideia, a kind of spoken encyclopedia, which provides the correctly pronounced words and their definitions for the current year's study list. It can be an excellent vocabulary builder on its own!

For 54 finalists in the 1992 National Spelling Bee, the championship was lost by misspelling one of these words:

alpestrine	effaceable	knurl	obloquy	synod
anathema	emolument	lilliputian	opsimath	tendresse
beleaguer	epistrophe	linguipotence	ossuary	tralatitious
burgherly	exscind	lorgnette	paroxysm	trattoria
cabochon	famulus	loupe	pellagra	trousseau
cappuccino	gentian	lycanthrope	pylorus	usurpation
catechism	grogram	mademoiselle	requital	venireman
condign	habiliment	marquee	rescissory	vitiate
crinoline	immolate	nacelle	serigraph	wainwright
diptych	ingenue	nefarious	sinecure	zweiback
doughty	jodhpur	nonpareil	sorbefacient	

Here are words that determined the champions for the last fifteen years.

1991—antipyretic	1996—vivisepulture	2001—succedaneum
1992—lyceum	1997—euonym	2002—prospicience
1993—kamikaze	1998—chiaroscurist	2003—pococurante
1994—antediluvian	1999—logorrhea	2004—autochthonous
1995—xanthosis	2000—demarche	2005—appoggiatura

LIST 155. SPELLING—TRADITIONAL TEACHING METHODS

Test–Study–Test Method

This book provides you the content, such as the Instant Words, Subject Words, or Phonograms, but you must use your own methods to teach spelling. Here are a few suggestions based on experience and research on using the test–study–test method.

1. **Give a spelling test at the beginning of the week.** For example, you might give a spelling test of the twenty words to all your fourth graders or five to ten words for first graders.

2. **Have the students correct their own papers.** Make sure they properly spell all the words they spelled incorrectly. During the first few weeks you should check their papers to see that they have both (1) found the words they misspelled, and (2) spelled them correctly. After a few weeks most students can do the self-correcting satisfactorily; however, there may be a few students who need frequent or continual supervision.

3. **Have the students carefully study the words that they missed,** paying careful attention to just the incorrect or missing letters, perhaps by circling the incorrect letter(s) and writing the word correctly from memory several times. See the *5-Step Word Study Method* below.

4. **Give a second spelling test on Wednesday.** Every student who gets either 100% or perhaps 90% (your choice) will not have to take the test again on Friday. They can read or write stories.

5. **A final test should be given on Friday** only for those students who did not score well on the Wednesday test. They should study just the words and letter(s) they missed. You can help them by pointing out phonics, syllabication, spelling patterns, suffix principles, or irregularities.

6. **Each student can keep a chart of final scores** achieved on his/her final spelling test (Wednesday or Friday).

7. **Add to the word list or spelling book lessons** some special words, such as words from social studies or math.

5-Step Word Study Method for Students

1. *Look* at the whole word carefully.

2. *Say* the word aloud to yourself.

3. *Spell* the word. (Say each letter to yourself.)

4. *Write* the word from memory. (Cover the word and write it.)

5. *Check* your written word against the correct spelling. (Circle errors and repeat the 5 steps.)

See also List 16, Instant Words; List 19, Homophones; List 23, Easily Confused Words.

The Reading Teacher's Book of Lists, Fifth Edition, © 2006 by John Wiley & Sons, Inc.

LIST 156. DOUBLE-LETTER SPELLING PATTERNS

Teachers often find it helpful to give a little explanation when they see a student making spelling errors. A common type of spelling error is failure to double a letter. The following spelling patterns might be helpful when used at the "teachable moment" in a classroom explanation. Linguists call consonant doubling "semination."

Spelling Pattern 1: Syllabication

Many double letters are explained by syllabication. If a syllable ends in a consonant and the next syllable begins with the same consonant, a double letter occurs. For example:

tt	little = lit tle
ll	follow = fol low
ff	office = of fice
pp	supper = sup per
ss	missal = mis sal
cc	occur = oc cur
zz	blizzard = bliz zard
rr	hurry = hur ry
nn	penny = pen ny

Spelling Pattern 2: Compound Words and Prefixes

A variation of Pattern 1, Syllabication, is the doubling of letters in compound words or when adding prefixes. The general rule in compounding or adding prefixes is that both keep their full spelling. For example:

kk	bookkeeper = book + keeper	**ee**	reenter = re + enter
tt	cattail = cat + tail	**mm**	commit = com + mit
ss	misspell = mis + spell	**nn**	unnatural = un + natural

Spelling Pattern 3: Vowel Digraphs

Two vowel digraphs OO and EE are a source of many double-letter spellings. For example:

oo	moon, room (long sound)
oo	look, cook (short sound)
ee	see, three (long sound)

Spelling Pattern 4: Prefix A

The prefix A followed by a root consonant often doubles the consonant. (The meaning of that prefix is "to or toward.") Take a look at these examples:

ac	accident, accord
af	affluent, affix
ag	aggrandize, aggregate
al	allege, alliance
an	annex, annual
ap	applause, appeal
ar	arrest, arrive
as	asset, associate
at	attach, attire

(Note: When the prefix A means "not," as in "atypical," you do not double the root consonant.)

DOUBLE-LETTER SPELLING PATTERNS CONTINUED

Spelling Pattern 5: Final Consonants F, L, and S

The letters F, L, and S are often doubled at the end of a word. For example:

f	cliff, off, staff
l	ball, mill, toll, dull
s	class, fuss, kiss

Spelling Pattern 6: Suffixes

Suffixes can be a bit confusing, but here is a basic doubling rule:

> "You double the final consonant when the words end in a single consonant preceded by a single vowel and the suffix begins with a vowel."

Phyllis Fischer (1993) developed a nice mnemonic that she calls "1+1+1," which means when one vowel (1) is followed by one consonant (+1), you add (double) one consonant (+1).

Examples that follow the basic doubling rule (1+1+1):

run—running   wet—wetted
big—bigger

Examples *not* following the basic doubling rule:

ring—ringed   kick—kicked   want—wanting

The Reading Teacher's Book of Lists, Fifth Edition, © 2006 by John Wiley & Sons, Inc.

Fun Facts About Words

Reduplication means "to double"
(re- means again, du- means two, ply- means fold or unit).

Reduplications are an interesting class of words,
which have some doubling of a sound
such as: dilly-dally, hanky-panky, itsy-bitsy, and fiddle-faddle.

See also List 15, Syllabication Rules; List 29, More Prefixes; List 31, More Suffixes; List 157, Spelling Rules for Adding Suffixes.

LIST 157. SPELLING RULES FOR ADDING SUFFIXES

There are a number of special spelling rules for adding suffixes that change the form of a word (tense of a verb, part of speech) or the meaning (root word + suffix). Most of them are aids to pronouncing the new word; that is, they help make the transition of sounds within the word smoother. Focus on one rule at a time and use lots of examples. (See List 158, Plurals, for additional information on spelling rules for forming plurals.) A spelling rule is that the suffix spelling never changes (except for plural -s to -es) but the root can change (make—making).

Basic rule for adding suffixes to change the verb form, compare adjectives, change a word to an adverb, or make a word plural: **Just add the suffix.**

want + s = wants	want + ing = wanting	want + ed = wanted
talk + s = talks	talk + ing = talking	talk + ed = talked
tall + er = taller	smart + er = smarter	slow + ly = slowly
tall + est = tallest	smart + est = smartest	quick + ly = quickly
chair + s = chairs	book + s = books	bill + s = bills

If a word ends in "e"

- If a word ends in "e," drop the final "e" if the suffix begins with a vowel.
  rose—rosy   dine—dining   name—named   note—notable
- If a word ends in "e," keep the final "e" if the suffix begins with a consonant.
  safe—safely   care—careful   tire—tireless   strange—strangeness
- If a word ends in "e," keep the final "e" if it is preceded by a vowel.
  see—seeing

If a word ends in "y"

- If a word ends in "y," change the "y" to "i" if the "y" is preceded by a consonant.
  carry—carried. Sometimes change the "y" to "ie." cry—cries   lady—ladies
- If a word ends in "y," keep the "y" if it is preceded by a vowel. joy—joyful
- If a word ends in "y," keep the "y" if the suffix begins with "i." marry—marrying

If a word ends in "c"

- If a word ends in "c," add a "k" before a suffix beginning with an "e," "i," or "y."
  picnic—picnicking panic—panicky

If a word ends in a single consonant

- If a one-syllable word ends in a consonant (or the final syllable is accented), double the final consonant. brag—bragged   (1 + 1 + 1 Rule)
- If the word ends in two consonants, do not double the final one.
  hard—harder   (Negative 1 + 1 + 1 Rule)
- If a word has a single vowel letter, double the final consonant. run—running. If it has a two-letter vowel, do not double the consonant. rain—rained   (1 + 1 + 1 Rule)
- If a word ends in a single consonant and the suffix begins with a vowel, double the consonant. bag—bagged
- If a word ends in "le" and the suffix is "ly," drop the final "le" before adding the suffix. able—ably. But if the word ends in "l," leave the "l" before adding "ly." cool—coolly

See also List 15, Syllabication Rules; List 156, Double-Letter Spelling Patterns; List 158, Plurals.

LIST 158. PLURALS

Mastery of these rules will help students in any grade. The irregular spellings must be memorized. Try a fast-paced spelling bee for practice.

Rules for forming plurals:

1. The plural form of most nouns is made by adding *-s* to the end of a word.

chair—chairs	floor—floors
president—presidents	desk—desks
face—faces	drill—drills

2. If the word ends in *-s, -ss, -sh, -ch, -x,* or *-z,* the plural is formed by adding *-es.*

boss—bosses	dish—dishes	gas—gases
bench—benches	fox—foxes	
waltz—waltzes	tax—taxes	

3. If the word ends in a *y* preceded by a consonant, the plural is formed by changing the *-y* to *-i* and adding *-es.*

city—cities	country—countries
variety—varieties	candy—candies
family—families	cherry—cherries

4. If the word ends in a *y* preceded by a vowel, the plural is formed by adding *-s.*

valley—valleys	turkey—turkeys
key—keys	play—plays
journey—journeys	boy—boys

5. The plurals of most nouns ending with *-f* or *-fe* are formed by adding *-s.*

gulf—gulfs	belief—beliefs
cuff—cuffs	roof—roofs
cliff—cliffs	

6. Some words that end in *-f* or *-fe* are formed by changing the *-f* to *-v* and adding *-es.*

knife—knives	wife—wives
leaf—leaves	elf—elves
thief—thieves	life—lives
loaf—loaves	wolf—wolves
half—halves	self—selves
calf—calves	dwarf—dwarves

7. If the word ends in an *o* preceded by a consonant, form the plural by adding *-es.*

hero—heroes	potato—potatoes
tomato—tomatoes	echo—echoes
zero—zeroes	cargo—cargoes

8. If the word ends in an *o* preceded by a vowel, form the plural by adding *-s.*

video—videos	radio—radios
studio—studios	patio—patios

The Reading Teacher's Book of Lists, Fifth Edition, © 2006 by John Wiley & Sons, Inc.

9. To form the plural of a compound word, make the base noun plural.

brother-in-law—brothers-in-law   bucketseat—bucketseats
sandbox—sandboxes   passerby—passersby
attorney general—attorneys general

10. Some words have irregular plural forms:

child—children   radius—radii
ox—oxen   tooth—teeth
louse—lice   brother—brethren
man—men   woman—women
basis—bases   goose—geese
crisis—crises   stimulus—stimuli
index—indices   medium—media
axis—axes   criterion—criteria
oasis—oases   focus—foci
die—dice   parenthesis—parentheses
foot—feet   datum—data
mouse—mice

11. Some words are used for both singular and plural meanings. These never use an *-s* or *-es* suffix. These are called invariable nouns.

cod	species	hay	sheep	gross
moose	deer	dirt	rye	Swiss
barley	bass	music	fish	British
traffic	mackerel	trout	wheat	aircraft
salmon	dozen	corps	series	

12. Some nouns look singular but are always plural.

police	vermin	livestock
people	folk	cattle

13. Note that "mass nouns" in List 25 do not have a plural form.

air	sand
soap	water

See also List 15, Syllabication Rules.

LIST 159. CAPITALIZATION GUIDELINES

Review these guidelines with your students and provide practice exercises for problem areas. Give "proofreading" assignments to help students become sensitive to the proper use of uppercase letters.

- Capitalize the pronoun I.
  I often sleep late on weekends.

- Capitalize the first word of any sentence.
  Kittens are playful.

- Capitalize the first word and all important words in titles of books, magazines, newspapers, stories, etc.
  The Lion, the Witch, and the Wardrobe

- Capitalize names of specific people, events, dates, and documents.
  Eunice Jones, Toronto, Fourth of July, Thanksgiving, September, the Constitution

- Capitalize the names of organizations and trade names.
  Ford Motor Company, Tide detergent

- Capitalize titles of respect.
  Mr. Cox, Ms. Blake, Judge Rand

- Capitalize names of races, languages, religions, and deity.
  Caucasian, Spanish, Catholic, the Almighty, Jehovah

- Capitalize the first word in a direct quotation.
  Ann inquired, "Where is the suntan lotion?"

- Capitalize abbreviations and acronyms, all or part.
  U.S., UNESCO, CA, St., Mr.

Optional Capitalization

- All letters in a title or sign.
  BOOK OF LISTS, THE JONES MARKET

- Special emphasis.
  She yelled, "STOP." SEND HELP IMMEDIATELY

- Subheads and outline words.

The Reading Teacher's Book of Lists, Fifth Edition, © 2006 by John Wiley & Sons, Inc.

See also List 182, Basic Sentence Patterns; List 89, Punctuation Guidelines; List 91, Proofreading Checklist—Elementary; List 92, Proofreading Checklist—Intermediate.

LIST 160. CONTRACTIONS

Contractions substitute an apostrophe for a letter or letters. You will find the grouping of contractions a good teaching strategy.

am	is, has	would, had	have	will or shall	not
I'm	he's	I'd	I've	I'll	can't
	she's	you'd	you've	you'll	don't
are	it's	he'd	we've	she'll	isn't
you're	what's	she'd	they've	he'll	won't
we're	that's	we'd	could've	it'll	shouldn't
they're	who's	they'd	would've	we'll	couldn't
who're	there's	it'd	should've	they'll	wouldn't
	here's	there'd	might've	that'll	aren't
us	one's	what'd	who've	these'll	doesn't
let's		who'd	there've	those'll	wasn't
		that'd		there'll	weren't
				this'll	hasn't
				what'll	haven't
				who'll	hadn't
					mustn't
					didn't
					mightn't
					needn't

Apostrophes are also used in some slang, dialect words, or old-fashioned words.

ain't (am not)   d'you (do you)

fo'c'sle (forecastle)   shan't (shall not)

br'er (dialect for brother)   y'all (you all)

See also List 15, Syllabication Rules; List 23, Easily Confused Words; List 204, Portmanteau Words.

LIST 161. COMPOUND WORDS

Compound words are made by joining two or more words to make another word. The joined words may be two nouns (watermelon, handcuff), two non-nouns (takeoff, checkup), or a noun and a non-noun (blackbird, sunrise). When they form a compound word, the two words do not always keep the same meaning as they had as separate words; for example: *brainstorm, shoelace.*

There are three types of compound words: closed compounds that have no spaces (*into, backpack*); open compounds that have spaces between the paired words (*tennis court, pitch hitter*), and hyphenated compounds (*fifty-five, merry-go-round*).

Many compound words build on a common base word to form **meaning families.** For example, here are some of the members of the "house" family: *birdhouse, clubhouse, doghouse, farmhouse, firehouse, greenhouse, schoolhouse,* and *warehouse.* Here are some members of the "some" family: *somebody, someday, somehow, someone, someplace, something, sometimes, somewhat,* and *somewhere.*

Closed Compounds

afternoon	barefoot	chalkboard
afterthought	baseball	checkout
airborne	basketball	churchgoer
airline	bathroom	citywide
airmail	bedrock	classmate
airplane	bedroom	cleanup
airport	bedspread	clipboard
airtight	beforehand	cockpit
anchorperson	benchmark	colorblind
another	birdhouse	cookbook
anybody	birthday	cooperative
anyone	blackbird	copperhead
anyplace	blackboard	copyright
anything	blowup	countryside
anytime	blueprint	cowboy
anyway	bookstore	crosswalk
anywhere	boyfriend	cupcake
applesauce	brainstorm	database
audiotape	breakdown	daydream
awestruck	breakfast	daylight
backache	breathtaking	daytime
backboard	broadcast	desktop
backbone	buildup	doorbell
backbreaking	bulldog	doorknob
backfire	burnout	downpour
background	buttermilk	downstairs
backlash	byproduct	drawbridge
backpack	campfire	driveway
backup	cannot	drugstore
backyard	caregiver	dugout
ballpark	carpool	earring
ballroom	carryover	earthquake

The Reading Teacher's Book of Lists, Fifth Edition, © 2006 by John Wiley & Sons, Inc.

earthworm	headache	network
easygoing	headlight	nevertheless
everybody	headquarters	newscast
everyday	headset	newspaper
everyone	heartwarming	nightgown
everything	herringbone	nobody
everywhere	herself	notebook
extracurricular	highway	nowhere
eyeball	hilltop	oatmeal
eyebrow	himself	ongoing
eyelid	homemade	online
fingernail	homeowner	ourselves
fingerprint	homesick	outcome
firefighter	homework	outfield
fireplace	however	outfit
fireproof	indoor	outlaw
firewood	infield	outline
fireworks	inside	outside
flashback	into	outsource
flashlight	itself	outstanding
flowchart	jellyfish	overalls
flowerpot	keyboard	overcoat
folklore	kickoff	overexposure
football	knucklehead	overkill
forever	ladybug	overlook
freelance	landlord	overpass
freshwater	leapfrog	pancake
frostbite	leftover	paperback
gentleman	lifeboat	paperwork
gingerbread	lifeguard	payoff
girlfriend	lifestyle	payroll
goldfish	lightheaded	peanut
grandchildren	lighthouse	peppermint
grandfather	lightweight	percent
grandmother	lipstick	pinball
grandparent	longshoreman	pinpoint
grapefruit	loudspeaker	playground
grasshopper	makeup	playmate
gridlock	marketplace	ponytail
groundwater	maybe	popcorn
grownup	meantime	postcard
haircut	meanwhile	pothole
hamburger	miniskirt	printout
handcuff	moonlight	proofread
handlebar	motorcycle	quarterback
handshake	myself	quicksand
haystack	nationwide	railroad

COMPOUND WORDS CONTINUED

rainbow	sometimes	turnpike
raincoat	somewhat	turtleneck
rattlesnake	somewhere	undercover
rawhide	spacewalk	underdog
redhead	spotlight	underground
redwood	spreadsheet	understatement
rollerblade	springtime	undertake
rollout	starfish	uproot
runway	statewide	upset
sagebrush	stepbrother	upstairs
sailboat	stepfather	uptown
sandpaper	stepmother	videotape
scarecrow	stepsister	vineyard
scatterbrain	storyteller	wastebasket
screwdriver	straightforward	watercolor
seacoast	strawberry	waterfall
seafood	sugarcoat	waterfront
seagull	suitcase	watermelon
seaport	summertime	weatherperson
seashell	sundown	Webpage
seaside	sunflower	weekday
seaweed	sunlight	weekend
seesaw	sunrise	wheelchair
shipwreck	sunset	whenever
shoelace	sunshine	whirlpool
shortstop	sunstroke	whiteboard
showdown	suntan	wholesale
showoff	superhighway	windmill
showroom	sweatshirt	windpipe
sidewalk	sweetheart	windshield
silverware	tablecloth	windsurfing
skateboard	teammate	wingspan
skyscraper	textbook	wiretapping
snowball	Thanksgiving	without
snowfall	themselves	woodland
snowflake	thunderstorm	woodpecker
snowman	timetable	workday
snowplow	tiptoe	workforce
snowshoe	today	workload
snowstorm	toenail	workplace
softball	together	workshop
somebody	toothbrush	workstation
someday	touchdown	wristwatch
somehow	trailblazer	wrongdoing
someone	tryout	yourself
someplace	tugboat	
something	turnaround	

Open Compounds

bottled water
car pool
cash flow
catcher's mitt
cell phone
chat room
child care
Christmas tree
civil rights
comic strip
common sense
course work
crossword puzzle
dirt bike
disc drive
disc jockey
dump truck
energy bar
fact sheet
fine arts
French fry
grass roots

health care
heart attack
heat lightning
help desk
high school
hockey puck
home page
hot dog
ice cream
key pal
life span
memory stick
New World
oven mitt
paper clip
photo ID
pitch hitter
post office
prime minister
real estate
remote control
rock band

role play
safety glasses
salad dressing
school day
school year
search engine
sleeping bag
sports drink
square root
tennis court
theme park
time line
time saver
tree house
vice president
voice mail
waiting room
walking stick
Web site
word processing
word wall
work boots

Hyphenated Compounds

able-bodied
A-frame
brother-in-law
check-in
clean-cut
close-up
co-op
editor-in-chief
empty-handed
father-in-law
follow-up
for-profit
free-for-all
front-runner
fund-raiser
get-together
hanky-panky
high-tech

ho-hum
hush-hush
in-depth
in-law
know-how
know-it-all
life-size
merry-go-round
mother-in-law
nitty-gritty
not-for-profit
off-site
one-sided
on-site
roly-poly
run-in
runner-up
self-concept

self-service
shrink-wrap
single-minded
strong-arm
thirty-nine
three-dimensional
tip-off
topsy-turvy
toss-up
two-thirds
U-turn
warm-up
well-being
well-to-do
word-of-mouth
worn-out
X-ray

LIST 162. SPELLING AND PRONUNCIATION

Pronouncing words properly can be a great help in spelling them correctly. Furthermore, you can sometimes exaggerate the pronunciation, even distort it a bit, to emphasize what letter should be used. A further help in pronunciation sometimes is to pronounce the word syllable-by-syllable. Here are a few other pronunciation suggestions:

1. Watch out for confusing words that have similar but not identical sounds; for example, celery—salary; finally—finely.

2. Don't add syllables that aren't there; for example, athlete (not athelete); laundry (not laundery).

3. Don't skip syllables that are there; for example, chocolate (not choclate); probably (not probly).

4. Don't skip letter sounds that are there; for example, arctic (not artic); government (not goverment).

5. Don't reverse letters; for example, perform (not preform); tragedy (not tradegy).

6. Watch out for the schwa /ə/ or unaccented vowel sound. Because it causes a lot of errors in spelling lessons, it is often helpful to temporarily exaggerate the unaccented vowel letter (thereby making it not a schwa sound). Example: doll*a*r; spons*o*r; ben*e*fit; def*i*nite.

7. For purposes of mnemonics or memory devices, it is sometimes helpful to even use a temporary incorrect pronunciation; for example, "Wednesday" might be pronounced "Wed-nes-day."

8. Take a little extra time with ESL students to see that they are pronouncing all the spelling words correctly.

The Reading Teacher's Book of Lists, Fifth Edition, © 2006 by John Wiley & Sons, Inc.

LIST 163. COMMON ABBREVIATIONS

Abbreviations are so widely used that it is important to know what the common ones stand for. In addition to being an advantage in reading comprehension, knowing and using abbreviations saves time, space, and energy when we write.

Streets and Roads

Blvd.	Boulevard
Dr.	Drive
St.	Street
Pkwy.	Parkway
Rd.	Road
Hwy.	Highway
Ln.	Lane

Titles

Dr.	Doctor
Esq.	Esquire
Hon.	Honorable
H.R.H.	Her (His) Royal Highness
Jr.	Junior
Pres.	President
Supt.	Superintendent
Rev.	Reverend
Sr.	Sister, Senior
Mr.	Mister
Mrs.	Mistress

Military Titles

Capt.	Captain
Lt.	Lieutenant
Col.	Colonel
Gen.	General
Sgt.	Sergeant

Degrees

B.A.	Bachelor of Arts
B.S.	Bachelor of Science
D.D	Doctor of Divinity
D.D.S.	Doctor of Dental Surgery
M.A.	Master of Arts
M.D.	Doctor of Medicine
Ph.D.	Doctor of Philosophy
Ed.D.	Doctor of Education
R.N.	Registered Nurse

Days of the Week

Sun.	Sunday
Mon.	Monday
Tues.	Tuesday
Wed.	Wednesday
Thur., Th.	Thursday
Fri., Fr.	Friday
Sat.	Saturday

Months of the Year

Jan.	January
Feb.	February
Mar.	March
Apr.	April
Jul.	July
Aug.	August
Sept.	September
Oct.	October
Nov.	November
Dec.	December

Parts of Speech

adj.	adjective
adv.	adverb
conj.	conjunction
n.	noun
prep.	preposition
v.	verb
art.	article
pn.	pronoun

Time

A.M.	ante meridiem (morning)
P.M.	post meridiem (afternoon/evening)
A.D.	Anno Domini (in the year of our Lord)
B.C.	before Christ
C.E.	Common Era
hr.	hour

COMMON ABBREVIATIONS CONTINUED

min.	minute	F	Fahrenheit
sec.	second	fem.	feminine
wk.	week	fig.	figure
mo.	month	freq.	frequency
yr.	year	ft.	foot

Other Abbreviations

acct.	account	g	gram
ad lib	ad libitum (improvise)	gal.	gallon
AKA	also known as	Gen.	General
amt.	amount	govt.	government
anon.	anonymous		
ans.	answer	H.M.S.	His (Her) Majesty's Ship
arith.	arithmetic		
assn.	association	hosp.	hospital
assoc.	association	ht.	height
asst.	assistant	ibid.	ibidem (in the same place)
atty.	attorney		
		id.	idem (the same)
bib.	bibliography	i.e.	id est (that is)
biog.	biography	illus.	illustration
bldg.	building	in.	inch
		Inc.	incorporated
C	Celsius	incl.	including
cap.	capital	intro	introduction
cc	cubic centimeter		
cert.	certificate	Jour.	Journal
chap.	chapter		
Chas.	Charles	K	Kelvin
cm	centimeter	kg	kilogram
Co.	company		
conj.	conjunction	lat.	latitude
Corp.	corporation	lb.	pound
cu	cubic	long.	longitude
dept.	department	mag.	magazine
diam.	diameter	masc.	masculine
div.	division	math	mathematics
doz.	dozen	mdse.	merchandise
		med.	medium
ea.	each	mg	milligram
ed.	edition	mgr.	manager
e.g.	exempli gratia (for example)	misc.	miscellaneous
		ml	milliliter
elec.	electric	mph	miles per hour
et al.	et alia (and others)		
etc.	et cetera (and others)	neg.	negative
		neut.	neuter
ex.	example	no.	number

opp.	opposite	St.	Saint
oz.	ounce	subj.	subject
p.	page	tel.	telephone
pd.	paid		
pkg.	package	univ.	university
pl.	plural	USA	United States of America
pop.	population		
pp.	pages		
prin.	principal	vet	veterinarian, veteran
pt.	pint	vocab.	vocabulary
		vol.	volume
qt.	quart	vs.	versus
recd.	received		
ref.	referee; reference	Wm.	William
		wt.	weight
sci.	science		
sing.	singular	yd.	yard
sq.	square		

See also List 57, U.S. States, Abbreviations, Name Meanings, and Capitals; List 217, Acronyms and Initializations.

13

THE INTERNET

LIST 164. TIPS FOR SEARCHING THE WEB

With information about everything available on the Web, what you are looking for is just a click or two away . . . well, maybe not. With more than 8 billion documents on the Web you could spend a lot of valuable time searching and sorting through hundreds of "matches" unless you master a few basic search techniques. Although search engines work somewhat differently from one another, these tips will work with nearly all. Be sure your students know them as well.

1. **"Bookmark" or save as a "favorite" at least four search engine sites.** A search engine is a large database that helps index the Webpages and other sites on the Internet. No one search engine indexes the whole Internet; in fact, Google has indexed only (!) about 4 billion of the 8 billion Webpages. Using both general and specialized search engines will help cover the field and find what you are looking for.

2. **Do a quick word web.** Jot down the search topic and related words, including its category, subcategories, type of information you are looking for, etc. For example, a word web for "collective nouns" might include: *grammar, elementary, list.* If the word has multiple meanings, add a few key words to distinguish the target from the others, such as: -farm, -agriculture. As you search, note the words that helped most so you can use them again if you need to use a second search engine.

3. **Use lowercase letters when entering your query.** Most search engines are case sensitive and will not give you matches for collective nouns if you queried *Collective* or *Noun* or *COLLECTIVE NOUN.*

4. **Use singular, not plural in your query.** A match is made when all of what you ask for is found. If your word has an *-s*, its singular form will not be counted as a match. Because the spelling of the singular is generally part of the plural, plurals will be found using the singular form.

5. **Use quotations marks to search for a specific phrase or multiword term.** For example: "collective noun." Otherwise, the search will find sites with either "collective" or "noun" but not those with the two words together.

6. **Use the plus (+) and minus (−) signs in your query.** The + and − signs show what to include or exclude from the search results. A search for *"collective noun"+ grammar+elementary+list−farm−agriculture* has a much different result from just using "collective noun." (Note: Do not leave space after the + or − sign.) Also using the + with two (or more) words will find sites that contain both words, but not necessarily together as in a phrase.

7. **Use the * as a wildcard.** The * at the end of a word will enable you to find variants of the word, including plurals. For example, "white water raft*" will locate raft, rafts, rafter, rafters, rafting. This is a technique that expands the catch of your search. For most search engines, the * will replace up to five contiguous letters.

8. **Look for titles.** Simple searches match your query to words anywhere in the site. To find sites that have your target word in the title, type *title:* followed by your topic. Here are two examples: *title:Caldecott   title:"Mother Goose"*

9. **Look for links.** Many of the best sites include links to other related Webpages, chat groups, etc., and often these are most important or useful additional sites. To find links from one site to another, type *link:* then the URL of the site you already know. For example, this query is for links about technology and learning online: *link:http://www.techlearning.com/*

See also List 165, Search Engines for Teachers and Students.

The Reading Teacher's Book of Lists, Fifth Edition, © 2006 by John Wiley & Sons, Inc.

LIST 165. SEARCH ENGINES FOR TEACHERS AND STUDENTS

Researchers at the Online Computer Library Center report that there are now more than 8.4 million unique sites on the Web with more than 7 billion Web documents. No single search engine or Web directory can sort through it all. The search engines listed below are easy to use and return the best results for educational and general information searches.

Yahooligans is especially good for students, but all are fairly easy to use once you've learned the basics. Bookmark at least four search engines or Web directories on your home and classroom computers: two for general purposes and two or more that focus on specific content information. Consult the search engine sites below if you need a specialized search.

General Search Engine Sites

About	http://www.about.com/
AltaVista	http://www.altavista.com/
Ask Jeeves	http://www.ask.com/
Dogpile	http://www.dogpile.com/
Excite!	http://www.excite.com/
Google	http://www.google.com/
Lycos	http://www.lycos.com/
WebCrawler	http://www.webcrawler.com/
Yahoo!	http://www.yahoo.com/

Specialized Information Sites

AltaVista Images	http://www.altavista.com/image/default
Artcylopedia	http://www.artcyclopedia.com/
Ask Jeeves for Kids	http://www.ajkids.com/
Awesome Library	http://www.neat-schoolhouse.org/awesome.html
Clip Art Search	http://www.webplaces.com/search/
Cybersleuth Kids	http://cybersleuth-kids.com/
Discovery Online	http://school.discovery.com/
Education Index	http://www.educationindex.com/
Encarta	http://uk.encarta.msn.com/
Fact Monster (from InfoPlease)	http://www.factmonster.com/
Federal Resources for Educational Materials	http://wdcrobcolp01.ed.gov/cfapps/free/displaysearch.cfm
Franklin Institute	http://sln.fi.edu/

Ivy's Search Engine Resources	http://www.ivyjoy.com/rayne/kidssearch.html#guides
KidsClick	http://kidsclick.org/
LookSmart—NetNanny	http://search.netnanny.com/?pi = nnh3&ch = kids
Museums of the World	http://vlmp.museophile.com/world.html
National Geographic	http://www.nationalgeographic.com/index.html
One Key	http://www.onekey.com/
Surfsafely	http://surfsafely.com/
TekMom Search Tools	http://www.tekmom.com/search/
The Search Page	http://www.accesscom.com/~ziegler/search.html
The Why Files (Science Behind the News)	http://whyfiles.org/
ThinkQuest Library	http://www.thinkquest.org/library
Thomas (U.S. Congress)	http://thomas.loc.gov/
WebSEEk Image Catalog	http://persia.ee.columbia.edu:8008/cgi-bin/walk?
White House	http://www.whitehouse.gov/
Wikipedia	http://en.wikipedia.org/wiki/Main_Page
Windows to the Universe	http://www.windows.ucar.edu/

Directory of All Search Engines

http://www.allsearchengines.com

LIST 166. WEB SITES FOR READING INSTRUCTION

Before the Web, teachers kept file drawers full of "best practice" ideas from workshops, lesson plans, articles from journals, publishers' catalogues, and more. Now, much of this information is available online, making it accessible anytime, anywhere. Bookmark your favorite spots or make a hot list of links to keep them in easy reach when you are planning lessons. Check out the specialized sites on the other lists as well. Note that most of the links provided in this book contain links to other reading resources. Take some time to surf through them. The rewards are worth it to you and your students.

Instructional Resources

Aaron Shepard's Readers' Theater Resources	http://www.aaronshep.com/rt/index.html
Annenberg/CPB	http://www.learner.org/about/aboutus.html
Apples for the Teacher Educational Activities	http://www.apples4theteacher.com/
Ask a Librarian Live	http://www.qandanj.org
Book Adventure	http://www.bookadventure.org/
Busy Teachers' Web Site	http://www.ceismc.gatech.edu/busyt/k-12
CEC Lesson Plans	http://www.col-ed.org/cur/
Club for Kids Who Love Books	http://www.scholastic.com/kids/index.asp
Connections +	http://www.mcrel.org/resources/plus/
English Pavilion	http://pen.k12.va.us/Anthology/Pav/LangArts/LangArts.html
Exemplary Reading Practices	http://reading.indiana.edu/ieo/bibs/rdprace.html
Federal Resources for Educational Excellence	http://www.ed.gov/free/index.html
Instructor Magazine	http://www.scholastic.com/Instructor/
Leanna Traill's Tutorial for Running Records	http://reta.nmsu.edu/bldg99/bridges/5-running/tutorial.htm
Lesson Plans	http://teachers.net/lessons/
Linguistic Funland	http://www.tesol.net/tesltext.html
List of Leveled Books	http://www.readinga-z.com/guided/leveled_list.html
Marco Polo Education Foundation	http://www.marcopolo-education.org/
Online Poetry Classroom	http://www.poets.org/page.php/prmID/6
Poetry Teachers	http://www.poetryteachers.com/
Read Between the Lions	http://www.pbskids.org/lions/
Read Write Think	http://www.readwritethinki.org/index.asp
Readers' Theater Scripts	http://www.teachingheart.net/readerstheater.htm

The Reading Teacher's Book of Lists, Fifth Edition, © 2006 by John Wiley & Sons, Inc.

Reading A to Z	http://www.readinga-z.com/
Reading Assessment and Evaluation	http://www.sarasota.k12.fl.us/MRC/assesseval.htm
Reading Recovery	http://www.readingrecovery.org/
SCORE Language Arts	http://www.sdcoe.k12.ca.us/score/cla.html
Study Tips and Resources	http://www.studytips.com/
Success for All	http://www.successforall.net/
Teaching Heart (Resources for Gr. 1–4)	http://www.teachingheart.net/
Teaching PreK–8	http://www.TeachingK-8.com/
The Educator's Reference Desk Lesson Plans and Resources	http://www.eduref.org/index.shtml
Whole Language Umbrella	http://www.ncte.org/wlu/

Reading Programs

Harcourt Brace	http://www.harcourtschool.com/
Houghton Mifflin	http://www.eduplace.com/catalog/rdg//
Macmillan/McGraw Hill	http://www.mhschool.com/reading/2005/student/
Open Court (SRA)	http://www.sra4kids.com
Pearson Scott Foresman	http://www.scottforesman.com/sfaw/

LIST 167. WEB SITES FOR WRITERS AND WORD LOVERS

Rhymes . . . Word histories . . . Help with research papers . . . Word puzzles and games . . . Places to publish student writing . . . Even a puzzlemaker for budding cruciverbalists. The following Web sites and their links are great for every student writer and word aficionado you know.

Words

A Word a Day	http://www.wordsmith.org/awad/themes.html
Analogy of the Day	http://www.factmonster.com/analogies
Australian Crossword Club	http://www.crosswordclub.org/ACCsite%20Site/ Word%20Lists/Intro.html
English Teacher	http://www.theenglishteacher.org/
English Tongue Twisters	http://www.uebersetzung.at/twister/en.htm
Funbrain.com	http://www.funbrain.com/vocab/index.html
People's Names and What They Mean	http://www.zelo.com/firstnames
Puzzlemaker	http://www.puzzlemaker.com/
Rhyming Dictionary	http://www.cs.cmu.edu/~dougb/rhyme.html
Syndicate	http://syndicate.com/
Word Central	http://www.wordcentral.com/dailybuzzword.html
Word Game of the Day	http://www.m-w.com/game/
Word of the Day from Dictionary.com	http://dictionary.reference.com/wordoftheday/
Word Play	http://www.wolinskyweb.net/word.htm

Writing

E-Pals	http://www.epals.com/
Inkspot for Young Writers	http://www.inkspot.com/young/
Intercultural E-Mail Classroom Connections	http://www.stolaf.edu/network/iecc
Poetry Gallery	http://www.kidlit@mgfx.com
Researchpaper.com	http://www.researchpaper.com/
The Grammar Lady	http://www.grammarlady.com/
The Quill Society	http://www.quill.net/
The Write Site	http://writesite.org/html/oti.html
Writing Links	http://andromeda.rutgers.edu/~jlynch/Writing/ links.html
Young Writers Resources	http://www.elisacarbone.com/index. 2ts?page=youngwriters

The Reading Teacher's Book of Lists, Fifth Edition, © 2006 by John Wiley & Sons, Inc.

LIST 168. WEB SITES FOR CHILDREN'S LITERATURE

These Internet sites offer an amazing array of useful and interesting information related to children's literature. The sites in the Authors section connect you with many favorite authors and illustrators and include one where you can contact authors. The Literature section offers book lists, online versions of classics, as well as specialty sites such as Myths and Legends and Cinderella stories. The Books list includes children's book publishers and online bookstores. Most sites have links and many include instructional activities and much more.

Authors

Ask the Author	http://www.ipl.org/youth/AskAuthor/
Author & Illustration Links	http://www.cbcbooks.org/navigation/teaindex.htm
Into the Wardrobe: The C.S. Lewis Site	http://cslewis.DrZeus.net/
Laura Ingalls Wilder Home Page	http://webpages.marshall.edu/~irby1/laura.html
Lewis Carroll Home Page Illustrated	http://www.cstone.net/library/alice/carroll.html
Mark Twain	http://etext.lib.virginia.edu/railton/index2.html
Winnie the Pooh Collection	http://www.penguinputnam.com/yreaders/pooh/winnie.htm
Judy Blume	http://www.judyblume.com/menu-main.html
Eric Carle	http://www.eric-carle.com/
Lewis Carroll	http://www.lewiscarroll.org/carroll.html
Tomie dePaola	http://www.tomie.com/main.html; www.bingley.com/
Ezra Jack Keats	http://www.lib.usm.edu/~degrum/keats/main.html; http://www.ezra-jack-keats.org
Lois Lenski	http://library.uncg.edu/depts/speccoll/lenski/
Jack London	http://sunsite.berkeley.edu/London/
Dr. Seuss	http://www.seussville.com/; www.randomhouse.com/seussville
The Scoop (multiple authors)	http://friendly.net/users/jorban/biographies/index.html
Meet Authors and Illustrators	http://www.childrenslit.com/f_mai.htm

Literature

Aesop's Fables Online Exhibit	http://www.pacificnet.net/~johnr/aesop/
American Library Association	http://www.ala.org/
Booktalks—Quick and Simple	http://www.concord.k12.nh.us/schools/rundlett/booktalks/
Carol Hurst's Children's Literature Site	http://www.carolhurst.com/
Children's Book Cooperative	http://www.soemadison.wisc.edu/ccbc/
Children's Book Council	http://www.cbcbooks.org/
Children's Literature	http://www.childrenslit.com/
Children's Literature & Language Arts Resources	http://falcon.jmu.edu/~ramseyil/childlit.html

WEB SITES FOR CHILDREN'S LITERATURE CONTINUED

Children's Literature Web Guide http://www.acs.ucalgary.ca/~dkbrown/index.html
Children's Literature—Resources for Teachers http://www.cynthialeitichsmith.com/index1.htm
Children's Literature Network http://www.childrensliteraturenetwork.org/
Cinderella Stories http://www.ucalgary.ca/~dkbrown/cinderella.html
Cinderella Studies www.dept.usm.edu/~engdept/cinderella/cinderella.html
Cyberkids http://www.cyberkids.com/
Database of Award-Winning Children's Literature http://www.dawcl.com/
Electric Library http://www.elibrary.com/
Fairrosa Cyber Library http://www.fairrosa.info/
Internet Public Library http://www.ipl.org/
Kay Vandergrift's Children's Literature Site http://www.scils.rutgers.edu/~kvander/
Kid's Web—A WWW Digital Library for School Kids http://www.kidvista.com/index.html
Literature for Children http://palmm.fcla.edu/juv/
The Little Red Riding Hood Project www.dept.usm.edu/~engdept/lrrh/lrrhhome.htm
Multicultural Book Review http://www.isomedia.com/homes/jmele/homepage.html
Mystery Readers Journal http://www.murderonthemenu.com/mystery/
Myths and Legends http://pubpages.unh.edu/~cbsiren/myth.html
New York Public Library http://www.nypl.org/
Notable Children's Trade Books http://www.ncss.org/resources/notable/home.html
The On-Line Books Page http://www.cs.cmu.edu/Web/books.html
Online Mystery Database http://www.mysteries.com
Project Bartleby Archive http://www.bartleby.com/
Tales of Wonder: Folk & Fairy Tales from Around the World http://itpubs.ucdavis.edu/richard/tales/

Books

AddALL (searches and compares 41 bookstores) http://www.addall.com/
Amazon.com http://www.amazon.com/
Barnes and Noble http://www.bn.com/
Books-a-Million http://www.booksamillion.com/
Borders' Children's Page http://www.amazon.com/exec/obidos/tg/browse/-/4/ref=bgi_bhp_tn_ki/002-4924673-8104052
Buy http://www.buy.com/
Cheap Books http://www.cheapbooks.info/
Powells http://www.powells.com/
Publishers of Children's Books http://www.acs.ucalgary.ca/~dkbrown/publish.html
Scholastic http://www.scholastic.com/
Tattered Cover http://www.tatteredcover.com/NASApp/store/IndexJsp
Wordsworth http://www.curiousg.com/

The Reading Teacher's Book of Lists, Fifth Edition, © 2006 by John Wiley & Sons, Inc.

LIST 169. KIDS' ZINES

Kids' zines are online counterparts of children's print magazines (see List 75, Kids' Magazines for Readers and Writers). Zines are accessible to all students with just a few mouse clicks. Their interactive nature is very engaging, and many provide access to features like real-time Webcams—something no print magazine can do. Some Web sites offer partial or full access to popular print magazines. Some zines are only published online. They also offer publication opportunities to young writers. As with print magazines, zines are a great source of high-interest material for reluctant and/or developing readers.

American Girl (general content for girls; ages 8–12)
http://www.americangirl.com/agmg/index.html

Boys' Life (general content for boys; ages 8–12)
http://www.boyslife.org/

Chickadee (some online activities; ages 5–9)
http://www.owlkids.com/chickadee/chickadee_this_month.html

Consumer Reports 4 Kids (kids products, consumer education; ages 8–18)
http://www.zillions.org/

Dig (earth science and archaeology; ages 9–14)
http://www.digonsite.com/

EEK: Environmental Education for Kids (outdoors, environment; ages 9–14)
http://www.dnr.state.wi.us/org/caer/ce/eek/index.htm

FootSteps: African American History (African American history; ages 8–14)
http://www.footstepsmagazine.com/

Kids' Castle (Smithsonian magazine for kids; ages 7–12)
http://www.kidscastle.si.edu/

MidLink Magazine (general topics, world links; ages 8–18)
http://www.cs.ucf.edu/~MidLink/

National Geographic Kids (wildlife, adventure, geography, science; ages 8–14)
http://www.nationalgeographic.com/ngkids/

National Geographic World (general interest; ages 7–14)
http://www.nationalgeographic.com/media/world/index.html

Odyssey (science themes, explorations; ages 10–16)
http://www.odysseymagazine.com/

Ranger Rick (nature, environment, outdoors; ages 7–10)
http://www.nwf.org/gowild/

Skipping Stones (international, multicultural themes; ages 8–16)
http://www.skippingstones.org/

Sports Illustrated for Kids Online (sports stars, teams, action photos; ages 7–14)
http://www.sikids.com/

Stone Soup (fiction, poetry, artwork, projects; ages 8–13)
http://www.stonesoup.com/

Time Magazine for Kids (current events, features, activities; ages 7–12)
http://www.timeforkids.com/TFK

Yak's Corner (news and general interest; ages 8–12)
http://www.freep.com/index/yak.htm

LIST 170. VIRTUAL REFERENCE LIBRARY

Every classroom (and every teacher) is just a click or two away from a world-class reference library. These sites and their links cover every school subject and then some. Create a hot list or bookmark individual sites to make browsing and using them easy.

Almanacs, Dictionaries, and Encyclopedias

A Web of On-Line Dictionaries	http://www.facstaff.bucknell.edu/rbeard/diction.html
A&E Biographical Dictionary	http://www.biography.com/
Artcyclopedia	http://www.artcyclopedia.com/
Biographical Dictionary	http://www.s9.com/
Cambridge Dictionaries	http://dictionary.cambridge.org/
CIA World Factbook	http://www.odci.gov/cia/publications/factbook
Encyclopedia Mythica	http://www.pantheon.org/mythica/
English Homophone Dictionary	http://www.earlham.edu/~peters/writing/homofone.htm
Events and Calendars of the Day	http://www.erebus.phys.cwru.edu/~copi/events.html
Fact Monster	http://sln.fi.edu/tfi/hotlists/hotlists.html
Information Please Almanac	http://www.infoplease.com/
Life Science Dictionary	http://biotech.icmb.utexas.edu/pages/dictionary.html
Literary Calendar	http://www.litcal.yasuda-u.ac.jp/
Little Explorers Picture Dictionary	http://www.LittleExplorers.com/dictionary.html
Merriam-Webster Dictionary	http://www.m-w.com/
Multilingual Picture Dictionary	http://www.EnchantedLearning.com/Dictionary.html
My Facts Page Dictionaries and Language Resources	http://www.refdesk.com/factdict.html
My Virtual Reference Desk	http://www.refdesk.com/
One Look Dictionary	http://www.onelook.com/
Online Dictionaries	http://www.dict.org; http://www.dictionary.com
Rhyming Dictionary	http://www.link.cs.cmu.edu/dougb/rhyme-doc.html
Roget's Thesaurus.com	http://www.thesaurus.com/
The Free Dictionary	http://www.thefreedictionary.com/
The Old Farmers Almanac	http://www.almanac.com/
The Oxford English Dictionary OnLine	http://www.oed.com/
Weather Glossary	http://www.weatherlabs.com
Wikipedia	http://www.wikipedia.org/

The Reading Teacher's Book of Lists, Fifth Edition, © 2006 by John Wiley & Sons, Inc.

Other Online Resources for Teaching and Learning

American History—Library of Congress	http://www.americastory.gov/
AOL Photo of the Day	http://reference.aol.com/photooftheday
Ašk ERIC	http://ericir.syc.edu/
Bartleby Library & Reference	http://www.bartleby.com/
Bartlett's Familiar Quotations	http://www.bartleby.com/quotations
Book Adventure	http://www.bookadventure.org/te/index.asp
Buster's Bookshelf on Reading Education	http://www.bustersbookshelf.com/
Carolyn's Corner Words and Spelling	http://www.spellingbee.com/cctoc.shtml
Common Errors in English	http://www.wsu.edu:8080/~brians/errors/errors.html
EdHelper	http://www.edhelper.com/
Elementary Writing	http://www.bcps.org/offices/lis/curric/elem/ElemLA/elawriting.html
Encyclopedia Smithsonian	http://www.si.edu/resource/faq/start.htm
Family Search	http://www.familysearch.org/
FamilyTreeMaker's Genealogy Site	http://www.familytreemaker.com/
Franklin Institute's Education Hot List	http://sln.fi.edu/tfi/hotlists/hotlists.html
Google Maps	http://maps.google.com/
Internet Archive	http://www.archive.org/
Internet Library for Librarians	http://www.itcompany.com/inforetriever/dict_eng.htm
Internet Public Library Youth Division	http://www.ipl.org/youth
Kodak Picture of the Day	http://www.kodak.com/eknec/PageQuerier.jhtml?pq-path=2549&pq-locale=en_US
Library of Blue Ribbon Learning Web Sites	http://www.kn.pacbell.com/wired/bluewebn/index.cfm
Liszt Directory of Newsgroups	http://www.liszt.com/news/
MapQuest	http://www.mapquest.com/
NASA Earth Images	http://modis.gsfc.nasa.gov/gallery/index.php
National Geographic Homework Help	http://www.nationalgeographic.com/education/homework/
National Spelling Bee	http://www.spellingbee.com/index.shtml
PC Webopedia	http://www.pcwebopedia.com/

VIRTUAL REFERENCE LIBRARY CONTINUED

Poetry Daily	http://www.poems.com/
Project Gutenberg	http://www.gutenberg.org/
Quote of the Day from Bookreporters.com	http://www.bookreporter.com/community/ quote/index.asp
Reading Rainbow	http://gpn.unl.edu/rainbow/
Reference Desk	http://www.refdesk.com/
Rick Walton Book Lists, Words, Fun and Curriculum Activities	http://www.rickwalton.com/
Robert's Rules of Order	http://www.bartleby.com/176/
Scholarly Journals Distributed World Wide via the Web	http://info.lib.uh.edu/wj/webjour.html
SciCentral	http://www.scicentral.com/index.html
Sites for Teachers	http://www.sitesforteachers.com/
Study Guides and Strategies	http://www.studygs.net/
Study WEB	http://www.studyweb.com/
The Human Languages Page	http://www.june29.com/HLP/
The Rhyme Zone	http://www.rhymezone.com/
The Weather Channel	http://www.weather.com/
Today in Literature	http://www.todayinliterature.com/
Tongue Twister Database	http://www.geocities.com/Athens/8136/ tonguetwisters.html
United Nations Cyber School Bus	http://cyberschoolbus.un.org/index.asp
U.S. and Worldwide Newspapers	http://www.refdesk.com/paper.html

The Reading Teacher's Book of Lists, Fifth Edition, © 2006 by John Wiley & Sons, Inc.

LIST 171. COMPUTER AND INTERNET TERMS

USB . . . MP3s . . . PDAs . . . plug and play . . . The language of computers and the Internet grows rapidly and being techno-literate is a basic requirement for today's teachers and students. This list of commonly used computer and Internet terms and their meanings will help you keep up or catch up with the latest.

Abort	To stop a program or function before it finishes.
Archive	To copy computer files onto a long-term storage device for safekeeping.
ASCII	American Standard Code for Information Interchange. A code for representing English letters as numbers, which makes it possible to transfer data from one computer to another.
Backbone	The main cable that connects devices on a computer network.
Bandwidth	The amount of data that can be transmitted in a fixed amount of time; e.g., bits per second.
Bit	Binary digit. The smallest unit of information used by computers. Each bit can represent only two values: 0 or 1.
Blog	The shortened form of Web-log and refers to any publicly accessible Web-based journal. Easy-to-use blogging software allows people with little or no computer skill to establish and maintain a blog.
Bluetooth	A wireless technology that enables communication between Bluetooth-compatible devices, such as PDAs, digital cameras, and cell phones, by using short-range radio technology. Bluetooth technology is defined by the Bluetooth Special Interest Group (http://www.bluetooth.com).
Bookmark	To mark a Web address or document for later retrieval.
Boolean Search	A search that uses *and*, *or*, and *not* to select matches for the search terms.
Boot	To start a computer by loading the operating system.
Broadband	A high-speed connection to the Internet. Broadband generally refers to any Internet connection using DSL, cable modems, or T1 or T3 lines.
Browser	Computer software used to search the Web and display information.
Bug	An error in the computer software or hardware that causes a malfunction.
Byte	Groups of eight bits that can be used to represent numbers and letters of the alphabet.
CAD	Computer Aided Design. Software used especially by architects and engineers that allows them to manipulate pictorial representations on the display screen.
CAM	Computer Aided Manufacturing. The use of computer systems to assist in automated manufacturing.

COMPUTER AND INTERNET TERMS CONTINUED

CD	Compact Disk. A disk (or disc) with one or more metal layers used to store digital information that is read by a laser.
CD-ROM	Compact Disk-Read Only Memory. A type of compact disk designed to have information read from it but not have information recorded on it.
Chat Room	An online location or address where people can login and "talk" to one another by posting messages and replying to others' posts.
Chip	An extremely small piece of silicon on which thousands of electronic elements are implanted.
Click	To tap a mouse button. "Click on" means to select an item on the screen by pointing the cursor at it and tapping the mouse button.
Clip Art	Electronic graphics, often part of a software package, and generally royalty-free, that can be inserted into a document.
Connectivity	The ability of a device or software to link with other devices or software.
Cookie	Information that is given to a Web browser by a server to identify a user when the server is accessed in the future.
CPU	Central Processing Unit. The main unit in a computer that contains the chip that makes the computer operate. It can be thought of as the brains of the computer.
Crash	A major failure in a computer resulting from a failure in the hardware or software.
CSS	Cascading Style Sheet. A recent feature that specifies the layout of Webpages. Web designers can create style sheets to define the appearance of various Web elements (such as font, heading, and links) and apply it to any Webpage. CSS is a convenient way to control the appearance of a large number of Webpages.
Cursor	A special symbol, usually blinking, that indicates where the next character will appear on the screen.
Cyberspace	Term invented by author William Gibson in his novel *Neuromancer*. It is now used as a metaphor to describe the virtual space created by computer systems.
Database	A computer file that holds an organized collection of data.
Debug	To find and remove errors from a program.
Default	A value or setting that is preset by the manufacturer or program and remains until changed.
Defragment	A process whereby scattered files on a disk are reorganized to make them contiguous and improve operating efficiency.
Desktop	The primary display screen with icons representing programs, files, etc.
Digitize	To convert from analog to digital format by sampling the original file. Computers use digital information. After converting an audio or video file from analog to digital at a high sampling rate, you

can use computer applications to edit, copy, and replay with little or no noticeable distortion.

Disk Drive	A device that reads and writes data to a disk.
Domain Name	A unique name to identify a Web site; for example, "apple.com" is the domain name of Apple Computer's Web site. Each domain name has a suffix or file extension that indicates its top-level domain. The most common extensions are: *gov* (government agencies), *edu* (educational organizations), *com* (commercial business), *org* (nonprofit organizations), and *net* (network organizations).
DOS	Disk Operation System. A collection of programs that form the operating system for the disk drives. Often refers to the operating system developed by Microsoft, i.e., MS-DOS.
Download	To copy a file, program, etc., from a main source such as the Internet or a mainframe computer to a local computer, printer, etc.
Drag	To drag an icon, object, or some text on the desktop, move the cursor over the desired element, then left-click and hold down the mouse button to capture it. Then, using the mouse, drag the icon to the desired destination, then let go of the mouse button to finish the action. Dragging can be used to resize windows or boxes, move text, and move unwanted material to the trash or recycle file. You can drag the scroll bar to move forward and back in a document, and you can drag files from one folder to another.
DVD	Digital Video Disc or Digital Versatile Disc. A type of optical disk technology similar to CD-ROM, but a DVD holds more data than CD-ROM. A single-layer, single-sided DVD holds 4.7 GB of data. This allows a DVD to carry a massive amount of data, such as a movie. A DVD player is required to play a DVD disk.
E-mail	Electronic mail. A message sent from one computer to another over a communication network.
ESC	Escape key on the computer keyboard.
Ethernet	The most common method to connect computers in a LAN. 10BaseT and 100BaseT are two widely-used forms of Ethernet. 10BaseT means data transfer speeds can reach up to 10 mbps (mega bits per second) through the copper cable, while a 100BaseT enables data transfer speed up to 100 mbps.
Execute	To run a program or perform a command or function.
Firewall	A system designed to prevent hackers from accessing a private network without authorization.
Floppy Disk	A disk designed to be removed from a computer, and thus is portable. This type of disk used to be in a sealed envelope and "flopped" when shaken. Now it is in a rigid shell.
Freeware	Software given away by the author, often available over the Internet.
FTP	File Transfer Protocol. The protocol used on the Internet for sending files.

COMPUTER AND INTERNET TERMS CONTINUED

GIF
Graphic Interchange Format. A common format for clip art graphic files. A GIF file is based on indexed colors, which is a palette of 256 colors. A GIF file size is small and can be downloaded quickly from the Internet.

Handhelds
Any of a number of small computers that can fit in your hand and are used to store data. The most popular uses are for PIM (personal information management) such as PDAs, or for use with probes and other sensors to allow mobile data collection.

Hard Disk
A rigid magnetic disk sealed inside the computer on which data can be stored.

Hardware
The actual physical computer and other objects—such as monitor, keyboard, printer, scanner, etc.—that are connected to it.

Hit
A match when searching a database, or the number of visitors a Web site receives in a given period.

Home Page
The main page of a Web site—often the first page accessed by visitors to the Web site.

Host
A computer that provides services (for example, e-mail, FTP) to other computers on a network. For example, a Web host provides service to allow other computers to access the Webpages stored on it.

HTML
HyperText Markup Language. The language used to create documents on the World Wide Web.

HTTP
HyperText Transfer Protocol. The way in which World Wide Web pages are transferred over the Internet.

Hypermedia
An extension of hypertext that includes sound and graphics in addition to text.

Hypertext
A system of writing and displaying text in which there are links that allow the reader to browse and find connections with related documents and text.

Instant Messaging
IM. A communication between two or more people who use the same IM client software (AOL IM or MSN IM, for example). It takes place in real time and works as a private chat room. It is sometimes referred to as IMing and users often employ acronyms and "txt msg" shorthand to speed things along.

Icon
A picture that represents an object, idea, action, or program.

Internet
A large number of computer networks that are interconnected and make it possible for millions of computers throughout the world to communicate with each other.

Intranet
A private computer network accessible within an organization that uses protocols like those of the Internet to allow the sharing of information among computer users.

IP Address
Also known as IP Number. A unique number consisting of four parts separated by dots; for example: 163.13.251.19. Every computer requires a unique IP address in order to connect to the Internet.

The Reading Teacher's Book of Lists, Fifth Edition, © 2006 by John Wiley & Sons, Inc.

JPEG
Joint Photographic Experts Group. A widely used format for image files. JPEG is a compressed image file format and is best for compressing photo images.

Key Logger
A type of spyware that records the user's keystrokes and transmits them to another computer. Key loggers are used by some identity thieves to record user's passwords, ID numbers, credit card numbers, and other data as the user types them.

Keyword Search
An Internet search that matches sites based on specific terms or key words that represent the topic.

Kilobyte
KB. Approximately 1,000 (actually 1,024) bytes.

LAN
Local Area Network. A computer network confined to a limited area.

Landscape
Printing or other printer output that is parallel to the long side of the paper.

Laptop
A small, portable computer.

Laser Printer
High-speed, high-resolution printer that uses a laser beam to print.

Link
An embedded connection, usually indicated by a blue line under text, that allows you to go to a Web site by clicking on the link.

Linux
A Unix-based operating system created by Linux Torvalds in 1991. Linux is freely distributed, and users can download the open source, customize it, or add changes to the operating system and then share with the public.

Listserv
A family of programs used to distribute messages to a list of members. Listservs usually are organized around a particular theme or interest. Members subscribe to a listserv in order to exchange information with people who share that interest.

Log Off
To terminate a session on a computer system.

Log On
To access a computer system by providing a password or other identification.

Mainframe
The largest computers to which terminals or personal computers may be linked.

Megabyte
MB. 2 to the 20th power or 1,048,576 bytes—approximately one million bytes.

Memory
Storage area in the computer.

Minimize
To shrink a window into an icon.

Modem
Modulator–Demodulator. A device that makes it possible for a computer to send and receive data over a cable, telephone, or other similar telecommunications line.

Monitor
A screen for displaying computer information.

Mouse
A small device connected to the computer that controls the movements of the cursor.

MP3
MPEG-1 Audio Layer-3. MP3 is the most popular compressed audio file format because the file size is about one-tenth of the original audio file and still remains nearly CD quality. An MP3 player or device is required to play MP3 file.

Computer and Internet Terms Continued

MPEG	Moving Picture Experts Group. MPEG is a set of standards used to compress video and audio to digital format and still remain original quality.
Multimedia	The use of computers to present voice, video, and data in an integrated way.
Multitasking	The ability to execute more than one task or program simultaneously.
Navigation	Aids that allow the user to move within a Web site or database.
Netiquette	Etiquette for posting messages on computer networks, particularly the Internet.
Network	Two or more computers linked together.
Newsgroup	Online discussion groups. Same as forum.
Notebook	A lightweight and portable computer. *See also* laptop.
Off-line	Not connected.
Online	Turned on and connected.
Operating System	The program that performs the most basic tasks of a computer, such as recognizing data from the keyboard, sending data to the display screen or other peripheral device, organizing files, etc.
Output	Anything that comes out from the computer.
Password	A series of characters that is kept secret and allows the user to gain access to files, computers, etc.
PC	Personal computer.
PDA	Personal data assistant. A pocket-sized computer that has an appointment book, address file, calculator, and many other features. PDAs are synchronized (synched) to the user's computer to update the files in both locations.
PDF	Portable Document Format. A file format developed by Adobe systems. PDF enables printing and viewing of documents with all the original formatting across platforms. The Adobe Reader application is required to view a PDF file. It can be downloaded for free from the Adobe Web site.
Peripherals	Add-on hardware not part of the computer proper, such as a scanner or printer.
Phishing	A surreptitious act by which a con artist tries to get your personal information. The most common method of phishing is to send an e-mail that appears to be from a legitimate source and ask the receivers to update their accounts and provide information for any field that is incorrect or empty. It is illegal to phish.
Personal Computer	PC. A microcomputer that has its central processing unit etched onto a single chip. This is the most common type of computer in use today. In recent years PCs have become extremely powerful.
Pixel	A picture element. A single point in a graphic.
Plug-and-Play	PnP. Protocols that allow peripherals to work with a computer without additional setup or applications.

The Reading Teacher's Book of Lists, Fifth Edition, © 2006 by John Wiley & Sons, Inc.

Plug-ins	Applications that enhance programs. For example, audio plug-ins allow users to play audio files.
Program	A series of instructions that tell a computer what to do.
Protocol	Any set of rules that allows different computers to communicate with each other accurately and reliably.
Purge	To remove or delete unneeded files.
Query	A request for information from a database.
RAM	Random Access Memory. The most common type of memory found in most computers.
Read-only	Capable of being displayed but not modified or deleted.
Real Audio	A World Wide Web plug-in program that allows the user to hear sound.
Registry	A Microsoft database file that stores configuration information for a computer.
ROM	Read Only Memory. Computer memory on which basic low-level programs have been prerecorded.
Save	To copy data from a temporary to a more permanent storage.
Screen Saver	A small program that takes over a display screen when it has not been used for a preset amount of time. Often displays decorative patterns.
Search Engine	A program that searches for information on the World Wide Web.
Server	A computer or other device that manages resources on a network.
SharePoint Site	A Web site or Web community that is an online collaborative environment set up for groups of individuals with common interests or jobs that allows document sharing, blogging, and other shared information. Users need a Web portal content management system from Microsoft.
Software	Computer programs and accompanying documentation.
SPAM	Junk e-mail or irrelevant postings to a forum.
Spreadsheet	Software used for working with data (both words and numbers) in rows and columns.
Spyware	Software that "spies" on users' computer to capture information without their knowledge.
Streaming	A technique that allows audio or video to be played back on users' computer without being completely downloaded first.
Surfing the Net	Exploring the Internet.
Tablet	A wireless PC that recognizes natural handwriting as well as keystrokes.
TCP/IP	Transmission Control Protocol/Internet Protocol. These two protocols are used to define the Internet and allow computers to communicate on the Internet.
Telnet	A program that allows users to login to a Unix computer with Unix commands. Users can access resources on the server such as e-mail and FTP files.

COMPUTER AND INTERNET TERMS CONTINUED

Trojan	A malicious software application that appears to be a text file, game, or other legitimate file, but when opened will write over or corrupt portions of your hard drive and disable your computer. A good virus protection software program will detect and delete Trojans. Do not open any file or attachment you think is suspicious. Once you open the Trojan the damage will be done.
Txt	A text file with no formatting or graphics.
Upload	To transmit information from a computer to a mainframe or network.
URL	Uniform Resource Locator. The address for accessing resources on the Internet.
USB	Universal Serial Bus. A type of serial connection for computers and peripherals.
USB Flash Drive	A portable flash memory card that can be used as a storage device through the USB port on a computer or digital devices, such as a digital camera. USB Flash drives are also known as key drives or USB drives.
Username	A name used to gain access to a computer.
Virus	Computer code that is introduced to the computer from an outside source without the user's knowledge and causes problems.
Web	*See* World Wide Web.
Webpage	A document on the World Wide Web.
Web Site	A collection of interrelated Webpages.
Webmaster	An individual who manages a Web site.
Wi-Fi	Wireless Fidelity. The form of wireless data transmission that is based on the Wi-Fi Alliance's standards. A "Wi-Fi certified" product (PDA, laptop) is tested and proved by the Wi-Fi Alliance to ensure it can be recognized by "Wi-Fi certified" access points.
Wiki Site	Allows visitors to add to and edit the site's content allowing for group work of any type. Wiki is short for "what I know is . . . "
Wild Card	A symbol used to substitute for others; wild cards allow the user to search using only part of a word. This is helpful because it will match terms with similar roots or common elements.
Wireless	Ability to connect to a network without a cable or other wired connection.
Word Processor	Computer software used to produce and edit text.
World Wide Web	A hypermedia system on the Internet that makes it possible to browse through information.
Worm	A computer virus that causes harm by replicating itself and using up memory, causing your computer to run slower and slower and eventually crash. Good virus protection software can detect and remove worms.
WYSIWYG	What You See Is What You Get. Computer software that shows on the display screen exactly what you will get when you print.
ZIP	A popular way of compressing data so that it takes less computer memory.

LIST 172. TEXT, CHAT, AND E-MAIL GLOSSARY

This list will help keep your online and text message communications flowing smoothly. These acronyms, abbreviations, and shorthand forms communicate a lot with very few keystrokes. The growing use of cell phone text messaging has encouraged the development of shorthand forms using letters and symbols to "spell" longer words. For example, CUL8R is used for "See you later." This phenomenon presents a good opportunity to talk about the arbitrariness of the conventions of language and spelling.

101 Beginner
121 One to one
143 I love you
14324*7 I love you 24 hours, seven days a week
14AA41 One for all and all for one
1dering Wondering
1dRfL Wonderful
1ns Once
2B or not 2B To be or not to be
2day Today
2l8 Too late
2moro Tomorrow
2nite Tonight
2U To you
404 Clueless
411 Information
4ever Forever
4get Forget
4giv Forgive
86 Over
A3 Anytime, anywhere, anyplace
AAMOF As a Matter of fact
AAYF As always, your friend
ADBB All done, bye bye
AFAIK As far as I know
AIMP Always in my prayers
AKA Also known as
amazn amazing
AML All my love
ApreC8 Appreciate
ASAP As soon as possible
ata2ud Attitude
AYT Are you there?
B/C Because
b3 Blah, blah, blah
B4 Before
B4N Bye for now
BBFBBM Body by Fisher, brains by Mattel
BBT Be back tomorrow
BCNU Be seeing you

BF Boyfriend
BFN Bye for now
BHL8 Be home late
bin Been
biz Business
bl$ Bless
BRB Be right back
bro Brother
BTW By the way
BW Best wishes
BYKT But you knew that
BzAR Bizarre
bzy Busy
c%l Cool
CB Chat brat
chocl@ Chocolate
CICO Coffee in, coffee out
CIO Check it out
cla$ Class
CMIIW Correct me if I'm wrong
cn Can
cnot Cannot
cofy Coffee
communic8 Communicate
complic8 Complicate
congr@ul8 Congratulate
cos Because
craZ Crazy
CT City
CU See you
CUL8R See you later
CUNS See you in school
D8 Date
Db8 Debate
Dcide Decide
DETI Don't even think it
DGT Don't go there
DIKU Do I know you?
DIY Do it yourself
doh Stupid me!
E123 Easy as one, two, three

TEXT, CHAT, AND E-MAIL GLOSSARY CONTINUED

EM? Excuse me?

enuf Enough

EOL End of lecture

ESO Equipment smarter than operator

EZ Easy

f%d Food

F2F Face to face

f8 Fate

FAB Features, attributes, benefits

fanC Fancy

FAQ Frequently asked question(s)

FF Friends forever

FISH First in, still here

FITB Fill in the blank

FOC Free of charge

FWIW For what it's worth

FYA For your amusement

FYI For your information

GBH Great big hug

gdby Goodbye

gf Girlfriend

GG Good game

GIGO Garbage in, garbage out

GL Good luck

GMTA Great minds think alike

gr@ Grand

gr8 Great

grr Angry

GTG Got to go

gudnite Good night

HAND Have a nice day

HbTU Happy birthday to you!

HTH Hope this helps

I 1DR I wonder

IAC In any case

IAE In any event

IC I see

ID10T Idiot

IDK I don't know

ILU I love you

IMO In my opinion

IOW In other words

IYKWIM If you know what I mean

JM2C Just my 2 cents

KEWL Cool

KISS Keep it simple stupid

kol Cool!

l8rg8r Later 'gater

L8R Later

LOL Laughing out loud

lv Love

LY Love you

MergNC Emergency

MHOTY My hat's off to you

moV Movie

Mt Empty

MYOB Mind your own business

nd And

NRG Energy

NRN No reply necessary

NUFF Enough said

OIC Oh, I see

ONNA Oh no, not again

OTOH On the other hand

plA Play

pls Please

POOF Good-bye

POV Point of view

ppl People

P-ZA Pizza

QL Quit laughing!

QT Cutie

r8 Right

ROF Rolling on the floor

ROTFL Rolling on the floor laughing

RSN Real soon now

Rtst Artist

RU Are you?

sis Sister

SITD Still in the dark

skool School

SLIRK Smart little rich kid

SNAFU Situation normal: all fouled up

SNAG Sensitive New Age guy

SOHF Sense of humor failure

SSDD Same stuff, different day

SWAK Sealed with a kiss

SYS See you soon

T+ Think positive

TIA Thanks in advance

TLK2UL8R Talk to you later

TPTB The powers that be

TTFN Ta ta for now

TTYL Talk to you later

TWIMC To whom it may concern

TY Thank you

TYVM Thank you very much
U&I You and I
U2 You, too
UC You see
UL You will
uok? Are you okay
URSpshl You are special
W/ With
W/O Without
WRT With respect to

WU? What's up?
WUF? Where are you from?
WWY? Where were you?
WYSIWYG What you see is what you get
wz Was
XI10 Exciting
XOXO Hugs and kisses
Y3 Yadda, yadda, yadda
zzz Sleeping, bored, tired

See also List 217, Acronyms and Initializations.

LIST 173. EMOTICONS

It's hard to get feelings across in the quick and cryptic messages of e-mail, text messaging, and other electronic media. Emoticons help get them across and head off miscommunications. The word "emoticon" is a portmanteau formed by combining the words *emotion* and *icon*. Emoticons are formed using regular letters and symbols on the computer keyboard. Although they are also called "smileys," they represent a wide range of feelings. The following emoticons are the most often used.

:-)	happy	:-()	bored
;-)	playful, winking	:-(	sad, unhappy, upset
:-<	miserable, frowning	:-D	laughing, joking
:-|	indifferent, who cares?	:-X	it's a secret, lips are sealed
(-:	left-handed writer	%-)	cross-eyed, exhausted
8-)	wearing sunglasses	::-)	wearing regular glasses
B-)	wearing dark-rimmed glasses	8:-)	girl, woman
:-)>═	boy, man	:-{)	has a mustache
:'-(	crying	:-/	confused, not sure, skeptical
:-#	wearing braces	:-o	talking
|-D	laughing out loud	:-O	shouting
:0	uh-oh!	:-@	screaming
:-&	tongue tied	:-]	grinning
|-O	yawning	:-P	sticking tongue out
|-I	sleeping	:-[	frowning, miserable
:->	smirk, joking, devilish	:-{}	wearing lipstick
{:-)	wearing a toupee	*<:-)	Santa or partygoer
*.o)	clowning around	[ ] **	hugs and kisses
{{{}}}	thinking it over	0:-)	angel, angelic
[:-]	robot	<:-)	dunce
[:-)	wearing earphones	<:3)~	mouse
3:]	pet, cat, dog, cow	8 :-)	wizard
$-)	greedy	:-*	kiss
@—)—	flower, rose	<()(—)≪	fish
:-)X	wearing a bow tie	(:::[ ]:::)	Band-aid
@(*0*)@	koala bear	_/7	cup of coffee

14

ENGLISH LANGUAGE LEARNERS (ESL OR ELL)

LIST 174. STUDENTS' LANGUAGE BACKGROUND

According to the Census Bureau, for 18% of the U.S. population over the age of five—some 48.4 million people—English is *not* the language they speak at home. This may seem surprising because 27.1 million of these individuals (55.9%) not only speak their native language but speak English very well. Children in many of these households develop competence in both languages as they grow up. In contrast, data submitted by states to the U.S. Department of Education identified 400 languages spoken by students who are limited English proficient (LEP). The first table below shows the top languages spoken in American homes. The second table shows the most common language groups of LEP students. Spanish is by far the most frequently spoken other language in either category, accounting for 61% of the non-English home language use and 79% of the language backgrounds of limited English proficient students.

Languages Spoken at Home

1. Spanish	7. Other Germanic	13. Other Slavic	19. Other Indic
2. French	8. Scandinavian languages	14. Armenian	20. Other Indo-European
3. Italian	9. Greek	15. Persian	21. Chinese
4. Portuguese	10. Russian	16. Gujarathi	22. Japanese
5. German	11. Polish	17. Hindi	23. Korean
6. Yiddish	12. Serbo-Croatian	18. Urdu	24. Khmer

Language Groups of LEP Students

1. Spanish	7. Arabic	13. Portuguese	19. Chinese (other)
2. Vietnamese	8. Russian	14. Urdu	20. Chamorro
3. Hmong	9. Tagalog	15. Serbo-Croatian	21. Marshallese
4. Cantonese	10. Navajo	16. Lao	22. Punjabi
5. Korean	11. Khmer	17. Japanese	23. Armenian
6. Haitian Creole	12. Mandarin	18. Chuukese	24. Polish

For additional information, visit the U.S. Census Bureau Web site at http://www.census.gov/ or the National Clearinghouse for English Language Acquisition Web site at http://www.ncela.gwu.edu/.

LIST 175. ENGLISH SOUNDS NOT USED IN OTHER LANGUAGES

The number of distinct speech sounds (phonemes) varies across languages. Hawaiian has very few at 13 and !Xóõ, an indigenous language in Africa, is known to have more than 140. English has about 41, depending on the dialect, and this number is greater than the average for modern spoken languages. Some sounds used in English are not used in other languages. For example, /th/ is one of the most common English sounds, but it does not occur in most other languages.

While children are physically capable of learning any of the phonemes, from birth they sort out and recognize those that are part of the language they hear. As a result, students whose primary language is not English may have difficulty recognizing or "hearing" the unfamiliar English sounds and, therefore, will have difficulty pronouncing words that use them.

To master the pronunciation of sounds not in their native languages, students need to practice recognizing the sounds, then producing them. Practice with minimal pairs—words that differ by one sound—to isolate the sound of interest. For example: pit/bit or pit/spit.

Language	English Sounds Not Used in the Language						
Spanish	dg	j	sh	th	z		
Chinese	b	ch	d	dg	g	oa	sh
	s	th	th	v	z		
French	ch	ee	j	ng	oo	th	th
Greek	aw	ee	i	oo	schwa		
Italian	a	ar	dg	h	i	ng	th
	th	schwa					
Japanese	dg	f	i	th	th	oo	v
	schwa						

See also List 9, Phonics Example Words; List 11, Phonograms.

The Reading Teacher's Book of Lists, Fifth Edition, © 2006 by John Wiley & Sons, Inc.

LIST 176. PROBLEM ENGLISH SOUNDS FOR ENGLISH LANGUAGE LEARNERS

English language learners (ELLs) frequently have difficulty pronouncing sounds that are not in their native language or that are used in different patterns from what they have previously heard and used. It is important to distinguish between a student who has difficulty pronouncing words correctly but understands their meaning when heard or read from a student who does not. For example, a Spanish-speaking student may be able to select the correct word—cap or cab—to match to a picture of a taxi but may not have learned to distinctly pronounce /p/ and /b/. It will help to practice pronouncing words with the target sounds first in initial, then final, and then medial positions. Use the words in List 9, Phonics Example Words, for practice.

Language	Problem English Sounds						
Spanish	b	d	dg	h	j	m	n
	ng	oo	p	r	sh	t	th
	u	v	w	z	s-clusters		
Chinese	b	ch	d	dg	f	g	j
	l	m	n	r	ō	sh	s̲
	th	t̲h̲	v	z	l-clusters	r-clusters	
French	ā	ch	ē	h	j	ng	oo
	oy	s̲	th	t̲h̲	s	schwa	
Italian	a	ar	dg	h	i	ng	r̲
	th	t̲h̲	v	schwa	l-clusters	end clusters	
Japanese	dg	f	h̲	i	l̲	th	t̲h̲
	oo	r	s̲h̲	s̲	v̲	w	schwa
	l-clusters	r-clusters					
Korean	b	l	ō	ow	p	r	sh
	t	t̲h̲	l-clusters	r-clusters			

LIST 177. SPANISH PHONICS

Phonics works just fine in Spanish because Spanish is a Latin-based language and English uses a Latin alphabet.

Latin is called a Romance Language not because of love, but because Latin was the language of ancient Rome. Knowing how to pronounce Spanish words, particularly the names of Spanish students, can be helpful to anyone. For example, in the common name Juan, the letter J sounds like /h/ in Harry, not like /j/ in John. The vowel diphthong UA is pronounced like the /wa/ in wand.

Spanish-speaking ELL students, particularly young ones, may not know how to read or write in Spanish. If they and their teachers knew some Spanish phonics (phoneme-grapheme correspondences), it might help their literacy in both Spanish and English.

VOWELS

Letter	English Pronunciation	Approximate Sound
a	Broad /ä/	Like *a* in English *far, father*, e.g., **casa, mano.**
e	Long /ā/	When *stressed*, like *a* in English *pay*, e.g., **dedo, cerca.**
	Short /e/	When *unstressed*, it has a shorter sound like in English *bet, net*, e.g., **estado, decidir.**
i	Long /ē/	Like *i* in English *machine* or *ee* in *feet*, e.g., **fin, sali.**
o	Long /ō/	Like *o* in English *obey*, e.g., **mona, poner.**
u	Long /o͞o/	Like *u* in English *rule* or *oo* in *boot*, e.g., **atún, luna.**
		It is silent in **gue** and **gui**, e.g., **guerra, guisado.** If it carries a diaeresis (ü), it is prounounced (see Diphthongs), e.g., **bilingüe, bilingüismo.**
		It is also silent in que and qui, e.g., **querer, quinto.**
y	Long /ē/	When used as a vowel, it sounds like the Spanish i, e.g., **y, rey.**

DIPHTHONGS

Diphthong	English Pronunciation	Approximate Sound
ai, ay	Long /ī/	Like *i* in English, light, e.g., **caign, hay.**
au	Diphthong /ou/	Like *ou* in English *sound*, e.g., **cauto, paular.**
ei, ey	Long /ā/	Like *ey* in English *they* or *a* in *ale*, e.g., **reina, ley.**
eu	Long /ā/ + Long /o͞o/	Like the *a* in English *pay* combined with the sound of *ew* in English *knew*, e.g., **deuda, feudal.**
oi, oy	Diphthong /oi/	Like *oy* in English *toy*, e.g., **oiga, soy.**
ia, ya	Blend consonant /y/ + vowel /är/	Like *ya* in English *yard*, e.g., **rabia, raya.**
ua	Blend consonant /w/ + vowel /ä/	Like *wa* in English *wand*, e.g., **cuatro, cual.**
ie, ye	Consonant /y/	Like *ye* in English *yet*, e.g., **bien, yeso.**

Diphthong	English Pronunciation	Approximate Sound
ue	Blend consonant /w/ + Long /ā/	Like *wa* in English *wake,* e.g., **buena, fue, bilingüe.**
io, yo	Blend Long /ē/ + Long /ō/	Like *yo* in English *yoke,* without the following sound of *w* in this word, e.g., **región, yodo.**
uo	Blend consonant /w/ + Long /ō/	Like *uo* in English *quote,* e.g., **cuota, oblicuo.**
iu, yu	Blend consonant /y/ + Long /o͞o/	Like *yu* in English *Yule,* e.g., **cuidad, triunfo, yunta.**
ui	Diphthong Long /o͞o/ + Long /ē/	Like *wee* in English *week,* e.g., **ruido, bilingüismo.**

TRIPHTHONGS

Triphthong	English Pronunciation	Approximate Sound
iai	/y/ /e/ /o/	Like *ya* in English *yard* combined with the *i* in *fight,* e.g., **estudiáis.**
iei	/y/ /ē/ /o/	Like the English word *yea,* e.g., **estudiés.**
uai, uay	/w/ /ī/ /ā/	Like *wi* in English *wide,* e.g., **averguáis, guay.**
uei, uey	/w/ /ā/	Like *wei* in English *weigh,* e.g., **amortigüéis, buey.**

CONSONANTS

Letter	English Pronunciation	Approximate Sound
b	/b/	Generally like the English *b* in *boar, bring, obsolete,* when it is at the beginning of a word or preceded by *m,* e.g., **baile, bomba.**
b	/v/	Between two vowels and when followed by *l* or *r,* it has a softer sound, almost like the English *v* but formed by pressing both lips together, e.g., **acaba, haber, cable.**
c	/k/	Before *a, o, u,* or a consonant, it sounds like the English *c* in *coal,* e.g., **casa, saco, cuba, acto.**
c	/s/ or /th/	Before *e* or *i,* it is pronounced like the English *s* in *six* in American Spanish and like the English *th* in *thin* in Castillian Spanish, e.g. **cerdo, cine.**
c	/ks/	If a word contains two *c*'s, the first is pronounced like *c* in *coal,* and the second like *s* or *th* accordingly, e.g., **acción.**
ch	/ch/	Like *ch* in English *cheese* or *such,* e.g., **chato, mucho.**
d	/d/	Generally like *d* in English *dog* or *th* in English *this,* e.g., **dedo, digo.** When ending a syllable, it is pronounced like the English *th,* e.g., **usted, libertad.**

SPANISH PHONICS CONTINUED

CONSONANTS

Letter	English Pronunciation	Approximate Sound
f	/f/	Like *f* in English *fine, life,* e.g., **final.**
g	/g/	Before *a, o,* and *u,* the groups *ue* and *ui* or a consonant, it sounds like *g* in English *gain,* e.g., **gato, gorra, aguja, guerra, guitar, digno.**
g	/h/	Before *e* or *i,* like a strongly aspirated English *h,,* e.g., **general, región.**
h	silent	Always silent, e.g., **hoyo, historia.**
j	/h/	Like *h* in English *hat,* e.g., **joven, reja.**
k	/k/	Like *c* in English *coal,* e.g., **kilo.** It is found only in words of foreign origin.
l	/l/	Like *l* in English *lion,* e.g., **libro, limite**. Same as English.
ll	/y/	In some parts of Spain and Spanish America, like the English *y* in *yet;* generally in Castillian Spanish like the *lli* in English *million;* e.g., **castillo, silla.**
m	/m/	Like *m* in English *map,* e.g., **moneda, tomo.**
n	/n/	Like *n* in English *nine,* e.g., **nuevo, canto, determinación.**
ñ	/ny/	Like *ni* in English *onion* or *ny* in English *canyon,* e.g., **cañon, pañon.**
p	/p/	Like *p* in English *parent,* e.g., **pipa, pollo.**
q(u)	/k/	Like *c* in English *coal.* This letter is only used in the combinations *que* and *qui* in which the *u* is silent, e.g., **queso, aqui.**
r	/rr/	At the beginning of a word and when preceded by *l, n,* or *s,* it is strongly trilled, e.g., **roca, alrota, Enrique, desrabar.**
r	/r/	In all other positions, it is pronounced with a single tap of the tongue, e.g., **era, padre.**
rr	/rr/	Strongly trilled, e.g., **carro, arriba.**
s	/s/	Like *s* in English *so,* e.g., **cosa, das.**
t	/t/	Like *t* in English *tip* but generally softer, e.g., **toma, carta.**
v	/v/	Like *v* in English *mauve,* but in many parts of
	/b/	Spain and the Americas, like the Spanish **b,** e.g., **variar, mover.**
x	/ks/	Before a consonant, it is sometimes pronounced like *s* in English *so,* e.g., **excepción, extensión.**
	/h/	In the word **México,** and in other place names of that country, it is pronounced like Spanish **j.**
y	/y/	When used as a consonant between vowels or at the beginning of a word, like the *y* in English *yet,* e.g., **yate, yeso, hoyo.**
z	/s/	Like *s* in English, e.g., **zapato, cazo, azul.**

See also List 1, Consonant Sounds; List 2, Vowel Sounds.

The Reading Teacher's Book of Lists, Fifth Edition, © 2006 by John Wiley & Sons, Inc.

LIST 178. SPANISH COMMON WORDS AND PHRASES FOR TEACHERS

Spanish-speaking students are the largest group of English Language Learners (ELL) in the public schools. Teachers should find the following words and phrases helpful in communicating with them.

English	Spanish
after (in position)	tras de
again	de nuevo, de vuelta, otra vez
a little more	y pico
all together	en conjunto, en junto
aloud	en vox alta, voz alta
ask a question (questions)	hacer una pregunta (preguntas)
at home	en casa
at last	a la poste, al fin, al fin y al cabo, por fin, pro ultimo
at the least	al menos, a lo menos, como minimo, menos mal, por lo menos
at once	ahora mismo, al instante, al punto, de pronto, de una vez, desde luego, en el acto, en seguida
at the end	al fin
at the very latest	a más tardar
backward(s)	al revés, hacia atrás
bad habits	malas tretas
bathroom	el baño
be ashamed	tener vergüenza
before	antes de que
begin	echarse a, ponerse a, romper a
be in a hurry	estar (or andar) de prisa, tener prisa
be in trouble	estar en un aprieto
be lucky	tener suerte, tocarle a uno la suerte
be mistaken	estar en un error
beneath	debajo de
be necessary	ser fuerza
be one's turn	tocarle a uno, tocarle a uno la suerte
be on vacation	estar de vacaciones
be pleased with	quedar contento con
be right	andar bien; tener razón
beside	a lado de, tras de
be sleepy	tener sueño
be successful	salir bien, tener éxito
be thirsty	tener sed
between	por entre
be wrong	estar en un error, no tener razón
blackboard	la pizarra
book	el libro
bookcase	el estante

SPANISH COMMON WORDS
AND PHRASES FOR TEACHERS CONTINUED

English	Spanish
by foot	a pie
by hand	a mano
by heart	de memoria
by itself	de por si
by oneself	por si solo, por su mano
by twos	de dos en dos
call the roll	pasar lista
carry away	cargar con
chair	la silla
chalk	la tiza
classmate	compañero (de clase)
classroom	sala de clase
desk	el escritorio
do. . .again	hacer. . .de nuevo, volver a. . .
do over	hacer de nuevo, hacer otra vez, volver a hacer
each one	cada cual, cada uno
each time	a cada rato, cada vez
either	el uno o el otro, uno u otro
everybody	todo el mundo
every day	todos los dias
everyone	todo hombre
everywhere	a todas partes, en todas partes, por todas partes, por todos lados
fail	dejar de, salir mal, venirse abajo
finally	al cabo, en fin, pro fin, por última vez, por último
first of all	ante todo
for sure	de seguro
for the last time	por última vez
get going	poner en marcha
get ready to leave	hacer las maletas
get up	ponerse de pie, ponerse en pie
give a report on	dar cuenta de
given name	nombre de bautismo, nombre de pila
give to	dar a
go on vacation	ir de vacaciones
half done	a medio hacer
halfway (to a place)	a medio camino
have a birthday	cumplir años

The Reading Teacher's Book of Lists, Fifth Edition, © 2006 by John Wiley & Sons, Inc.

English	Spanish
have a good day	que lo pase bien
have a good time	pasar un buen rato
help	dar la mano
help yourself	sirvase usted
hurry	darse prisa
ill behaved	mal mandado, muy mandado
in a moment	en un improviso
incomplete	a medio hacer
indoors	bajo techo, en casa
in front of	al frente de, delante de, frente a
in the evening	en la noche, por la noche
in the same way	del mismo modo
in turn	en rueda
in writing	por escrito
it is all right	está bien
it is better . . .	más vale . . .
it is forbidden	se prohibe
it is time for	es (la) hora de
it is time to go	es (la) hora de partir
it's not important	no tiene importancia
it's time to . . .	ya es hora de . . .
it's too late now	ya es tarde
just right	al centavo, al pelo
keep silent	guardar silencio
last month	el mes pasado
last week	la semana pasada
last year	el año pasado
late	a fines de
learn by heart	aprendier de memoria
lend	dar prestado
lesson	la lección
less than	menos de, menos que
little by little	poco a poco
little more	y pico
long time	largos años
look	pues, mire
lots of	a mar de
lunch	el almuerzo
majority of the people	el comun de las gentes
make a deal	hacer un trato
make a mistake	no dar pie con bola
make an appointment	dar una cita
make a poor showing	hacer mal papel

SPANISH COMMON WORDS
AND PHRASES FOR TEACHERS CONTINUED

English	Spanish
make fun of	burlarse de, hacer cuco a, hacer burla de
make good	tener buen éxito
make no difference	dar lo mismo, no erle ni venirle a uno
make trouble	dar guerra
make up	inventar, imaginar
many years	largos años
mature	hecho y derecho
maybe	a lo mejor, tal vez
more than	más de, más que
most of	la mayoria de, la mayor parte de
move over	hacerse a un lado
naturally	claro que si
nearly	por poco
neatly dressed	bien arreglado(a)
never mind	no importa!, no se ocupe!
next to	al lado de, junto a
no . . . (smoking, eating, etc.)	se prohibe . . . (fumar, comer, etc.)
nobody else	ningún otro
no comment	sin comentarios
nonsense	de dónde!, salida de pie de banco
nothing at all	nada en absoluto
not much	poca cosa
not to open one's mouth	no despegar los labios
not to say a word	perder cuidado
not to worry	perder cuidado
not yet	aún no, todavia no
occasionally	de cuando en cuando, de vez en cuando
of course	claro que si, cómo no?, desde luego, por supuesto, seguro que si, ya se ve
often	a menudo
okay (to approve)	dar el visto bueno
on an average	pro término medio
once again	una que otra vez
once in a while	de uno en uno, uno a la vez
one way	de un solo sentido
one week from today	de hoy en ocho dias
on foot	a pie
only	nada más, no más que
only yesterday	ayer mismo
on the following day	al dia siguiente, al otro dia
on the inside	por dentro
on the other side of	al otro lado de

English	Spanish
on the outside	por fuera
on time	a buena hora, a tiempo
on top of	por encima de
opposed to	en contra de
ordinary	de ordinario
others	los (las) demás
over and over again	repetidas veces, una y otra vez
overnight	de la noche a la mañana
over there	por ahi, por allá
pack	hacer las maletas
paper	el papel
partly	en parte
pay attention (to)	dar atención, fijarse en, hacer caso (a or de), prestar atención
pen (ballpoint)	el bolígrafo
pencil	el lópiz
perhaps	a lo mejor, tal vez
plain	a secas
play fair	jugar limpio
proud	de copete
publicly	a las claras
pull	tirar de
put in writing	hacer por escrito
question	poner den duda
quickly	al trote, de prisa, de un salto, en un salto
rapidly	a escape
rather late	algo tarde
reflect on (think about)	parar mientes en
remember (or recollect)	hacer memoria
repeat mechanically	repetir de carretilla
right away	en el acto
right here	aqui mismo
right now	ahora mismo, en seguida, más ahorita
rise	pomerse en pie
same as (the)	el (or lo) mismo que, igual que
save time	ganar tiempo
say to oneself	decir para si
school	la escuela
scissors	las tijeras
seldom	por rareza, rara vez, raras veces
several times	varias veces
shake hands (with)	dar la mano, darse la mano, estrechar la mano (a)
sharp (on time)	en punto
shortly	en breve
show off	darse farol, hacer teatro

Spanish Common Words
and Phrases for Teachers Continued

English	Spanish
similar	algo por el estilo, parecido a
simply	a secas
slowly	a la larga
somebody else	algún otro
sometimes	algunas veces, de cuando en cuando
somewhere	en alguna parte
so much the better	tanto mejor
so much the worse	tanto peor
so-so	asi asi, tal cual
speak loudly	hablar alto, hablar en voz alta
stand still	estarse parado
stop talking	dejar de hablar
stop the excuses	dejarse de rodeos
study hard	quemarse las pestañas (or las cejas)
table	la mesa
take (something)	quedarse con (una cosa)
take a walk	pasear a pie
take care	tener cuidado (con)
take care of	preocuparse de
take it easy	tomarlo con calma
take place	tener lugar
take seriously	tomar a pecho(s)
take time off	tomar tiempo libre
talk too much	hablar por los codos
teacher	el maestro (male), la maestra (female)
team	el equipo
tease	tomarle el pelo
there's no hurry	no hay prisa
the same as	asi como, el (or lo) mismo que
they say	se dice
think (be of the opinion)	tener para si
think about	pensar en
this way	por acá, por aqui
this will do	asi está bien
thoroughly	por completo
(a) thousand thanks	mil gracias
together	a la vez
tomorrow afternoon	mañana por la tarde
tomorrow morning	mañana por la mañana
tomorrow night	mañana por la noche
tonight	a la noche, por la noche
too bad	que lástima!
to oneself	consigo mismo
towards the end of (a period of time)	a fines de

The Reading Teacher's Book of Lists, Fifth Edition, © 2006 by John Wiley & Sons, Inc.

English	Spanish
truly or truthfully	a la verdad, de veras, de verdad, en verdad
trust	confiar en
try to (attempt)	tratar de, ver de, ver que
turn around	dar(se) la vuelta
turn the page	darle vuelta a la hoja
two by two	de dos en dos
two weeks from today	de hoy en quince dias
under	debajo de
understand that . . .	tener entendido que . . .
unequaled	sin igual
unfortunately	por desgracia
unless	a menos que, a no ser que, como no
unneccessary	de sobra
until	hasta que
unusual	fuera de lo corriente
upon	encima de
up to now	hasta aqui, hasta ahi, hasta la fecha
usual	de ordinario
various times	repetidas veces
very close	a quema ropa, a quemarropa
very much	con (or en or por) extremo, de lo lindo
very often	con mucha frecuencia, muy a menudo
very soon	poco rato, ya mero
wait in line	hacer cola
walk	ir a pie
watch out (for)	tener cuidado (con)
water	agua
week before last	la semana antepasada
weekday(s)	dia(s) de semana, dia de trabajo, di hábil
weekend	el fin de semana
Well done!	Asi se hace!
What a mess!	Qué batingue!
What a pleasure!	Qué gusto!
What does it mean?	Qué quiere decir? qué significa?
What happened?	Qué pasó?
What is the date?	A cuánto(s) estamos?
What's new?	Qué hay de nuevo?
What's the difference?	Qué más da!
What time is it?	Qué hora es? qué horas son?
whenever	cuando quiera, siempre que, todas las veces (que)
while	en tanto que
whisper	hablar en secreto
whispering	en voz baja
win	salir ganando
with	junto con

SPANISH COMMON WORDS
AND PHRASES FOR TEACHERS CONTINUED

English	Spanish
within a week	dentro de una semana
without	sin que
with your permission	con permiso
wonderfully well	a las mil maravillas
work hard	dar bateria, sudar la gota gorda
work well	andar bien
worse than	peor que
years ago	hace años
yes, of course	ya lo creo
yesterday afternoon	ayer por la tarde
you're welcome	de nada, no hay de que

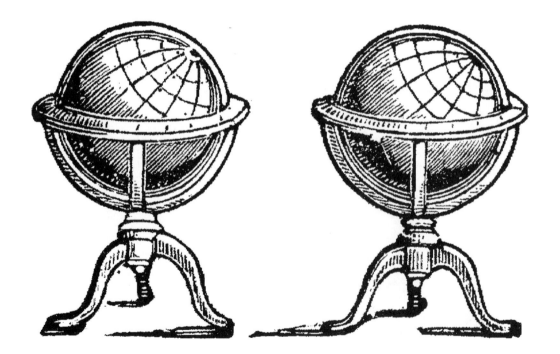

The Reading Teacher's Book of Lists, Fifth Edition, © 2006 by John Wiley & Sons, Inc.

LIST 179. DICHOS—SPANISH PROVERBS

Proverbs of all languages express a broad range of cultural ideas and wisdom. Most are not meant to be taken literally. Proverbs often have distinctive rhythms or rhymes that make them easy to remember. Many familiar English sayings have Spanish counterparts that are almost identical. Other Spanish dichos convey similar sentiments but use phrasing and words that express differences in culture as well.

The dichos below include some that are very similar to American English proverbs and some that are unique to Spanish language. Use them as part of your class discussion of how proverbs convey wisdom and culture.

Dichos	Meaning
Más vale tarde que nunca.	Better late than never.
Quien mucho duerme, poco aprende.	If you sleep much, you learn little.
No nació quien erró	No one born has not erred.
Los pájaros de la misma pluma vuelan juntos.	Birds of the same feather fly together.
En boca cerrada, no entran moscas.	In a closed mouth, no flies will enter.
Cuanto mas estudio, tanto más sabe.	The more you study, the more you know.
Del dicho al hecho, hay mucho trecho.	Between the word to the deed, there is a great gulf.
Donde hay gana, hay maña.	Where there's the desire, there's the ability.
El mal escribano le echa la culpa al la pluma.	The poor writer blames the pen.
El que mucho habla, mucho yerra.	He who speaks much, errs much.
La palabra es plata, el silencio oro.	The word is silver, silence gold.
Por el árbol se conocce el fruto.	By the tree, the fruit is known.
Querer es poder.	To want to is to be able to.
Mejor solo que mal acompañado.	Better alone than in poor company.
Los genios pensamos iqual.	Great minds think alike.
Excusa no pedida, la culpa manifiesta.	He who excuses himself, accuses himself.
Quien quiera saber, que compre un viejo.	If you seek wisdom, ask an old man.
Amigo y vino, el mas antiguo.	Friends and wine improve with age.
La risa es el major remedio.	Laughter is the best medicine.
Quien compra ha de tener cien ojos; a quien vende le basta uno solo.	The buyer needs a hundred eyes; the seller only one.
Ha ropa tendida.	Walls have ears.

15

LANGUAGE

The Reading Teacher's Book of Lists, Fifth Edition, © 2006 by John Wiley & Sons, Inc.

LIST 180. PARTS OF SPEECH

Over the centuries that English has been spoken and written, patterns of word usage have developed. These patterns form the grammar or syntax for the language and govern the use of the eight parts of speech.

Noun. A word that names a person, place, thing, or idea. It can act or be acted upon.
Examples:
> Roger, Father McGovern, bowlers, cousins, neighborhood, Baltimore, attic, Asia, LaGuardia Airport, Golden Gate Bridge, glove, class, triangle, goodness, strength, joy, perfection

Proper Noun. A specific name for a person, place, or thing. Proper nouns are capitalized and usually do not have a plural form.
Examples:
> Bill, London, Kleenex

Pronoun. A word that is used in place of a noun.
Examples:
> he, you, they, them, it, her, our, your, its, their, anybody, both, nobody, someone, several, himself, ourselves, themselves, yourself, itself, who, whom, which, what, whose

Adjective. A word that is used to describe or qualify a noun or pronoun, telling what kind, how many, or which one.
Examples:
> green, enormous, slinky, original, Italian, some, few, eleven, all, none, that, this, these, those, third

Verb. A word that shows physical or mental action, being, or state of being; a word used for saying something about a noun or pronoun.
Examples:
> swayed, cowered, dance, study, hold, think, imagine, love, approve, considered, am, is, was, were, has been, seems, appears, looks, feels, remains

Adverb. A word that is used to describe a verb, telling where, how, or when; a word that can qualify any part of speech except a noun or pronoun. Adverbs frequently end in *-ly*.
Examples:
> quietly, lovingly, skillfully, slyly, honestly, very, quite, extremely, too, moderately, seldom, never, often, periodically, forever

Conjunction. A word that is used to join words or groups of words.
Examples:
> and, or, either, neither, but, because, while, however, since, for, yet, still

Preposition. A word used to show the relationship of a noun or pronoun to another word.
Examples:
> across, below, toward, within, over, above, before, until, of, beyond, from, during, after, at, against

Interjection. A word that is used alone to express strong emotion.
Examples:
> Heavens! Cheers! Oh! Aha! Darn!

See also List 182, Basic Sentence Patterns; List 88, Build-a-Sentence.

LIST 181. IRREGULAR VERB PATTERNS

Most rules have exceptions, and exceptions can cause problems. Here is an extensive list of verbs and their principal parts that do not follow the regular pattern. (Regular verbs form the past or past participle by simply adding *-d* or *-ed*. For example: *call, called, has called*.)

Present	Past	Past Participle*
am	was	been
are (pl.)	were	been
beat	beat	beaten
become	became	become
begin	began	begun
bend	bent or bended	bent or bended
bet	bet	bet
bite	bit	bitten
bleed	bled	bled
blow	blew	blown
break	broke	broken
bring	brought	brought
build	built	built
burst	burst	burst
cast	cast	cast
catch	caught	caught
choose	chose	chosen
come	came	come
cost	cost	cost
creep	crept	crept
cut	cut	cut
dig	dug	dug
dive	dived or dove	dived
do	did	done
draw	drew	drawn
dream	dreamed or dreamt	dreamed or dreamt
drink	drank	drunk
drive	drove	driven
eat	ate	eaten
fall	fell	fallen
feed	fed	fed
feel	felt	felt
fight	fought	fought
fly	flew	flown
forbid	forbade	forbidden
forget	forgot	forgotten
forgive	forgave	forgiven
freeze	froze	frozen

*Note: The past participle also needs one of the following verbs: was, has, had, is.

Present	Past	Past Participle
get	got	got or gotten
give	gave	given
go	went	gone
grow	grew	grown
grind	ground	ground
hang	hung or hanged	hung
has	had	had
hear	heard	heard
hide	hid	hidden
hit	hit	hit
hold	held	held
hurt	hurt	hurt
is	was	has been
keep	kept	kept
kneel	kneeled or knelt	kneeled or knelt
know	knew	known
lay	laid	laid
leap	leaped or leapt	leaped or leapt
leave	left	left
lend	lent	lent
let	let	let
lie	lay	lain
light	lit	lit
lose	lost	lost
make	made	made
mean	meant	meant
mow	mowed	mowed or mown
put	put	put
quit	quit	quit
read	read	read
ride	rode	ridden
ring	rang	rung
rise	rose	risen
run	ran	run
saw	sawed	sawed or sawn
say	said	said
see	saw	seen
sell	sold	sold
set	set	set
sew	sewed	sewed or sewn
shake	shook	shaken
shed	shed	shed
shine	shined or shone	shined or shone
shoot	shot	shot
show	showed	shown or showed
shrink	shrank or shrunk	shrunk

IRREGULAR VERB FORMS CONTINUED

Present	Past	Past Participle
shut	shut	shut
sing	sang	sung
sink	sank	sunk
sit	sat	sat
sleep	slept	slept
slide	slid	slid
slit	slit	slit
sow	sowed	sowed or sown
speak	spoke	spoken
spend	spent	spent
spin	spun	spun
spit	spit	spit
split	split	split
spread	spread	spread
spring	sprang or sprung	sprung
stand	stood	stood
steal	stole	stolen
stick	stuck	stuck
sting	stung	stung
strike	struck	struck
string	strung	strung
swear	swore	sworn
sweat	sweat or sweated	sweat or sweated
sweep	swept	swept
swim	swam or swum	swum
swing	swung	swung
take	took	taken
teach	taught	taught
tear	tore	torn
tell	told	told
think	thought	thought
throw	threw	thrown
thrust	thrust	thrust
understand	understood	understood
wake	woke or waked	woken or waked
wear	wore	worn
weave	wove	woven
weep	wept	wept
wet	wet	wet
win	won	won
wind	wound	wound
write	wrote	written

The Reading Teacher's Book of Lists, Fifth Edition, © 2006 by John Wiley & Sons, Inc.

See also List 182, Basic Sentence Patterns.

LIST 182. BASIC SENTENCE PATTERNS

Parts of speech are put together to form sentences. The list of basic sentence patterns and variations shows the most common arrangements of words. Remember that every sentence must have at minimum a noun (or pronoun) and a verb. This is sometimes called a subject and a predicate.

N/V	noun/verb	*Children sang.*
N/V/N	noun/verb/noun	*Bill paid the worker.*
N/V/ADV	noun/verb/adverb	*Ann sewed quickly.*
N/LV/N	noun/linking verb/noun	*Arthur is President.*
N/LV/ADJ	noun/linking verb/adjective	*Chris looks sleepy.*
N/V/N/N	noun/verb/noun/noun	*Chuck gave Marie flowers.*

Variations of Basic Sentence Patterns

Affirmative to Negative—*It is raining./It is not raining.*

Affirmative to Question—*The bottle is empty./Is the bottle empty?*

Use of "there"—*A man is at the door./There is a man at the door.*

Request—*You mow the grass./Mow the grass.*

Active to Passive—*The dog chased the fox./The fox was chased by the dog.*

Possessive—*Juan owns this car./This is Juan's car.*

Prepositional phrase added—*This is Juan's car in the garage.*

Adverbial phrase added—*Birds fly quietly together.*

Present to Past—*I live in Miami./I lived in Miami.*

Simple Past to Progressive Past—*I live in Miami./I was living in Miami.*

Past to Future—*I lived in Miami./I will live in Miami.*

Certain to Uncertain—*I will do it./I might do it.*

See also List 88, Build-a-Sentence; List 180, Parts of Speech.

LIST 183. COMMON WORD IDIOMS

Idioms—expressions that have unique meanings and cannot be understood from the individual meanings of their components—are challenging for all readers. They are particularly difficult for English language learners. Many of these word idioms have multiple meanings which only add to the confusion. *Back up*, for example, may refer to a clogged drain, a traffic jam, moving in a backwards direction, to give support for someone, evidence, duplication of work, alternative plan, or a tense disposition. Use the following list as a start for exploring idioms.

all	all along, all at once, all ears, all eyes, all hours, all in all, all out, all over, all set, all systems go, all there, all thumbs, all wet
back	back down, back out, back up, back and forth, back off, back street, backseat driver
blow	blow up, blow out, blow one's lines, blow over, blow the whistle, blow the lid off
break	break down, break in, break a promise, break out, break the ice, break the news, break up, break even, break ground, break one's heart, break one's neck, break through
bring	bring about, bring down the house, bring in, bring off, bring on, bring one to do something, bring out, bring up
burn	burn one's bridges, burn out, burn rubber, burn the candle at both ends, burn up
call	call attention to, call for, call in, call names, call on, call out, call up, call a strike, call it quits, call it a day, call the shots, call to order
catch	catch cold, catch on, catch one's breath, catch one's eye, catch up
check	check in, check out, check on, check over, check up, check with
come	come about, come again, come alive, come a long way, come back, come by, come clean, come across, come around, come down on, come into, come into your own, come off it, come out, come up to, come upon, come-on, come over, come to, come through, come to think of it
cut	cut across, cut corners, cut in, cut out, cut someone out, cut out for, cut into, cut off
eat	eat away, eat like a bird, eat like a horse, eat your heart out, eat your words, eat your hat, eat out of your hand, eat it up
fall	fall down, fall flat, fall for, fall out, fall over each other, fall short, fall through, fall behind, fall back on, fall over backwards, fall head over heels
get	get along, get away with, get back at, get even with, get into, get on someone's nerves, get your back up, get out of, get over, get the hang of, get up, get ahead, get around to, get lost, get off the ground, get up and go
give	give away, give in, give of, give out, give up, give a hand, give oneself up
go	go all out, go by, go easy, go far, go for, go in for, go into, go off the deep end, go on, go out, go over, go with, go without, go ahead, go back on a promise, go broke
hang	hang around, hang on, hang out, hang up, hang in there
head	head of a company, head of lettuce, head of the line, head of a pimple, have a good head, air head, head of a coin, head of a river, head of a nail, head to head, head lock, well head, head between our legs, head food server, heads or tails

The Reading Teacher's Book of Lists, Fifth Edition, © 2006 by John Wiley & Sons, Inc.

The Reading Teacher's Book of Lists, Fifth Edition, © 2006 by John Wiley & Sons, Inc.

hit   hit the books, hit the roof, hit the headlines, hit the high points, hit the nail on the head, hit bottom, hit and run, hit it off, hit the road, hit the jackpot, hit the spot, hit the bull's eye

hold   hold a candle to, hold on, hold down, hold back, hold everything, hold your fire, hold out, hold up, hold your own

keep   keep a straight face, keep on, keep your head above water, keep your word, keep the pot boiling, keep up with, keep it down, keep one's chin up, keep one's nose clean, keep track, keep one's fingers crossed

look   look down on, look down your nose at, look for, look into, look out, look up, look up to someone, look after, look back, look over

make   make a move, make a play for, make certain, make ends meet, make fun of, make good, make believe, make a point, make friends, make sense of, make it, make over, make sure, make the grade, make up, make up for, make up your mind, make up with

pull   pull off, pull your weight, pull strings, pull through, pull together, pull up, pull the wool over your eyes, pull rank, pull it together, pull the rug out from under

put   put away, put an end to, put in one's place, put one's foot down, put to bed, put to use, put down, put off, put on, put out, put two and two together, put up, put up with

run   run into, run away, run down, run in, run out of, run over, run through, run the risk of, run away with, run short, run wild

see   see about, see into, see through, see to, see daylight, see off, see red, see to it

set   set a table, set of dishes, all set, set out, set in, set upon, set a clock, set apart, set a trap, set a time, set your mind to something, set a fast pace, set a gem

sit   sit on, sit out, sit pretty, sit tight, sit up, sit back, sit in

take   take aim, take after, take a bath (shower), take advantage of, take in, take by surprise, take effect, take care, take it easy, take for granted, take in, take it from me, take it hard, take it out on someone, take note of, take off, take on, take your time, take out, take over, take the cake, take the trouble, take it upon yourself, take a breath, take a breather

throw   throw a curve, throw a party, throw in the sponge, throw off, throw one's weight around, throw out, throw up

turn   turn off, turn one's stomach, turn the clock back, turn over a new leaf, turn down, turn in, turn loose, turn on, turn your head, turn out, turn over, turn the tables on someone, turn to, turn up

LIST 184. IDIOMATIC EXPRESSIONS

Idiomatic expressions cannot be understood from the literal meanings of their words. Instead, these interesting phrases must be "translated." Idiomatic expressions are part of our conversations and informal writing; however, most are not appropriate for formal writing. Idiomatic expressions can vary across the regions of the United States, which makes them even more of a challenge for English language learners. Teach the following expressions as you would teach single vocabulary words in context.

If we want our team to win, we all need *to stick together*.

Because Darin was such a good swimmer, his coach *went to bat for* him.

You can tell by her beautiful garden that Kathy *has a green thumb*.

It's been a long day, so I think I'll *hit the hay*.

Cynda and Jason *burned the midnight oil* getting their project done.

Please *don't monkey around* with that because it's fragile and may break.

Michael had to *be on the road* early, so he *called it a night* before Camille returned.

He *lost his temper* for no reason. He has to learn to stay calm.

Gloria arrived *on the dot* for the noon meeting and *got the ball rolling*.

"*There, there*," Emily said to Hanna. "*No use crying over spilled milk.*"

Mike *lucked out* and got tickets to the Super Bowl game.

Sam didn't *know the ropes* and there was no one willing to help her.

Chuck had them *rolling in the aisles* with his stories.

It *sounds fishy* to me. We'd better *check it out*.

Things ran smoothly while Jim was *head honcho* in the department.

I *get cold feet* when it comes time to make a speech.

Tom said it was *a piece of cake*, but I still wondered how he *pulled it off*.

It took *forever and a day* to get to the front of the line.

Grace *had us in stitches* when she showed up in costume.

Hang on. I'm almost ready to leave.

Drop me a line when you're on vacation.

Off the top of my head, I'd say it weighed a ton.

Tell me what you know about him, *I'm all ears*.

The weather report said there's only a *slim chance* of rain.

Michael wanted *to sleep on it*. Moving to New Jersey was a big decision.

You're *barking up the wrong tree*.

Don't bother me, I need my *beauty sleep*.

Nick *got a kick* out of the way Jared and Alex decorated the room.

Ryan *caught some Z's* on his *flight* to California.

Eve *had her hands full* getting everyone ready to leave on time.

After taking a long nap, I *felt like a million dollars*.

Phil *did a bang-up job* when he built the cabinet.

He always *roots for the underdog*, and sometimes they win.

The Reading Teacher's Book of Lists, Fifth Edition, © 2006 by John Wiley & Sons, Inc.

Nancy *kept an eye out for* Marie as she walked through the crowd.

Debbie couldn't *make heads or tails out of* the note Art left on the door.

Kathryn and Fred were ready for some *R and R* after putting the new floor in the house.

Pat had *to cut out* to meet her friends.

Adam *drove a hard bargain* and *ended up with* a good deal.

Christopher's new car *hugged the road* as it *took the curve*.

I wonder where Candi gets her *get-up-and-go*.

Jamie had a lot to do, so Jessica *gave her a hand*.

Nicole *changed her mind* about the job and stayed in the city.

Steven was *glued to his seat* watching the movie.

You can tell this is Jenn's favorite book of poems; it has *dog-eared* pages.

Clayton and Garret were so excited to make the team that they were *on cloud nine*.

It's supposed to be a surprise, so don't *let the cat out of the bag*.

No, I'm not ill; I've just *got a frog in my throat*.

Chris and Tom *grabbed a bite* to eat before going to the show.

The green dress in the store window *caught Lisa's eye*.

It was *raining cats and dogs* when Meg arrived with David and Andrew.

Mike has a *state-of-the-art* video camera; it even takes pictures underwater.

This one has to be perfect. Remember to *dot all the i's and cross all the t's*.

The ball Philip wanted to buy Jacob was *out of stock*, so he asked for a *rain check*.

Benjamin knew the code *backwards and forwards*.

Marianne *crunched the numbers* and said it was a good deal.

Dru was *skating on thin ice* when he asked Ari to do him another favor.

Gerry *caught a bad cold*, even though she took vitamins.

Joe was *down in the dumps* after losing the game.

The solution to my problem finally *dawned on me*.

She was *like a fish out of water* in the city. It was so different from her farm.

When Larry found out what I did, he gave me *a piece of his mind*.

Marly was so grouchy, we knew she had gotten up on the *wrong side of the bed*.

David was so serious that I couldn't get him *to crack a smile* no matter how hard I tried.

You have to climb up the ladder to get a *bird's eye view* of the yard.

LIST 185. PROVERBS

Proverbs are common, wise, or thoughtful sayings that are short and often applicable to different situations. Every culture and language has its own, from the ancient Chinese Confucian "A picture is worth a thousand words" to the American "A stitch in time saves nine." You and your students might enjoy adding to this collection. Proverbs can also be used as prompts for writing assignments, or you may want to ask your students to complete the end of a proverb. Don't be surprised if the result is humorous. For example, one teacher reported that her first grader completed "A penny saved is . . ." with "not much."

Relationships

A friend in need is a friend indeed.

Absence makes the heart grow fonder.

All's fair in love and war.

Better to have loved and lost than never to have loved at all.

Familiarity breeds contempt.

Good fences make good neighbors.

If you can't beat them, join them.

Like father, like son.

Love will find a way.

Marry in haste, repent at leisure.

Misery loves company.

Short visits make long friends.

Action and Determination

A faint heart never won a fair lady.

A quitter never wins and a winner never quits.

A rolling stone gathers no moss.

A stitch in time saves nine.

Actions speak louder than words.

All things come to those who wait.

Confession is good for the soul.

He/She who hesitates is lost.

He/She who sits on the fence is easily blown off.

If you can't stand the heat, get out of the kitchen.

If you want something done, ask a busy person.

Leave no stone unturned.

Make hay while the sun shines.

Never put off 'til tomorrow what you can do today.

No pain, no gain.

Sometimes you have to run just to stay in place.

Strike while the iron is hot.

When the going gets tough, the tough get going.

Where there's a will, there's a way.

Caution

Better safe than sorry.

Don't cross the bridge until you come to it.

Forewarned is forearmed.

Haste makes waste.

Learn to walk before you run.

Look before you leap.

Waste not, want not.

Encouragement

Every cloud has a silver lining.

The darkest hour is just before the dawn.

The first step is the most difficult.

Appearances

Beauty is in the eye of the beholder.

Beauty is only skin deep.

The grass is always greener on the other side of the fence.

You can't tell a book by its cover.

Good Deeds

Charity begins at home.

Civility costs nothing.

Do right and fear no one.

Do unto others as you would have them do unto you.

Give credit where credit is due.

Great oaks from little acorns grow.

One good turn deserves another.

The Reading Teacher's Book of Lists, Fifth Edition, © 2006 by John Wiley & Sons, Inc.

To err is human; to forgive, divine.

Two wrongs don't make a right.

Words

A picture is worth a thousand words.

A soft answer turneth away wrath.

A tongue is worth little without a brain.

A word spoken is not an action done.

Ask a silly question and you get a silly answer.

Ask no question and hear no lies.

Bad news travels fast.

Brevity is the soul of wit.

Sticks and stones may break my bones but names can never hurt me.

Still waters run deep.

The pen is mightier than the sword.

The squeaky wheel gets the grease.

There's many a slip between cup and lip.

Animals

A bird in the hand is worth two in the bush.

Birds of a feather flock together.

Curiosity killed the cat.

Don't change horses in midstream.

Don't count your chickens before they're hatched.

Let sleeping dogs lie.

One camel doesn't make fun of another camel's hump.

The early bird catches the worm.

When the cat's away, the mice will play.

You can lead a horse to water but you can't make it drink.

You can't teach an old dog new tricks.

Money

A fool and his/her money are soon parted.

A penny saved is a penny earned.

All that glitters is not gold.

Early to bed, early to rise makes a man/woman healthy, wealthy, and wise.

He/She who pays the piper calls the tune.

Lend your money and lose your friend.

Money burns a hole in your pocket.

They who dance must pay the fiddler.

Time is money.

Food

An apple a day keeps the doctor away.

Don't cry over spilt milk.

Half a loaf is better than none.

He/She who would eat the fruit must climb the tree.

Honey catches more flies than vinegar.

The apple never falls far from the tree.

The proof of the pudding is in the eating.

There's no such thing as a free lunch.

Too many cooks spoil the broth.

You can't have your cake and eat it too.

Miscellaneous

A good beginning makes a good ending.

A house divided cannot stand.

A hovel on the rock is better than a palace on the sand.

A little knowledge is a dangerous thing.

A rising tide lifts all boats.

A watched pot never boils.

Adversity makes strange bedfellows.

All good things come to an end.

An idle brain is the devil's workshop.

Beggars can't be choosers.

Better late than never.

Different strokes for different folks.

Don't get mad—get even.

Everybody's business is nobody's business.

Experience is the father/mother of wisdom.

Fact is stranger than fiction.

Fool me once, shame on you. Fool me twice, shame on me.

For every joy there is a price to be paid.

He/She gives twice who gives quickly.

He/She who lives by the sword, dies by the sword.

If it isn't broken, don't fix it.

If the shoe fits, wear it.

If you're not part of the solution, you're part of the problem.

16

ALPHABETS
AND
SYMBOLS

ABC 123

ABC 123

ABC 123

ABC 123

שׂב־ 123

AЂB 123

LIST 186. HANDWRITING CHARTS

Have you ever needed a handwriting chart for a student and couldn't quickly locate one? The Zaner–Bloser and D'Nealian manuscript and cursive alphabet charts are here to help you out in just such a situation.

Zaner-Bloser Manuscript Alphabet

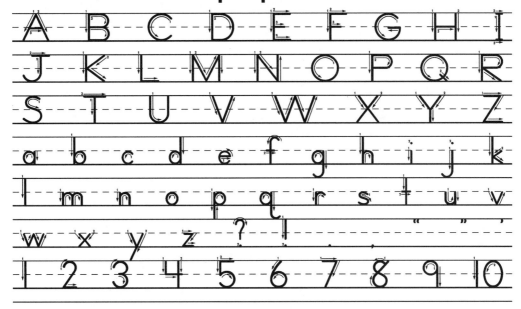

Copyright © Zaner-Bloser, Inc.

Zaner-Bloser Cursive Alphabet

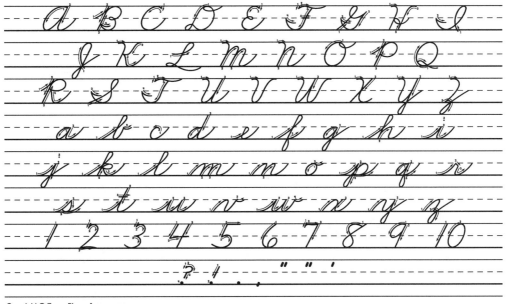

Copyright © Zaner-Bloser, Inc.

HANDWRITING CHARTS CONTINUED

D'Nealian® Cursive Alphabet

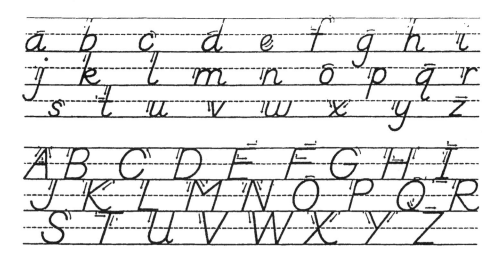

D'Nealian® Numbers

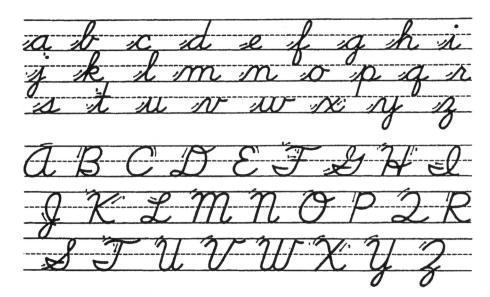

See also List 187, Alphabet Letter Frequency.

The Reading Teacher's Book of Lists, Fifth Edition, © 2006 by John Wiley & Sons, Inc.

LIST 187. ALPHABET LETTER FREQUENCY

What are the most common letters? Put another way, which letters are the most useful, that beginners need to read and write? Which letters should you teach first?

Here is one suggestion based on a count of over a million words taken from 15 categories of American English writing.

Letters 1–5	Letters 6–10	Letters 11–15
e	n	d
t	s	c
a	r	u
o	h	m
i	l	f

Letters 16–20	Letters 21–26
p	v
g	k
w	x
y	j
b	q
	z

Where does the word "alphabet" come from? *Alpha* is the first letter and *beta* is the second letter of the Greek alphabet. *Alef* and *beit* are the first two letters of the Hebrew alphabet.

In English we frequently speak of learning the alphabet as learning the ABC's. An alphabet is a set of symbols that stand for speech sounds or phonemes. The Greeks got the idea of writing using sound symbols from the Phoenicians, who lived in the Near East in the 11th century B.C. From "Phoenician" we get such words as *phonics*, *phonetic*, *phoneme*, and *telephone*.

Alpha and omega is a phrase meaning all-encompassing. It includes everything from the first to the last. Alpha is the first letter of the Greek alphabet and omega is the last letter of the Greek alphabet.

LIST 188. ALPHABET AND SYMBOLS WEB SITES

Check out these web sites for activities centered around alphabets and symbols.

AlphaBites

Activities for every letter of the alphabet.
http://www.alphabet-soup.net/alphabite.html

Mrs. Alphabet

Alphabet worksheets, activities, book ideas, and more.
http://www.mrsalphabet.com/links.html

Letter Songs, Rhymes and Chants

Lyrics for ABC songs, rhymes and chants
http://www.littlegiraffes.com/lettersongsrhymes.html

Alphabet Preschool Activities and Crafts

Worksheets, traceables, flashcards, activities for each letter of the alphabet.
http://www.first-school.ws/theme/alphabet.htm

Alphabet Activities – Preschool

Crafts and other activities to teach letter names.
http://www.preschoolrainbow.org/alphabet.htm

ABCTeach

Flashcards, worksheets, puzzles, dot to dot, and more
http://www.abcteach.com/directory/basics/abc_activities/

Billy Bear's Online Alphabet Games

Online activities for learning the alphabet
http://www.billybear4kids.com/games/online/alphabet/abc.htm

Online Animal Alphabet Book

Yellowstone National Park's Kids Web Site with pictures and information about animals a to z
http://www.billybear4kids.com/games/online/alphabet/abc.htm

Alphabet Writing Sheets

D'Nealian, Zaner-Bloser, and Cursive Alphabet Reproducible Worksheets with image and traceable letters
http://www.learningpage.com/free_pages/menu_basics/alpha_dnealian.html

Alphabet Action

Click a letter and see a picture and hear the letter name
http://www.learningplanet.com/act/fl/aact/index.asp

Your Name in Hieroglyphs

Translates your name into hieroglyphs
http://hieroglyphs.net/0301/cgi/pager.pl?p=42

Egyptian Hieroglyphs – Kids Site

Numbers, Fractions, Writing, and More
http://www.greatscott.com/hiero/

The Reading Teacher's Book of Lists, Fifth Edition, © 2006 by John Wiley & Sons, Inc.

LIST 189. FOREIGN ALPHABETS

The following table of alphabets shows how some other languages are written. Your students will enjoy writing their names and other messages using the different alphabets.

TABLE OF ALPHABETS

Because it is more convenient to use a single system of spelling to represent the speech sounds of many different languages, words from languages that use other writing systems are usually transliterated into Roman characters. The transliterations shown here are those used in the etymologies in this Dictionary for four of the most important non-Roman alphabets. The names of the Hebrew and Greek letters are also entered and defined in the Dictionary as English nouns. (In some cases the English spelling differs from the transliterated letter name shown here, chiefly in the absence of diacritical marks—for example English **omega** versus Greek **ōmega**.) The Cyrillic letters shown are those used in modern Russian. For the history of the English alphabet, see "Development of the Alphabet."

HEBREW

Forms	Name	Sound
א	'aleph	'
ב	bēth	b
ג	gimel	g
ד	dāleth	d
ה	hē	h
ו	vāv, wāw	w
ז	zayin	z
ח	ḥeth	ḥ
ט	ṭeth	ṭ
י	yodh	y
כ	kāph	k
ל	lāmedh	l
מ	mēm	m
נ	nūn	n
ס	samekh	s
ע	'ayin	'
פ	pē	p
צ	ṣadhe	ṣ
ק	qōph	q
ר	rēsh	r
שׂ	sin	ś
שׁ	shin	š
ת	tāv, tāw	t

ARABIC

	Forms			Name	Sound
1	2	3	4		
ا	ا			'alif	'
ب	ب	ب	ب	bā	b
ت	ت	ت	ت	tā	t
ث	ث	ث	ث	thā	t̲
ج	ج	ج	ج	jīm	j
ح	ح	ح	ح	ḥā	ḥ
خ	خ	خ	خ	khā	ḫ
د	د			dāl	d
ذ	ذ			dhāl	d̲
ر	ر			rā	r
ز	ز			zāy	z
س	س	س	س	sīn	s
ش	ش	ش	ش	shīn	š
ص	ص	ص	ص	ṣād	ṣ
ض	ض	ض	ض	ḍād	ḍ
ط	ط	ط	ط	ṭā	ṭ
ظ	ظ	ظ	ظ	ẓā	z̧
ع	ع	ع	ع	'ayn	'
غ	غ	غ	غ	ghayn	ġ
ف	ف	ف	ف	fā	f
ق	ق	ق	ق	qāf	q
ك	ك	ك	ك	kāf	k
ل	ل	ل	ل	lām	l
م	م	م	م	mīm	m
ن	ن	ن	ن	nūn	n
ه	ه	ه	ه	hā	h
و	و			wāw	w
ي	ي	ي	ي	yā	y

GREEK

Forms	Name	Sound
Α α	alpha	a
Β β	bēta	b
Γ γ	gamma	g (n)
Δ δ	delta	d
Ε ε	epsīlon	e
Ζ ζ	zēta	z
Η η	ēta	ē
Θ θ	thēta	th
Ι ι	iōta	i
Κ κ	kappa	k
Λ λ	lambda	l
Μ μ	mū	m
Ν ν	nū	n
Ξ ξ	xī	x
Ο ο	omīkron	o
Π π	pī	p
Ρ ρ	rhō	r (rh)
Σ σ, ς	sīgma	s
Τ τ	tau	t
Υ υ	upsīlon	u
Φ φ	phī	ph
Χ χ	chī, khī	kh
Ψ ψ	psī	ps
Ω ω	ōmega	ō

CYRILLIC

Forms	Sound
А а	a
Б б	b
В в	v
Г г	g
Д д	d
Е е Ё ё	e, ë[1]
Ж ж	zh
З з	z
И и Й й	i, ĭ
К к	k
Л л	l
М м	m
Н н	n
О о	o
П п	p
Р р	r
С с	s
Т т	t
У у	u
Ф ф	f
Х х	kh
Ц ц	ts
Ч ч	ch
Ш ш	sh
Щ щ	shch
Ъ ъ	[2]
Ы ы	y
Ь ь	[3]
Э э	e
Ю ю	yu
Я я	ya

The Reading Teacher's Book of Lists, Fifth Edition, © 2006 by John Wiley & Sons, Inc.

FOREIGN ALPHABETS CONTINUED

Vowels are not represented in normal Hebrew writing, but for certain purposes they are indicated by a system of subscript and superscript dots. The transliterations with subscript dots are pharyngeal consonants as in Arabic. The second forms shown are used when the letter falls at the end of a word.

The different forms in the four numbered columns are used when the letters are in: 1. isolation; 2. juncture with a previous letter; 3. juncture with letters on both sides; 4. juncture with a following letter.

Long vowels are represented by the consonants ʼalif (for ā), wāw (for ū), and yā (for ī). Short vowels are not usually written; they can, however, be indicated by the following signs: ʼfatha (for a), ‚kesra (for i), and ʼ damma (for u).

Transliterations with subscript dots represent "emphatic" or pharyngeal consonants, which are pronounced in the usual way except that the pharynx is tightly narrowed during articulation. When two dots are placed over the hā, the new letter thus formed is called tā marbūta, and is pronounced (t).

The superscript on an initial vowel or rhō represents aspiration or "rough breathing," and is transliterated by h. Lack of aspiration on an initial vowel is indicated by the superscript ʼ, called the smooth breathing. When gamma precedes kappa, xī, khī, or another gamma, it has the value ng (as in Engl. sing) and is transliterated n. The second lowercase form of sigma is used only in the final position.

[1]The variant ë occurs only in stressed position, and is pronounced as (ô) or (yô).

[2]This letter, called the "hard sign," is very rare in modern Russian. It indicates that the previous consonant remains hard (not palatalized) even when followed by a front vowel.

[3]This letter, called the "soft sign," indicates that the previous consonant is soft (palatalized) even when a front vowel does not follow.

The Reading Teacher's Book of Lists, Fifth Edition, © 2006 by John Wiley & Sons, Inc.

LIST 190. ANCIENT EGYPTIAN ALPHABET—HIEROGLYPHS

For many years archaeologists could not read or understand ancient Egyptian writing. All they saw was a jumble of little pictures. It turns out that it wasn't picture writing at all but a phonetic alphabet similar to ours.

Maybe you could try writing your name in hieroglyphs. Don't worry if you have to leave out some vowels; other Middle East languages such as Hebrew or Arabic do, too.

Hieroglyph	Picture	Transliteration	Pronunciation
	Egyptian vulture	$ȝ$	a (aleph)
	reed leaf	i	i or y
	double reed leaf	y	i or y
	lower arm	c	a (ayin)
	quail chick	w	w or u
	leg	b	b
	wicker stool	p	p
	viper	f	f
	owl	m	m
	water	n	n
	mouth	r	r
	courtyard (plan)	h	h
	twisted flax wick	$ḥ$	h (emphatic h)*
	placenta	$ḫ$	k (soft kh: German *ich*)

*In the English text of this book, this sound will be written h.

Hieroglyphics from *Hieroglyphs without Mystery: An Introduction to Ancient Egyptian Writing* by Karl-Theodor Zauzich; translated and adapted for English-speaking readers by Ann Macy Roth. Copyright © 1992. By permission of the University of Texas Press and Thames & Hudson Ltd., London.

Ancient Egyptian Alphabet—Hieroglyphs Continued

Hieroglyph	Picture	Transliteration	Pronunciation
	animal belly	$\underline{h}$	k (hard kh: German *ach*)
	door bolt	z	z
	folded cloth	s	s
	pool	$š$	sh
	sandy slope	k	k (q without u: *qaf*)
	basket	k	k
	jar stand	g	g
	bread loaf	t	t
	tether rope	$\underline{t}$	ch
	hand	d	d
	cobra	$\underline{d}$	j

Some Alternate Forms:

	two strokes	y	i or y
	red crown	n	n
	jar stand and bolt	gs	ges
	from the cursive form	w	w

The Reading Teacher's Book of Lists, Fifth Edition, © 2006 by John Wiley & Sons, Inc.

LIST 191. NATIVE AMERICAN SYMBOLS

The earliest writings of the Native American Indians were those of signs and symbols. These symbols are also apparent in their handicraft and jewelry.

 HORSE (Journey)

 MAN (Human Life)

 SUN RAYS (Constancy)

 LASSO (Captivity)

 THUNDERBIRD (Sacred Bearer of Happiness Unlimited)

 CROSSED ARROWS (Friendship)

 ARROW (Protection)

 ARROWHEAD (Alertness)

 FOUR AGES (Infancy, Youth, Middle, and Old Age)

 CACTUS (Sign of the Desert)

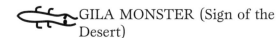 GILA MONSTER (Sign of the Desert)

 CACTUS FLOWER (Courtship)

 SADDLE BAGS (Journey)

 BIRD (Carefree, Lighthearted)

 LIGHTNING SNAKE (Defiance, Wisdom)

 SNAKE (Defiance, Wisdom)

 THUNDERBIRD TRACK (Bright Prospects)

 DEER TRACK (Plentiful Game)

 BEAR TRACK (Good Omen)

 RATTLESNAKE JAW (Strength)

 HEADDRESS (Ceremonial Dance)

 COYOTE TRACKS (Good Prospects)

The Reading Teacher's Book of Lists, Fifth Edition, © 2006 by John Wiley & Sons, Inc.

NATIVE AMERICAN SYMBOLS CONTINUED

 RAIN CLOUDS (Good Prospects)

 LIGHTNING AND LIGHTNING ARROW (Swiftness)

 DAYS AND NIGHTS (Time)

 MORNING START (Guidance)

 SUN SYMBOLS (Happiness)

 RUNNING WATER (Constant Life)

 RAINDROP—RAIN (Plentiful Crops)

 TEPEE (Temporary Home)

 SKY BAND (Leading to Happiness)

 MEDICINE MAN'S EYE (Wise, Watchful)

 MOUNTAIN RANGE

 HOGAN (Permanent Home)

 BIG MOUNTAIN (Abundance)

 HOUSE OF WATER

 FENCE (Guarding Good Luck)

 ENCLOSURE FOR CEREMONIAL DANCES

 EAGLE FEATHERS (Chief)

 WARDING OFF EVIL SPIRITS

 PATHS CROSSING

 BROKEN ARROW Peace

BUTTERFLY (Everlasting Life)

LIST 192. FINGER SPELLING ALPHABET

Many people who have hearing impairments use this alphabet to spell individual words to others. Each letter is represented by a particular arrangement of the fingers, and some letters include movement as well. Finger spelling is used in addition to sign language which communicates whole ideas through gestures and hand signs.

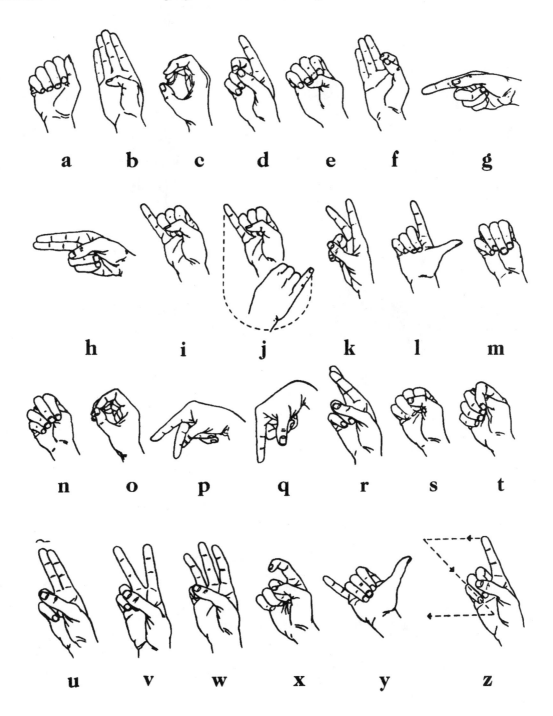

LIST 193. SIGN LANGUAGE EXAMPLES

Words are communicated by hand positions and movement.

Go

Stop

Good

Bad

Smart

Stupid

Stand up

Sit down

Yes

No

The Reading Teacher's Book of Lists, Fifth Edition, © 2006 by John Wiley & Sons, Inc.

LIST 194. BRAILLE ALPHABET

People who are blind or visually impaired learn to read the alphabet by feeling raised dots with their fingers.

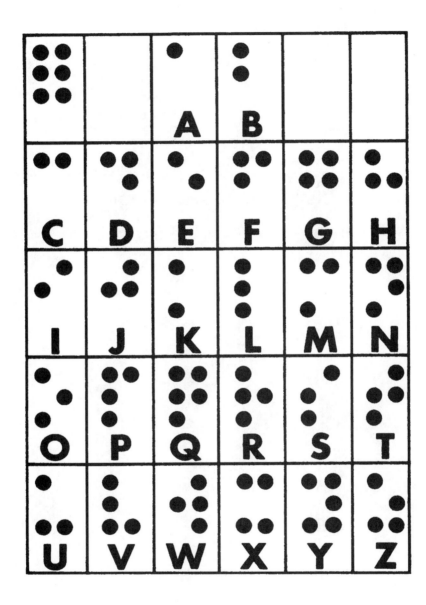

LIST 195. RADIO VOICE ALPHABET

This international alphabet is used by airplane pilots, ship personnel, ham radio operators, and many others who speak over the radio when they need to spell out words or give call letters.

Alfa	**H**otel	**O**scar	**V**ictor
Bravo	**I**ndia	**P**apa	**W**hiskey
Charlie	**J**uliett	**Q**uebec	**X**-ray
Delta	**K**ilo	**R**omeo	**Y**ankee
Echo	**L**ima	**S**ierra	**Z**ulu
Foxtrot	**M**ike	**T**ango	
Golf	**N**ovember	**U**niform	

LIST 196. MORSE CODE

The Morse Code is still used by some radio hams. With practice, it is possible for amateurs to use it to send flashlight messages.

A	.—	L	.—..	W	.——	1	.————
B	—...	M	——	X	—..—	2	..———
C	—.—.	N	—.	Y	—.——	3	...——
D	—..	O	———	Z	——..	4	....—
E	.	P	.——.	Á	.——.—	5	.....
F	..—.	Q	——.—	Ä	.—.—	6	—....
G	——.	R	.—.	É	..—..	7	——...
H	....	S	...	Ñ	——.——	8	———..
I	..	T	—	Ö	———.	9	————.
J	.———	U	..—	Ü	..——	0	—————
K	—.—	V	...—				

,	(comma)	——..——	- (hyphen)		—....—
.	(period)	.—.—.—	apostrophe		.————.
?		..——..	parenthesis		—.——.—
;		—.—.—.	underline		..——.—
:		———...			
/		—..—.			

The Reading Teacher's Book of Lists, Fifth Edition, © 2006 by John Wiley & Sons, Inc.

LIST 197. TRAFFIC SIGNS

As international travel has become more common, the United States has adopted traffic signs that use pictures and symbols. These help overcome language barriers. Understanding traffic signs is important for safety for drivers and pedestrians.

Shapes have meaning. Diamond-shaped signs signify a warning; rectangular signs with the longer dimension vertical provide a traffic regulation; rectangular signs with the longer dimension horizontal contain guidance information; an octagon means stop; an inverted triangle means yield; a pennant means no passing; a pentagon shows the presence of a school; and a circle warns of a railroad crossing.

TRAFFIC SIGNS CONTINUED

Regulatory Signs

Black and white signs are for posting regulations. Red signifies stop, yield or prohibition. The red circle with a diagonal slash always indicates a prohibited movement.

Left turns may be allowed for traffic coming from opposing directions in the center lane of a highway. There are two types of signs used to identify these locations. One is a word message and the other is a symbol sign showing opposing left turn arrows with the word "Only."

Turns are permitted in many states at traffic signals when the red traffic signal is on. There are two types of laws which permit this movement. One permits the turn only with posting of the sign "Right Turn on Red After Stop." The other law allows turns at any intersection unless specifically prohibited by displaying the sign "No Turn on Red."

The pennant-shaped warning sign supplements the rectangular regulatory, "Do Not Pass" sign. The pennant is located on the left side of the road at the beginning of the no-passing pavement marking.

A "Restricted Lane Ahead" sign provides advance notice of a preferential lane which has been established in many cases to conserve energy by the use of high occupancy vehicles such as buses and carpools. The diamond symbol displayed on the sign is also marked on the pavement to further identify the controlled lane.

The Reading Teacher's Book of Lists, Fifth Edition, © 2006 by John Wiley & Sons, Inc.

Guide Signs

Green background signs provide directional information. Diagrams on some signs are being introduced to help motorists find the correct path through complicated interchange ramp networks. Roadside mileage markers will assist in trip planning and provide locational information. In addition mileage numbers (mile post numbers) are used to identify interchanges and exits. The number for an exit is determined from the nearest roadside mileage marker preceding the crossroad. Green signs also point the way of such items as trails for hiking and places for parking.

The brown background sign provides information pertaining to access routes for public parks and recreation areas.

Signs for Bicycles

Bicycles are used by many persons on portions of heavily traveled roadways. This mixing of bicycles and motor vehicles is extremely dangerous and wherever possible, separate facilities are being provided for the bicycles.

TRAFFIC SIGNS CONTINUED

Service Signs

The blue color of these signs indicates that they provide direction to motorist service facilities. Word message signs generally are used to direct motorists to areas where service stations, restaurants, and motels are available. Logo signs are optional.

Signs in Construction Areas

The color orange has a special use. It appears on signs and barricades in construction and maintenance areas as a constant warning to motorists of possible dangers.

See also List 44, Daily Living Words.

The Reading Teacher's Book of Lists, Fifth Edition, © 2006 by John Wiley & Sons, Inc.

17

WORD PLAY

LIST 198. JUMP-ROPE RHYMES

Jump-rope rhymes or street poems are fun. Nearly every youngster knows at least some of these. Many are learned at camp and in after-school programs and activities. Use jump-rope rhymes to discuss cadence, rhyme, rhythm, and the uses of chants in our culture.

A Horse, a Flea, and Three Blind Mice

A horse, a flea, and three blind mice,

Sat on a curbstone shooting dice.

The horse, he slipped and fell on the flea.

The flea said, "Whoops, there's a horse on me."

The flea, he slipped and fell on the mice

And no one knows what became of the dice.

Cinderella

Cinderella, dressed in yellow, went upstairs to kiss a fella.

Made a mistake and kissed a snake.

How many stitches did it take?

1, 2, 3, 4, 5, etc.

I Like Coffee

"I like coffee, I like tea, I'd like (name) to come in with me."

(Repeat, with the first person leaving, and second person picking a name.)

I like coffee, I like tea,

I like the boys and the boys like me.

Yes, no, maybe so; Yes, no, maybe so, etc.

Doctor, Doctor

Doctor, doctor, can you tell, what will make poor Anna well?

Is she sick and going to die? That would make poor Tommy cry.

Tommy, Tommy, don't you cry. You will see her by and by.

Dressed in pink or white or blue, waiting at the church to marry you.

Ice Cream Soda

Ice cream soda, cherry on top! Who's your new friend? I forgot.

A, B, C, D, E, etc. (instead of new friend, could be boyfriend, best friend, girlfriend)

Last Night, the Night Before

Last night, the night before, my old friend took me to the candy store.

He bought me an ice cream, he bought me some cake,

Then he brought me home with a belly ache.

Mama, Mama, I feel sick. Call the doctor quick, quick, quick!

Doctor, Doctor will I die?

No you won't, you're bound to survive!

The Reading Teacher's Book of Lists, Fifth Edition, © 2006 by John Wiley & Sons, Inc.

JUMP-ROPE RHYMES CONTINUED

Lemon Lime

Lemon lime, be on time,

1, 2 (first person jumps in and out); 3, 4 (the next person jumps in and out), etc.

Miss Mary Mack

Miss Mary Mack, Mack, Mack; All dressed in black, black, black

With silver buttons, buttons, buttons; All down her back, back, back.

She asked her mother, mother, mother; For 50 cents, cents, cents

To see the elephants, elephants, elephants; Jump over the fence, fence, fence.

They jumped so high, high, high; They reached the sky, sky, sky

And they didn't come back, back, back; 'Til the 4th of July, ly, ly!

School, School

School, school, and the golden rule

Spell your name and go to school.

(Person jumps and spells name, then continues to jump counting the grades 1–12)

Miss Polly Had a Dolly

Miss Polly had a dolly who was sick, sick, sick,

So she called for the doctor to be quick, quick, quick.

The doctor came with his bag and his hat,

And he knocked at the door with a rat-a-tat-tat.

He looked at the dolly and he shook his head,

And he said "Miss Polly, put her straight to bed."

He wrote out a paper for a pill, pill, pill,

"That'll make her better, yes it will, will, will!"

Teddy Bear, Teddy Bear

Teddy Bear, Teddy Bear, turn around.

Teddy Bear, Teddy Bear, touch the ground.

Teddy Bear, Teddy Bear, show your shoe.

Teddy Bear, Teddy Bear, that will do!

Teddy Bear, Teddy Bear, go upstairs.

Teddy Bear, Teddy Bear, say your prayers.

Teddy Bear, Teddy Bear, turn out the lights.

Teddy Bear, Teddy Bear, say good-night!

The Reading Teacher's Book of Lists, Fifth Edition, © 2006 by John Wiley & Sons, Inc.

LIST 199. ANAGRAMS

Anagrams—words formed by rearranging the letters of another word—are fun and they help students pay close attention to spelling and spelling patterns.

Primary

act—cat	flow—wolf	ring—grin
aide—idea	god—dog	sink—skin
ape—pea	mars—rams	slip—lips
are—ear	meat—team	tab—bat
arm—ram	meats—steam	tar—rat
bare—bear	nap—pan	tea—eat
beak—bake	night—thing	urn—run
best—bets	note—tone	use—sue
boss—sobs	ours—sour	war—raw
café—face	pat—tap	was—saw
care—race	pea—ape	wed—dew
case—aces	pear—reap	who—how
earth—heart	pins—spin	won—now
fast—fats	pots—spot	yap—pay

Elementary/Intermediate

avenge—Geneva	limped—dimple	panels—Naples	skills—kills
balm—lamb	loin—lion	parks—sparks	snail—nails
blot—bolt	looted—Toledo	pools—spool	sober—robes
blow—bowl	lump—plum	ports—sport	soil—oils
brag—grab	march—charm	posts—stops	solo—Oslo
chum—much	mash—hams	races—cares	spray—prays
coal—cola	meals—males	reap—pear	stack—tacks
counts—Tuscon	meals—Salem	reef—free	stick—ticks
diagnose—San Diego	mean—mane	robed—bored	stops—posts
diary—dairy	melon—lemon	rock—Cork	strip—trips
domains—Madison	moist—omits	room—moor	study—dusty
dottier—Detroit	more—Rome	ropes—pores	team—meat
fired—fried	needs—dense	saint—stain	ticks—stick
fringe—finger	nerved—Denver	sales—seals	tooled—Toledo
hasten—Athens	none—neon	salts—lasts	votes—stove
iced—dice	nude—dune	salvages—Las Vegas	waits—waist
inch—chin	ocean—canoe	sharp—harps	wasps—swaps
keen—knee	pace—cape	shrub—brush	wells—swell
lamp—palm	pairs—Paris	siren—rinse	west—stew
last—salt	pale—leap	skids—disks	what—thaw

ANAGRAMS CONTINUED

Advanced

an aisle—is a lane

atom—bomb

considerate—care is noted

conversation—voices rant on

a decimal point—I'm a dot in place

departed this life—He's left it, dead; R I P

dormitory—dirty room

dynamite—may end it

eleven plus two—twelve plus one

Fourth of July—joyful fourth

gold and silver—grand old evils

HMS Pinafore—name for ship

limericks—slick rime

monasteries—Amen stories

a near miss—an air miss

the earthquakes—that queer shake

the Morse Code—here come dots

the nudist colony—no untidy clothes

the public art galleries—large picture halls, I bet

old England—golden land

restaurant—runs a treat

saintliness—least in sins

Semolina—is no meal

signature—a true sign

Statue of Liberty—built to stay free

the tennis pro—he in net sport

Valentine poem—pen mate in love

Year Two Thousand—a year to shut down!

See also List 111, Games and Methods for Teaching; List 202, Onomatopoeia; List 203, Palindromes.

LIST 200. DOUBLESPEAK

Here's something both you and your students can enjoy. Select in any order one word from Column A, one from Column B, and one from Column C. Now copy them on scratch paper in the order they were selected.

A	B	C
1. social	1. involvement	1. objectives
2. perceptual	2. motivation	2. activity
3. developmental	3. accelerated	3. curriculum
4. professional	4. cognitive	4. concept
5. homogeneous	5. effectiveness	5. evaluation
6. interdependent	6. maturation	6. processes
7. exceptional	7. integration	7. approach
8. instructional	8. orientation	8. articulation
9. individual	9. guidance	9. utilization
10. sequential	10. creative	10. resources
11. environmental	11. culture	11. adjustment
12. incremental	12. relationship	12. capacity

EXAMPLES: (A-10) sequential, (B-1) involvement, (C-2) activity;
(A-3) developmental, (B-4) cognitive, (C-7) approach

Now that you have the hang of it, enjoy your new status by sprinkling a few common words between the phrases like this:

> Social involvement objectives in today's schools are realized by combining an accelerated developmental curriculum with professional effectiveness utilization and creative instructional evaluation.

> The motivation of interdependent activity in an environmental adjustment culture is not easy when one takes into account the perceptual maturation processes of the individual.

> The utilization of instructional guidance resources will enable students to employ a sequential orientation approach to social integration.

After you have mastered this creative incremental approach to educationalese (also called "jargon") you will realize that happiness is social effectiveness through concept articulation. Infectious, isn't it?

See List 120, Comprehension Thesaurus, for additional terms and jargon.

Excerpt from *Doublespeak Terms* by William Lutz. Reprinted by permission of the author and Jean V. Naggar Literary Agency, Inc.

Used with permission from William Lutz.

LIST 201. HINK PINKS AND JOKES

Word games and jokes help increase vocabulary and verbal fluency. Some word games such as Hink Pinks also help increase phoneme awareness. Besides that, they are fun! Use a few of these for starters, then make up some of your own. *Hint:* The list of example words in List 9 will help you.

What is a single speech machine?	*lone phone*
What is an uncovered seat?	*bare chair*
What is a library burglar?	*book crook*
What is a strong beautiful plant?	*power flower*
What is an entrance to a shop?	*store door*
What is a boring singing?	*long song*
What is a skyway to heaven?	*air stair*
What is a weak bird?	*frail quail*
What is a container for wood fasteners?	*nail pail*
What is a resting place for ducks?	*quack rack*
What is an unhappy father?	*sad dad*
What is an old marine mammal?	*stale whale*
What is a chicken enclosure?	*hen pen*
What is a beach party-giver?	*coast host*
What is a hip place of learning?	*cool school*
What is a journey by boat?	*ship trip*
What is bad air in a swamp?	*bog smog*
What is a fat behind?	*plump rump*
What is a closed-up shack?	*shut hut*
What is a beginning prophet?	*new guru*
What is a house mortgage?	*home loan*
What is a skinny hotel?	*thin inn*
What is a cheap medieval soldier?	*tight knight*

Hink Pinks have one-syllable word answers, but the more advanced Hinky Pinkies have two-syllable word answers, and Hinkety Pinketys have three-syllable answers.

Hinky Pinkies

What do you call a rabbit that tells jokes?	*funny bunny*
What do you call a dog that fell in the river?	*soggy doggie*
What is sunshine in the high mountains?	*alpine sunshine*
What is a student who doesn't like to pay?	*cheapskate classmate*

Hinkety Pinketys

What is a love affair?	*affection connection*
What do rich people eat off of?	*millionaire dinnerware*

The Reading Teacher's Book of Lists, Fifth Edition, © 2006 by John Wiley & Sons, Inc.

JOKES

Knock knock.
Who's there?
Doris.
Doris who?
Doris locked, that's why I knocked.

Knock knock.
Who's there?
Olive.
Olive who?
Olive across the street.

Knock knock.
Who's there?
Police.
Police who?
Police stop telling these silly knock-knock jokes.

Waiter, there is a fly in my soup.
That's all right, sir, he won't drink much.

Waiter, what's this fly doing in my soup?
I believe he is doing the backstroke, miss.

Waiter, this soup is terrible. Please call the manager.
He won't drink it either, sir.

Patient: Doctor, my little brother is really crazy. He thinks he is a chicken.
Doctor: How long has this been going on?
Patient: About six years.
Doctor: Good heavens. Why have you waited so long to come for help?
Patient: Because we needed the eggs.

Why did the doctor take her eye chart into the classroom?
Because she wanted to check the pupils.

See also List 206, Riddles.

LIST 202. ONOMATOPOEIA

Onomatopoeic words resemble the sound to which they refer. For example, a cow *moos*. The word "onomatopoeia" comes from Greek and means "name making." These words are favorites with poets and comic-strip writers because they help describe the sounds for the actions in the stories and poems. Entertainers also love them, and children's authors use them regularly. Your students will enjoy them and probably add some to this list.

If your students have different language backgrounds, an interesting multicultural lesson is to compare the sounds animals make in different languages. For example, a dog doesn't say "bow wow" in all languages. Instead they say "gnaf gnaf" (French), "wang wang" (Chinese), and "wan wan" (Japanese).

aaaaah	boo	crackle
ah choo	boo-hoo	crackling
ahem	boom	crash
arf arf	boom-boom-bang	creak
argh	bow-wow	crinkle
aw	braap	croak
baa	bray	crunch
ba-da-bam	brrrrrh	cuckoo
ba-da-bing	brrrrring	ding-a-ling
bah	bump	ding dong
bam	burble	ding-ding
bang	burp	drip
bang-bang	bur-ring	drone
bark	buzz	drop
bash	caw	dum-dum-da-dum
bawl	cheep	eek
bay	chirp	fizz
beep	chirrup	flap
beep-beep	chitter	flip flop
belch	chomp	flump
bing	choo choo	flutter
bing-bong	chug	giggle
blab	chuga-chuga	glub-glub
blabber	clang	gong
blare	clank	goosh
blast	clap	grate
blather	clash	grind
bleat	clatter	groan
bleep	click	growl
bling	clickety clack	grunt
blink	clink	guffaw
blop	clip clop	gurgle
blubber	clomp	gush
blurt	cluck	hahaha
boing	conk	harrumph
bong	coo	hee haw
bonk	crack	hiccup

The Reading Teacher's Book of Lists, Fifth Edition, © 2006 by John Wiley & Sons, Inc.

hiss	purr	tinkle
ho-hum	puttputt	tom tom
honk	quack	toot
hoot	rat a tat	twang
howl	rattle	tweet
huff	ring	twitter
huff 'n puff	ring-a-ling	varoom
hum	rip	va-va-voom
hurrah	roar	wahoo
hush	rumble	wail
jabber	rush	whack
jangle	rustle	wham
jingle	screech	whang
ka-blam	shriek	wheeze
kerchoo	sigh	whimper
kerplunk	sizzle	whine
klomp	slop	whir
knock	slurp	whirr
knock-knock	slush	whish
lisp	smack	whiz
lub-dub	smash	whoo whoo
meow	snap	whoop
mew	sniff	whoopee
moan	sniffle	woof woof
moo	snort	woosh
mumble	splash	wop
murmur	splat	wow
neigh	splish-splash	wowee
oink	sploosh	yahoo
oops	splutter	yech
ooze	sputter	yelp
ouch	squeak	yikes
patter	squeal	yip
peal	squish	yippity yap
peep	stomp	yuck
phew	swish	yum
ping	swoosh	yum-yum
pitter patter	szhoom	zap
plink	thrum	zing
plop	thud	zip
pop	thump	zonk
pow	thwap	zoom
puff	tick tock	zzzzzzzzzz

LIST 203. PALINDROMES

Palindromes are words or sentences that read the same way forward and backward. They are enjoyed by people of all ages who like to have fun with words. Some word palindromes have been known for hundreds of years.

Word Palindromes

aha	ere	madam	racecar
Anna	eve	mom	radar
bib	ewe	mum	refer
bob	eye	noon	sees
civic	gag	nun	solos
dad	hah	Otto	SOS
deed	Hannah	peep	toot
did	kayak	pep	tot
dud	level	pop	wow

Sentence and Phrase Palindromes

. . . and DNA and DNA . . .
A man, a plan, a canal, Panama!
A Santa at NASA.
A Toyota's a Toyota.
Able was I ere I saw Elba.
Are we not drawn onward to new era?
Borrow or rob?
Camp Mac
Cigar? Toss it in a can, it is so tragic.
Dee saw a seed.
Delia failed.
Did Dean aid Diana? Ed did.
Did Hannah see bees? Hannah did.
Do geese see God?
Don't nod.
Dot sees Tod.
Ew! Eat a ewe?
Go, dog!
He did, eh?

I did, did I?
I Love Me, Vol. I
I prefer pi.
Is it I? It is I!
Lee had a heel.
Live not on evil.
Ma has a ham.
Madam I'm Adam.
my gym
navy van
Never odd or even
No lemons, no melon.
Now I won.
Nurses run.
Rise to vote, sir.
Was it a car or a cat I saw?
Was it a rat I saw?
We sew.

Emordnilap Words

Emordnilap (palindrome spelled backward) words are words that read differently in reverse. For example, "keep" read backward is "peek." Sometimes they are called reverse pairs. They are often used to form phrase or sentence palindromes.

am	bard	buns
are	bat	but
avid	bats	cod
bad	bonk	dab
ban	bud	dam

The Reading Teacher's Book of Lists, Fifth Edition, © 2006 by John Wiley & Sons, Inc.

decaf	loots	sleep
decal	ma	sloop
deer	maps	snug
deliver	may	span
denim	mood	spat
Dennis	moor	spoons
desserts	mug	spots
devil	naps	stab
dial	net	star
diaper	nip	step
doc	no	stool
dog	Noel	stop
doom	not	stops
dot	now	strap
draw	nuts	stressed
drawer	on	stun
edit	pal	tang
eel	pals	tap
emit	parts	taps
evil	peek	tar
flog	peels	ten
flow	pets	time
gals	pins	tip
garb	pit	Tod
gas	pools	ton
gnat	pot	top
golf	pots	trap
gum	rat	tub
keels	rats	war
keep	reed	ward
lager	regal	was
laid	reviled	wed
lap	reward	wets
leg	saw	won
Leon	sinned	yam
liar	slap	yap
live	sleek	

LIST 204. PORTMANTEAU WORDS

Alice, in *Alice in Wonderland*, asks Humpty Dumpty what "slithy" (from the Jabberwocky) means. He tells her that it means "lithe" and "slimy." "You can see there are two meanings packed into one word." *Portmanteau* is French for suitcase. The words in the comprehensive list below are called "portmanteau words" because they have two parts that fold into one, just as the two parts of a suitcase fold into one piece of luggage. Your students will have fun with these, and understanding the derivations of the words will enhance their comprehension. They may even enjoy making up portmanteau words of their own and quizzing each other on how they were derived.

alphabet	alpha + beta	**cyborg**	cybernetic + organism
alphanumeric	alphabetic + numeric	**daisy**	day's + eye
animatronics	animation + electronics	**dancercise**	dance + exercise
autobus	automobile + bus	**ditsy**	dizzy + dotty
avionics	aviation + electronics	**docudrama**	documentary + drama
bash	bang + smash	**dumbfound**	dumb + confound
beefalo	beef + buffalo	**econometric**	economy + metric
bionic	biology + electronic	**edutainment**	education + entertainment
bit	binary + digit	**electrocute**	electronic + execute
bleep	blankout + beep	**e-mail**	electronic + mail
blimp	B category + limp	**emoticon**	emotion + icon
blog	Web + log	**escalator**	escalade + elevator
blotch	blot + botch	**e-zine**	electronic + magazine
blurt	blow + spurt	**fantabulous**	fantastic + fabulous
boost	boom + hoist	**farewell**	fare + ye + well
brash	bold + rash	**flabbergast**	flap + aghast
breathalyser	breath + analyser	**flare**	flame + glare
brunch	breakfast + lunch	**flaunt**	flout + vaunt
buffeteria	buffet + cafeteria	**flop**	flap + drop
bumble	bungle + stumble	**flounder**	flounce + founder
camcorder	camera + recorder	**flunk**	flinch + funk
caplet	capsule + tablet	**flurry**	flutter + hurry
cellophane	cellulose + diaphane	**flush**	flash + gush
chocoholic	chocolate + alcoholic	**fortnight**	fourteen + nights
chortle	chuckle + snort	**freeware**	free + software
chump	chunk + lump	**galumph**	gallop + triumph
chunnel	channel + tunnel	**gasohol**	gasoline + alcohol
cineplex	cinema + complex	**gerrymander**	Gerry + salamander
clash	clap + crash	**glimmer**	gleam + shimmer
clump	chunk + lump	**glitterati**	glitter + literati
con man	confidence + man	**glitz**	glamour + ritz
contrail	condensation + trail	**glob**	globe + blob

glop	goo + slop	**scrawl**	scribble + sprawl
goodbye	God + be (with) + ye	**scrunch**	squeeze + crunch
goon	gorilla + baboon	**scuzzy**	scrummy + lousy
guesstimate	guess + estimate	**seascape**	sea + landscape
hassle	haggle + tussle	**simulcast**	simultaneous + broadcast
hazmat	hazardous + materials	**sitcom**	situation + comedy
hi-fi	high + fidelity	**skort**	skirt + short
humongous	huge + monstrous	**skyjack**	sky + hijack
infomercial	information + commercial	**skylab**	sky + laboratory
intercom	internal + communication	**slang**	slovenly + language
Internet	international + network	**slather**	slap + lather
jamboree	jam + soiree	**slosh**	slop + slush
kidvid	kids + video	**smash**	smack + mash
Medicare	medicine + care	**smog**	smoke + fog
meld	melt + weld	**snazzy**	snappy + jazzy
modem	modulator + demodulator	**soundscape**	sound + landscape
moped	motor + pedal	**splatter**	splash + spatter
motel	motor + hotel	**splurge**	splash + surge
motocross	motor + cross country	**sportscast**	sports + broadcast
motorcade	motor + cavalcade	**squash**	squeeze + crash
multiplex	multiple + complex	**squawk**	squall + squeak
Muppet	marionette + puppet	**squiggle**	squirm + wiggle
netiquette	Internet + etiquette	**swipe**	wipe + sweep
netizen	Internet + citizen	**tangelo**	tangerine + pomelo
outpatient	outside + patient	**taxicab**	taximeter + cabriolet
pang	pain + sting	**telecommuter**	telecommunication + commuter
paratroops	parachute + troops		
petrochemical	petroleum + chemical	**telegenic**	television + photogenic
pixel	picture + element	**telethon**	telephone + marathon
pluot	plum + apricot	**televangelist**	television + evangelist
podcasting	iPod + broadcasting	**Tex-Mex**	Texan + Mexican
prequel	precede + sequel	**transistor**	transfer + resistor
prissy	prim + sissy	**travelogue**	travel + monologue
pro-am	professional + amateur	**twiddle**	twist + fiddle
prod	poke + rod	**twinight**	twilight + night
pulsar	pulsating + star	**twirl**	twist + whirl
rubbage	rubbish + garbage	**waddle**	wade + toddle
satisfice	satisfy + suffice	**workaholic**	work + alcoholic

LIST 205. CLIPPED WORDS

These are words that have been shortened or clipped by common use, as in *sub* for *submarine*. This shortening is called *Zipf's Principle* and is well known in the study of languages.

ad	advertisement	memo	memorandum
auto	automobile	miss	mistress
bike	bicycle	mod	modern
burger	hamburger	movie	moving picture
bus	omnibus	mum	chrysanthemum
bust	burst	pants	pantaloons
cab	cabriolet	pen	penitentiary
canter	Canterbury gallop	pep	pepper
cent	centum	perk	percolate
champ	champion	perk	perquisite
chemist	alchemist	phone	telephone
clerk	cleric	photo	photograph
coed	coeducational student	pike	turnpike
con	convict	plane	airplane
copter	helicopter	pop	popular
cuke	cucumber	prof	professor
curio	curiosity	prom	promenade
deb	debutante	ref	referee
doc	doctor	scram	scramble
dorm	dormitory	specs	spectacles
drape	drapery	sport	disport
exam	examination	stat	statistics
fan	fanatic	stereo	stereophonic
fax	facsimile	still	distill
flu	influenza	sub	submarine
fridge	refrigerator	tails	coattails
gab	gabble	taxi	taxicab
gas	gasoline	teen	teenager
grad	graduate	tie	necktie
gym	gymnasium	trig	trigonometry
hack	hackney	trump	triumph
iron	flatiron	tux	tuxedo
jet	jet aircraft	typo	typographical error
lab	laboratory	van	caravan
limo	limousine	varsity	university
lube	lubricate	vet	veteran
lunch	luncheon	vet	veterinarian
margarine	oleomargarine	wig	periwig
mart	market	zoo	zoological garden
math	mathematics		
mend	amend		

See also List 163, Common Abbreviations.

LIST 206. RIDDLES

Youngsters love riddles and other kinds of Word Play. These riddles, like many other types of humor, rely on the definitions of key words. The Word Play makes good use of a word's denotation (literal definition), connotation (special meaning in context), or one of a word's multiple meanings. Word Play helps students focus on details, shades of meaning, and figurative language. Post a riddle-a-day for your class to solve and encourage students to share others

Where do fish sleep? *in water beds*

What do you call a burning jacket? *a blazer*

Which is faster, hot or cold? *hot because you can catch a cold*

What never gets locked out? *a piano; it has 88 keys*

What kind of room has no windows? *a mushroom*

What do you call a horse that stays up very late? *a nightmare*

What question did the owl ask the turtle about the winner of the race? *Who? Who?*

What do computers eat? *computer chips*

What kind of house is always hot? *a firehouse*

Why did the boy close the refrigerator door quickly? *because he saw the salad dressing*

Where do fish keep their money? *in the river bank*

What is the quietest sport? *bowling because you can hear a pin drop*

What did one eye say to the other eye? *between you and me, something smells*

Why is a river rich? *because it has two banks*

When is a door not a door? *when it is ajar*

Who sleeps with his shoes on? *a horse (horseshoes)*

Where do frozen ants come from? *Antarctica*

Where do dogs refuse to shop? *at flea markets*

What sounds better the more you beat it? *a drum*

Why did the robber take a bath? *so he could make a clean get away*

What kind of house weighs the least? *a lighthouse*

Why did the puppy take a nap? *because he was dog tired*

What kind of key won't work in the lock? *a monkey*

What did the car have on its toast this morning? *traffic jam*

Where do big black birds hang out? *at crowbars*

When is a car not a car? *when it turns into a driveway*

What happened when the frog parked its car in a "no parking" zone? *it was toad away*

What did one wall say to the other wall? *I'll meet you at the corner*

What kind of bird goes "Bang Bang"? *a fire quacker*

What goes tick-tick, woof-woof? *a watch dog*

What do you get if you cross a cat and a lemon? *a sour puss*

What year do frogs like best? *leap year*

What does an eagle like to write with? *a bald point pen*

See also List 201, Hink Pinks and Jokes.

LIST 207. CHILDREN'S HUMOR: WHAT KIDS SAY

Humorists, comedians, and pundits often bemoan the work involved in being funny. Yet, as all teachers know, kids do it innocently and without a moment's effort. Here is a collection of children's answers, observations, and thoughts that prove the point.

- Where is Alaska? Alaska is not in Canada.
- Oceania is a continent that contains no land.
- One by-product of cattle raising is calves.
- Actually, Homer was not written by Homer but by another man of that name.
- Algebraical symbols are used when you do not know what you are talking about.
- Bach was the most famous composer in the world and so was Handel.
- Before giving a transfusion, find out if the blood is negative or affirmative.
- Charles Darwin was a naturalist who wrote the Organ of the Species.
- Benjamin Franklin produced electricity by rubbing cats backwards.
- The process of turning steam back into water again is called conversation.
- Parallel lines never meet, unless you bend one or both of them.
- A circle is a line which meets its other end without ending.
- A triangle which has an angle of 135 degrees is called an obscene triangle.
- It is a well-known fact that a deceased body harms the mind.
- A super saturated solution holds more than it can hold.
- In the west, farming is done mostly by irritating the land.
- In what general direction to the rivers of France flow? From the source to the mouth.
- Many dead animals in the past changed to fossils while others preferred to be oil.
- Mushrooms always grow in damp places and so they look like umbrellas.
- Chaucer wrote many poems and verses and also wrote literature.
- Respiration is composed of two acts, first inspiration, and then expectoration.
- South America has cold summers and hot winters, but somehow they manage.
- The French Revolution was caused by overcharging taxies.
- The skeleton is what is left after the insides have been taken out and the outsides have been taken off.
- There are 26 vitamins in all, but some of the letters are yet to be discovered.
- Vacuums are nothings. We only mention them to let people know they're there.
- Water vapor gets together in a cloud. When it is big enough to be called a drop, it does.
- To most people solutions are answers. To chemists they are things that are all mixed up.
- Under the constitution the people enjoyed the right to bare arms.
- The difference between a green light and a red light? The color.
- It is always darkest before Daylight Savings Time.
- The red-brick wall was the color of brick-red crayon.
- Ancient Egypt was inhabited by mummies.
- Her vocabulary was as bad as, like, whatever.

The Reading Teacher's Book of Lists, Fifth Edition, © 2006 by John Wiley & Sons, Inc.

CHILDREN'S HUMOR: WHAT KIDS SAY CONTINUED

- History called them Romans because they moved around a lot.
- When you smell an odorless gas, it is probably carbon monoxide.
- The future of "I give" is "I take."
- Climate lasts all the time, but weather lasts just a few days.
- Terminal illness: getting sick at the airport.
- Spelling doesn't madder.
- In Pittsburgh, they make iron and steal.
- Julius Caesar extinguished himself on the battlefield.
- You know when you know, you know?
- At the bottom of Lake Michigan is Chicago.
- I can wait to fall in love—fourth grade is hard enough.
- No, it's not a right angle—it's a left angle.
- H_2O is hot water, CO_2 is cold water.
- The sun never set on the British Empire because the British Empire is in the East and the sun sets in the West.
- Imports are ports very fair inland.
- When you breathe, you inspire. When you do not breathe, you expire.
- Never trust your dog to watch your food.
- In the Olympic games, Greeks ran races, jumped, hurled biscuits, and threw java.
- Denver is just below the "o" in Colorado.
- Involuntary muscles are not as willing as voluntary ones.
- Who draws the lines around the countries?
- The spinal column is a long bunch of bones. The head sits at the top and you sit at the bottom.
- I'd explain it to you, but your brain would explode.
- A fossil is an extinct animal. The older it is, the more extinct it is.
- The general direction of the Alps is up.
- Hot lather comes from volcanoes. When it cools, it turns into rocks.
- In some rocks we find the fossil footprints of fishes.
- Love is the most important thing in the world, but baseball is pretty good, too.
- The earth makes a resolution every 24 hours.
- When driving through fog, use your car.
- The four seasons are salt, pepper, mustard, and ketchup.
- Why is "abbreviation" such a long word?
- Water is melted steam.

LIST 208. TONGUE TWISTERS

Tongue twisters are great fun. Try a different one each week. Tongue twisters are great practice for auditory awareness, sound discrimination, and articulation. They can be especially helpful for students who are learning English as a second language. Many of these tongue twisters are used by actors and announcers as elocution exercises.

Repeaters (Try saying these three times quickly.)

A regal rural ruler	Pug puppy
Baboon bamboo	Red leather, yellow leather
Cheap ship trips	Smashed shrimp chips
Crisco crisps crusts	Three free throws
Girl gargoyle, guy gargoyle	Tiny orangutan tongues
Greek grapes	Toy boat
Knapsack strap	Truly plural
Lemon liniment	Urgent detergent
Peggy Babcock	

One Liners

A box of mixed biscuits, a mixed biscuit box.

A noisy noise annoys an oyster.

An icehouse is not a nice house.

Andy ran from the Andes to the Indies in his undies.

Black bugs bleed black blood.

Do drop in at the Dewdrop Inn.

Even Edith eats eggs.

Five minutes to eight, not five minutes to wait.

For fine fish phone Phil.

Friday's Five Fresh Fish Specials.

Give me some ice, not some mice.

How much wood would a woodchuck chuck if a woodchuck could chuck wood?

Is there a pleasant peasant present?

Lesser leather never weathered lesser wetter weather.

Lesser weather never weathered lesser wetter leather.

Lot lost his hot chocolate at the loft.

Mrs. Smith's Fish Sauce Shop.

Seven silly Santas slid on the slick snow.

Seven silly swans swam silently seaward.

She sells seashells by the seashore, and the shells she sells are seashells.

Sheep shouldn't sleep in a shack. Sheep should sleep in a shed.

Silly Sally slid down a slippery slide.

Six sharp smart sharks.

Six sick snakes sit by the sea.

Six thick thistle sticks.

Strong sharks sink ships.

The Reading Teacher's Book of Lists, Fifth Edition, © 2006 by John Wiley & Sons, Inc.

Ten tiny tin trains toot ten times.

That bloke's back brake-block broke.

The big black-backed bumblebee.

The cat catchers can't catch caught cats.

The myth of Miss Muffet.

The sheik's sixth sheep's sick.

The summer school, not a summer's cool.

The sun shines on shop signs.

Thin sticks, thick bricks.

Three free thugs set three thugs free.

Which witch wished which wicked wish?

Whistle for the thistle sifter.

Stories

A big black bug bit a big black bear and the big black bear bled blood.

A big bug bit the little beetle but the little beetle bit the big bug back.

A flea and a fly flew up in a flue. Said the flea, "Let us fly!" Said the fly, "Let us flee!"
So they flew through a flaw in the flue.

A tree toad loved a she-toad that lived up in a tree. She was a three-toed tree toad, but
a two-toed toad was he.

Betty Botter had some butter. "But," she said, "this butter's bitter. If I bake this bitter
butter, it would make my batter bitter."

Fuzzy Wuzzy was a bear, Fuzzy Wuzzy had no hair. Fuzzy Wuzzy wasn't fuzzy, was he?

I thought a thought. But the thought I thought wasn't the thought I thought I thought.

On two thousand acres, too tangled for tilling, where thousands of thorn trees grew thrifty
and thrilling, Theophilus Twistle, less thrifty than some, thrust three thousand thistles
through the thick of his thumb!

Once upon a barren moor there dwelt a bear also a boar. The bear could not bear the boar.
The bear thought the boar a bore. At last that bear could bear no more of that boar that
bored him on the moor and so one morn' he bored that boar. That boar will bore the
bear no more.

Our Joe wants to know if your Joe will lend our Joe your Joe's banjo. If your Joe won't lend
our Joe your Joe's banjo, our Joe won't lend your Joe our Joe's banjo when our Joe has a
banjo!

Two witches bought two wrist watches, but which witch wore which wrist watch?

Unique New York, you need New York, you know you need unique New York.

Whether the weather is hot. Whether the weather is cold. Whether the weather is either
or not. It is whether we like it or not.

**See also List 127, Speech Sound Development; List 162, Spelling and
Pronunciation.**

LIST 209. WACKY WORDIES

A. The object in solving is to discern a familiar phrase, saying, cliché, or name from each arrangement of letters and/or symbols. For example, box 1a depicts the phrase "just between you and me." Box 1b shows "hitting below the belt." The puzzles get more diabolical as you go.

	a	b	c	d	e	f
1	you just me	belt hitting	lo head heels ve	V I O L E T s	B A E D U M R	agb
2	cry milk	· — c 3 σ · — ↵	Symphon	ʎddɐǝuıd cake	arrest you're	timing tim ing
3	O TV	night fly	S T I N K	injury + insult	r o rail d	my own heart a person
4	at the · of on	dothepe	wear long	strich grround	lu cky	the market
5	worl	the x way	word YYY	search and	go off coc	no ways it ways
6	oholene	t o e a r t h	ooo circus	1 at 3:46	late n e v er	get a word in
7	let gone gone be gone gone	a chance n	O MD BA PhD	wheather	world world world world	lo ose
8	lines reading lines	chicken	y fireworks	L D Bridge	pace k	danc t e s c etno

The Reading Teacher's Book of Lists, Fifth Edition, © 2006 by John Wiley & Sons, Inc.

Reprinted from *Games* magazine (19 West 21st St., New York, NY 10010). Copyright © 1979, 1981 Playboy Enterprises, Inc.

B. The object in solving is to discern a familiar phrase, saying, cliché, or name from each arrangement of letters and/or symbols. For example, box 1a depicts "sleeping on the job." Box 1b shows a "cornerstone." Sounds easy, but wait until you see the others.

	a	b	c	d	e	f
1	sleeping job	s t one	jink jink jink	gnitteg da wn	Roger	escape
2	right = right	house prairie	goodbye	milk	c c garage r r	c o m i c
3	e L u l c l i	clou	ieieceiie	neegr geren ngree regen	t i o n a i n l f	pölkä
4	MIRROR	momanon	clams she	ma√il	1.D 2.R 3.A 4.C 5.U 6.L 7.A	ca se case
5	TRN	ping willow	animation	sugar Please	hair —	L V O R E E A T
6	bus	age a g e age	TU↗L OIP€S	m ce m ce m ce	eyebrows	ri poorch
7		morning	socket	TORTILLA	12safety345	s d r k i n house

Reprinted from *Games* magazine (19 West 21st St., New York, NY 10010). Copyright © 1979, 1981 Playboy Enterprises, Inc.

WACKY WORDIES CONTINUED

C. The object in solving is to discern a familiar phrase, saying, cliché, or name from each arrangement of letters and/or symbols. For example, box 1a depicts the phrase "eggs over easy." Box 1b shows "Trafalgar Square."

	a	b	c	d	e	f
1	eggs easy	T R A F A L G A R	told tales told	e^{ttr} k_{cit}p_i	new leaf (inverted)	sītky
2	price	L +O SS	swear bible bible bible bible	league	bridge wa↑er	school
3	–attitude	hoppin	century (curved)	E^{RC} T N U_O	orseman	D UC K
4	set one's teeth	or or O	bet one's dollar	tpmerhao	what must	way yield
5	t o 2 par n	dictnry	rifle rifle rifle rifle	pAI**NS**	everything pizza	L Y I N G JOB
6	tr ial	prosperity (curved)	monkey O	busines	writers	moon sonata
7	power	mesnackal	Wilson (inverted)	pit	wheel wheel wheel drive wheel	✓✓ ✓ cöunter

black

The Reading Teacher's Book of Lists, Fifth Edition, © 2006 by John Wiley & Sons, Inc.

D. The object in solving is to discern a familiar phrase, saying, cliché, or name from each arrangement of letters and/or symbols. For example, box 1a depicts "once over lightly." Box 1b shows "gossip column."

	a	b	c	d	e	f
1	once lightly	g o s s i p	ᴡᴀᴠᴇ radio	c a p t a i n	noon good	bathing suit
2	ee ch sp	God nation ✸	✓ yearly	ses ame	d deer e r	hold second
3	r − i × s + k	ᴘᴏx	strokes *strokes* **strokes**	n P y o c m a	law of returns	e a p s p u a l
4	hou se	age beauty	harm on y	encounters encounters encounters	breth	hearted
5	p a r t i c i p	**MAN** campus	momanon	ᴜld block	"Duty!" and beyond	day	day
6	sigh	qonpɟ	skating ɪᴄᴇ	inflat10n	g o s p e l	enemy enemy
7	to ngue ngue	gettingitall	e a v e s	c m ᴄ e a ban ana	e e q u a l s m c	aluminum

WACKY WORDIES CONTINUED

WACKIE WORDIES—ANSWERS

A

1a Just between you and me
1b Hitting below the belt
1c Head over heels in love
1d Shrinking violets
1e Bermuda Triangle
1f A mixed bag
2a Cry over spilt milk
2b Lying in wait
2c *Unfinished Symphony*
2d Pineapple upside-down cake
2e You're under arrest
2f Split-second timing
3a Nothing on TV
3b Fly-by-night
3c Raise a big stink
3d Add insult to injury
3e Railroad crossing
3f A person after my own heart
4a At the point of no return
4b The inside dope
4c Long underwear
4d Ostrich with its head in the ground
4e Lucky break
4f Corner the market
5a World without end
5b Way behind the times
5c Word to the wise
5d Search high and low
5e Go off half-cocked
5f No two ways about it
6a Hole-in-one
6b Down-to-earth
6c Three-ring circus
6d One at a time
6e Better late than never
6f Get a word in edgewise
7a Let bygones be bygones
7b An outside chance
7c Three degrees below zero
7d A terrible spell of weather
7e World Series
7f Cut loose
8a Reading between the lines
8b Chicken Little
8c Fourth of July fireworks

8d London Bridge
8e Change of pace
8f Square dance contest

B

1a Sleeping on the job
1b Cornerstone
1c High jinks
1d Getting up before the crack of dawn
1e "Roger, over and out"
1f Narrow escape
2a Equal rights
2b *Little House on the Prairie*
2c Waving goodbye
2d Condensed milk
2e Two-car garage
2f Stand-up comic
3a Lucille Ball
3b Partly cloudy
3c "I before E except after C"
3d Mixed greens
3e Spiraling inflation
3f Polka-dotted
4a Full-length mirror
4b Man in the moon
4c Clams on the half-shell
4d "The check is in the mail"
4e Count Dracula
4f Open-and-shut case
5a No U-Turn
5b Weeping willow
5c Suspended animation
5d "Pretty please with sugar on top"
5e Receding hairline
5f Elevator out of order
6a Double-decker bus
6b Middle-age spread
6c "Tiptoe Through the Tulips"
6d "Three Blind Mice" (without their i's)
6e Raised eyebrows
6f Steal from the rich and give to the poor
7b Top of the morning
7c Light socket
7d *Tortilla Flat*
7e Safety in numbers
7f Round of drinks on the house

The Reading Teacher's Book of Lists, Fifth Edition, © 2006 by John Wiley & Sons, Inc.

C

1a   Eggs over easy
1b   Trafalgar Square
1c   *Twice-Told Tales*
1d   Round-trip ticket
1e   Turn over a new leaf
1f   Pie in the sky
2a   *The Price is Right*
2b   Total loss
2c   Swear on a stack of Bibles
2d   Little League
2e   Bridge over troubled water
2f   High school
3a   Negative attitude
3b   Shopping center
3c   Turn-of-the-Century
3d   Counterclockwise
3e   Headless Horseman
3f   Sitting duck
4a   Set one's teeth on edge
4b   Double or nothing
4c   Bet one's bottom dollar
4d   Mixed metaphor
4e   What goes up must come down
4f   Yield right of way
5a   Not up to par
5b   Abridged dictionary
5c   Repeating rifle
5d   Growing pains
5e   Pizza with everything on it
5f   Lying down on the job
6a   Trial separation
6b   Prosperity is just around the corner
6c   Monkey around
6d   Unfinished business
6e   Writer's cramp
6f   *Moonlight Sonata*
7a   Power blackout
7b   Between-meal snack
7c   Flip Wilson
7d   Bottomless pit
7e   Four-wheel drive
7f   Checkout counter

D

1a   Once over lightly
1b   Gossip column
1c   Short-wave radio
1d   Captain Hook
1e   Good afternoon
1f   Topless bathing suit
2a   Parts of speech
2b   One nation, under God, indivisible
2c   Yearly checkup
2d   Open sesame
2e   Deer crossing
2f   Hold on a second
3a   Calculated risk
3b   Smallpox
3c   Different strokes
3d   Mixed company
3e   Law of diminishing returns
3f   Round of applause
4a   Split-level house
4b   Age before beauty
4c   Three-part harmony
4d   *Close Encounters of the Third Kind*
4e   A little out of breath
4f   Light-hearted
5a   Dangling participle
5b   Big man on campus
5c   Man in the moon
5d   Chip off the old block
5e   Above and beyond the call of duty
5f   Day in and day out
6a   No end in sight
6b   Shadow of a doubt
6c   Skating on thin ice
6d   Double-digit inflation
6e   Spread the gospel
6f   Archenemies
7a   Forked tongue
7b   Getting it all together
7c   Eavesdropping
7d   Banana split with whipped cream topping
7e $E = mc^2$
7f   Aluminum siding

LIST 210. EUPHEMISMS

These euphemisms might help at report-card time or in preparing for parent interviews. They are a reminder that there are polite ways to express negative observations. Students enjoy euphemisms; share some of these with your class and have them add to the list.

BLUNT TRUTH	EUPHEMISM
Lies	Shows difficulty in distinguishing between imaginary and factual material.
Is a klutz	Has difficulty with motor control and coordination.
Needs nagging	Accomplishes task when interest is constantly prodded.
Fights	Resorts to physical means of winning his or her point or attracting attention.
Smells bad	Needs guidance in development of good habits of hygiene.
Cheats	Needs help in learning to adhere to rules and standards of fair play.
Steals	Needs help in learning to respect the property rights of others.
Is a wiseguy (or -gal)	Needs guidance in learning to express ideas respectfully.
Has weird hair	Unconventional hairstyle draws negative attention
Is lazy	Requires ongoing supervision in order to work well.
Is rude	Lacks a respectful attitude toward others.
Is selfish	Needs help in learning to enjoy sharing with others.
Is gross	Needs guidance in developing the social graces.
Has big mouth	Needs to develop quieter habits of communication.
Eats like a pig	Needs to develop more refined table manners.
Bullies others	Has qualities of leadership, but needs to use them more constructively.
Is babyish	Shows lack of maturity in relationships with others.
Hangs out	Seems to feel secure only in group situations; needs to develop sense of identity and independence.
Is disliked by others	Needs help in developing meaningful peer relationships.
Is often late	Needs guidance in developing habits of responsibility and punctuality
Wastes time	Needs to improve time management skills

The Reading Teacher's Book of Lists, Fifth Edition, © 2006 by John Wiley & Sons, Inc.

Is truant	Needs to develop a sense of responsibility in regard to attendance.
Only wants to play	Needs to develop greater interest in academic subjects
Wears wild clothes	Clothing choices draw negative attention
A snail is faster	Has difficulty completing tasks in allotted time
Has a mind like a sieve	Demonstrates difficulty with recall
Is a regular spin doctor	Selectively responds to questions to avoid negative consequences
Uses others as scapegoats and go-fers	Demonstrates leadership among peers
Got caught reading comics again	Is an avid recreational reader
Hangs with a gang	Has formed a strong social network
Drew unflattering but recognizable caricatures of teacher on board	Shows interest in developing artistic skills
Skips class a lot	Engages in frequent undocumented extracurricular activities
Leaves school premises	Seeks extramural enrichment without approval

LIST 211. POPULAR FIRST NAMES

One interesting thing about first names is their change in popularity. Another is their meanings. Names may have mythological or religious roots, like "Cassandra" and "Abraham." Some are toponyms—based on a place name—like "Brittany" or "Trent." Others are descriptors of traits or ideas, like "Felicity" or "Charity." And some, have origins in parents' creativity.

The first list below shows names that have remained in the "top 20" for babies born in the United States from 1990 to 2005. The shorter list of girls' names shows their popularity changes much more quickly than for boys' names.

The second list shows the most popular boys' and girls' names for 2004. To find the rankings of more than 1000 names for the last 100 years, go to www.ssa.gov/OACT/babynames/. There are also many good sources for the meanings of names from around the world, including www.behindthename.com/ and www.babynamesworld.com/

Boys' and Girls' Names in the Top 20 from 1990 to 2005

Andrew	Jacob	Matthew
Anthony	James	Michael
Christopher	John	Nicholas
Daniel	Joseph	Ryan
David	Joshua	William
Ashley	Kayla	Samantha
Elizabeth	Lauren	Sarah
Emily		

75 Most Popular Boys' Names

1. Jacob
2. Michel
3. Joshua
4. Matthew
5. Ethan
6. Andrew
7. Daniel
8. William
9. Joseph
10. Christopher
11. Anthony
12. Ryan
13. Nicholas
14. David
15. Alexander
16. Tyler
17. James
18. John
19. Dylan
20. Nathan
21. Jonathan
22. Brandon
23. Samuel
24. Christian
25. Benjamin
26. Zachary
27. Logan
28. Jose
29. Noah
30. Justin
31. Elijah
32. Gabriel
33. Caleb
34. Kevin
35. Austin
36. Robert
37. Thomas
38. Connor
39. Evan
40. Aidan
41. Jack
42. Luke
43. Jordan
44. Angel
45. Isaiah
46. Isaac
47. Jason
48. Jackson
49. Hunter
50. Cameron
51. Gavin
52. Mason
53. Aaron
54. Juan
55. Kyle
56. Charles
57. Luis
58. Adam
59. Brian
60. Aiden
61. Eric
62. Jayden
63. Alex
64. Bryan
65. Sean
66. Owen
67. Lucas
68. Nathaniel
69. Ian
70. Jesus
71. Carlos
72. Adrian
73. Diego
74. Julian
75. Cole

The Reading Teacher's Book of Lists, Fifth Edition, © 2006 by John Wiley & Sons, Inc.

75 Most Popular Girls Names

1. Emily
2. Emma
3. Madison
4. Olivia
5. Hannah
6. Abigail
7. Isabella
8. Ashley
9. Samantha
10. Elizabeth
11. Alexis
12. Sarah
13. Grace
14. Alyssa
15. Sophia
16. Lauren
17. Brianna
18. Kayla
19. Natalie
20. Anna
21. Jessica
22. Taylor
23. Chloe
24. Hailey
25. Ava
26. Jasmine
27. Sydney
28. Victoria
29. Ella
30. Mia
31. Morgan
32. Julia
33. Kaitlyn
34. Rachel
35. Katherine
36. Megan
37. Alexandra
38. Jennifer
39. Destiny
40. Allison
41. Savannah
42. Haley
43. Mackenzie
44. Brooke
45. Maria
46. Nicole
47. Makayla
48. Trinity
49. Kylie
50. Kaylee
51. Paige
52. Lily
53. Faith
54. Zoe
55. Stephanie
56. Jenna
57. Andrea
58. Riley
59. Katelyn
60. Angelina
61. Kimberly
62. Madeline
63. Mary
64. Leah
65. Lillian
66. Michelle
67. Amanda
68. Sara
69. Sofia
70. Jordan
71. Alexa
72. Rebecca
73. Gabrielle
74. Caroline
75. Vanessa

LIST 212. FUN NAMES

Word Play motivates, entertains, and helps students attend to meaning, spelling, context, idiom, as well as elements of humor. Challenge students to think of other fun names, and encourage students to draw suitable "portraits" of this cast of characters.

Adam Zapple	Doug Graves	Mark Thyme
Alf Abett	Dusty Rhode	Mel Lowe
Ann Chovy	Earl E. Byrd	Mike Rowave
Ann Natome	Eileen Dover	Miss B. Haven
Ann T. Lope	Ella Gantt	Moira Less
Ann Teak	Ella Vator	Myles Long
Armand Hammer	Evan L. Puss	Noah Zark
Arthur I. Tuss	Ferris Wheeler	Norman Conquest
Barb Dwyer	Gail Storm	Oliver Sudden
Bea Keeper	Gracie Mansion	Otto Mattick
Bea Lowe	Gustav Wynde	Pearl E. Gates
Bea Sharpe	Herb Alty	Penny Sillan
Bill Ding	Howard Ino	Penny Wise
Bill E. Club	Hugh Donnit	Percy Veer
Bill Folde	Hugo N. Furst	Pete Moss
Bob Katz	Ike Entell	Polly Dent
Brock Lee	Ima Hogg	Polly Ester
Candy Cotton	Isabel Ringing	Ray On
Carmen Geditt	Jack B. Quick	Rob Storrs
Carrie Oakey	Jack Pott	Rocky Shore
Cherry Tree	Jean Poole	Rose Bush
Chester Drawers	Jo Kerr	Sally Forth
Chris P. Bacon	Jo King	Sally Mander
Claire Voyant	June Moon	Sandy Beach
Cole Dazice	Justin Kase	Stan Tupp
Curt N. Rodd	Justin Tyme	Terry Cloth
Cy Burnett	Lee King	Tim Burr
Dawn Early	Lois Bidder	Uneeda Life
Dee Lited	Lois Teem	Vic Tree
Dee Zaster	Lorne Mowers	Walter Mellon
Della Ware	Lou Brickint	Warren Peas
Donna N. Blitzen	Lou Pole	
Dora Jarr	Lynn Oleum	

The Reading Teacher's Book of Lists, Fifth Edition, © 2006 by John Wiley & Sons, Inc.

LIST 213. PROVERBS IN DISGUISE

Students, and teachers too, have a good time translating these popular proverbs from verbose to customary versions. This is a good exercise for getting students interested in more sophisticated language. Have students create new ones using a thesaurus and challenge their classmates to a contest figuring them out. Can you translate all of these? If you're stuck, the answers follow the list.

1. Accelerated execution often produces faulty results.
2. Surveillance should precede saltation.
3. Pulchritude possesses solely cutaneous profundity.
4. It is futile to attempt to indoctrinate a superannuated canine with innovative maneuvers.
5. Male cadavers are incapable of yielding any testimony.
6. Neophyte's serendipity
7. Eschew the implementation of correction and vitiate the scion.
8. The stylus is more potent than the rapier.
9. Individuals who make their abodes in vitreous edifices would be advised to refrain from catapulting petreous projectiles.
10. A revolving lithic conglomerate accumulates no congeries of small, green, biophytic plants.

TRANSLATION

1. Haste makes waste.
2. Look before you leap.
3. Beauty is only skin deep.
4. You can't teach an old dog new tricks.
5. Dead men tell no tales.
6. Beginner's luck
7. Spare the rod and spoil the child.
8. The pen is mightier than the sword.
9. People who live in glass houses shouldn't throw stones.
10. A rolling stone gathers no moss.

See also List 179, Dichos—Spanish Proverbs; List 185, Proverbs.

LIST 214. STRANGE READING RESEARCH

Can you read and understand the paragraph below? Most proficient readers can. Although not part of an actual research study at Cambridge University or any other university, it demonstrates the mind's ability to recognize intended words from context and sentence structure, even when many are misspelled.

> I cdnuolt blveiee taht I cluod aulaclty uesdnatnrd waht I was rdanieg. The phaonmneal pweor of the hmuan mnid. Aoccdrnig to a rscheearch at Cmabrigde Uinervtisy, it deosn't mttaer in waht oredr the ltteers in a wrod are, the olny iprmoatnt tihng is taht the frist and lsat ltteer be in the rghit pclae. The rset can be a taotl mses and you can sitll raed it wouthit a porbelm. Tihs is bcuseae the huamn mnid deos not raed ervey lteter by istlef, but the wrod as a wlohe. Amzanig huh? Yaeh, and I awlyas thought slpeling was ipmorantt.

Note: Along this line it is worth noting that Semitic languages, like Hebrew and Arabic, are usually not written with vowel letters. However, vowel symbols (really letters) are often added for beginning readers.

The Reading Teacher's Book of Lists, Fifth Edition, © 2006 by John Wiley & Sons, Inc.

18

REFERENCE

LIST 215. READING ORGANIZATIONS AND JOURNALS

Reading and literacy education is dynamic and there is always something new to learn or share with reading colleagues. Keep abreast of research, trends, best practices, and promising innovations by being an active member of one or more professional associations in reading and by reading journals and publications in the field. The organizations have local and regional affiliates and sponsor national conferences. Their web sites have current information, links to reading sites, and much more.

Organizations

International Reading Association (IRA)
Box 8139
Newark, DE 19711
http://www.ira.org/
Annual meeting, early May

National Reading Conference (NRC)
122 S. Michigan Ave.
Suite 1100
Chicago, IL 60603
www.oakland.edu/~mceneane/nrc/nrcindex.html
Annual meeting, early December

College Reading and Learning
Association (CRLA)
P.O. Box 382
El Dorado, KS 67042
http://www.crla.net/
Annual meeting, late October

National Council of Teachers
of English (NCTE)
1111 Kenyon Road
Urbana, IL 61801
http://www.ncte.org/
Annual meeting, mid-November

Journals

Many journals are available through membership in the reading associations listed above. Your school librarian can contact the associations for library subscription information. Visit *Reading OnLine,* the electronic journal of the International Reading Association, at www.readingonline.ort/about/welcome.index.

English Education (CEE/NCTE)
English Journal (NCTE)
Journal of Adolescent & Adult Literary (IRA)
Journal of College Research & Learning (CRLA)
Journal of Literacy Research (NRC)
Language Arts (NCTE)
Primary Voices (NCTE)

Reading Research Quarterly (IRA)
Reading Teacher (IRA)
Research in the Teaching of English (NCTE)
Talking Points (WLU/NCTE)
The Reading News (CRA)
Voice from the Media (NCTE)

IRA Presidents

2000–2001	Carmelita K. Williams	2004–2005	Mary Ellen Vogt
2001–2002	Dona M. Ogle	2005–2006	Richard Allington
2002–2003	Jerry Johns	2006–2007	Timothy S. Shanahan
2003–2004	Leslie Morrow	2007–2008	Linda B. Gambrell

NRC Presidents

2000	Taffy E. Raphael	2005	Donald J. Leu
2001	Peter B. Mosenthal	2006	Victoria Purcell-Gates
2002	Deborah R. Dillon	2007	Patricia Edwards
2003	Lee Gunderson	2008	Norman Stahl
2004	Lea McGee		

LIST 216. EDUCATION ABBREVIATIONS

The field of education has its share of abbreviations. Here are some widely known ones that you may find useful.

AAHPERD	American Alliance for Health, Physical Education, Recreation and Dance
AASA	American Association of School Administrators
AD/HD	Attention Deficit/Hyperactivity Disorder
AFT	American Federation of Teachers
AP	Advanced Placement
ASCD	Association for Supervision and Curriculum Development
CEC	Council for Exceptional Children
CEEB	College Entrance Exam Board
EH	Emotionally Handicapped
ELL	English Language Learner
ERIC	Educational Resources Information Center
ESL	English as a Second Language
ETS	Educational Testing Service
GED	General Educational Development Test (high school equivalency test)
IEP	Individualized Education Plan
IRA	International Reading Association
LEP	Limited English Proficiency
LD	Learning Disabled
LDA	Learning Disabilities Association
LRE	Least Restrictive Environment
MENC	National Association for Music Education
MH	Mentally Handicapped
NAEA	National Art Education Association
NAEP	National Assessment of Educational Progress
NAESP	National Association of Elementary School Principals
NAEYC	National Association for the Education of Young People
NASSP	National Association of Secondary School Principals
NCATE	National Council for Accreditation of Teacher Education
NCEA	National Catholic Educational Association
NCES	National Center for Educational Statistics
NCPT	National Congress of Parents and Teachers
NCSS	National Council for the Social Studies
NCTE	National Council of Teachers of English
NCTM	National Council of Teachers of Mathematics
NEA	National Education Association
NSF	National Science Foundation
NSTA	National Science Teachers Association
SAT	Scholastic Aptitude Test

LIST 217. ACRONYMS AND INITIALIZATIONS

Everyone knows about TGIF, but what about MMB? Acronyms and initializations are used frequently in media and everyday communication. They are "shortcuts" that refer to multi-word names and phrases. Both initializations and acronyms are formed from the first letters of the words they represent; however, they are pronounced differently. An initialization is pronounced using the letters that form it (e.g., ABC) whereas an acronym is pronounced as a word (e.g., AIDS). In both cases, periods signifying abbreviations are usually omitted. Entire dictionaries are now devoted to acronyms and a Web search will turn up more than you will ever need. This list includes commonly used acronyms and initializations. Acronyms are noted by *(acr)* following the definition. Additional computer-related acronyms and initializations can be found in List 171, Computer and Internet Terms, and List 172, Text, Chat, and E-mail Glossary.

ABC	American Broadcasting System
ADA	Americans with Disabilities Act
AIDS	Acquired immune deficiency syndrome *(acr)*
AKA	Also known as
ATM	Automated teller machine
ASAP	As soon as possible
AWOL	Absent without leave *(acr)*
BBC	British Broadcasting Corporation
BLT	Bacon, lettuce, and tomato
BMOC	Big man on campus
BTO	Big-time operator
CBS	Columbia Broadcasting System
CD	Compact disk; certificate of deposit
CEO	Chief executive officer
CIA	Central Intelligence Agency
COD	Cash on delivery
CPA	Certified public accountant
DA	District attorney
DINK	Dual income no kids *(acr)*
DJ	Disk jockey
DOA	Dead on Arrival
DVD	Digital video disk
EEOC	Equal Employment Opportunity Commission
EDP	Electronic Data Processing
EKG	Electrocardiogram
ELL	English language learner
EPCOT	Experimental Prototype Community of Tomorrow *(acr)*
ERA	Equal rights amendment
ESL	English as a second language
EU	European Union

The Reading Teacher's Book of Lists, Fifth Edition, © 2006 by John Wiley & Sons, Inc.

ACRONYMS AND INITIALIZATIONS CONTINUED

FedEx	Federal Express (*acr*)
FYI	For your information
GIGO	Garbage in, garbage out (*acr*)
GNP	Gross national product
GPA	Grade point average
HIV	Human immunodeficiency virus
HMO	Health maintenance organization
HQ	Headquarters
IOU	I owe you
IQ	Intelligence quotient
IRA	International Reading Association; Irish Republican Army
IRS	Internal Revenue Service
KISS	Keep it simple stupid (*acr*)
LASER	Light amplification by stimulated emission of radiation (*acr*)
LIFO	Last in, first out (*acr*)
MIA	Missing in action
MIT	Massachusetts Institute of Technology
MMB	Monday morning blues
MO	Modus operandi
MRI	Magnetic resonance imaging
MYOB	Mind your own business
NA	Not applicable; North America
NAACP	National Association for the Advancement of Colored People
NASA	National Aeronautics and Space Administration (*acr*)
NATO	North Atlantic Treaty Organization (*acr*)
NBC	National Broadcasting System
NIMBY	Not in my backyard (*acr*)
NRP	National Reading Panel
OPEC	Organization of Petroleum-Exporting Countries (*acr*)
PA	Public address
PBS	Public Broadcasting System
PC	Personal computer; politically correct
PDQ	Pretty darn quick
PIN	Personal identification number (*acr*)
POSH	Port out starboard home (*acr*)
POV	Point of view
POW	Prisoner of war
PR	Public relations
PS	Post script; public school
PTA	Parent–Teacher Association
RADAR	Radio detecting and range (*acr*)

The Reading Teacher's Book of Lists, Fifth Edition, © 2006 by John Wiley & Sons, Inc.

RAM	Random access memory (*acr*)
RIP	Rest in peace
ROM	Read-only memory (*acr*)
RSVP	Répondez s'il vous plaît
RV	Recreational vehicle
SASE	Self-addressed stamped envelope
SAT	Scholastic Aptitude Test
SCUBA	Self-contained underwater breathing apparatus (*acr*)
SNAFU	Situation normal: all fouled up (*acr*)
SONAR	Sound navigation ranging (*acr*)
SOS	Save our ship
SRO	Standing room only
SUV	Sports utility vehicle
SWAK	Sealed with a kiss (*acr*)
SWAT	Special weapons action team (*acr*)
TBA	To be arranged; to be announced
TDD	Telecommunications device for the deaf
TEFLON	Tetrafloroethylene resin (*acr*)
TGIF	Thank God it's Friday
TLC	Tender loving care
TNT	Trinitrotoluene
TV	Television
UFO	Unidentified flying object
UN	United Nations
UNICEF	United Nations International Children's Emergency Fund (*acr*)
UPS	United Parcel Service
USA	United States of America
VCR	Video cassette recorder
VIP	Very important person
WASP	White Anglo-Saxon Protestant (*acr*)
ZIP	Zone Improvement Plan (*acr*)

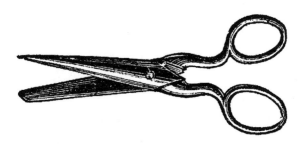

See also List 116, Comprehension Strategy Initialization; List 172, Text, Chat, and E-mail Glossary.

LIST 218. PUBLISHERS OF READING MATERIALS AND TESTS

AGS Publishing

4201 Woodland Road
Circle Pines, MN 55014
http://www.agsnet.com/

Allyn & Bacon

75 Arlington Street, Suite 300
Boston, MA 02116
http://ablongman.com/

**Association for Supervision &
    Curriculum Development**

1703 North Beauregard Street
Alexandria, VA 22202
http://ascd.org/

Books on Tape, Inc.

Attn: Customer Service
400 Hahn Road
Westminster, MD 21157
http://library.booksontape.com/

Boyds Mills Press

815 Church Street
Honesdale, PA 18431
http://BoydsMillsPress.com/

Carson-Dellosa Publishing

P.O. Box 35665
Greensboro, NC 27425-5665
http://carsondellosa.com/

Continental Press/Seedling Publications

520 East Bainbridge Street
Elizabethtown, PA 17022
http://www.continentalpress.com/

Creative Teaching Press

15342 Graham Street
Huntington Beach, CA 92649-1111
http://creativeteaching.com/

Curriculum Associates, Inc.

153 Rangeway Road
North Billerica, MA 01862
http://curriculumassociates.com/

Educators Publishing Service

P.O. Box 9031
Cambridge, MA 02139-9031
http://epsbooks.com/

Evan-Moor Educational Publishers

18 Lower Ragsdale
Monterey, CA 93940
http://www.evan-moor.com/

Glencoe/McGraw-Hill

8787 Orion Place
Columbus, OH 43240-4027
http://glencoe.com/

Guilford Publications

72 Spring Street
New York, NY 10012
http://www.guilford.com/

Harcourt Assessment

19500 Bulverde Road
San Antonio, TX 78259-3701
http://HarcourtAssessment.com/

Harcourt School Publishers

6277 Sea Harbor Drive
Orlando, FL 32887
http://harcourtschool.com/

Heinemann Publishers

361 Hanover Street
Portsmouth, NH 03801
http://heinemann.com/

Highlights for Children

1800 Watermark
P.O. Box 269
Columbus, OH 43216
http://www.highlights.com/

Holt, Rinehart and Winston

10801 North Mopac Expressway
Building 3
Austin, TX 78759
http://hrw.com/

The Reading Teacher's Book of Lists, Fifth Edition, © 2006 by John Wiley & Sons, Inc.

Houghton Mifflin Company

222 Berkeley Street
Boston, MA 02116
http://eduplace.com/

International Reading Association

800 Barksdale Road
P.O. Box 8139
Newark, DE 19714-8139
http://ira.org/

Jamestown Education

130 East Randolph Street, Suite 900
Chicago, IL 60601
http://jamestowneducation.com/

John Wiley and Sons

111 River Street
Hoboken, NJ 07030
http://www.wiley.com/

Jossey-Bass, A Wiley Imprint

989 Market Street
San Francisco, CA 94103-1741
http://www.josseybass.com/

Kendall/Hunt Publishing Company

4050 Westmark Drive
Dubuque, IA 52002
http://kendallhunt.com/

Macmillan/McGraw-Hill

Two Penn Plaza, 23rd Floor
New York, NY 10121
http://mhschool.com/

National Council of Teachers of English

1111 West Kenyon Road
Urbana, IL 61801
http://www.ncte.org/

National Geographic School Publishing

1145 17th Street NW
Washington, D.C. 20036
http://www.ngschoolpub.org/

Pearson Education

1 Lake Street
Upper Saddle River, NJ 07458
http://www.pearsoneducation.com/

Pearson Learning

299 Jefferson Road
Parsippany, NJ 07054-2827
http://pearsonlearning.com/

Pearson Scott Foresman

1900 East Lake Avenue
Glenview, IL 60025
http://scottforesman.com/

Penguin Group USA

375 Hudson Street
New York, NY 10014
http://us.penguingroup.com/

Reading Recovery Council of North America

400 West Wilson Bridge Road, Suite 250
Worthington, OH 43085
http://readingrecovery.org/

Riverside Publishing

425 Spring Lake Drive
Itasca, IL 60143
http://www.riverpub.com/

Scholastic Inc.

557 Broadway
New York, NY 10012
http://scholastic.com/

SRA/McGraw-Hill

8787 Orion Place
Columbus, OH 43240-4027
http://sraonline.com/

Teacher Created Materials

P.O. Box 1040
Huntington Beach, CA 92647
http://www.tcmpub.com/

PUBLISHERS OF READING MATERIALS AND TESTS CONTINUED

Teacher Created Resources

6421 Industry Way
Westminster, CA 92683
http://teachercreated.com/

Thomson/Peterson's

2000 Lenox Drive
Lawrenceville, NJ 08648
http://thomson.com/

Weekly Reader Corporation

200 First Stamford Place
Stamford, CT 06912-0023
http://weeklyreader.com/

Weekly Reader Early Learning Library

330 West Olive Street, Suite 100
Milwaukee, WI 53212
http://earlyliteracy.org/

Wikki Stix Company (Omnicor Inc.)

2432 West Peoria, #1188
Phoenix, AZ 85029
http://www.wikkistix.com/

Wright Group/McGraw-Hill

1 Prudential Plaza
Chicago, IL 60601
http://wrightgroup.com/

Zaner-Bloser Educational Publishers

P.O. Box 16764
Columbus, OH 43216-6764
http://www.zaner-bloser.com/

The Reading Teacher's Book of Lists, Fifth Edition, © 2006 by John Wiley & Sons, Inc.

Index